INTRODUCTION TO INSURANCE

PRACTICAL GUIDES

Other titles in this series are:

Marine Claims
2nd edition
by Christof Lüddeke

Maritime Law
4th edition
by Christopher Hill

Arbitration
by Michael Reynolds

International Shipping
by Bruce Farthing

Insurance Regulation in Europe
by Clifford Chance

Chartering Documents
by Harvey Williams

Introduction to P&I
2nd edition
by Christopher Hill,
Bill Robertson,
Steven Hazelwood

Professional Negligence and Insurance Law
by Neil F. Jones & Co.

INTRODUCTION TO INSURANCE

BY

D S HANSELL
FCII
Chartered Insurance Practitioner

LLP

LONDON NEW YORK HONG KONG
1996

LLP Limited
Legal Publishing Division
27 Swinton Street
London WC1X 9NW
Great Britain

USA AND CANADA
LLP Inc.
Suite 308, 611 Broadway
New York, NY 10012, USA

SOUTH-EAST ASIA
LLP Asia Limited
Room 1101, Hollywood Centre
233 Hollywood Road
Hong Kong

British Library Cataloguing in Publication Data

A catalogue record
for this book is available
from the British Library

ISBN 1-85978-053-9

Text set in 10/12pt Plantin by
Selwood Systems,
Midsomer Norton
Printed in Great Britain by
WBC Limited,
Bridgend, Mid-Glamorgan

AUTHOR'S FOREWORD

The end of the twentieth century is an exciting time in the insurance world and particularly for the United Kingdom. There are many "hot potatoes", presenting challenges not totally resolved. Let me mention a number of them, in alphabetical order only:

"Banking v Insurance"	the narrowing of differences between insurance, banking and other financial activities, with the possibility of the "financial supermarket" replacing separate identities.
Direct Insurance	the threat to traditional sales and intermediary services, now concentrated in personal lines: but where will it stop?
Europe	some E.C. Directives are now part of our law affecting insurance, but what of wider issues implied with a fully developed "common market"?
Information Technology	we used to say we had computers working for us: must we now say that we are working for them (if we still have a job!)?
Insurance education	will the industry be able to retain its identity in this field, in the light of NVQs and other government pressures, coupled with the threat of "creeping academia"?
Lloyd's	how will the present "troubles" be resolved: can we really foresee an insurance world without Lloyd's of London?
Politics	at home, increasing trends towards "privatisation" may lead to opportunities in the medical and pension fields; abroad, the enigmas of Eastern Europe and, further afield, China.

Reinsurance	with the great growth and then decline of reinsurance capacity in the last quarter of the century, to what extent will reinsurers call the tune?
Self-insurance	the growth of risk management in the United States and elsewhere, with the realisation that it may not be essential for risk to be carried by a commercial insurer, presents interesting possibilities.
Staff	the "slimming down" of staffing levels is certainly producing "leaner" organisations, but to what extent are they "fitter"?

These are all fascinating topics, providing ample scope for assignments and projects for insurance students (and perhaps many PhDs for their mentors). I have touched upon several of these topics, in passing. They all deserve deeper thought and attention.

During some 35 years in insurance education/training I have cherished the famous quotation "Education is not filling pails, it is lighting fires". May this be better understood and my contribution be a help.

U.K. April 1996 D S HANSELL

PREFACE

It is with considerable pleasure that I am able to present this book, through LLP Limited.

In very large measure this is effectively a new edition of my book *Elements of Insurance*, which first appeared in 1970. Since that time the world of insurance has seen many changes. It was therefore with some hesitation that I approached this further production, not knowing whether to adopt a completely new format or to represent the material much as before. I decided on the latter, updating where appropriate, but giving the new title.

Retaining so much of the old text will not please all. Also, I am quite sure there will be obsolete things which should have been removed or modified, but which I have overlooked. I will be sincerely grateful to have them pointed out, with other suggestions.

Over many years I have had a large number of people who have helped and encouraged me in the field of insurance education/training. It is not feasible to attempt a full list, but I would like to pay tribute to various insurance Institutes: particularly the CII in London, the AII in Melbourne, the Insurance Institute of Bermuda, the IIA/CPCU Institutes in Malvern, USA, the Singapore College of Insurance and the Insurance Institute of Hong Kong. It has been my pleasure to be associated or to have very friendly contact with them all.

In addition to my long-suffering wife Molly and daughter Anna, may I also mention some individuals? Looking back, I was influenced into going into insurance teaching more than either of us knew by Clem Aldridge, a former colleague and now long-retired, but happily still a friend and neighbour. Finally, my appreciation once more to my students over the years, and in more recent times to Mrs Irene Wong and my other excellent young Training Officers at the Insurance Training Centre (Vocational Training Council), Hong Kong.

D S HANSELL

ABOUT THE AUTHOR

Stanley Hansell has a wide and long experience in insurance and particularly in technical insurance education/training.

He began his career with the Norwich Union, where he spent over 12 years, mostly in claims work, in the Overseas Department. He was next a casualty claims inspector with the Eagle Star for two years, and later claims manager for J S Johnson & Co, the leading insurance broker in the Bahamas, for three years.

His involvement in insurance education/training began almost immediately after he qualified as an FCII in 1959. He helped as a part-time lecturer in insurance in Norwich and became an examiner/senior examiner for the Chartered Insurance Institute. The latter role he had to relinquish when he entered full-time employment as an insurance lecturer. For over ten years he was at Norwich City College in the United Kingdom. He was later to be in charge of training centres, for four years with the Bermuda Insurance Institute in Hamilton, Bermuda, and for over nine years with the Vocational Training Council in Hong Kong.

His experience therefore embraces tariff and non-tariff insurers, brokers, and insurance education/training establishments in a number of jurisdictions. He has also travelled widely and is known in several international insurance educational centres.

After completing his contract in Hong Kong, he is now semi-retired, but hopes to be able to write a little more and still help out to some extent in the profession to which he remains committed.

CONTENTS

Author's foreword v
Preface vii
About the author ix
List of illustrations xix
Table of cases xxi
Table of statutes xxiii

PART ONE: INSURANCE GENERALLY 1

1 **Basically What It Is** 3
A) Risk 5
B) Reaction to Risk 6
C) Risk Management 7
D) The Functions of Insurance 10
E) Progress Test

2 **Limitations and Classifications of Insurance** 13
A) Limitations on the Scope of Insurance 13
B) Classifications of Insurance 16
C) Progress Test 2 20

Part One: Objective Tests and Assignments 22

PART TWO: MAJOR CLASSES OF BUSINESS 23

3 **Marine Insurance** 25
A) The Development of Marine Insurance 25
B) The Scope of Marine Insurance 29
C) The Importance of Marine Insurance in Trade 32
D) Progress Test 3 33

4 **Life Assurance** 35
A) The Development of Life Assurance 35
B) Industrial Life Assurance 39
C) The Scope of Life Assurance 41

D) Some Features Peculiar to Life Assurance 45
E) Progress Test 4 49

5 **Fire Insurance** 51
A) The Development of Fire Insurance 51
B) The Scope of Fire Insurance 55
C) Progress Test 5 58

6 **Accident Insurance** 61
A) General Observations 61
B) Fidelity Guarantee Insurance 62
C) Personal Accident Insurance 65
D) Employer's Liability Insurance 66
E) Public Liability Insurance 68
F) Theft Insurance 69
G) Other Types of Insurance 70
H) Summary 71
I) Progress Test 6 72

7 **Motor Insurance** 75
A) The Development of Motor Insurance 75
B) The Motor Tariff 76
C) The Scope of Motor Insurance 77
D) The Road Traffic Acts 1930–1991 79
E) E.C. Directives 81
F) The Motor Insurers' Bureau 81
G) Progress Test 7 83

8 **Engineering Insurance** 85
A) The Development and Scope of Engineering Insurance 85
B) Progress Test 8 87

9 **Aviation Insurance** 89
A) The Development and Scope of Aviation Insurance 89
B) Progress Test 9 91

10 **More Recent Developments** 93
A) Newer Types of Insurance 93
B) Progress Test 10 97

Part Two: Objective Tests and Assignments 99

PART THREE: THE INSURANCE MARKET 101

11 **Insurers** 103
A) Introduction 103
B) Types of Insurers 103
C) Other Insurer Classifications 106

	D) Reinsurers	106
	E) Advantages and Disadvantages of Self-Insurance	107
	F) Captive Insurance Companies	108
	G) Tariff Organisations	109
	H) Progress Test 11	110
12	**Lloyd's**	113
	A) Formation and Structure	113
	B) Placing an Insurance Risk at Lloyd's	115
	C) Links with the Past	117
	D) Shipping Intelligence and Publications	118
	E) Progress Test 12	120
13	**Insurance Intermediaries**	123
	A) General Observations	123
	B) Agents and Brokers	124
	C) Legal Considerations	126
	D) Recent UK Developments	129
	E) Progress Test 13	130
14	**UK Insurance Market Associations**	133
	A) The Chartered Insurance Institute (CII)	133
	B) The Association of British Insurers (ABI)	134
	C) Lloyd's	134
	D) British Insurers' International Committee (BIIC)	135
	E) Other Insurer Organisations	135
	F) Life and Related Insurance Organisations	136
	G) Other Intermediary Organisations	136
	H) Risk Management	137
	I) Claims and Surveying Organisations	137
	J) Educational and Charitable	138
15	**The Late Twentieth Century**	139
	A) Miscellaneous Observations	139
	B) Product and Other Innovations	139
	C) Other Market Features in the United Kingdom	141
	D) General Market Features	143
	E) Progress Test 15	147
	Part Three: Objective Tests and Assignments	149
PART FOUR: BASIC PRINCIPLES		151
16	**The Insurance Contract**	153
	A) General Observations	153
	B) Simple Contracts	154
	C) Speciality Contracts	156

	D) Contracts which are Defective	157
	E) Stamp Duty	157
	F) Subject Matter of the Insurance, and of the Contract	158
	G) Progress Test 16	158
17	**Insurable Interest**	161
	A) General Observations	161
	B) Insurable Interest and the Law	162
	C) How Insurable Interest Arises	164
	D) Insurable Interest Affected by Statute	167
	E) Miscellaneous Legal Features	168
	F) When Insurable Interest Must Exist	169
	G) The Transfer of Insurable Interest (Assignment)	170
	H) Progress Test 17	172
18	**Utmost Good Faith**	175
	A) General Observations	175
	B) Utmost Good Faith and the Law	176
	C) Material Facts	177
	D) Duty of Disclosure	179
	E) Representations	179
	F) Warranties	180
	G) Distinction Between Representations and Warranties	181
	H) The Inherent and Contractual Duties of Utmost Good Faith	182
	I) Breaches of Utmost Good Faith	182
	J) Effect of Legislation	184
	K) Law Reform and Case Law	185
	L) Progress Test 18	187
19	**Indemnity**	189
	A) General Observations	189
	B) How Indemnity is Assessed	192
	C) Methods of Providing an Indemnity	193
	D) Reinstatement of the Sum Insured	195
	E) Policies which Modify Indemnity	197
	F) Special Considerations in Marine Insurance	199
	G) Progress Test 19	200
20	**Subrogation**	203
	A) General Observations	203
	B) How Subrogation Rights Arise	204
	C) How the Common Law Position is Sometimes Modified	207
	D) When Subrogation Rights are Sometimes Waived	207
	E) Miscellaneous Legal Considerations	208
	F) Progress Test 20	209

21 **Contribution** 211
A) General Observations 211
B) The Operation of Contribution 212
C) Modifications of the Basic Principle 214
D) Contribution Not Applicable where Different Interests Exist 215
E) Different Meaning of "Contribution" in Insurance 217
F) Progress Test 21 217

22 **Proximate Cause** 219
A) General Observations 219
B) Legal Considerations 220
C) General Rules of Application 222
D) Amendment of the Position by Policy Condition 225
E) Progress Test 22 226

23 **Insurance and Wagering** 229
A) Insurance and Wagering in the Past 229
B) Similarities Between Insurance and Gambling 229
C) Differences Between Insurance and Gambling 230
D) Progress Test 23 233

Part Four: Objective Tests and Assignments 234

PART FIVE: INSURANCE IN PRACTICE 237

24 **Underwriting** 239
A) Some Basic Observations 239
B) Steps in Underwriting 240
C) Features to be Considered by the Underwriter 242
D) Underwriting Remedies 244
E) Underwriting in the Different Classes 245
F) Progress Test 24 246

25 **Physical and Moral Hazard** 249
A) Introduction 249
B) Physical Hazard 249
C) Underwriting Remedies for Bad Physical Hazard 250
D) Moral Hazard 251
E) Adverse Moral Hazard and its Remedies 252
F) Progress Test 25 254

26 **Proposal Forms** 255
A) General Observations 255
B) Use in the Major Classes of Business 256
C) Structure of Most Proposal Forms 257
D) Progress Test 26 260

27	**Policy Forms**	263
	A) General Observations	263
	B) Structure of a Scheduled Policy Form	264
	C) Classifications of Policy Conditions	267
	D) Rectification	270
	E) Cover Notes and Certificates	271
	F) Endorsements	272
	G) Progress Test 27	272
28	**Premiums**	275
	A) General Observations	275
	B) How Premiums are Calculated	277
	C) Short-Period Premium Scales	279
	D) Returns of Premiums	280
	E) Reserves	283
	F) Terminology of Premiums	285
	G) Ratios	286
	H) Progress Test 28	287
29	**Renewals**	289
	A) General Observations	289
	B) Underwriting Considerations Arising at Renewal	289
	C) General Renewal Procedure	291
	D) Progress Test 29	294
30	**Claims and Disputes**	295
	A) Claims Generally	295
	B) Claims Procedure	296
	C) *Ex Gratia* Claim Payments	297
	D) Claims in the Major Classes of Business	298
	E) Disputes over Claims	299
	F) Arbitration and Mediation	300
	G) Insurers' Arbitration Services	302
	H) Fraudulent Claims	303
	I) Claims Results	304
	J) Progress Test 30	305
31	**Average**	307
	A) Average in Marine Insurance	307
	B) Average in Fire Insurance	308
	C) Average in Accident Insurance	311
	D) Average in Life Assurance	312
	E) Progress Test 31	312
32	**Reinsurance**	315
	A) General Observations	315

B) Types of Reinsurance 316
C) Some Difficulties Examined 320
D) Reinsurance and Co-Insurance 321
E) Present Day Reinsurance 322
F) Progress Test 32 324

Part Five: Objective Tests and Assignments 326

PART SIX: INSURANCE AND THE STATE 329

33 State Supervision and Regulation 331
A) Why the State is Interested 331
B) Historical Developments in the United Kingdom 331
C) The Insurance Companies Acts 1974–1982 333
D) The Policyholders Protection Act 1975 337
E) Other Government "Intervention" 338
F) Why not Nationalise? 339
G) Compulsory Insurance in the United Kingdom 341
H) Progress Test 33 342

34 UK Supervisory Bodies and Insolvency 345
A) The UK Philosophy of Insurance Supervision 345
B) Government and Other Supervisory Bodies 346
C) Insolvency 348
D) The "Failure" of an Insurer 349
E) The "Failure" of an Insurance Intermediary 350
F) The "Failure" of an Insured 351
G) Progress Test 34 352

Part Six: Objective Tests and Assignments 353

Answers to the Progress and Objective Tests 355

Index 357

LIST OF ILLUSTRATIONS

1	Classification of insurance (1)	17
2	Classification of insurance (2)	19
3	Classification of insurance (3)	19
4	The development of marine insurance	27
5	The development of life assurance	36
6	The development of fire insurance	52
7	The development of accident insurance	62
8	The insurance market	104
9	Comparison between insurance agents and insurance brokers	126
10	The essentials of a simple contract	154
11	The essentials of insurablc interest	162
12	Breaches of utmost good faith	183
13	Methods of providing an indemnity	194
14	How subrogation arises	206
15	The essentials of contribution	213
16	The application of proximate cause	223
17	Classification of policy conditions	269
18	Returns of premiums	282
19	Comparison between reinsurance and co-insurance	323

TABLE OF CASES

Burnand *v.* Rodoconachi (1882) 7 App Cas 333 204
Carter *v.* Boehm (1766) 3 Burr 1905; 97 ER 1162 176
Castellain *v.* Preston (1883) 11 QBD 380 (CA) 158, 204
Commercial Union *v.* Hayden [1977] QB 804 213
Container Transport International Ltd. *v.* Oceanus Mutual Underwriting Association [1982] 2 Lloyd's Rep 178; [1984] 1 Lloyd's Rep 476 (CA) 186
Coxe *v.* Employers' Liability Assurance Corpn. [1916] 2 KB 629 226
Dalby *v.* The India & London Life Assurance Co. (1854) 15 CB 365 . . . . 163, 169
Darrell *v.* Tibbits (1880) 5 QBD 560 (CA) 205
De Hahn *v.* Hartley (1786) 1 TR 343 181
De Vaux *v.* Salvador (1836) 4 Ad & El 420 31
Edwards (John) & Co. *v.* Motor Union Ins. Co. Ltd. [1922] 2 KB 249 . . . . 166, 209
Etherington and the Lancashire & Yorkshire Accident Ins. Co., Re [1909] 1 KB 591 (CA) 223
Gaskarth *v.* Law Union (1876), Bunyan's *Fire Insurance*, 6th edn., p. 155 221
Godsall *v.* Boldero (1807) 9 East 72 163
Johnston *v.* West of Scotland Ins. Co. (1828) 7 Shaw 52 221
Lambert *v.* Co-operative Ins. Society Ltd. [1975] 2 Lloyd's Rep 485 185
Leppard *v.* Excess Ins. Co. Ltd. [1979] 2 Lloyd's Rep 91 191
Leyland Shipping Co. Ltd. *v.* Norwich Union Fire Ins. Co. Ltd. [1918] AC 350 220
London General Omnibus Co. Ltd. *v.* Holloway [1912] 2 KB 72 (CA) 176
Lucena *v.* Crauford (1806) 127 ER 630 (HL) 168
Marsden *v.* City & County Assurance Co. (1866) LR 1 CP 232 . . . . 221, 225
Morley *v.* Moore [1936] 2 QB 359 (CA) 204
Murfitt *v.* Royal Ins. Co. Ltd. (1922) 10 Ll L Rep 191 128
Newsholme Brothers *v.* Road Transport & General Ins. Co. [1929] 2 KB 365 (CA) 127
North British & Mercantile *v.* London, Liverpool & Globe Ins. Co. (1877) 5 Ch D 569 . . . 212, 216
Pan Atlantic Ins. Co. Ltd. *v.* Pine Top Ins. Co. Ltd. [1993] 1 Lloyd's Rep 496 (CA) 186
Pawsey *v.* Scottish Union & National, *The Times*, 17 October 1908 219
Priestley *v.* Fowler (1837) 3 M & W 1 67
Rozanes *v.* Bowen (1928) 32 Ll L Rep 98 (CA) 177
St. Paul Fire & Marine Co. (U.K.) Ltd. *v.* McConnell Dowell Constructors Ltd. [1995] 2 Lloyd's Rep 116 186
Scher & Ackman *v.* Policyholders' Protection Board [1993] 3 All ER 384 (HL) 337
Tootal Broadhurst Lee Co. *v.* London & Lancashire Fire Ins. Co., *The Times*, 21 May 1908 224
Yorkshire Dale S.S. Co. *v.* Minister of War Transport [1942] AC 691 221
Yorkshire Ins. Co. Ltd. *v.* Nisbet Shipping Co. Ltd. [1962] 2 QB 330 208

TABLE OF LEGISLATION

Arbitration Act 1950 300
Assurance Companies Act 1909 332
Assurance Companies Act 1946 333
Assurance Companies (Winding Up) Acts 1933–35 333
Boiler Explosions Act 1882 86
Carriage of Goods by Sea Act 1924 168
Carriers Act 1830 168
Civil Aviation Act 1949 90
Companies Acts 1862–1985 .... 104, 105
Court of Arbitration Act 1601 28
E.C. Directives
  Motor Insurance Directives 81, 83, 215
  Life Directive 334
Employers' Liability Act 1880 67
Employers' Liability (Compulsory Insurance) Act 1969 .... 68, 341
Employers' Liability Insurance Companies Act 1907 332
Factories Acts 1937–61 86
Financial Services Act 1986 .... 129, 338
Fires Prevention (Metropolis) Act 1774 195
Friendly Societies Act 1955 172
Gaming Act 1845 .... 164, 229
Health & Safety at Work Act 1974 68
Hotel Proprietors Act 1956 168
Industrial Assurance & Friendly Societies Acts 1948–58 .... 39, 165, 167
Industrial Assurances Act 1923 .... 39, 332
Insurance Brokers (Registration) Act 1977 .... 129, 338, 341
Insurance Companies (Accounts & Statements) Regulations 1983 334
Insurance Companies Act 1958 90
Insurance Companies Acts 1958–82 333
Insurance Companies Acts 1974–82 .... 18, 333
Insurance Companies Act 1982 .... 106, 334, 349
Insurance Companies Regulations 1981 334
Law Reform (Contributory Negligence) Act 1945 67
Law Reform (Personal Injuries) Act 1948 67
Life Assurance Act 1774 .... 38, 163, 169, 186, 229
Life Assurance Companies Act 1870 .... 39, 332
Limitation Acts 1939–75 296
Lloyd's Act 1982 .... 113, 115
Marine Insurance Act 1745 163
Marine Insurance Act 1788 163
Marine Insurance Act 1906 .... 29, 154, 164, 169, 171, 176, 199, 200, 211
Marine Insurance (Gambling Policies) Act 1909 .... 29, 164, 166, 229
Married Women's Policies of Assurance (Scotland) Act 1880 172
Married Women's Property Acts 1870–1882 48

Married Women's Property Act 1882 . . . 165, 167, 172, 351
Merchant Shipping (Oil Pollution) Act 1971 . . . 341
National Insurance (Industrial Injuries) Act 1946 . . . 68
Nuclear Installations Act 1965 . . . 94, 341
Policies of Assurance Act 1867 . . . 171
Policyholders Protection Act 1975 . . . 283, 337
Railway Fires Act (1905) Amendment Act 1923 . . . 206
Rehabilitation of Offenders Act 1974 . . . 184
Repair of Benefice Buildings Measure 1972 . . . 167
Riding Establishments Act 1964 . . . 341
Riot (Damages) Act 1886 . . . 206
Road Traffic Acts 1930–91 . . . 78, 79, 80
Road Traffic Act 1930 . . . 76, 341
Sale of Goods Act 1893 . . . 175
Settled Land Act 1925 . . . 167
Solicitors Act 1974 . . . 341
South Sea Company Act 1720 . . . 28
Stamp Act 1891 . . . 157
Statute of Frauds 1677 . . . 154
Theft Act 1968 . . . 70
Third Parties (Rights Against Insurers) Act 1930 . . . 351
Unfair Contract Terms Act 1977 . . . 182, 184, 339
Unfair Terms in Consumer Contracts Regulations 1994 . . . 338
Workmen's Compensation Act 1897 . . . 68

PART ONE

INSURANCE GENERALLY

CHAPTER 1

BASICALLY WHAT IT IS

1.1 Definition of insurance

Insurance may be defined as a social device providing financial compensation for the effects of misfortune, the payments being made from the accumulated contributions of all parties participating in the scheme.

Thus, it may be seen as a kind of fund, into which all who are insured will pay an assessed contribution (called a *premium*). In return, those insured will have the right to call on the fund for any appropriate payment should the insured event occur.

1.2 The position of the insurer

If the above definition is accepted, the insurer may be considered as the custodian, or treasurer, of the fund. This is an imperfect illustration, in that the insurer is more than a treasurer. He is also the owner of the fund. Further, he assesses the contribution payable by each individual member, and should the claims on the fund exceed the sources available he must make good any deficiency from his own assets. Nevertheless, regarding the insurer as treasurer of a central fund does illustrate the basic principle behind all insurances.

1.3 Insurance is to do with risk

It may be seen already that insurance exists to combat the adverse effects of risk. Risk is inseparable from life and nobody is exempt from it. Obviously, some people are exposed to greater dangers or risks than others, by virtue of their occupation, physical condition, geographical situation or any of countless reasons, but each and all of us are subject to what Shakespeare's Hamlet called "the slings and arrows of outrageous fortune". To a greater or lesser extent, the risks of fire, flood, theft, negligence of others and ourselves and many other perils are constantly with us.

For various reasons, studied in this and the next chapter, we do not or cannot insure all the risks to which we are exposed.

A. RISK

1.4 Risk and chance

Both terms relate to uncertainty. Risk, in insurance, is generally used in a pessimistic sense, with the possibility of loss or misfortune in mind (compare "crossing the road without looking is a risky business"). Chance tends to be regarded more optimistically (compare "what are my chances of getting that job?"). Thus, in life assurance, it may be said that at a given age the risk of death in the next year is 2 per cent, whereas the chance of survival is 98 per cent.

1.5 Two classifications of risk

There are different kinds of risk, some of which may be insured, according to the nature and possible consequences of the hazard involved. The following classifications of risk should be noted:

(a) pure and speculative risks;
(b) fundamental and particular risks (see below).

1.6 Pure risks

Bearing in mind the pessimistic connotation of risk mentioned above, a pure risk offers no prospect of gain. It offers only the possibility of loss, or at best the preservation of the *status quo*. Examples of pure risk are fire, flood, accident, death, etc. These are the kinds of risk which may normally be the subject of insurance, although individual risks may not meet insurability criteria (see Chapter 2).

1.7 Speculative risks

Also called *entrepreneurial risks*, these offer the possibility of gain or of loss. Trading risks fall within this category. Generally, speculative risks are not insurable. Provision against the possibilities of loss with this type of risk is usually made by commercial transactions, such as the purchase of "futures", or by specific management decisions, such as diversifying business activities, etc.

1.8 Fundamental risks

These are risks which tend to affect large sections of society or even the world, rather than individuals. Thus, a fundamental risk has within it the element of catastrophe. Examples are war, famine, earthquake, pollution, etc. Where fundamental risks have a tremendously widespread disaster potential they are generally regarded as uninsurable commercially. Instead, they are considered to be problems of society as a whole, to be dealt with at government or international level.

1.9 Particular risks

These are risks the consequences of which are comparatively restricted. Most insurable risks are particular risks, likely to result in loss for a relatively small number of individuals when they happen.

B. REACTION TO RISK

1.10 Generally

How we react to risks to which we are exposed depends largely on our awareness of them and our mental approach generally, or on the practicability of doing anything about them.

1.11 Some risks we accept

Total elimination of risk is impossible in every instance. Willingly or not, some risks we accept (or may be said to *assume*). This will take place where:

(a) *There is no practical means of avoidance.* The remote but possible risk of being struck by an object falling from an aircraft cannot be totally avoided, within practical reason.
(b) *We are unaware of the risk.* Many people are unaware of their legal obligations towards visitors or employees under various statutes, for instance. Such potential liability risks are thus accepted (or assumed) in ignorance.
(c) *The likely consequences are not serious.* Minor losses will not cause economic distress. Thus, insuring articles of very small value is not worth the premium involved.
(d) *The consequences of risk avoidance are unacceptable.* Few of us are prepared to stop riding in motor vehicles to avoid the obvious risks thereby involved.
(e) *The risk is actively desired.* Some hobbies and pastimes (and even jobs) have an element of danger and risk that is an essential attraction to those participating.

1.12 Some risks we avoid or reduce

Generally, we prefer to avoid or reduce risks which threaten our life and well-being. This is true for individuals and society. We will look before crossing a road; society will have a police force and hospitals, for instance. In the economic realm also, strenuous efforts have been made to avoid or reduce risks. The efforts include:

(a) *Improving methods.* The use of more modern machinery or equipment may remove financial risks by ensuring competitive prices. Risk of injury to operators is also improved.
(b) *Spreading the risk.* Reducing net loss by:
   (i) *Diversification.* "Keeping all one's eggs in one basket" by relying on a single product or process is hazardous.
   (ii) *Amalgamations or mergers.* Widely practised for years, these result in greater security for all, since risks are spread over a wider field and greater resources.
   (iii) *Insurance.* The risk is transferred to the insurance fund from the individual. And this is what insurance is all about: transferring the risk which is upon the individual to the shoulders of the whole insuring community, "so that the loss lighteth rather easily on the many, than heavily upon the few", as an old statute said.

NOTE: i. The term "assurance" may also be met. There is no essential difference. "Insurance" tends to be used where a claim is only potential ("in case" needed), e.g. fire, and "assurance" where a claim seems certain ("as sure" as can be), e.g. most life assurance contracts.

ii. Insurance may also be seen as *funding* a loss. That is, ensuring beforehand that funds will be available to cover the financial consequences of risk. This seeks to ensure continuity and indeed survival in the face of economic loss.

iii. The reactions to risk described in **1.11** and **1.12** are not "either/or" possibilities. We can retain part of a risk, take care and have insurance all at the same time, for instance.

C. RISK MANAGEMENT

1.13 The risk manager

Many industrial and commercial firms have appointed a risk manager. His primary function is to see that his management is aware of pure risks threatening the organisation and to recommend steps to combat them. A large part of his responsibilities is the insurance programme for the firm. It must be said, however, that insurance is only part of the risk management process (see **1.15**).

1.14 Risk management

This is a recently developed science, highly organised in the United States and of increasing significance elsewhere in the world. Full consideration of it is beyond the scope of this study, but the basic steps in risk management are:

(a) *Identifying risk.* Until you know what your problems are you cannot deal with them. Statistical research, experience and knowledge, personal interviews and physical inspections are all needed to achieve this end.
(b) *Quantifying risk.* Knowing the financial impact of risk is essential in order to make intelligent recommendations. It must be understood, however, that financial impact is a relative term, since financially strong organisations can more easily absorb losses than less well financed organisations.
(c) *Recommendations.* Once risks have been identified and measured, appropriate recommendations to management may be made. Some of the alternatives available are outlined in **1.11** and **1.12**.
(d) *Monitoring results.* This differentiates the manager from the visiting consultant. It is vital to check and monitor the effect of decisions, so that improvements may be made. It often happens that good ideas have to be modified in practice because of unforeseen consequences.

1.15 Insurance is only one tool of the risk manager

It is increasingly being realised that insurance, far from being an end in itself, is but one reaction to risk and just a part of a total risk-management programme. Much more attention, especially by larger organisations, is being paid to risk reduction and part or even total *risk retention*, as we shall see in later chapters.

D. THE FUNCTIONS OF INSURANCE

1.16 Primary function

The primary function of insurance is to spread the financial losses of insured members over the whole of the insuring community, by compensating the unfortunate few from the fund built up from the contributions of all members.

Basically, there are two elements in deciding an equitable contribution from the individual into the fund. One, the *amount* likely to be taken from the fund (a more valuable property will normally cost more to insure). Two, the *likelihood* of a claim on the fund (a wooden property is more likely to produce a fire claim than a concrete one, etc.). This is self-evident but it is a profound, if simplified, truth behind all premium calculations.

1.17 Benefits of the primary function

Benefits accrue to both the individual insured and the insurer from the proper fulfilment of the primary function. The insured is secure in the knowledge that the protection of the fund is behind him in misfortune. This is of considerable value, since confidence and removal of fears in this way have important subsidiary benefits (see **1.21**).

The insurer, as owner of the fund, benefits from investment income and any profits made.

1.18 Secondary functions

The practice of insurance provides many obvious, and some less obvious, benefits to the individual and society generally. These may be considered under several heads, as set out below.

1.19 Releasing funds otherwise tied up in reserves

No prudent industrialist would consider investing large sums of money in a project without some suitable safeguards. In the absence of insurance, one of these might be a substantial reserve fund, so that misfortune would not bring financial ruin. Insurance has the effect of releasing these reserves for further investment and development. This promotes trade and industry.

1.20 Investment by insurers

Over the years, insurers have accumulated vast resources from the various insurance funds. A very large proportion of such resources are invested in the nation, either in the government or in private enterprise. This helps considerably in the overall development of the economy.

1.21 Removing fear and establishing confidence

This was touched upon in **1.17**, and must not be underrated. It is of considerable importance to the individual, for instance, to know that his life assurance will provide for his dependants in the event of his premature death. This is a factor that is difficult to evaluate, but the benefit is very real.

The business world also benefits from the confidence which insurance inspires. Without insurance, many business ventures would never begin, as those involved would scarcely risk financial ruin by the chance happening of fire, etc. The quotation in **1.12**(b)(iii) is taken from the preamble to an ancient statute concerning marine insurance, and it goes on to say that the effect of insurance is that "all merchants, specially the younger sort, are allured to adventure more willingly and more freely".

1.22 A means of saving

Most people find it difficult to save, but an insurance policy is often a very suitable way of providing for the future. This type of policy is found particularly in life assurance, and will be examined in more detail in a later chapter. Clearly, such savings have a beneficial effect both for the individual and for the nation.

1.23 Reducing the cost of social services

This is partly evidenced by **1.22**, but as with any cases of want or distress relieved by payments under an insurance policy there is an indirect benefit to society. If it were not for such payments, there could well be additional demands on social security and similar funds.

A vivid example of this is seen in the compensation paid to the victims of motor accidents. In the absence of insurance, it is doubtful whether more than a very small percentage of negligent motorists could afford to pay the compensation due to their victims, so there might well be pressure on the State to provide some relief.

1.24 Invisible exports

In Britain, for example, a very valuable contribution towards its balance of payments is made by *invisible exports*. These include banking, shipping and other services, as well as insurance transacted abroad by British insurers.

Some students have difficulty in seeing overseas insurance as an export. It may be considered in the following manner: the insurer is selling a commodity, namely security, to an overseas buyer. Although this commodity is invisible, it is an export in the same way as any material goods. The profits received from overseas insurance may therefore be considered as invisible exports.

NOTE: In some instances, local legislation prohibits or restricts the flow of currency from the country concerned. Where the profits are not remitted, for whatever reason, they are invariably invested locally, thus helping to advance the standard of living there.

1.25 Reduction of losses

By action taken or recommendations made during the course of their business, insurers have a considerable effect on the reduction of losses, both in their incidence and extent. More detailed comment will be made on certain aspects of this when considering the various classes of insurance business: see later. In outline, however, the practice of insurance reduces losses in the following ways:

(a) *Rating*. Rating means the assessment of the premium payable by the insured. By charging extra for bad features and less for good, insurers can induce the insured to make improvements which have a beneficial effect on losses. This can clearly be seen, for example, in fire insurance, where the installation of good fire-fighting equipment, such as a sprinkler system, receives considerable reward by way of reduced premiums.

(b) *Surveys and inspection services.* Insurers frequently inspect premises which are proposed for insurance, and their trained surveyors make safety and other recommendations. When carried out, these recommendations render losses less likely or less severe.

In engineering insurance, there is a very detailed programme for regular inspection of boilers and similar installations. These inspections ensure that equipment is in good order, and must reduce losses considerably.

(c) *Loss and salvage experts.* These technical experts on the staff of insurers or independent organisations are employed after losses have occurred, but they have an appreciable effect on reducing the size of losses and, by their recommendations, preventing recurrence.

(d) *Central organisations.* Various organisations and associations of insurers exist and the advisory and statistical work performed by them materially assists in loss reduction.

E. PROGRESS TEST 1

PART 1—SHORT ANSWERS (Answer in one or two sentences)

1. Define insurance. **(1.1)**
2. Give, with examples, two alternative classifications of risk. **(1.5–1.9)**
3. Risk is incidental to life. Explain the various ways in which people may react to risk. **(1.11–1.12)**
4. What are the steps usually taken in the science of risk management? **(1.14)**
5. In what ways may insurance benefit the individual and society generally? **(1.18–1.25)**

PART 2—MULTIPLE CHOICE (Choose the most correct option)

1. Calling the insurer the treasurer of the insurance fund is not quite accurate because:
   (a) the fund really belongs to the policyholders;
   (b) he is really the owner of the fund;
   (c) the fund is managed by government rules;
   (d) he is not elected by the policyholders. **(1.2)**
2. A risk manager is concerned with:
   (a) the trading results of his employer;
   (b) the control of his company's insurance programme;

   (c) the management of pure risks affecting his company;
   (d) the investment portfolio of his company. **(1.13)**

3. The final step in the risk management process is:
   (a) implementing risk control recommendations;
   (b) quantifying risks threatening the company;
   (c) identifying risks threatening the company;
   (d) monitoring the results of risk management decisions. **(1.14)**

4. The primary function of insurance may be said to be:
   (a) spreading financial losses over the insuring community;
   (b) providing profit to the insurer and taxes to government;
   (c) giving employment to many people;
   (d) the collection of premiums. **(1.16)**

5. Insurance helps to reduce the number or amount of losses by:
   (a) the system of rating and other means;
   (b) refusing to insure people again after a loss;
   (c) promising a discount or refund if there are no claims;
   (d) collecting data to help analyse how losses occur. **(1.25)**

(*For multiple choice answers, see page 355.*)

CHAPTER 2

LIMITATIONS AND CLASSIFICATIONS OF INSURANCE

A. LIMITATIONS ON THE SCOPE OF INSURANCE

2.1 All risks cannot be insured

While insurance exists, in principle, to combat risk, there are certain legal, commercial and moral considerations which make it impossible to insure every conceivable kind of risk. In particular, the conditions outlined below must be fulfilled. (These criteria are sometimes described under the general term *the insurability of risk*.)

2.2 There must be an insurable interest

This is a fundamental principle of insurance and is studied in much greater detail later: see Chapter 17. Basically, it means that the person seeking the insurance must be legally entitled to insure the article or event. If no such entitlement exists, any insurance so arranged is void, entirely destitute of legal effect.

2.3 Insurance is limited to financial value

Insurance can only provide *monetary* compensation. Sentimental value and esteem cannot be replaced in the event of loss. Thus, the scope of insurance is limited to the intrinsic value of the article concerned, or to the precise financial consequences of an insured event.

To some extent life assurance is a modification of this general rule, in that life cannot be measured precisely in financial terms. Also, there are insurances arranged on an *agreed value* or some other basis intended to represent commercial rather than intrinsic compensation in the event of loss.

2.4 There must be a large number of similar risks

It has often been said that insurance is subject to "the law of large numbers". If an insurance fund were made up from the contributions of a relatively small number of members, the contributions by individuals might have to be so high as to be totally unacceptable.

In motor insurance, for example, it is not uncommon for a single claim to run into hundreds of thousands of pounds. If a motor insurance fund consisted of merely a hundred or so contributors, it can be seen that the individual contributions would have to be very high. This would tend to make the fund unworkable and economically impracticable.

2.5 It must be possible to calculate the risk of loss

Most risks are said to have a mathematical value. That is, a close examination of past occurrences and statistics enables the likelihood and probable extent of loss to be reasonably predictable. The science of this lies behind all insurance, and where such a possibility does not exist insurance is not feasible. An example of a risk which cannot be insured for this reason is the risk of loss through changes of fashion or the operation of competitors.

NOTE: Life assurance may be said to be the most mathematically calculable (see **28.7**), but calculations are made with all classes of business to arrive at the *pure premium* (i.e. that which must be charged merely to meet losses. To this must be added loadings for expenses and profit, possibly taking into account anticipated interest on investments).

2.6 Losses must not be catastrophic

Very large risks, such as the consequences of a jumbo jet crashing, or of an earthquake, may be insured, but some risks are of such magnitude that insurance funds, at least on a commercial scale, would be quite inadequate. The risks of death or property damage on a national level as a result of war are so enormous, particularly with nuclear war, that they could only be insured by governments, if at all. Therefore, with certain exceptions, it is usual to find a standard exclusion regarding war risks in all insurance contracts.

2.7 Losses must not be "too small"

With **2.6** we may say that losses must not be "too big" for commercial insurance to handle. Conversely, very minor losses are not a practical insurance proposition. Minor losses are expensive administratively to the insurer and the premium that must be charged for such losses would be disproportionately high. Thus, policies are often subject to an *excess/deductible*, which means that small losses are uninsured. "Small" will of course be relative to the wealth of the individual or company concerned, but it has been said that insurance is not sensible unless the potential loss would cause significant economic distress.

2.8 Losses must be reasonably unexpected

Where the possibility of loss is so high as to be a near certainty, insurance in the commercial sense is not possible. For this reason, it is very rare to find insurance covering the risk of shop theft (shoplifting). Also, with insurances on individuals, normally it is impossible to arrange life assurance for a person suffering from a serious heart condition, for example.

The proper functioning of an insurance fund depends upon claims being comparatively rare, so that it is indeed an "unfortunate few" being compensated by the contributions of all.

NOTE: Life assurance would again seem to be a modification of the general rule. Nevertheless, although death is sure to happen, the time it occurs with the individual is unknown and this element of uncertainty renders insurance possible.

2.9 Losses must be accidental

Losses arising through the deliberate acts of the insured, or at his instigation, cannot be insured. Of course, the wilful acts of others, such as theft, malicious damage and bodily harm, may be insured, but the loss must be fortuitous as far as the insured is concerned.

NOTE: Life assurance once more provides an exception, in that suicide is covered by most life policies. However, there is usually a limitation period, often one year, after the commencement of the contract, during which suicide is excluded. This is intended to frustrate the deliberate arranging of an insurance policy when suicide is contemplated, but will not penalise dependants should the policyholder's mind subsequently become disturbed to the extent that he takes his own life.

2.10 It must be consistent with public policy

The insurance effected must not offend the public conscience. This, of course, has proved flexible over the years. For example, at one time it was thought immoral that a person could insure against his legal liability for injury or damage to others. The ability to insure against loss of business profit following a fire was also considered to be wrong. Both are important sectors of insurance business today, but there are still some risks which cannot be insured because they are considered to be against public policy. The insurance against fines imposed for motoring offences is one example.

NOTE: "Contrary to public policy" does not necessarily mean that the insurance is illegal. Rather, it denotes a reluctance of the courts to enforce a contract which is perceived to be against the public interest. On the other hand, some such insurances have been made illegal by statute. For example, in some countries *kidnap and ransom insurance* (see **10.2**) has been made illegal.

B. CLASSIFICATIONS OF INSURANCE

2.11 Meaning of classification

Many students seem to be confused over the very term *classification*, and when asked to supply a classification of insurance will answer by giving one or two examples of different types of policy. To classify means to subdivide the whole subject into a series of headings or categories, into which any given example may be fitted.

2.12 Three main ways of classifying insurance

These are as follows:

(a) by the function it performs;
(b) by the main classes of business;
(c) as under the Insurance Companies Act 1974: see below.

2.13 By the function it performs (See Fig. 1.)

This categorises insurance according to the object or event insured, and may be considered as follows:

(a) *Insurance of the person of the policyholder.* This involves insurance in connection with the life, limbs or health of the person insured. Life assurance and personal accident insurance fall within this category.
(b) *Insurance of the property of the policyholder.* The term property in this context refers to all possessions rather than mere premises. Examples are fire insurance and hull (vessel) policies in marine insurance.
(c) *Insurance of the liability of the policyholder.* The insured person may become liable at law for the death, injury or disease of another person, or may have legal liability for damage to their property. Public liability and certain aspects of motor insurance are examples.
(d) *Insurance of the rights or financial interest of the policyholder.* More often now termed *pecuniary insurance*, this is a rather miscellaneous category to describe those insurances which do not fall conveniently within any of the previous three subdivisions. Examples are fidelity guarantee and credit insurances.

NOTE: i. It will be realised that some insurances involve more than one of the above categories. Pedal cycle insurance, for instance, frequently covers loss or damage to the machine insured as well as liability arising from the use of the cycle. Motor insurance provides an even more striking example, in that the private car comprehensive policy may well include some personal accident cover in addition to insurance of the vehicle and liability arising from the use thereof.

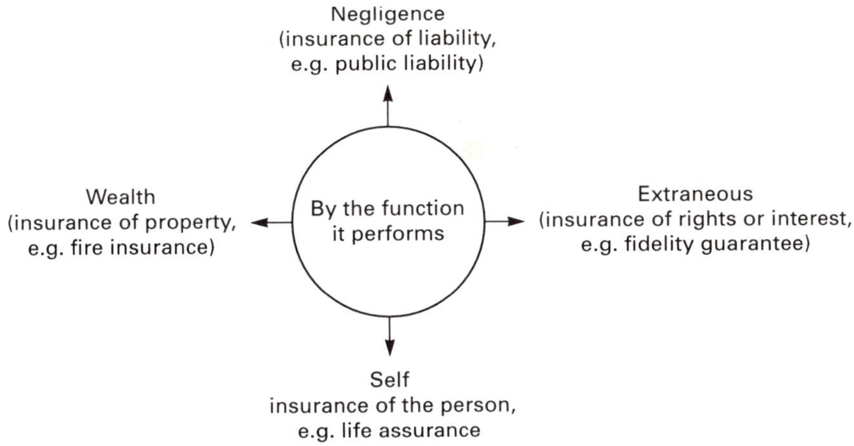

Fig. 1 Classification of insurance (1)

ii. The functional basis of insurance classification is rather academic, often used in examination syllabuses, but would probably not be found in practical use within insurance companies.

2.14 By the main classes of business (See Fig. 2.)

Traditionally insurance has been categorised on the following broad departmental basis:

(a) *Marine insurance.* Maritime trade and the perils of the sea have been with man since time immemorial. Marine insurance, in keeping with man's long association with the sea, is many centuries old. Examples of marine insurance are:
  (i) *hull* policies, which insure the actual vessel and its equipment;
  (ii) *cargo* policies, which are self-explanatory.
(b) *Life assurance.* One of the deepest desires of the prudent man is to ensure that his dependants are provided for, especially in the event of his premature death. Thus, life assurance is also of very ancient origin, and the present-day practice may be sub-divided into:
  (i) ordinary life assurance;
  (ii) industrial life assurance; and
  (iii) annuities (see Chapter 4).
(c) *Fire insurance.* Concerned primarily with one of the four elements thought by the ancient world to comprise the whole of created matter, fire insurance as we know it is something like 300 years old. In addition

to the risk of destruction by fire, *loss of profits* (or *consequential loss*) insurance is an example within this category.

(d) *Accident insurance.* This is a somewhat miscellaneous term applied to all classes of business not covered by the three previous subsections. *Personal accident* insurance and *theft* insurance are two examples.

Because of enormous growth or technical complexity of the class concerned, most insurers now regard (e), (f) and (g) below as separate departments, although with composite insurers they were formerly considered to be within the accident field.

(e) *Motor insurance.* The growth of this class of business, especially in recent decades, has been so phenomenal that most insurers now regard it as a department in its own right. Its name is, of course, self-explanatory.

(f) *Engineering insurance.* Apart from actual cover given, a sizeable proportion of the efforts made by insurers in connection with this class of insurance is the loss preventive work of surveys and inspections of boilers and the like.

(g) *Aviation insurance.* This is another class of business which has seen enormous growth recently, and which is highly specialised. Insurances may be arranged covering damage to the aircraft, legal liabilities and personal accident benefits, among others.

NOTE: i. All the above classes of business are dealt with in greater detail in chapters specifically devoted to the development and scope of each one: see later.

ii. Risks involving the use of atomic energy (for peaceful purposes) might be considered a separate class, but these are not undertaken by individual insurers: see later.

2.15 As under statute (In the United Kingdom the Insurance Companies Acts 1974–82.) (See Fig. 3.)

A totally different classification of insurance arose from these statutes, largely influenced by E.C. requirements. A comprehensive study of this legislation is not within the scope of this book, but further comments are given in **33.12–33.23**.

2.16 Alternative classifications

Statutory requirements may compel insurers to report and collate statistics under a specific classification, but the internal organisation of an insurer is entirely its own concern and various different ways of classifying business have developed in recent years. These will include:

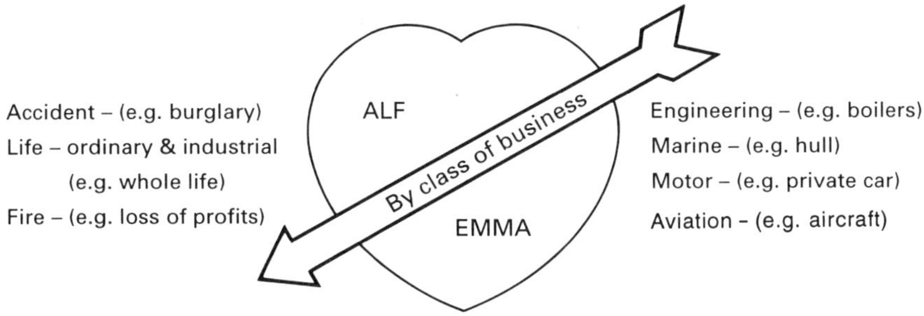

Fig. 2 Classification of insurance (2)

As under the Insurance Companies Act 1982			
LONG TERM			
Class I	Life and annuity	Class V	Tontines
Class II	Marriage and birth	Class VI	Capital redemption
Class III	Linked long term	Class VII	Pension fund management
Class IV	Permanent health		
GENERAL			
Class 1	Accident	Class 10	Motor vehicle liability
Class 2	Sickness	Class 11	Aircraft liability
Class 3	Land vehicles	Class 12	Liability for ships
Class 4	Railway rolling stock	Class 13	General liability
Class 5	Aircraft	Class 14	Credit
Class 6	Ships	Class 15	Suretyship
Class 7	Goods in transit	Class 16	Misc. financial loss
Class 8	Fire & natural forces	Class 17	Legal expenses
Class 9	Damage to property	Class 18	Assistance

Fig. 3 Classification of insurance (3)

(a) Business being sub-divided into *commercial* and *personal* lines (a "line" of business is another name for a class of business), indicating whether the insured is a private individual or a business organisation.
(b) Sub-divisions according to the source of the business concerned, i.e. *direct business, broker-produced* and *agent-produced.*

There may well be others. Insurers are quite free to develop their own systems and students should seek comparisons between various insurers.

2.17 Miscellaneous insurances

A very limited market exists for what might be termed *extraordinary risks.*

Within this category would fall such examples as a policy covering the loss of a stage performer's peculiarly shaped front teeth, or disfigurement or loss of the shapely limbs of a film star. An unusual risk placed in the British insurance market was insurance by a cinema against the risk of patrons dying from heart attack during what was said to be an unusually terrifying horror film. A Greek insurer issued a policy in respect of the three astronauts who took part in the historic first man-landing on the moon, the cover including such contingencies as death caused by extra-terrestrial beings!

These insurances, often arranged solely for publicity reasons, account for only an infinitesimal fraction of the business transacted by insurers.

C. PROGRESS TEST 2

PART 1—SHORT ANSWERS (Answer in one or two sentences)

1. Briefly indicate why all risks cannot be insured. **(2.1–2.10)**
2. When can one claim for the results of a deliberate act? **(2.9)**
3. What is meant by an insurance being against public policy? **(2.10)**
4. Give two alternative classifications of insurance. **(2.11–2.16)**
5. Differentiate between *commercial lines* and *personal lines.* **(2.16)**

PART 2—MULTIPLE CHOICE (Choose the most correct option)

1. All risks cannot be insured commercially because:
   (a) insurers do not have the staff to cope with this;
   (b) certain criteria are necessary for commercial and legal reasons;
   (c) the government has a monopoly on some types of insurance;
   (d) the policy documents would be too complicated. **(2.1–2.10)**
2. Insurance depends upon the "law of large numbers" because:
   (a) only thus are losses reasonably predictable;
   (b) it is not worth insuring only a few risks;
   (c) government requires a minimum amount of business by insurers;
   (d) small claims are not worth insuring. **(2.4)**
3. Viable insurance requires losses to be reasonably unexpected because:
   (a) no-claim discounts would otherwise not be earned;
   (b) claims staff would be inundated with work;
   (c) only then would premium rates be at acceptable levels;
   (d) it is impossible to insure any event which is expected. **(2.8)**
4. The functional classification of insurance:
   (a) means that business is categorised by the subject matter insured;
   (b) identifies the authorised classes of insurance for an insurer;
   (c) indicates which classes of business are profitable;
   (d) is the classification required by law. **(2.13)**

5. A statutory classification of insurance:
   (a) requires all insurers to follow this system in their internal administration;
   (b) is a suggested way of categorising business, but with no obligation to use the system in any respect;
   (c) will only apply to compulsory classes of insurance;
   (d) is to be used for statistical data supplied to government for control purposes. **(2.15)**

(For multiple choice answers, see page 355.)

PART ONE: OBJECTIVE TESTS (see Answers, page 356) AND ASSIGNMENTS

1.1 State whether the following statements are *true* or *false*:
- (a) A businessman may insure all his business risks.
- (b) Fundamental risks are never commercially insurable.
- (c) A risk manager is employed by insurance companies as a consultant for large business customers.
- (d) Insurance cannot be arranged against the consequences of deliberate acts.
- (e) Specialist insurers concentrate on a single type of insurance.

1.2 Select the most correct answer for the following questions:
- (a) The meaning of a pure risk is: (i) an insurance where the policyholder's honesty is beyond reproach; (ii) a potentiality which offers only the prospect of a loss; (iii) a risk which is insurable.
- (b) The definition of a speculative risk is: (i) a bet on a horse race; (ii) launching a new product; (iii) an uncertainty from which profit, loss or *status quo* might result.
- (c) The mathematical value of a risk is: (i) the premium charged; (ii) the statistical possibility of calculating its predictability; (iii) the sum insured as a percentage of total sums insured by that insurer.
- (d) If an insurance is contrary to public policy: (i) insurers will rarely grant it; (ii) it would be considered immoral by most members of the public; (iii) both insurer and policyholder are liable to criminal charges.
- (e) Classification of insurance by the function performed: (i) outlines the different classes of insurance transacted by insurers; (ii) gives broad categories of insurance crossing traditional departmental boundaries; (iii) summarises the main purposes of insurance.

1.3 Assignments:
- (a) Write an essay on the types of risk a businessman is likely to face and the manner and extent to which he might seek to safeguard himself from the effects of them.
- (b) Discuss the suggestion that (i) motor insurance and (ii) life assurance relate to fundamental risks and that they should not be left to the option of the individual.
- (c) Make enquiries with local insurance organisations to ascertain the way they classify the insurances they deal with (e.g. their usual departmental divisions) and compare these practical examples with each other and the classification for your examination purposes.

PART TWO

MAJOR CLASSES OF BUSINESS

CHAPTER 3

MARINE INSURANCE

A. THE DEVELOPMENT OF MARINE INSURANCE

3.1 History

Marine insurance is the oldest known type of insurance. Something akin to it was practised at least 1,000 years before the Christian era. The early Phoenician traders were probably the first to adopt insurance-like practices, although the present form of marine insurance probably began in Northern Italy in the eleventh or twelfth century. One of the earliest records of a marine policy relates to a Mediterranean voyage in 1347.

3.2 Early insurance-like practices

Long before modern insurance methods were introduced, maritime ventures were sometimes subject to practices similar in form or intent to insurance. These were as follows:

(a) *Bottomry and respondentia bonds.* Bottomry originally concerned a loan to the owner of a vessel, made in order to finance a venture. Later (and the practice survived until the early twentieth century), it concerned loans advanced to the master of a vessel in a time of emergency to enable a venture to be completed. In both cases, the vessel was pledged against the loan, on the understanding that the loan was not repayable if the vessel did not survive the voyage. A "premium", or charge for interest on the loan, was added to the amount to be repaid, to cover the risk that had been borne by the lender.

In one way, a bottomry bond may be considered as *insurance in reverse.* That is, the amount payable is paid at the outset and retained if misfortune occurs (the "premium" not then being paid), whereas insurance involves the prior payment of the premium with no recovery unless misfortune occurs.

A *respondentia bond* was the same, in principle, as a bottomry bond, except that the cargo and not the vessel was pledged against the loan.

(b) *General average.* This is a marine practice which still survives today, and most marine policies include *general average contributions* within the cover provided. Basically, the practice means that the owner of goods or property deliberately damaged or sacrificed in a successful attempt to save a marine venture receives compensation from all interested parties for the loss suffered.

For a more detailed consideration of general average, see **31.4**.

3.3 Development in the United Kingdom

Marine insurance was introduced to England in the fourteenth or fifteenth century by the Lombards from Northern Italy. They were great traders, and in addition to their goods they brought with them their business methods and practices, such as banking and insurance. Their place in British commercial history is recorded in the name of Lombard Street in the City of London.

The rest of this chapter devoted to the development of this class of business will be confined to development within the United Kingdom, which rapidly became and is still a leading world centre of marine insurance (see Fig. 4).

3.4 Not originally a full-time occupation

In the early days of marine insurance merchants would engage in such activities as an adjunct to their normal trading. They would assume part of the risks in ventures undertaken by their colleagues, who would reciprocate for the merchants' own ventures. This achieved the primary function of spreading the risk, and much of the necessary administrative work was performed by brokers. They would draw up details of a proposed marine venture and ask merchants to sign their name or initials underneath, indicating what proportion of the risk they would be prepared to bear and at what rate of premium. This practice has survived to the present day, and is basically the procedure adopted with insurances placed, for example, with Lloyd's underwriters (see **3.9**).

3.5 "Underwriter" and "underwriting"

These terms are very frequently used in all forms of insurance, although originating in marine insurance. Their meaning should be understood as follows:

(a) *"Underwriter"*. This term arose quite literally from the fact that a merchant prepared to assume part of a risk would "write under" the details of the risk his name and the proportion accepted. It still has this ancient meaning of one who is prepared to accept insurance risks. In this sense, therefore, every insurer, whether a company or an individual, is an underwriter. The term is more usually applied to insurers who are individuals, namely Lloyd's underwriters (see **3.9**).

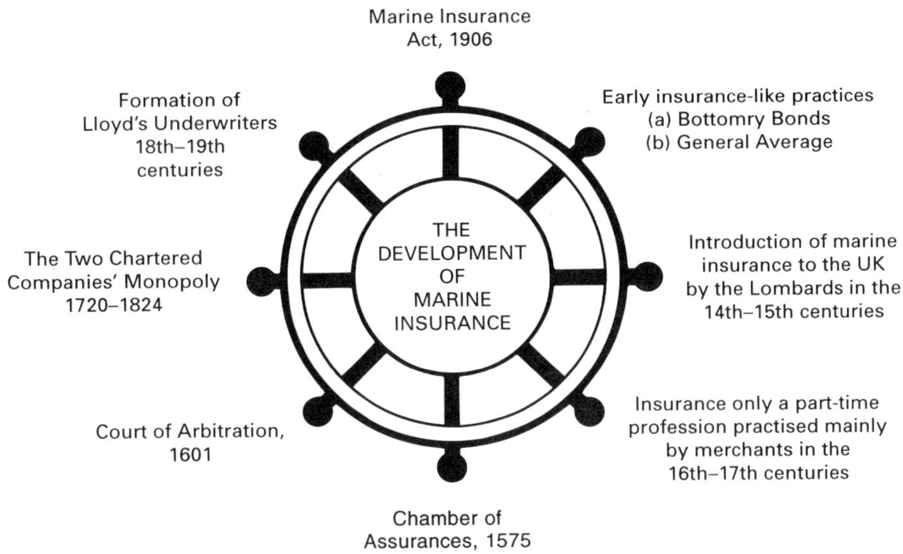

Fig. 4 The development of marine insurance

NOTE: it is the custom for insurance companies to appoint certain officials with the authority to decide whether or not to accept risks proposed. These officials are in the true sense underwriters, and are often termed as such in their title, e.g. the marine underwriter, who would be a senior official corresponding to the motor manager or the fire manager in other classes of business. Indeed, these latter officials might equally be termed motor and fire underwriters.

(b) *"Underwriting"*. This is performing the function of an underwriter, in assessing a risk and deciding the premium and other terms to be applied. By custom, the term has also come to mean all action associated with the processing and servicing (excluding claims and accounting work) of new and existing insurances. Thus, for example, in accident insurance the theft underwriting department will be engaged in all the above activities for theft and associated policies.

NOTE: A shortened version of the word, i.e. to "write" business, will mean the transaction of insurance. Thus, a company which "writes" marine business is one which transacts this class of insurance, and will normally be prepared to quote a premium rate for such risks.

3.6 The Chamber of Assurances, 1575

In the reign of Elizabeth I, England was greatly involved in exploration and trade abroad. This encouraged the great growth of marine insurance, but as it was transacted on less formal lines disputes were extremely common under marine policies. The Chamber of Assurances was opened in the Royal Exchange for the registration of marine policies. Having policies registered gave the immense advantage of proving the existence and terms of the contracts when disputes arose. However, not every policy was registered, and disputes were still fairly commonplace.

3.7 The Court of Arbitration, 1601

An Act of Parliament relating to marine insurance was passed in 1601, setting up a Court of Arbitration, which was to deal with disputes under marine policies and which met in the Chamber of Assurances.

The effect of this court and the Chamber of Assurances, apart from reducing the number of disputes reaching the Admiralty Court, was to give a degree of permanence to marine insurance customs, which have largely survived to this day. Even the form of marine insurance policy used became standardised and survived for some 300 years (although the basic wording was brought up to date by "clauses" attached to the document). However, for various reasons the Chamber of Assurances gradually became less important. It finally outlived its usefulness about 100 years after its formation.

3.8 The two chartered companies' monopoly

Gradually the practice of marine insurance had become more specialised, and by the early eighteenth century it was established as a full-time profession. However, it was still practised by individuals rather than by corporations. Indeed, the so-called "Bubble Act" (The South Sea Company Act 1720) restricted the authority to provide insurances to individuals. Nevertheless, by a substantial financial inducement to the King, the London Assurance and the Royal Exchange Assurance obtained the rare privilege of a royal charter to transact marine insurance. This was in the same year, 1720, and the charters also prohibited all except individuals from engaging in marine insurance.

This monopoly, together with the further growth in marine ventures, gave great impetus to individual underwriters, many of whom banded together and later formed the organisation called Lloyd's (see **3.9**). After a number of abortive attempts, the monopoly was repealed in 1824 and the number of companies transacting marine insurance grew enormously thereafter.

3.9 Formation of Lloyd's underwriters

With the establishment of full-time insurance specialists, it became customary for these "underwriters" and merchants seeking or dealing in marine insurance to have regular meeting places. Very frequently these were at the newly fashionable coffee houses, which were important centres of social and business life in the seventeenth and eighteenth centuries.

One such coffee house in London was opened by Edward Lloyd about 1680. This became a great centre for marine business and insurance transactions. Gradually a close-knit association of underwriters emerged and, although various changes of premises took place, the association became incorporated as Lloyd's by an Act of Parliament in 1871. For a more detailed examination of Lloyd's, see Chapter 17. It should be noted at this stage, however, that the individual underwriters forming the corporation of Lloyd's constitute an important part of the insurance market.

3.10 The Marine Insurance Act 1906

Over the years, marine insurance law developed an increasing wealth of recorded cases and customs. The Marine Insurance Act 1906 concentrated this into a single statute, which codifies the practice of marine insurance. In many ways the statute conforms to its oft-quoted description as "the Bible of marine insurance", and it is not possible to study marine insurance in the United Kingdom without a detailed knowledge of the contents of that Act.

The 1906 Act was followed by the Marine Insurance (Gambling Policies) Act 1909, adding some safeguards particularly in the area of possible speculation with marine insurance policies. The 1906–1909 Acts remain the only ones for commercial insurances on the statute book, and still largely govern the practice for this class of business. Indeed, having the full authority of statute, they also continue to influence other classes of insurance.

B. THE SCOPE OF MARINE INSURANCE

3.11 Perils covered

All insurance is intended to provide financial compensation for injury, loss or damage sustained. Marine insurance fulfils this general aim in respect of losses arising from maritime trade and ventures. "Perils of the sea" is a famous phrase with former marine insurance contracts, and includes collision, fire, theft and stranding. In fact any loss due to the actions of the sea and of an unexpected and fortuitous nature would normally be covered. War risks may also be insured on special terms.

It is now common for insurances to be arranged on an "all risks" basis, which implies that loss or damage arising from any risk will be covered unless the policy contains a specific exclusion deleting cover therefor. The alternative form of cover would be on a "specified perils" basis, whereby only loss or damage from the perils specified would be covered (again subject to any policy exclusions).

3.12 Insurance of property

The insurance of property in marine insurance may be considered under three headings:

(a) *Hull.* This relates to insurance of the actual vessel and its machinery (often termed "Hull and Machinery" coverage). Such policies are normally arranged on an annual basis, and may offer cover on an "all risks" basis.
(b) *Cargo.* As the name suggests, this relates to goods or merchandise carried by the ship. Policies may be arranged for the duration of a voyage, or on other bases (see **3.14**). War risks can be insured (sometimes under a separate policy) although the basic cover will be provided under Institute Cargo Clauses A, B or C (see **3.13**).
(c) *Freight.* The term "freight" when used on the railways means the same as "cargo" above, but in the maritime world it refers to the cost of transporting the goods. Alternatively, it is used for the hire of a vessel.

If the cost of transportation (i.e. freight) has been prepaid, this is usually merged with the value of the goods being carried, and insured under the cargo policy. Freight may be insured separately where it is at the risk of the shipowner. That is, where it is totally or partially lost should the ship fail to reach destination.

NOTE: i. *Liability risks*: these present an unusual feature in marine insurance and are considered in **3.15**.
ii. *Drilling rigs*: these offshore installations present specialist insurance needs. The London Drilling Rig Committee was formed to cater for these needs in formulating appropriate types of cover.

3.13 The policy document

For nearly 300 years the basic marine policy wording used by companies and Lloyd's underwriters was virtually unchanged. (The latter's policy form was known as the "SG" or "Ships-Goods" form, since it could be used for hull or cargo insurances.) This had the considerable legal advantage of continuity and agreed interpretation. But by the early 1980s the demands of international markets required the substitution of a more modern wording.

The archaic wording of the SG and company forms was replaced with more modern terminology and format in what became known as the "MAR" form, supplemented by clauses, termed *institute* clauses (so named from their origins with the Institute of London Underwriters). For cargo insurances, Clauses A ("all risks") B or C (specified perils) are now issued and are accepted and understood by the marine insurance market throughout the world.

3.14 Policy variations

The main types of cover available differ according to the period for which the insurance operates, as follows:

(a) *Time policy.* As the name suggests, this policy is for a predetermined period of time, usually not exceeding 12 months. Hull insurances are frequently on this basis.
(b) *Voyage policy.* Again the name is virtually self-explanatory, cover being operative from the port of departure to destination, irrespective of any time element. Nevertheless, cargo insured on this basis is normally subject to a "warehouse to warehouse" clause, and cover would in any event terminate 60 days after unloading at destination.
(c) *Mixed policy.* This cover is a combination of time and voyage insurance, a longer period of time being allowed after the vessel arrives at destination.
(d) *Building risk policy.* Another self-explanatory term; such a policy covers a vessel from the time its construction commences until its trials are completed.
(e) *Floating policy.* Although this is a term which seems particularly suited to marine insurance, its meaning is not as self-evident as those above. It relates to a type of cargo insurance, which is effected for a relatively large lump-sum insured. The cover applies to any shipments made by the policyholder, who makes a declaration as to the precise amount involved with individual shipments. These declarations are set against the floating policy, reducing the sum insured by that amount, until the full sum insured is exhausted.

    This type of policy is no longer in common use but it was a very convenient way of avoiding the issue of separate policies for every shipment. A floating policy must be distinguished from an *open cover.* This relates to an agreement by a marine insurer to accept insurance on proposed shipments by a given assured. For each of such shipments, a separate policy is subsequently issued. These arrangements are now very common with important clients or brokers.

NOTE: The term "assured" is used for the policyholder in marine insurance, not "insured". This is rather anomalous, but it is a practice of very long standing in this class of business.

3.15 Insurance of liability

At one time it was thought that the policy issued by marine insurers also covered liabilities of the shipowner in connection with a collision between two vessels. This was not the intention of the insurers, and the case of *De Vaux* v. *Salvador* (1836) held that the underwriters were not liable under their policy.

This was at a time when the insuring of one's liability was thought to be contrary to public policy: see **2.10**. However, it was realised that heavy liabilities could be incurred for damage, injury or death, including such liabilities for goods or persons being carried on the insured vessel. Consequently, a compromise was effected and thereafter it became customary to insure three-quarters of a shipowner's liability for collision damage. This was achieved by attaching an appropriate clause to the hull policy. The remaining quarter of any such liability was covered by what may be termed a self-insurance fund set up by an association of shipowners, known as "The Club", or, more usually, as the Protection and Indemnity (P & I) Club.

Liabilities other than the result of collisions are normally all covered by the Protection and Indemnity Club, rather than by marine insurers.

C. THE IMPORTANCE OF MARINE INSURANCE IN TRADE

3.16 General

It has already been seen that merchants and shipowners would be very reluctant to allow their substantial investments to be hazarded in marine ventures without the protection of insurance. This very situation occurred in the early part of the First World War, when shipowners refused to allow their ships to leave port before some form of war risks insurance could be arranged. This was achieved by the government giving considerable assistance in arranging a suitable scheme.

This reluctance of traders can be well understood when one considers that a large ocean-going vessel such as the *Queen Elizabeth 2* can easily represent an investment of over £100 million, quite apart from the immense potentialities of any liabilities arising from her use.

Disasters like those in which the *Titanic* in 1912 and more recently the *Amoco Cadiz* and the *Exxon Valdez* were involved demonstrate how enormous potential risks can become realities. Marine insurance played a very great part in compensating the financial results of such catastrophes.

3.17 Insurance required by banks

The great majority of international commercial transactions are financed by the banks or similar institutions. Those lending money will normally insist that the venture is covered by marine insurance. Indeed, it is customary for the marine insurance policy to be considered one of the "documents of title" that must be produced before banks will discount the bills of exchange through which most international trading is financed. The insurance policy is lodged with the bank as *collateral security* against the money advanced.

D. PROGRESS TEST 3

PART 1—SHORT ANSWERS (Answer in one or two sentences)

1. What were bottomry and respondentia bonds? **(3.2)**
2. Write briefly on:
   (a) The origin of the word "underwriter". **(3.5)**
   (b) The Chamber of Assurances. **(3.6)**
   (c) The chartered companies' monopoly. **(3.8)**
3. What is the significance of the Marine Insurance Act 1906? **(3.10)**
4. What different types of policy are found in marine insurance? **(3.12, 3.14)**
5. Why is marine insurance important in trade and commerce today? **(3.16, 3.17)**

PART 2—MULTIPLE CHOICE (Choose the most correct option)

1. General average is:
   (a) an ancient practice seeking to share certain losses fairly;
   (b) an ancient practice requiring all insurers to pay equal shares;
   (c) a policy provision requiring the assured to bear a share of the loss;
   (d) a system of sharing blame for a collision at sea. **(3.2)**
2. Underwriting is a term used to describe:
   (a) the authorisation of an insurer to transact insurance;
   (b) the assessment of risks proposed for insurance;
   (c) a guarantee that the insurer will not suffer heavy losses;
   (d) a process of determining the premium for a proposed risk. **(3.5)**
3. Lloyd's underwriters are:
   (a) part of the Lloyd's insurance company;
   (b) individuals employed by Lloyd's to assess insurance risks;
   (c) independent underwriters based at Lloyd's of London;
   (d) not authorised to transact business on their own account. **(3.9)**
4. The old "SG" form used in marine insurance:
   (a) is still the most common form of policy used today;
   (b) was used only for the insurance of ships;
   (c) could be used either for insuring ships or cargo;
   (d) was quickly replaced by a more modern form. **(3.13)**
5. The insurance of liability risks in marine insurance:
   (a) forms part of each marine insurance policy;
   (b) is never found in any marine insurance policy;

(c) is a compulsory requirement by law;
(d) is mostly insured by Protection and Indemnity Clubs. **(3.15)**

(For multiple choice answers, see page 355.)

CHAPTER 4

LIFE ASSURANCE

A. THE DEVELOPMENT OF LIFE ASSURANCE

4.1 History

Providing for one's dependants has been a consideration of all prudent people throughout the ages. Doing this, or at least providing for the cost of one's funeral, on a collective basis was a concept of the ancient world. Funeral clubs and similar benevolent societies, invariably as an adjunct to religious associations, existed in ancient Greece and Rome. As understood today, however, life assurance was not practised as a commercial venture until medieval times.

NOTE: The term life "assurance" is traditional in the U.K. market, but in more recent times and in most other markets life "insurance" is more commonly used. There is no practical difference, but in deference to traditional terminology the former term will be used here.

4.2 Development in the United Kingdom

The early development of life assurance was closely linked with that of marine insurance. Indeed, the first life assurers were marine insurance underwriters, policies often being written on the life of a merchant sailing with his goods. It is convenient, therefore, to study the historical development from the late sixteenth century (see Fig. 5). The first recorded life policy was in 1583.

NOTE: The first policy recorded was subject to a dispute over payment, the policyholder having died within one week of the calendar anniversary of the policy. The underwriters contended that the policy period of "12 months" related to lunar months, which had expired. The court ruled that payment must be made. This decision underlined the legal principle, known briefly as the *contra proferentem* rule, that the party drawing up a document is responsible for it and any ambiguity in it will be construed against him.

4.2 Life Assurance

THE DEVELOPMENT OF LIFE ASSURANCE

Ordinary Life Assurance		Industrial Life Assurance
Short-term policies & Mutual Associations	16th-17th centuries	
The Amicable Society	1705	
Dodson's Mortality Table	1755	
The Equitable	1762	
The Life Assurance Act	1774	The Industrial Revolution
The Westminster	1794	Many friendly societies and industrial life assurers
The Life Assurance Companies Act	1870	
Associated action		
Life Offices Association	1889	
	1901	Industrial Life Offices Association
	1923	Industrial Assurance Act
	1948-58	Industrial Assurance and Friendly Societies Act

Fig. 5 The development of life assurance

4.3 Early forms of life assurance

In the sixteenth and seventeenth centuries the following types of life assurance were practised:

(a) *Short-term assurances.* As the name indicates, these policies were for a limited period, covering the risk of death within that period only. They were particularly used for merchants and others on voyages, or on the lives of debtors as security against loans.

(b) *Mutual assurance associations.* These were generally societies which were in effect self-insurance clubs, whereby all participating members contributed a fixed sum, the total of which (less administration expenses) was available for distribution to the dependants of members dying during the year. Thus, the amount payable on death varied according to the number of members and number of deaths in that year.

(c) *Annuities.* An annuity is a form of pension, providing an income for a fixed period or for life. Unfortunately, a number of the early annuity schemes were fraudulent in intent. However, many were not and considerable relief was afforded particularly by the earliest schemes, which were devised to provide for widows on the death of their husbands.

4.4 Mortality tables

Statistics form a vital part in the transaction of all types of insurance, especially life assurance. In the earliest days of the business these statistics were not available, or their importance was not realised. Consequently, life assurance was written on very unscientific lines and many assurance schemes and assurers collapsed because of this.

Actuarial science, known to the ancient world in part, was being developed, and it began to be realised that this highly technical form of mathematics was eminently suited to life assurance. This became apparent with the compilation of *mortality tables*, the first of which was produced as early as 1693. A more important one was compiled in 1755 by one Dodson, who showed that it was possible to charge the same premium per year throughout a life assurance contract (these are termed *level premiums*), it being graduated according to the assured's age on entry. These mortality tables, and the introduction of actuarial science, revolutionised the whole practice of life assurance.

4.5 Important early societies

In the historical development of life assurance the following should be noted:

(a) the Amicable Society;
(b) the Equitable Life Assurance Society;
(c) the Westminster Society: see below.

4.6 The Amicable Society

Formed in 1705, with the rare privilege of a royal charter, the Amicable was undoubtedly the most successful mutual assurance association (see **4.3**(b)). Despite being run on what are now regarded as unscientific lines, the society prospered; so much so that in 1757 it felt justified in guaranteeing a minimum sum payable at death. This boldness brought further prosperity, but the sound logic of the modern methods was unanswerable, and a new charter was obtained in 1807 for the society to transact business on an actuarial basis in line with present-day practice.

In 1866 the Amicable was acquired by the Norwich Union Life.

4.7 The Equitable Life Assurance Society

The Equitable was formed in 1762 specifically to transact life assurance on an actuarial basis, following the recommendations of Dodson. For many years it led the way, and it is claimed by some that the history of the Equitable is the history of life assurance. This may be an exaggeration, but certainly that society was the pioneer in modern methods, introducing many features which are now standard practice in life assurance.

4.8 The Westminster Society

The Westminster, formed in 1792, was not of great importance except in so far as it was the first proprietary company with share capital to transact life assurance. It was soon followed by many similar organisations, such as the Pelican Life Office in 1797. The Westminster was amalgamated with the Guardian in 1861.

4.9 Life Assurance Act 1774

At the time life assurance was consolidating itself with the introduction of sound scientific methods, society generally was becoming engulfed by a wave of gambling and speculation. This was particularly evident in the multitude of highly speculative companies floated during this period (many of which were fraudulent, and nearly all of which collapsed). Life assurance also became the focus of attention for many gambling contracts, in the form of assurances on the lives of others, perhaps a notorious criminal or a famous soldier, in the hope that their early demise would bring the policyholder a quick reward.

This practice violated the common law principle of *insurable interest* (see Chapter 17), but the principle tended to be ignored as wagering assumed the proportions of a national scandal. However, the nation reacted in the passing of the Life Assurance Act 1774, which prohibited all insurance on lives except "where persons insuring shall have an interest on the life or death of the person insured". Thus the common law requirement was reinstated with statutory authority.

4.10 Life Assurance Companies Act 1870

The speculative, and indeed fraudulent, element associated with life assurance had never been completely eliminated, and it became increasingly clear, following the failure of many assurers, that further statutory action was required. The Life Assurance Companies Act sought to stabilise the business. To do this it required, among other things, life assurers to deposit £20,000 as security and to comply with Board of Trade regulations as to the maintenance and publication of accounts.

State regulation and intervention in the affairs of insurers generally is considered later: see Chapter 33.

4.11 Co-operation between assurers

Prompted by the wish to improve their business generally, and by the realisation that exchange of information and ideas could only have a beneficial effect, life assurers formed various associations in the nineteenth century. Perhaps the largest of these was the Life Offices' Association (LOA).

B. INDUSTRIAL LIFE ASSURANCE

4.12 Origins

As its name suggests, industrial life assurance had its beginnings in the "industrial" or working classes created by the Industrial Revolution, especially during the nineteenth century.

For the most part, the working classes were ignorant of life assurance, and in any event could scarcely have afforded a lump sum payment for the customary annual premium. Nevertheless, the desire to provide at least the cost of one's funeral was still there, and to meet this need literally thousands of friendly societies were created. It was from these societies that the practice of industrial life assurance grew, producing in due course such giants in the insurance world as the Prudential.

4.13 Legislation

As with ordinary life assurance, industrial life assurance became subject to statutory regulations. In addition to legislation applicable to insurance generally, this class of business is affected by the Industrial Assurances Act 1923 and the Industrial Assurance and Friendly Societies Act 1948 (with a similar amending Act in 1958). The 1923 Act created the post of Industrial Assurance Commissioner, who is also the Registrar of Friendly Societies, and one of whose duties is to hear and decide disputes.

4.14 Co-operation between industrial assurers

The advantages of associated action over matters of common interest were not overlooked, and in 1901 the Industrial Life Offices Association (ILOA) was formed.

4.15 Comparison with ordinary life assurance

Although the two classes of business are basically the same, industrial life assurance originated with the poorer classes of society, which meant that certain basic differences in practice were necessary. The following comparison should be noted:

(a) *Industrial life assurance* (known as "IB"—Industrial Branch):
  (i) Premiums payable weekly, fortnightly or monthly.
  (ii) Premiums collected from the policyholder at his home.
  (Hence the modern title *home service assurance* for this class of business.)
  (iii) Premiums of very low amounts, perhaps a few pence only per week.
  (iv) Sums payable correspondingly limited, perhaps under £20–£30 (originally intended to cover funeral costs).
  (v) Unit of cover is the premium (i.e. the policyholder decides what he wants to pay, which will indicate the cover obtained).
  (vi) The agent collecting the premiums is usually employed by the assurer, remunerated partly by commission.

(b) *Ordinary life assurance* (known as "OB"—Ordinary Branch):
  (i) Usually payable annually (quarterly or monthly payments can be arranged at extra cost).
  (ii) Usually paid by cheque or banker's order direct to the assurer.
  (iii) Usually involves premiums of many pounds.
  (iv) Sums assured normally reckoned in hundreds or thousands of pounds.
  (v) Unit is the sum assured (i.e. the premium is calculated from the amount of cover required).
  (vi) Agent not an employee; may be a solicitor, insurance broker, etc.

4.16 Relative decline of IB business

Industrial life assurance has seen a great decline in popularity over recent decades. There are several reasons for this, for example the growing affluence of society, but a major modern influence has been the cost factor involved in the labour-intensive process of collecting small sums of money on a frequent and regular basis.

C. THE SCOPE OF LIFE ASSURANCE

4.16 Basic types

A great variety of contracts are offered by life assurers, but virtually all of them can be considered within four basic descriptions:

(a) Term assurances.
(b) Whole-life assurances.
(c) Endowment assurances.
(d) Annuities: see below.

4.17 Term (or temporary) assurances

These are the oldest form of policy, payment being made by the assurer only if the life assured dies within the specified period. Suitable for businessmen on journeys, or as temporary cover to secure an outstanding debt (e.g. a mortgage loan), this is the cheapest form of life cover available, but of course its scope is very limited.

4.18 Whole-life assurances

As the name suggests, these policies last for the whole of the assured's life, the sum being payable at death only. Premiums may be payable throughout life, or cease at a given age, say sixty-five. These policies are useful to provide against death duties, and for persons of normal health quite substantial benefits can be obtained for relatively low premiums.

4.19 Endowment assurances

A feature of the policies in **4.17–4.18** is that the assured can never benefit personally from the proceeds of the policy. The endowment policy provides for the sum assured to be paid either at death or after a fixed number of years, whichever comes first. (The number of years is selected by the assured when effecting the policy.)

This is a particularly suitable form of policy for the family man. In the event of his premature death, his dependants are provided for; if he survives the term (when perhaps he no longer has family commitments), the policy moneys will be available for him to use as he wishes.

4.20 Variations of assurances described above

The number of adaptations and modifications of the basic forms in **4.17–4.19** is enormous, prompted both by the very competitive nature of this class of business and by the complex needs of society today. Some typical examples of variations which have been devised over the years are given below.

4.21 Convertible term

This is a normal term assurance (see **4.17**), but with the valuable provision that the assured has the option to convert the policy into a whole-life (**4.18**) or endowment assurance (**4.19**). This option must be exercised within a specified number of years during the term assured.

Such a policy is very useful to the young man who has family commitments. In the early years, when his resources may be rather limited, he has the protection, which can be converted to a wider form of cover (without further evidence of good health) should his resources improve.

4.22 House purchase

With more and more people borrowing money to buy their own house, many schemes have been effected to give assistance, especially where the borrower dies before the loan has been repaid. Basically, there are two types:

(a) *Decreasing term assurance.* This is a term assurance, but the amount payable in the event of death diminishes each year. This form of policy is not exclusively found in connection with house purchase, but it is particularly suited to this, in that the sum assured can be geared to the amount of the original loan, reducing as the loan is being repaid by the borrower (as with most mortgage loans advanced by building societies). By this method, the amount outstanding on the loan is covered at all times and would be cleared by the policy moneys in the event of a premature death. (This form of cover is the cheapest available and is sometimes known as a *mortgage protection policy.*)

(b) *Endowment assurance.* Under this method, a normal endowment policy is effected, with the policy moneys made payable to the lender. The sum assured is made equal to the amount of the loan, which is never reduced during the currency of the policy. The borrower makes no capital repayments to the lender until the policy moneys become available to clear the whole debt. In the meantime, of course, the borrower pays interest charges on the full loan, plus the annual premiums for the life policy.

A modern variation of this is where a "with profits" (see **4.32**) endowment is effected with the basic sum assured representing only a proportion, perhaps only 50 per cent, of the loan, the balance to be provided by the bonus allocations during the policy period. Linked with the policy is a decreasing term assurance (see (a) above), to pay the balance of the loan in the event of premature death.

4.23 Family income

There are several variations of this type of policy, which is known by different names with different assurers. The basic provisions, however, are that in the event of the death of the life assured a capital sum is paid, plus an income, payable monthly (or quarterly or annually, as arranged), for the remainder of a specified number of years from the inception date of the policy.

Such a policy forms a combination of whole-life or endowment (lump sum) and a decreasing term assurance, see **4.22**(a), payable by instalments (the income benefits). This is a very suitable policy for the family man with young dependants. An early death would result in the lump sum payment plus additional protection for the family during the years of its growing up.

Because full cover is costly, it is quite common for policies to provide income benefits only (i.e. deleting the lump sum benefit, thus substantially reducing the premium since a claim is no longer certain).

4.24 Assurances for children

Various types of policy have been devised with the welfare of children specifically in mind. Two examples are:

(a) *Child's deferred assurance.* This policy is effected on the life of the parent for a selected number of years, terminating with an option date, when the child reaches *vesting age* (often 18). Until that time, the premium is paid by the parent, but then the child has the option of having the assurance vested in his name and on his life, as a normal whole-life or endowment policy, regardless of the child's medical condition.

Should the child die before the vesting age, the premiums are returned to the parent, often with interest. Should the parent die before the option date, no further premiums are payable and the option can be exercised by the child at the appropriate time. If it is decided not to continue the policy beyond the option date, it is treated as a form of endowment which has *matured*, and a cash sum is allowed.

(b) *Educational endowment.* This is little more than an ordinary endowment policy, maturing by instalments, to provide income to meet school and/or university fees. Again, the policy would be on the life of the parent.

NOTE: It is not unusual for ordinary endowment policies to be effected by parents, godparents or relatives on their own lives for the ultimate benefit of children, the policies being designed to mature at the child's coming of age or some other suitable time. As far as the assurer is concerned, such policies are simply endowment contracts.

4.25 Pure endowments

These are a rare form of life assurance, in that no benefit is payable should death occur during the policy term. The provisions are that a certain sum of money will be paid to the assured in the event of his surviving a certain period.

Basically, this is merely a form of saving, but with relatively high rates of interest and many other savings schemes outside life assurance, this form of policy is of limited application today.

The contract may provide for a return of all or part of the premiums paid in the event of death before the policy matures. In this sense, a child's deferred assurance (see **4.24**(a)) incorporates a form of pure endowment (i.e. the premiums are returned if the child dies before vesting age).

4.26 Group life assurances

As the name suggests, these are policies on a collective basis, assuring the members of a particular group of persons, such as the employees of a firm. This kind of policy is becoming increasingly popular in all types of insurance, and the individual members are not always required to contribute towards the premiums (which are paid by the employer or by the group organisation). Where the scheme is non-contributory, such a policy could well provide a very useful "fringe benefit" for employees.

The policies may be on a whole-life or endowment basis, and cover for the individual is dependent upon his remaining a member of the group. However, provision is often made for an individual withdrawing from the group to arrange a continuation assurance on his own life.

4.27 "More than one life" assurances

The intriguing title of these types of policy conjures up interesting possibilities, but it merely means that there is a joint assurance on two or more persons. They are often called "joint-life assurances". The sum assured can be made payable on the death of the first life assured, or on that of the last survivor. The former arrangement is particularly useful with certain forms of partnership, where the death of one person can have serious financial repercussions for the other(s), e.g. theatrical performers.

4.28 Unit trusts

In recent decades a great emphasis has been given by assurers to the development of life assurance which is in some way linked with unit trusts or other commercial share schemes. The variations are numerous, but with an increasing growth in commercial investment and in times of high investment returns, this aspect of life assurances is always likely to prove popular. Such schemes may involve whole-life or endowment assurances.

4.29 Annuities

Strictly speaking, annuities are not contracts of life assurance. They are a form of pension whereby, in return for a certain sum of money (paid in a lump sum or by instalments) the assurer agrees to pay the *annuitant* an annual amount (an *annuity*) for a specified period or for the remainder of the annuitant's life. There are various forms of annuity:

(a) *Annuity for life.* This is a straightforward "pension", payable as long as the annuitant lives.
(b) *Annuity certain.* This means that the annuity is payable for a fixed number of years, even if the annuitant dies before the period is complete.
(c) *Guaranteed annuity.* The annuity is payable for a fixed number of years or until the annuitant dies, whichever comes later.
(d) *Reversionary annuity.* Payments to the annuitant do not commence until the death of another specified person.
(e) *Joint and survivor.* Two persons (often husband and wife) are named as the annuitants and on the death of one of them payments are continued to the other, usually, but not always, at a reduced rate.

NOTE: i. All annuities may be considered under two basic categories: (1) *immediate annuities*, where payments commence as soon as the lump sum is received by the assurer; (2) *deferred annuities*, where payments commence at some time in the future. With both types payments are normally half yearly, in arrears.

ii. A form of annuity now obsolete in the United Kingdom (but still to be found among the long-term statutory classes of business: see Fig. 3) is the *tontine*. This related to a group of persons who shared the annuity amongst those who were still surviving, until the last member of the group died.

D. SOME FEATURES PECULIAR TO LIFE ASSURANCE

4.30 Purpose

With all other types of insurance the policy is intended to give financial protection against the unforeseen or unexpected mishap. With life assurance, apart from term assurances, the assured event must happen (i.e. death or the expiry of a period of years). Thus, while other insurances are designed to compensate the policyholder in person for financial loss, the traditional role of life assurance was primarily to protect dependants or others in the event of the policyholder's death.

NOTE: Endowments and annuities are exceptions to this general statement, but they may be considered as indicating a second purpose for life assurance, namely as a form of saving and providing for one's own future.

4.31 Long-term contracts

Nearly all life policies are intended to continue until the assured's death, or at least for several years. Other forms of insurance policies may be renewed many times, but are usually 12-month contracts, which may be terminated by either party, or have their terms varied, at the anniversary dates. Bearing in mind the purpose of life policies (see **4.30**), it would be inequitable to allow an assurer to terminate such a policy at the anniversary date or at any other time. If this were possible, a policyholder of advancing years or declining health could find himself or his dependants deprived of the very security intended by the contract. Normally, the policyholder has the right to terminate a life policy at any time, but if he wishes the contract to continue it must do so, provided he continues to pay the premiums and complies with any policy conditions.

4.32 "With profits" policies

The standard scale of premiums for a life policy, purchasing the specified cover only, would acquire what is termed a *"without profits"* policy. A scale of premiums at an increased rate would not only acquire the appropriate cover but would also entitle the policyholder to some extent to participate in the profits of the assurer; hence *"with profits"* policies.

Such policies, which are sometimes termed *"participating"* policies, would participate in a declared bonus, proportionate to their sums assured. The bonus is declared annually (with some assurers every three or five years) as a rate per cent. There is no guarantee that a bonus will be paid, but for practical purposes a bonus of some sort may always be expected.

Bonuses are seldom payable at once (if they are, they are called *cash bonuses* and are for much lower amounts). Instead, they are added to the sum assured and paid when the sum assured is paid, i.e. at death or policy maturity. As with interest on a bank account, bonuses may be:

(a) *Simple.* This means that the addition of bonuses to the sum assured does not affect the calculations for future bonuses, which are based solely on the sum assured.

(b) *Compound.* Here the bonuses and sum assured are aggregated for the purpose of future bonus calculations.

(c) *Terminal bonuses.* In times of high interest earnings on investments, assurers have found it possible to add an extra bonus (usually as a percentage of existing bonus entitlement) when the policy payment is due because of death or maturity. These are now an established feature, even though investment earnings have declined in recent years.

NOTE: i. Bonuses are more correctly termed *reversionary bonuses*. A reversionary interest is one which is possessed by its owner but with the enjoyment of it deferred until a future time or event.

ii. In many countries bonuses, as such, are not provided. Instead, participating policies receive *dividends*. These are immediate cash entitlements, similar to dividends received on other financial investments. Such dividends are usually calculated as a percentage of the premium paid, rather than on the sum assured. They may be received as cash or left, at interest, with the insurer.

4.33 Level premiums

Actuarial science and the use of mortality tables have proved that it is possible to issue life policies with a constant premium during the whole policy period: see **4.4**. Naturally, the amount payable will depend upon the age of the assured at policy inception, but as the policyholder ages the premium does not change, even though the risk is increasing. With any other class of business such an increase in risk would invariably mean higher premiums or policy termination.

Normally, premiums are payable throughout the currency of the policy, but *limited payment assurances* can be arranged, with premiums ceasing at a given age. These are found almost exclusively with whole-life assurances.

4.34 Surrender values

With a level premium system (see **4.33**) the amount paid in the early years will be more than sufficient to cover the risk presented. This must be so to balance the later years when the risk has deteriorated but the premium is unchanged. In addition, a policy may be "with profits" (see **4.32**), which would mean that after a short while certain bonuses will have accrued.

These two facts make it possible to make a refund or payment to the assured who decides to terminate his policy before maturity date. With no other type of insurance is it possible to obtain a refund of premium paid in respect of past years.

A life policy will acquire a *surrender value* (i.e. a monetary worth or value on its surrender by the assured) after perhaps two years' currency. Prior to that, all of the premiums and bonuses are reckoned to be fully absorbed by the risk run and the expenses of issuing the policy, such as commission, stamp duty and document preparation. Naturally, the amount of a surrender value will be less than the premiums paid and bonuses earned, because of the expenses mentioned above and the risk already borne by the assurer. (In many countries the surrender value is called the *cash value*.)

This surrender, or cash, value of the policy is extremely important with life assurances and has given rise to a number of further features, considered below.

4.35 Loans

Because life policies acquire a surrender value, they provide a first-class security for loans up to that figure. Provided a legal attachment is made on the surrender value in favour of the lender, it is always certain that money will be available to extinguish the debt. For this reason, life assurers and others are normally prepared to lend policyholders money on life policies, perhaps up to 90 per cent of the surrender value. Of course, interest is payable on such loans.

4.36 Fully paid-up policies

These represent an alternative to surrender values where a policyholder wishes to terminate his policy, or at any rate does not wish to pay any more premiums. As the name implies, no further premiums are payable. The policy continues in force, however, on the same terms as the original contract, except for a reduced benefit. The latter will depend on the premiums paid and the period (or likely period) remaining. The policy may continue to participate in bonus distributions. These policies are particularly valuable when the maturity date is near.

4.37 Non-forfeiture clause

This clause, when applicable, causes the existing surrender value automatically to be used in payment of future premiums when premiums due cease to be paid without any request for policy termination. It is a useful provision which keeps the policy in force should the policyholder inadvertently omit to pay premiums. The money so used represents a charge against the policy should a claim be payable and once all the surrender value is used the policy will lapse.

4.38 State recognition

Life assurance has been said to have a sacred purpose in providing for dependants. This is a great benefit to the whole of society, and the State has recognised this by certain concessions; in particular:

(a) *Income tax relief*. Claim benefits and bonuses paid under life policies do not count as income for tax purposes. U.K. policies incepting before the 1984 budget (subject to certain qualifications) are also entitled to *life assurance premium relief* (LAPR). LAPR, however, does not apply to policies issued after that time.

(b) *Tax exemption*. Under certain circumstances, particularly under the Married Women's Property Acts, it is possible for a life policy to be effected on oneself, but expressly for the benefit of others, and for that policy to be considered separate from one's estate for the purposes of tax and other liabilities.

E. PROGRESS TEST 4

PART 1—SHORT ANSWERS (Answer in one or two sentences)

1. Why are mortality tables important in the history of life assurance? **(4.4)**
2. Write brief notes on:
   (a) the Amicable Society; **(4.6)**
   (b) the Equitable; **(4.7)**
   (c) the Life Assurance Act 1774. **(4.9)**
3. How does industrial life assurance differ from ordinary life assurance? **(4.15)**
4. What types of life assurance policy would you recommend for:
   (a) a young man with little money and family commitments; **(4.17–4.21)**
   (b) a rich man wishing to provide for inheritance tax; **(4.18)**
   (c) an aged widow with no dependants who is afraid to spend her capital, lest she should outlive her resources; **(4.19)**
   (d) a 30-year-old bachelor? **(4.19)**
5. Explain the following terms in life assurances:
   (a) "with profits" policy; **(4.32)**
   (b) surrender value; **(4.34)**
   (c) fully paid-up policy. **(4.36)**

Show how they are connected with each other. **(4.31–4.36)**

PART 2—MULTIPLE CHOICE (Choose the most correct option)

1. Mortality tables:
   (a) are of limited relevance to life assurance;
   (b) enable life assurers to calculate premiums more accurately;
   (c) will enable life assurers to know exactly when people will die;
   (d) have only been available since computers were invented. **(4.4)**
2. The Life Assurance Act 1774:
   (a) made life assurance compulsory in the United Kingdom;
   (b) legalised gambling in the form of life assurance;
   (c) was designed to combat gambling in the form of life assurances;
   (d) completely removed speculation with life assurances. **(4.10)**
3. Industrial life assurance:
   (a) was only available to people working in industrial firms;
   (b) is very much more expensive than ordinary life assurance;
   (c) was primarily designed for the accumulation of savings;
   (d) met a real need among lower paid workers. **(4.12–4.16)**
4. Term assurances:
   (a) are designed to meet a temporary need for life assurance;
   (b) are designed as a form of savings for the life assured;

(c) pay the benefit at the end of the stated term;
(d) are the dearest form of life assurance. **(4.17)**

5. "With profit" life assurance policies:
(a) only pay the sum assured in the event of a claim;
(b) allow the assured to participate in the profits of the assurer;
(c) guarantee a profit for the assurer;
(d) guarantee that a bonus will be paid every year. **(4.2)**

(*For multiple choice answers, see page 355.*)

CHAPTER 5

FIRE INSURANCE

A. THE DEVELOPMENT OF FIRE INSURANCE

5.1 History

It has been said that fire is a magnificent servant but a terrible master. From the time that man first discovered it, fire in the wrong place or out of control has proved to be a scourge. Even today, hundreds of lives are lost and millions of pounds worth of damage are still caused by it each year. Fire insurance can only deal with the financial aspects, but even if the owner of fire-ravaged property is compensated, the community is worse off to the extent of the damage sustained. This intrinsic or net loss is termed *fire waste*, which for the United Kingdom alone costs hundreds of millions of pounds annually.

Trying to compensate for the damage done by fire seems to have originated in Western Europe in the thirteenth century. This was on a community rather than a commercial basis, and in Britain schemes similar in intent were organised by the guilds for their members, or by religious organisations in the Middle Ages. Later charitable donations formed the basis of any compensation available, but abuses led to regulating legislation in the early eighteenth century.

5.2 The Great Fire of London, 1666

There is little doubt that this notorious disaster prompted the formation of fire insurance in this country, although marine and life policies had been issued commercially for many years before. The exact date of the first fire insurance commercially transacted is debated, but the Fire Office, later called the Phenix (no connection with the Phoenix of today), is generally reckoned to have been the pioneer company, in 1680.

Many other offices and insurance schemes followed, both in London and the provinces, with varying degrees of success.

5.3 The industrial revolution

The transformation of England from a country of predominantly rural communities to the first leading industrial nation was accelerated between approximately 1780 and 1850. Although some have challenged the term, it was indeed a revolution, making radical and permanent changes.

The new situation, with much greater concentrations of buildings and machinery and the accumulation of vast stocks of raw materials and goods, meant more wealth and more risks needing the protection of fire insurance. The industrial revolution gave impetus to virtually every class of insurance, but to fire insurance particularly.

5.4 Features of early development

Various features of the practices and situation in the early days of fire insurance are of interest, and are as follows (see Fig. 6):

(a) *Private fire brigades.* The community at large had not seen the need to appoint a co-ordinated fire fighting service. This deficiency had been cruelly exposed by the Fire of London, but for nearly two centuries

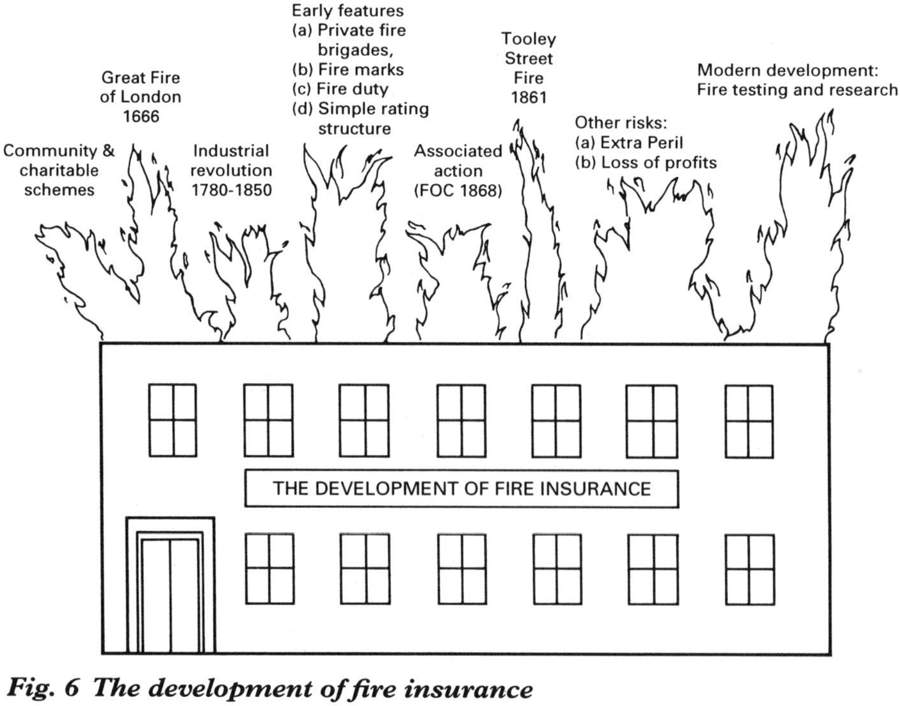

Fig. 6 The development of fire insurance

thereafter it remained for private firms or individuals to supply men and equipment for fire fighting. This was done largely by the leading fire insurers, but with no centralised control of the different brigades these, too, were inadequate for other than comparatively minor outbreaks.

(b) *Fire marks.* As a form of advertising, and possibly as a guide to their fire brigade as to which building to direct their attention, fire insurers issued *fire marks*, which were a form of insignia made of metal, leather or wood, attached to the exterior of buildings insured by the company indicated. These relics of the past are much sought by collectors today.

(c) *Fire insurance duty.* Between 1782 and 1896, in addition to stamp duty, a duty was imposed on every fire policy according to its sum insured. This had a useful effect in providing details of the amount of business transacted during that period, quite apart from its basic intention of providing revenue.

(d) *Simple rating system.* Until experience proved the necessity for a very sophisticated rating system, insurers merely classified risks as *common*, *hazardous*, or *extra hazardous*. While this had the great attraction of simplicity, subsequent events were to expose the inadequacy of such a system.

5.5 Associated action

Competition between fire offices, coupled with the effect of an inadequate system of rating, was having serious results for many insurers, and it became obvious that co-operation and a measure of associated action were needed for the good of all. Co-operation was particularly shown by:

(a) *Tariff association.* Needless competition and inconsistency in risk classification were combining to produce uneconomic rates of premium and the real danger of instability of fire insurers. Consequently, from time to time, usually after a particularly bad run of results, fire offices agreed minimum rates for particular risks and were prepared to share statistical information. The earliest moves in this direction took place in about 1820, but Scotland had the first formal association, following the meetings of Scottish Fire Office Managers, in 1829. After years of negotiation and liaison with the Scottish offices, a single Association of English and Scottish offices was formed in 1860. In 1868 it changed its name to the Fire Offices Committee. Membership was not compulsory, so there were many non-tariff companies. Lloyd's underwriters were also not members.

(b) *Salvage corps.* Substantial savings can be effected once a fire has occurred by undertaking suitable remedial action, for example, restoring damaged goods and safeguarding goods and property against theft, weather or water damage, once a fire has started. The Liverpool Fire Salvage Association was formed in

1829 following a particularly bad fire in that city a few years earlier. Subsequently, salvage corps were also established in London and Glasgow. The three organisations were maintained for many years, but were eventually disbanded in 1984.

(c) *Common fire brigade.* The limitations of separate fire-fighting forces were realised by the fire offices in London and a single brigade was formed there in 1832. This was an improvement, but even so it proved inadequate: see below.

5.6 The Tooley Street fire, 1861

This was the second major conflagration in London to become a landmark in the history of fire insurance. The fire caused damage of well over £1 million (an enormous sum in 1861) among wharves and warehouses which with one exception had been considered of the highest classification. Panic rating measures were immediately adopted by fire insurers, although these were modified following a stormy public meeting, but in several respects this fire formed the critical point in fire insurance in Britain. In particular:

(a) the recently formed association of fire insurers was seriously challenged and, had it collapsed, serious long-lasting results could have ensued. Happily, the difficulties were surmounted and the foundations for solid growth were laid;

(b) the old, somewhat rudimentary, rating system was abandoned in favour of the more scientific approach of penalising bad features and rewarding good, so that owners were encouraged to improve the fire risk of their buildings;

(c) *Common fire brigade.* The limitations of separate fire-fighting forces were realised by the fire offices in London and a single one was formed under the present title of the London Wharf and Warehouse Committee;

(d) the joint brigade of the fire offices was shown to be inadequate for major fires, and the community accepted the fact that fire fighting was the concern of all. In 1865 an Act was passed entrusting the task of fire fighting in London to publicly provided services;

(e) important new fire insurance companies were formed, for example the Commercial Union.

5.7 Risks other than fire

As fire insurance developed, various additional risks were included within the cover of a fire policy, or could be added by the payment of an additional premium. These included *special* (or *extra*) *perils*, such as earthquake, riot and civil commotion, impact damage to buildings, flood, storm, etc.: see **5.11**. Lightning damage with or without fire had long been included.

About the turn of the century *consequential loss* (also known as *loss of profits* or *business interruption*) insurance was introduced: see **5.14**. This provided compensation for profits lost through interruption of business following a fire, and was not introduced without some opposition. Such an insurance was formerly considered to be contrary to public policy, being considered somewhat immoral.

5.8 Fire testing and research

Fire insurers have shown a considerable interest in all types of research into fire and fire fighting. Various organisations were set up or directly supported by the fire insurance industry, but much of the work is now under the auspices of the national *Loss Prevention Council.*

B. THE SCOPE OF FIRE INSURANCE

5.9 General

Although this book mainly confines its study to insurance in the United Kingdom, fire insurance particularly is highly developed abroad by British insurers. Well over half the premium income of British fire insurers is thought to be in respect of risks overseas. Home or overseas, fire insurance concerns insurance of property, although consequential loss insurance (see **5.14**) relates to *pecuniary insurance*.

5.10 Standard fire policy

The basic intention of the fire policy is obvious: to compensate for loss or damage caused by burning. To form a valid claim under the policy there must have been actual ignition ("no claim without flame") which was unintended and accidental as far as the insured was concerned. The standard fire policy, which is issued for virtually all commercial risks (Lloyd's underwriters use a form which is very little different), also covers damage by lightning and, to a limited extent, explosion.

5.11 Special (or extra) perils

For additional premiums, the standard fire policy may be extended to cover any of the following:

- (a) bursting or overflowing of water tanks, apparatus or pipes;
- (b) earthquake;
- (c) explosion (wider cover than in the standard policy);

(d) flood;
(e) hail;
(f) impact damage by vehicles, animals, or articles from the air, including aircraft;
(g) riot and/or civil commotion. The latter would include damage done by strikers, locked out workers and some forms of malicious damage;
(h) storm and tempest;
(i) spontaneous combustion, self-heating or fermentation;
(j) subsidence, landslip and heave (see **15.11**);
(k) subterranean fire;
(l) thunderbolt.

NOTE: i. Some of these perils, as far as the United Kingdom is concerned, are very remote possibilities and the additional premium to cover the risk would be small.

ii. Most insurers require a *policy excess* for some of the above perils. That is, the insured is required to bear the first £100 (or other stated amount) of each and every loss. Practice varies, but (a), (d) and (h) above are usually subject to an excess.

5.12 Combined policies

It has increasingly become the practice for insurers to grant policies which cover many or all of the perils mentioned in **5.10–5.11**, and also include certain accident insurance risks, such as theft, public liability, etc. Having many forms of cover within the same document is of great benefit to the policyholder, and a *commercial "all risks" policy* is now common.

Such combined insurances may be found both with commercial premises, such as a *trader's combined policy* (or commercial "all risks"), and private dwellings, in the *householder's* or *house-owner's policy* (which can cover buildings and/or contents).

5.13 Sprinkler leakage policies

A very effective form of fire-fighting equipment, earning a substantial premium discount when installed, is an approved *sprinkler system*. As the name suggests, this comprises a network of sprinkler valves, usually set in the roof or ceiling, which operate automatically when a certain abnormally high temperature is reached (at the same time usually ringing a warning bell).

Should the sprinkler system operate accidentally, considerable water damage could result and insurance against such a possibility can be arranged. There are a number of exclusions to such a policy, particularly if the system operates through the insured's neglect or in the normal course of a fire. Such a policy is quite separate from the standard or other policies covering the insured premises (although the cover is sometimes one of the extra perils (see **5.11)** in some countries).

5.14 Consequential loss (or loss of profits, or business interruption) policies

The physical loss or damage caused by fire can be compensated for by insurances outlined above. However, in addition to any material damage there are almost invariably other losses to commercial firms, resulting from disruption of business activities and lack of production while repairs are in hand or alternative premises are sought. Loss of profits insurance, when arranged on a correct basis, can remedy this by paying:

(a) any *net profit lost*;
(b) all *standing charges* (i.e. expenses that are still incurred during the period of disruption, such as salaries, certain wages, rents and rates, etc.);
(c) any necessary *additional expenses* incurred in minimising the loss (e.g. extra clerical help in rewriting records, renting temporary accommodation).

5.15 Other insurances

Several other types of policy are issued by fire insurers. For example:

(a) *Rent.* Such an insurance may constitute a separate policy, or be included within other forms of cover, and may be effected by the following persons:
   (i) The *owner*, if the tenant is not obliged to continue payment while the premises are uninhabitable because of fire. (This is automatically the case in Scotland, but not necessarily so elsewhere.)
   (ii) The *tenant*, if his obligation to pay rent does not cease in the event of a fire or if his tenancy agreement requires such insurance.
   (iii) An *owner-occupier*. In the event of fire, the policy moneys would enable him to pay for alternative accommodation while repairs or reinstatement were in hand.

(b) *Building in course of erection.* This is another type of insurance where certain accident insurance risks, such as theft, are included. The widest forms of cover available for this type of insurance are for large-scale builders and contractors, and the policies are more usually today written in the accident department under the name *contract works* or *contractors all risks*.
(c) *Stock policies.* The normal form of fire policy is not suitable for policies covering stock, where fluctuations in the value at risk can occur throughout the policy period. To cover this situation special policies can be arranged. One example provides for an estimated sum insured, based on the maximum amount thought likely to be at risk; 75 per

cent of the premium is paid provisionally, and the actual amounts at risk during the year are submitted in periodic declarations. At the end of the year the average stock at risk is calculated and the final premium based on that, with a refund or extra premium payable as necessary when compared with the provisional payment. Such a policy is termed a *stock declaration policy* and is found in accident insurance as well.

(d) *Reinstatement insurances*. This is a form of policy where the insurer may pay more than the actual worth of the article damaged or destroyed by fire, effecting settlement on a "new for old" basis. For further consideration of this, see **19.20–19.21**.

C. PROGRESS TEST 5

PART 1—SHORT ANSWERS (Answer in one or two sentences)

1. Explain what is meant by "fire waste". **(5.1)**
2. Outline some features of the early days of fire insurance, and try to explain why they have not survived to the present time. **(5.4)**
3. What two major fires in London profoundly affected fire insurance in the United Kingdom and how were they important? **(5.2, 5.6)**
4. Name six special perils that may be added to a standard fire policy. **(5.11)**
5. By whom may rent be insured? **(5.15)**

PART 2—MULTIPLE CHOICE (Choose the most correct option)

1. The simple rating system in the early days of fire insurance:
   (a) is still appropriate today;
   (b) ensured that a fair premium was paid for each policy;
   (c) was cruelly exposed by the Great Fire of London, 1666;
   (d) was cruelly exposed by the Tooley Street Fire, 1861. **(5.4–5.6)**
2. Special perils added to a standard fire policy are also known as:
   (a) extra perils;
   (b) supplementary perils;
   (c) extensive perils;
   (d) additional premium perils. **(5.7)**
3. Sprinkler leakage policies are designed to cover:
   (a) the water damage caused when fighting a fire;
   (b) the negligence of the contractor who installed the system;
   (c) the accidental discharge of water from the system;
   (d) the cost of maintaining the sprinkler system. **(5.13)**
4. Business interruption (or loss of profits) insurance:
   (a) is an extension to the standard fire policy;
   (b) is considered immoral and is therefore illegal;

(c) mainly covers net profit, standing charges and extra costs;
(d) covers all income lost as a result of fire. **(15.5)**

5. Stock declaration policies:
   (a) are intended for situations with a fluctuating value at risk;
   (b) cover farmers for the loss of livestock by lightning;
   (c) require the insured to declare his stock values once a year;
   (d) adjust the premium every three years. **(5.15)**

(For multiple choice answers, see page 355.)

CHAPTER 6

ACCIDENT INSURANCE

A. GENERAL OBSERVATIONS

6.1 Meaning

The term *accident insurance* is not precise, embracing what may be described as a miscellany of only slightly connected different classes of business. The exact constitution of an accident department will vary between insurers, but this book will regard accident insurance as comprising the following classes (see Fig. 7):

(a) fidelity guarantee (including contingency insurance);
(b) personal accident and sickness;
(c) employers' liability;
(d) public liability;
(e) burglary (or theft);
(f) other types of insurance:
  (i) livestock;
  (ii) glass;
  (iii) miscellaneous (credit, rainfall, hail, licences).

NOTE: i. An important omission from the above list is motor insurance. This class of business has grown to such an extent that most insurers are regarding it as separate from their general accident portfolio (i.e. total amount of business). For its consideration see Chapter 7.

ii. In the United Kingdom the term "accident" insurance is becoming less used, although it is still employed in other insurance markets (mostly Commonwealth countries). One more modern approach is to sub-divide the accident portfolio into *property* and *casualty* business (although this would embrace fire insurance in the former category). However, we shall continue to use the term "accident" insurance for the purposes of this study.

6.2 History

Of somewhat diverse composition, accident insurance as such cannot be said to have had the measurable historical development of marine, life or fire, nor are its origins anywhere near so deep-rooted. The earliest classes of accident insurance

6.2 Accident Insurance

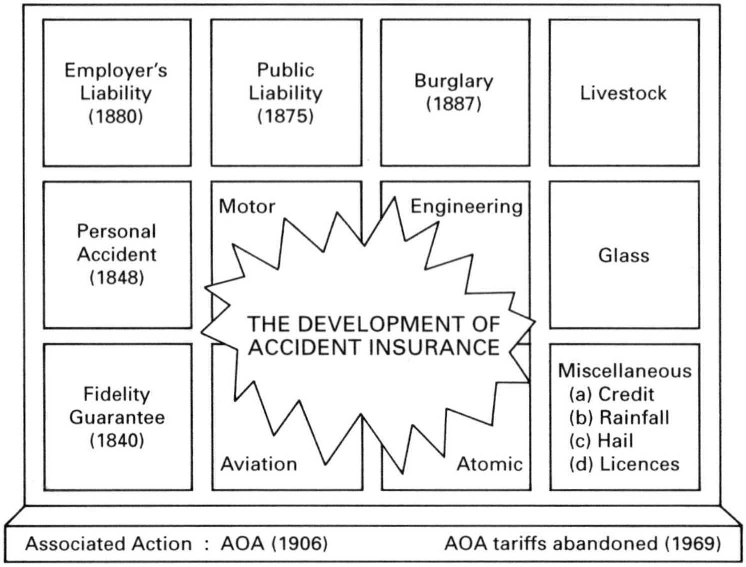

Fig. *7* ***The development of accident insurance***

written in the United Kingdom happened approximately in the mid-nineteenth century. By that time the other three major classes were well established as quite separate professions. The number of composite offices at that time was relatively small, with the result that the various classes of accident business tended to be transacted by specialist new insurers, or to be regarded as a new miscellaneous department of fire insurers, but scarcely regarded seriously.

The beginning of the twentieth century saw the realisation by fire insurers of the importance and permanence of accident business, if only because not writing it could well have led to their own fire connections being threatened by composite offices which were able to offer the wider service. About that time, therefore, accident insurance developed considerably, with many specialist companies being merged with fire offices to make composite insurers.

Particular historical comment will be made as appropriate when considering the different classes of business.

B. FIDELITY GUARANTEE INSURANCE

6.3 Insurance of rights or pecuniary interest

This class of business comes under the classification of *pecuniary interest* (see **2.13**(d)). Different types of contract are issued in this department, but the commercial fidelity guarantee, for instance, is intended to compensate an employer for losses due to the dishonesty of employees.

6.4 Types of contract

Although the fidelity department is not the largest in the accident field, it involves a wide variety of contracts, both policies and bonds.

NOTE: An insurance policy is legally a simple contract, which does not have to be evidenced in writing. A bond is a specialty contract or deed, which has to be signed, sealed and delivered. The major types of contract issued are: (1) *commercial guarantees*; (2) *court bonds*; (3) *government bonds*; (4) miscellaneous, including *building society guarantees*; (5) *contingency* risks: see below.

6.5 Modern practice

Because of the high degree of trust and confidence needed in this type of business, the selection of risks was very stringent. Partly because of competition, granting such cover is now more readily given and wider policy terms are prevalent (such as including misappropriation of stock as well as cash with commercial guarantees: see **6.6**).

6.6 Commercial guarantees

The need for persons in positions of responsibility to provide security against their default has been apprcciated for literally thousands of years. Formerly, such security was provided by means of one or more private sureties, who would guarantee to make good the defaults of the person concerned. Such a system was often highly embarrassing, and sometimes ruinous, to the surety. The Book of Proverbs in the Bible warns against acting as surety. Secular wisdom, in the person of one of the seven wise men of ancient Greece, similarly observes, "Suretyship is the forerunner of ruin."

NOTE: In some countries this class of business is known as *surety insurance*, which gives a clear understanding of its major function.

Corporate suretyship (i.e. a company acting as surety) has many advantages, and the Guarantee Society was the first company to offer this in 1840. Many other insurers began, or were formed, to write this class of business, which has rendered private suretyship obsolete. There are several different kinds of policy, on an individual or group basis.

6.7 Court bonds

The name indicates that these are bonds, rather than policies, and they are issued to cover losses from dishonesty or mishandling of assets entrusted to a person appointed by the court to perform certain duties. Examples of court bonds are:

(a) *Court of Protection bonds.* These are issued to persons handling the estate of persons incapable of managing their own affairs through insanity or other reasons.
(b) *Queen's Bench guarantees* and *Chancery guarantees.* These are types of guarantee required in connection with the appropriate division of the High Court.

6.8 Government bonds

These are also bonds, issued to cover losses not only arising from the bonded person's dishonesty but also his failure to comply with the requirements of the appropriate government department. Some examples are:

(a) *Bankruptcy bonds.* As the name suggests, these cover trustees or special managers in bankruptcy, during their official duties.
(b) *Customs and Excise bonds.* These bonds ensure that the appropriate authorities do not sustain a loss of duty should the bonded persons fail to meet their obligations in this respect.

6.9 Miscellaneous

Various other bonds and policies are issued in the fidelity department, but the most important not mentioned above are *building society* (or *mortgage*) *guarantees.* These have constituted a large proportion of the premium income and business portfolio of the fidelity department in recent years. The policies guarantee building societies against loss arising through the default of borrowers, particularly where the amount borrowed is above the lender's normal maximum for that type of property. (It should be noted that the economic recession and dramatic fall in property prices in the United Kingdom in the early 1990s resulted in enormous losses to insurance companies heavily involved in this type of business.)

6.10 Contingency risks

A "contingency" is a possible happening. In that sense all accident and most other kinds of insurance are contingency insurances. The technical use of the term, however, is reserved for a minor class of risks, which is usually written in the fidelity department for convenience, and which does not conveniently fall within any other major class of business. Such policies provide compensation, or *indemnity* (see later), in respect of rather unusual risks or liabilities, such as:

(a) *missing or lost documents*: the risk of loss to a company as a result of issuing duplicate share certificates to replace lost originals;
(b) *missing beneficiaries*: the risk of loss because a missing beneficiary entitled to part of a deceased's estate turns up and claims after his share has been distributed among others;
(c) *"twins" insurance*: a multiple birth can bring financial complications, and an insurance policy can be effected to provide a cash benefit in the event of this mixed blessing.

C. PERSONAL ACCIDENT INSURANCE

6.11 Origins

It has been said that the culmination of the industrial revolution was the railways, and they gave rise to accident insurance. In a sense this is true. Although fidelity guarantee insurance was in fact earlier in time, personal accident insurance is thought by many to be the real start of accident insurance, and there is no doubt that the railways prompted its beginnings.

The early railways were dangerous; a fact that was dramatically illustrated in 1830 when the then Leader of the House of Commons was killed by an engine while opening a railway line. To provide compensation for death or injury sustained in railway accidents, the first personal accident insurer, the Railway Passengers Assurance Company (later to be merged with the Commercial Union), began business in 1848.

NOTE: i. The importance of personal accident insurance, which gave accident insurance its name, may be seen in that certain statutes (e.g. the Assurance Companies Act 1909, now replaced) used the term "accident insurance" when alluding to personal accident business.

ii. The association of personal accident insurance with the railways continues today, in that travellers purchasing tickets for long-distance rail travel are still able to purchase such insurance for the journey, at nominal cost.

6.12 Types of policy

The scope of this class of business rapidly spread beyond railway accidents, and the following types of policy are found, both on an individual and on a group basis:

(a) *Accidents only*. The name speaks for itself, compensation only being provided for death or injury arising from "accidental, violent, external and visible means". A capital sum is normally payable for death, with lesser sums for loss of limbs or eyes, and a weekly benefit for a specified maximum period in respect of full or partial disability. Increasingly, a prospective policyholder is allowed to select his own table of benefits, at appropriate premiums.

(b) *Accidents and specified diseases.* This form of cover is also virtually self-explanatory. In addition to the accident benefits mentioned in (a) above, a weekly benefit is payable for disablement from any of a specified list of diseases. (There is no death benefit for disease.) This policy is somewhat obsolete in the United Kingdom, although it is sometimes used for cover in other countries, or when the insured's health is such that full sickness cover cannot be granted.

(c) *Accidents and all sickness.* Again with no cover for death, other than by accident, this type of policy is an extension of (b) above. The benefits received, as with all personal accident (and life) policies, are additional to any entitlement under state schemes.

(d) *Permanent sickness policies.* The name is a little misleading, as it is the policy and not the sickness which is "permanent" in nature. For this reason, most insurers call this class of business permanent *health* insurance.

The basic provisions are that the insured receives an income during any period of total disability for as long as the disability lasts or until a stipulated age limit is reached. Once the policy has commenced it takes on something of the nature of a life policy, in that only the insured has a right to terminate it, even though his health may deteriorate and numerous claims are made. This, of course, is subject to the insured continuing to pay the annual premiums. Because the contract is long-term, and because of the other similarities with life policies, many insurers in fact write this class of business within their life departments.

This type of contract has great appeal for the policyholder and is currently being actively promoted by insurers.

(e) *Aviation and travel.* This is another section of personal accident insurance which has increased enormously in recent years; these policies are much in demand because of the great volume of international travel. Cover can be much as with (c) above, with the most important addition of compensation for medical expenses. Some types of policy are available in coupon form, obtainable from machines at airports. Frequently travellers will effect this type of policy including some cover for loss or damage to their luggage as well: see **6.21**(f).

D. EMPLOYER'S LIABILITY INSURANCE

6.13 Beginnings

This form of insurance began in Europe approximately in the middle of the nineteenth century. In the United Kingdom, curious as it may seem today, there was great opposition to any scheme for insurance of this kind. It was thought by many that such insurance would make compensation easier to get and therefore have a weakening effect on the moral fibre of the nation. These objections on matters of principle applied also to other classes of insurance: see e.g. **8.1**.

6.14 The nineteenth century

In the United Kingdom, the plight of a man suffering from an industrial injury or disease, or of his dependants if he was killed, was indeed wretched throughout the nineteenth and early twentieth centuries. The industrial revolution had brought an enormous increase in production through the use of machinery, but working conditions and particularly safety standards left a lot to be desired. Accidents were commonplace, and the toll in human misery and suffering was appalling. Moreover, the existing attitude of society and the law was such that an employee had little hope of success in any legal action against his employer, even if he had the courage and finance to get an action started. Some measure of the hopelessness of the injured workman's position may be seen from the following facts:

(a) It was the belief of the courts that an employer owed no greater duty to his workmen than he owed to himself (as held in *Priestley v. Fowler* (1837)). Thus, the attitude was that in taking reward for the work (in wages) the workman accepted any risks involved and could not complain later.
(b) A common law defence available to an employer, where an injury was caused to an employee by the negligence of one of the victim's colleagues, was called *common employment*. If this were pleaded and accepted, the claim failed. (This principle also applied in *Priestley v. Fowler*, see (a) above. The defence was abolished by the Law Reform (Personal Injuries) Act 1948.)
(c) Another common law doctrine, which survived until abolished by the Law Reform (Contributory Negligence) Act 1945, was that if a claimant was in any degree himself negligent in the accident, the action failed completely. The position now is that a claim is not thus defeated, but that damages are reduced in proportion to the claimant's own negligence.

6.15 Legislation

Gradually, the national conscience was awakened to the injustice of the injured workman's position. The milestones in resulting statutes were as follows:

(a) Employers' Liability Act 1880. This Act was the first step towards remedying the unjust situation and meant that certain classes of workmen now had hopes of succeeding with claims for industrial injuries. The Act did not make insurance compulsory, but obviously the demand was there and in the same year the Employers' Liability Assurance Corporation was created specifically to meet it.

(b) Workmen's Compensation Act 1897. An injured workman had to prove negligence before he could obtain compensation, but this Act established the principle of compensation *irrespective of negligence*, laying down a scale of benefits applicable to all workmen. Clearly, such an enactment gave enormous impetus to workmen's compensation insurance, as it was called. About this time fire offices realised that accident insurance was here to stay and could not be ignored: see **6.2**.

(c) National Insurance (Industrial Injuries) Act 1946 (which came into force on 5 July 1948). This Act abolished workmen's compensation as such and took from commercial insurance a sizeable amount of business by setting up the now familiar national insurance scheme.

(d) Employers' Liability (Compulsory Insurance) Act 1969: see **6.16**.

6.16 Present position

Injured workmen retain the right to claim damages at common law or through breach of statutory duty. After workmen's compensation as such was abolished, employer's liability claims became much more common, aided by trade unions and general claims consciousness. The importance of this type of claim was illustrated by the Employers' Liability (Compulsory Insurance) Act 1969, which required an employer to be insured for at least up to £2 million. In making compulsory such insurance, society has almost totally reversed previous attitudes to people injured at work: see **6.13**, **6.14**.

NOTE: The growing social consciousness and concern for safety were further reflected in the Health and Safety at Work etc. Act 1974, which made stringent provisions for all to take more care in avoiding occupational injury and disease.

E. PUBLIC LIABILITY INSURANCE

6.17 Development

Public liability insurance developed with employers' liability insurance. Once the morality of being able to insure against one's liability was accepted, and the existence of such insurance became known, business grew rapidly.

The earliest policies were in respect of horse-drawn vehicles, covering the owner's liability for death, injury or property damage to the general public. They were issued in about 1875 and the business developed as builders, contractors, shopkeepers and others realised its importance.

6.18 Scope

Basically, the policy cover is simple, providing compensation for legal liability for death, injury, disease or damage to non-employees (employees should be covered by an employer's liability policy). In addition, as with employers' liability insurance, attendant legal costs are covered.

The different kinds of policy in use include:

(a) industrial and commercial risks;
(b) pedal cyclists;
(c) private individuals (a pedestrian, for example, can incur heavy liabilities by causing a serious road accident);
(d) "products" liabilities. This concerns manufacturers and distributors for defects in the goods supplied, such as foreign bodies in foodstuffs, etc.;
(e) professional people, such as solicitors, accountants, etc. This covers liabilities arising from errors and omissions by them or their staff;
(f) property owners (e.g. unsafe premises causing injury, etc.);
(g) public authorities (e.g. accidents in parks, museums, etc.);
(h) sportsmen (e.g. golfers);
(i) directors' and officers' (D & O) liabilities.

NOTE: i. This form of cover may include, or be included with, other risks. For example, a *householder's policy* covering loss or damage to the buildings and/or contents usually extends to cover the personal liability of the owner and his family towards the public.

ii. Liability arising from the use of motor vehicles, water-craft and aircraft is always excluded, and must be covered by separate insurances.

6.19 Combined liability policies

In line with an increasing desire to simplify with "package" types of cover, many insurers now issue a single *liability insurance policy*, which has separate sections covering employer's liability, public liability and products liability. The last has become of great significance in recent years, particularly on the international market, with increasing consumer claims consciousness and a tendency towards high damages being awarded in the courts.

F. THEFT INSURANCE

6.20 Development

The first real development of this class of business was when a Lloyd's underwriter extended a fire policy to cover the risk of burglary in 1887. The practice caught on and in the next 25 years several different types of associated risks were covered: see **6.21**.

The term "burglary insurance" has persisted, despite the fact that different risks such as larceny, housebreaking and even mere loss, were covered by this class of business. With the abolition of legal definitions of the various forms of theft, in the Theft Act 1968 (which came into effect on 1 January 1969), however, most insurers have tended to adopt the more modern term theft insurance.

6.21 Scope

The major sections of business written in the theft department may be considered as follows:

(a) *Householders.* This is a combined form of policy, written by many insurers in the fire department, covering several different types of loss. It is in respect of private dwellings and has become such a popular form of policy that the burglary private house policy is now obsolete.
(b) *Business premises.* With the increase in crime, this form of cover is of considerable importance. Stock declaration policies (see **5.15**(c)) are often arranged for risks where the value at risk varies over the period insured.
(c) *"All risks".* This is a somewhat unfortunate title, in that not every risk is covered (hence the term is usually shown in inverted commas). However, such policies cover not only criminal loss or damage but also losses from accidental means. Originally intended only for jewellery and other valuables, the scope of this section has been widened considerably, to cover both personal and business insurances.
(d) *Money.* This is of comparatively recent development, as money was at one time thought to be uninsurable because of the hazard presented. This has been proved wrong, and insurance on "all risks" lines is arranged, for cash both in transit and elsewhere.
(e) *Transit.* A large part of this section relates to cash in transit, but goods are also insured, again on an "all risks" basis. The experience in this type of business has been rather unsatisfactory in recent years, being particularly costly when whole lorryloads of expensive merchandise have been stolen.
(f) *Travel.* This has developed along with related personal accident business (see **6.12**(e)). Cover is for selected units of £1,000 (or other figure) on an "all risks" basis, covering the traveller's baggage and personal effects.

G. OTHER TYPES OF INSURANCE

6.22 Livestock insurance

Although many clubs and associations had been formed to compensate owners of animals which died, livestock insurance did not begin commercially in the

United Kingdom until towards the end of the nineteenth century. Basically, policies cover only the death of insured animals through accident or disease, and the main types of risk are:

(a) *Horses and bloodstock.* Death from humane slaughter is regarded as an accident within the meaning of the policy. This is an important consideration where valuable racehorses are insured.
(b) *Cattle.* Various forms of accidental death and disease cover are available, including policies for foot-and-mouth disease and anthrax.

6.23 Glass insurance

This form of insurance has been in existence for many years, and its basic intention is simple. A feature of the insurance is that most claims are settled on a replacement basis, the speed of service being particularly valuable to traders. Premiums are based on the area of glass exposed to risk. Policies are available for private premises, but naturally business risks predominate.

6.24 Miscellaneous types of insurance

Different types of miscellaneous insurance that may be considered are:

(a) *Credit insurance.* This protects traders from default by customers obtaining goods on hire-purchase or similar credit facilities. The much greater risks involved with overseas trading are largely insured at governmental level, through the Export Credits Guarantee Department.
(b) *Rainfall* (or *"pluvius"*). This form of insurance will provide a stipulated benefit in the event of at least a specified amount of rain during a particular period. This is useful to the organisers of outdoor events, or for individuals in respect of holiday periods.
(c) *Hail.* This provides compensation for crops ruined by hailstorm. (It may also include glass damage to greenhouses, etc.)
(d) *Licence insurance.* This protects against financial loss through the forfeiture or non-renewal of a licence to sell liquor.

H. SUMMARY

6.25 Different types of risk

As will be appreciated from the wide scope of accident insurance, this is a class of business which embraces different kinds of risks, comprising all classifications: insurance of the person, of property, of liability, and of rights or interest (see **2.13**).

6.26 Associated action

In earlier days, fierce competition between accident insurers made a central organisation impracticable. However, insurers saw the need for co-operation and in 1906 The Accident Offices' Association (AOA) was formed, principally to arrange tariffs in workmen's compensation insurance. Motor insurance, livestock and some fidelity business also became subject to tariffs, but the original intentions of these, particularly in respect of fixed minimum rates and standardised forms of cover, were later deemed unnecessary. All AOA tariffs were abolished as from 31 December 1968.

6.27 Reduction of losses

If there is an equivalent in accident insurance to fire waste (see **5.1**), accident insurers certainly help to reduce *accident waste*. The number and extent of accident claims is substantially affected by the direct and indirect action taken by insurers, in particular by the following activities:

(a) *Inspection services and surveys*. Surveys, much as in fire insurance, are carried out by experts employed or appointed by insurers considering risks proposed for theft, employer's liability and public liability insurance. Also detailed consideration of systems of check are carried out when a fidelity guarantee risk is contemplated. Any weaknesses or unsatisfactory features are pointed out and remedial action suggested. Sometimes insurance is refused unless the improvements are made.

(b) *Rating methods*. By imposing heavier terms because of adverse features, or a poor claims record, improvements are encouraged.

(c) *Education*. Insurers are very much involved with crime prevention education, in co-operation with the police, as well as safety measures and precautions for the home and industry. This is very much a part of insurers' public relations work.

I. PROGRESS TEST 6

PART 1—SHORT ANSWERS (Answer in one or two sentences)

1. What are the major classes of business in accident insurance? **(6.1)**
2. What types of business are transacted by the fidelity department? **(6.4–6.10)**
3. What is the connection between the railways and personal accident insurance, and what are the main sections of this class of business? **(6.11–6.12)**
4. What important legislation affected employers' liability insurance? **(6.14–6.15)**

5. What principal types of policy are written in the theft department? **(6.20)**

PART 2—MULTIPLE CHOICE (Choose the most correct option)

1. Fidelity guarantee insurance:
   (a) will ensure that employees never defraud their employer;
   (b) was invented long before private suretyship was practised;
   (c) covers liabilities arising from the negligence of staff members;
   (d) covers losses caused by staff dishonesty. **(6.3)**
2. Personal accident and sickness insurance:
   (a) covers liabilities arising from acts of carelessness;
   (b) was one of the last types of accident insurances to develop;
   (c) covers death from accident but not from sickness;
   (d) developed at the same time as life assurance. **(6.11–6.12)**
3. Employer's liability insurance:
   (a) covers legal liability for death or injury to staff members;
   (b) covers liabilities to the public arising from staff carelessness;
   (c) is exactly the same as workmen's compensation insurance;
   (d) was replaced by national insurance in the United Kingdom. **(6.13–6.16)**
4. Public liability insurance:
   (a) covers legal liability towards members of the public;
   (b) will include liability arising from motor accidents, etc.;
   (c) covers loss or damage caused by members of the public;
   (d) covers legal liability towards staff members. **(6.17–6.18)**
5. "All risks" insurance is usually shown in inverted commas because:
   (a) it is the widest form of property insurance available;
   (b) there are some types of risk not covered by the insurance;
   (c) it is the newest form of property insurance;
   (d) it does not indicate the type of property insured. **(6.21)**

(For multiple choice answers, see page 355.)

CHAPTER 7

MOTOR INSURANCE

A. THE DEVELOPMENT OF MOTOR INSURANCE

7.1 Part of accident insurance

When motor insurance developed in the early twentieth century it formed part of the accident department. In the second half of the century, however, for reasons we shall mention, it had developed to such an extent that it became a branch in its own right, with premium volume greater than all other accident insurance classes combined.

7.2 Beginnings

Soon after the "horseless carriages" of the late nineteenth century were liberated from very restrictive legislation on their use, the need for insurance arose, although motor insurance was not at that time compulsory and motoring was a luxury enjoyed by very few people. One or two pioneer attempts at such insurance failed, and the first leading motor insurers in the United Kingdom were the Law Accident and the General Accident, before the end of the century. They were soon followed by the Car and General (1903) and the Motor Union (1906).

NOTE: Motor insurance was part of the developing accident insurance field, and the early motor insurers are good examples of specialist companies brought into being for the express purpose of transacting the new classes of business: see **6.2**.

7.3 The First World War and after

The First World War saw a great increase in the use of motor transport and introduced motoring to thousands. After the war, mass production and the development of the hire-purchase system resulted in an enormous growth in motor vehicles, including motor cycles. Motor cycles in fact constituted a much higher proportion of motor vehicles in the 1920s than they do today. Whatever the vehicle, the need for insurance grew correspondingly.

7.4 Compulsory insurance

Unfortunately, the increasing need for insurance was comparatively seldom satisfied. In many cases this was due to the fact that the users of vehicles, which were often being acquired on hire-purchase, were unable to afford the additional "luxury" of insurance. This same lack of funds resulted in serious hardship to the victims of motor accidents, who were often left without effective remedy against negligent motorists of slender resources.

Motor accident casualties per vehicle on the road were in fact much higher in the 1920s than they are today. Coupled with the fact that comparatively few of the road accident victims were able to obtain adequate compensation for their injuries, the number of deaths and injuries provoked the realisation that motor insurance was a social necessity. This necessity was met by the introduction of compulsory insurance of liabilities for death or injuries to others, outlined in the Road Traffic Act 1930. Following the lead given by this country, some form of compulsory motor insurance has become a feature of virtually every developed country in the world. Naturally, such legislation produces a great increase in that class of business.

7.5 After the Second World War

The past 50 years or so have seen a transformation in the form of personal and business transport. From being a luxury, the private car is now seen as something of a social necessity for all old enough to drive (at least in the developed world). Commercial land transport has reflected a similar growth, often at the expense of the railways. This has resulted in a tremendous increase in motor insurance.

B. THE MOTOR TARIFF

7.6 Formation and abolition

Motor insurers soon realised the importance of associated action. Over the years many motor insurers have failed, to the great detriment of policyholders, accident victims, and the insurance profession generally. To reduce the possibility of such disasters, the Accident Offices Association, which began in 1906 with primary concern for the rapidly developing employer's liability insurance (see **6.13–6.16**), formed a strong tariff organisation which survived until the end of 1968. Two dominant reasons for the abolition of the tariff were the increasing strength of tariff offices and vigorous competition by non-tariff insurers in what had become a very large market indeed.

7.7 Effects of the tariff abolition

There is no doubt that the abolition of the motor tariff was a momentous occasion and there were some effects immediately visible when the market became an open one at the beginning of 1969. There were several completely new schemes and policies offered, particularly for the private motorist, with very favourable terms indeed being available, at least for experienced motorists of good record.

The element of fierce competition in a very large premium market has never disappeared, despite the fact that motor insurance has never proved easy to write profitably. The sheer size of the market, with implications for other types of business from policyholders, just cannot be ignored.

C. THE SCOPE OF MOTOR INSURANCE

7.8 Classification of risks

A moment's thought about the many different types of motor vehicle to be seen on the roads and in industry today will indicate the very wide variety of risks within the scope of motor insurance. These risks, however, have been classified by motor insurers into the following categories:

(a) *Private cars.* This section of the business has seen phenomenal growth in recent decades, and is the subject of the fiercest competition among insurers today.

(b) *Motor cycles.* This section includes motor scooters, mopeds and the like.

(c) *Commercial vehicles.* All vehicles used for transporting goods or passengers for commercial purposes, including hire-cars and taxis, are within this section.

(d) *Agricultural and forestry vehicles.* Although they are primarily commercial vehicles, the restricted and specialised use of these vehicles gives rise to separate insurance considerations.

(e) *Special types.* As the name indicates, this is a rather miscellaneous term given to vehicles which are of unusual construction or adaptation. This section includes such vehicles as mobile cranes, earth-moving equipment, ambulances, etc. (Vehicles which are really *tools of trade* may in fact be insured under a public liability rather than a motor policy when used as such, or if they never travel on public roads.)

(f) *Motor trade.* Individuals and firms operating within the motor trade have particular insurance needs. Forms of cover quite different from anything used in (a) to (e) above are made available to meet those needs.

7.9 Types of policy (excluding motor traders)

The standard types of policy available for motor vehicles are as follows:

(a) *"Act" only.* This is the minimum form of cover, providing insurance sufficient only to comply with the provisions of the Road Traffic Acts (to be considered below). This is a form of cover seldom advertised by insurers, as it is very limited in scope. With certain bad insurance risks insurers may sometimes offer this restricted type of policy rather than refuse insurance altogether.

NOTE: Although for practical purposes motor insurance is compulsory, insurers are not obliged to accept every such insurance offered to them.

(b) *Third party only (sometimes called full third party).* There are two parties involved with an insurance contract: the insurer and the insured. Accordingly, any other person who may become linked in some way with the insurance (e.g. a claimant) is regarded as a third party. A third party only policy covers the insured's legal liability towards other people, arising out of the use of the motor vehicle. However, such cover is more extensive than "Act" cover, including higher or unlimited cover for property damage liability.

NOTE: There may be several persons other than the insured and insurer interested in the motor policy, as for example where many passengers or pedestrians are injured. Each other person, however, is separately regarded as a third party, rather than as the fourth party, fifth party, etc.

(c) *Third party, fire and theft.* In addition to the full third party cover mentioned in (b) above, this policy includes loss or damage, *arising from fire or theft only,* to the insured vehicle.

(d) *Comprehensive.* This is a term in very common usage, but in some ways it is an unfortunate one. *Comprehensive* implies that every conceivable risk is covered, which is not the case with this type of policy. It is the widest form of cover available, but certain forms of loss, such as wear and tear or loss of use of the vehicle, are usually excluded.

The term means slightly different things with the different classes of vehicle (see **7.8**), but it always includes full third party cover, as in (b) above, and *virtually all accidental loss or damage* to the insured vehicle.

The private car comprehensive policy gives the widest form of cover; it includes such benefits as:

(i) personal accident insurance, providing a death benefit and various benefits for specified serious injuries, such as loss of limbs, etc. in respect of the insured. Many insurers also extend the benefits to the insured's spouse;

(ii) medical expenses, for a limited amount for any occupant of the insured car. This is quite separate from any legal liability upon the driver for such expenditure. That is covered by the third party section;

(iii) personal effects. A limited sum is available for loss of or damage to such articles while carried in the car. This is a form of "all risks" cover and, again, any legal liability of the driver for this will be covered by the third party section.

7.10 Motor traders' policies

Because of their rapid turnover of vehicles and the particular needs of their business, motor traders have separate types of policy. Basically, there are three types:

(a) *Road risks.* This grants cover for any vehicle owned by, or in the custody or control of, the motor trader, while they are away from the insured's premises. It can be on a comprehensive or third party basis: see above.
(b) *Internal risks.* This is little more than a public liability policy: see **6.17–6.18**. As the name suggests, the policy concerns risks on the trader's own premises.
(c) *Combined road and garage.* This is a combination of (a) and (b) above, with the addition of further cover, such as damage to petrol pumps, etc.

D. THE ROAD TRAFFIC ACTS 1930–1991

7.11 Motor insurance not technically compulsory

We are so accustomed to the thought that we need insurance before we can drive a motor vehicle that it may come as a surprise to realise that the law does allow two alternatives. The existing legislation provides that a deposit made into court is sufficient to permit driving without having any insurance (although since 1991 that deposit has been £500,000).

The other alternative allows vehicle owners not to have compulsory insurance if they are protected by a *security.* This is effectively a *solvency guarantee.* It must be issued by an approved body and provide a guarantee for as little as £25,000 in connection with public service vehicles and only £5,000 with other vehicles. These securities are very rare and by present money standards of very limited use. If found, they would be issued through the fidelity guarantee department of insurance companies, but they are considered by many to be totally anomalous today.

There may be a few very large organisations which take advantage of the former concession, as the deposit will apply to all vehicles owned by them and they may consider that the deposit will be cheaper than the premiums over a period for a large fleet of vehicles. Such organisations, however, are their own insurers for any misfortunes that may arise (as indeed would be all vehicle owners covered by a security), and once any part of the deposit is withdrawn from court, permission to use the motor vehicles on a road is also withdrawn. For practical purposes, therefore, insurance for motor vehicles is compulsory and this chapter regards it as such.

NOTE: In addition to the permitted alternatives to insurance, certain vehicles and vehicle users are exempt from compulsory insurance, e.g. vehicles belonging to the police.

7.12 Road Traffic Acts 1930–1991

The first Act laying down "compulsory" insurance requirements was a historic document that was to have a profound effect on the development of motor insurance.

The basic intention of the legislation was to ensure that funds would be available to compensate innocent victims killed or injured in road accidents. At first it was not thought necessary to include liability for property damage, but this was introduced some decades later.

Because the intentions of compulsory insurance were sometimes defeated by technical breaches of the insurance conditions by the policyholder, enabling the insurer to avoid liability under the policy, further legislation was quickly provided to limit the ability of insurers to decline claims.

7.13 Compulsory insurance requirements

Under the Road Traffic Acts it is now an offence to use or permit the use of a motorised vehicle on a road unless there is in force a policy of insurance covering the following:

(a) *Liability for death or bodily injury to third parties.* No limit for such liability is provided. Therefore unlimited liability cover must be given. This applies in respect of persons inside or outside the vehicle.
(b) *Liability for property damage to third parties.* Such liability must be insured, up to a minimum limit of £250,000.
(c) *Hospital charges.* Where a claim payment is made under a motor policy in respect of death or injury, any hospital attending to the injured person is entitled to claim from the insurer up to £2,780 for in-patient treatment and up to £255 for out-patient treatment;
(d) *Emergency treatment fees.* The hospital or qualified doctor first treating a person injured in a road accident is entitled to claim from the motor insurer £20.10 per person treated, plus a small mileage charge for travelling distances over two miles.

NOTE: The monetary amounts shown above are as applying in 1995. These are modified as appropriate from time to time.

E. E.C. DIRECTIVES

7.14 Motor Directives

Membership of the European Community has meant that U.K. legislation has to be changed from time to time to accord with mandatory instructions or *directives*. To date there have been three such directives affecting motor insurance, as follows:

(a) *First E.C. Motor Insurance Directive*: this directs all E.C. motor insurers automatically to provide at least the compulsory insurance required whilst the insured vehicle is in the member country concerned;
(b) *Second E.C. Motor Insurance Directive:* this requires all E.C. motor insurances to provide third party property damage liability cover; also, policies have to provide at least compulsory insurance cover for any driver of an insured vehicle;
(c) *Third E.C. Motor Insurance Directive*: this requires all E.C. motor insurances to grant at least compulsory insurance cover for *all* passengers (previously in the United Kingdom employees did not have to be included for death or injuries arising out of and in the course of their employment).

F. THE MOTOR INSURERS' BUREAU

7.15 Need for a central fund

The Cassel Committee on Compulsory Insurance submitted its report in 1937 recommending, *inter alia*, the establishment of a central fund to provide the compensation envisaged by the Road Traffic Acts for those victims of road accidents who, despite the legislation, were still unable to have their claims satisfied. This situation arose when:

(a) the motorist refused or failed to obtain any insurance;
(b) the insurance was in some way defective, enabling the insurer to deny liability under the policy;
(c) injuries were caused by an unidentified "hit and run" motorist.

7.16 Establishment of the MIB

The recommendations for a central fund could not be implemented before the Second World War. In 1946, however, the voluntary association known as the *Motor Insurers' Bureau* was set up. (Membership of the MIB is now compulsory for all motor insurers operating in the United Kingdom.)

The MIB is not a charitable fund. Innocent victims injured in road accidents by motor vehicles may sue the MIB for satisfaction of judgments in respect of the injuries if the motorist or his insurer does not pay. Even where the latter is not known, as with "hit and run" victims, the MIB still bears responsibility.

7.17 MIB agreements

The MIB functions by means of various agreements, two with the Secretary of State for Transport and one internal agreement among MIB members. These are:

(a) *Uninsured Drivers Agreement.* If a court judgment in respect of "Act" injuries remains unsatisfied seven days after it is enforceable the victim may proceed against the MIB, who must pay.

(b) *Untraced Drivers Agreement.* This is to provide compensation for the "hit and run" victim. It operates under two different procedures:

(i) *Procedure "A"* This is a simplified procedure intended for relatively small claims (up to £50,000). There is no appeal against the MIB decision and there are certain other requirements.
(ii) *Procedure "B"* This is for claims larger than £50,000 or involving public transport vehicles.

(c) *The "Domestic Agreement".* This agreement is between members of the bureau, which involves every motor insurer, and deals with cases where a policy of insurance issued by a member was in existence but for some reason was not effective in respect of the accident in question. The member who issued the policy is regarded as the "domestic agreement insurer" (formerly "insurer concerned") and makes any necessary payments, without subsequent recovery from the central fund of the MIB.

NOTE: It is important to remember that the MIB is solely concerned with liabilities required to be covered by compulsory insurance . Further, payment by the MIB or by any "domestic agreement insurer" does not relieve the motorist of his primary liability. The MIB or "domestic agreement insurer" has a right of recovery against the negligent motorist personally. In practice, this right is usually of little value.

7.18 Third party property damage liability

When property damage liability became compulsory following the Second E.C. Motor Insurance Directive (see **7.14**), the MIB agreed to include such claims within the provisions of the various agreements. However, in order to avoid minor cases, a £175 excess applies to such claims.

7.19 The Green Card system

This is an international extension of the MIB concept. Virtually all European countries have established national bureaux equivalent to the MIB. The *Green Card system* involves motorists travelling between member countries being provided with a Green Card which is accepted at frontiers as establishing at least the existence of the home country's compulsory motor insurance. The National Bureau of the country visited guarantees payment of liabilities subject to compulsory insurance, recovering from the National Bureau of the motorist, and thence from his insurer.

The E.C. Directive requiring all motor policies to give automatic compulsory cover within the Community (see **7.14**) has much reduced the need for Green Cards, but not all countries in the Green Card system are covered by the Directive. Green Cards are still issued, therefore, when the motorist visits such other countries or where he wants wider than minimum compulsory cover.

G. PROGRESS TEST 7

PART 1—SHORT ANSWERS (Answer in one or two sentences)

1. Outline the important stages in the development of motor insurance. **(7.1–7.5)**
2. What are the main sections of motor insurance business? **(7.8)**
3. What different types of cover are provided by motor insurers? **(7.9)**
4. A motorist has an "Act only" policy and negligently causes an accident to a cyclist. Which of the following are recoverable from his insurers:
   (a) damage to his own car;
   (b) damage to the cycle;
   (c) injury to the cyclist;
   (d) bill from the hospital treating the cyclist;
   (e) emergency treatment to the cyclist by a doctor at the scene of the accident? **(7.12)**
5. What is the MIB? Why was it formed, and how does it operate? **(7.15–7.19)**

PART 2—MULTIPLE CHOICE (Choose the most correct option)

1. In the development of motor insurance:
   (a) compulsory insurance cover was always required;
   (b) compulsory insurance had very little effect;
   (c) the tariff association was not of great importance;
   (d) the tariff association was of great importance. **(7.4)**
2. The motor insurance tariff:

(a) was a voluntary association of competing insurers;
(b) had compulsory membership for all motor insurers;
(c) only applied to compulsory motor insurance cover;
(d) required all members to charge the same premiums. **(7.6)**

3. Third party, fire and theft motor insurance:
   (a) is wider than "Act" cover, but less than "comprehensive";
   (b) does not cover any damage to the insured vehicle;
   (c) only covers fire and theft damage to third party vehicles;
   (d) is the minimum cover now required by law. **(7.9)**
4. The minimum requirements of compulsory motor insurance:
   (a) are at least some cover for the insured's own vehicle;
   (b) must cover injury and property liability for unlimited amounts;
   (c) apply wherever the motor vehicle is being used or worked upon;
   (d) include unlimited death and injury liability cover. **(7.13)**
5. The Motor Insurers' Bureau:
   (a) now has compulsory membership for all motor insurers;
   (b) still has voluntary membership;
   (c) deals with all claims denied by motor insurers;
   (d) is a charitable fund, which can refuse to contribute. **(7.16)**

CHAPTER 8

ENGINEERING INSURANCE

A. THE DEVELOPMENT AND SCOPE OF ENGINEERING INSURANCE

8.1 Part of accident insurance

Accident insurance has been described as a coalition of quasi-independent classes of business, many of which were specialist in nature. This is particularly true of engineering insurance, which formed perhaps the most obvious product of the industrial revolution and was not brought into being without considerable controversy.

8.2 Early situation

The industrial revolution had produced an enormous increase in the use of machinery of all kinds, including steam-powered machines. Unfortunately, the standards of use had the main result that accidents, sometimes involving violent explosions, were common. Public concern was aroused over the accidents and loss of life, and in 1854 the Manchester Steam Users' Association was formed to provide an inspection service for boilers.

However, the weight of public opinion at the time and particularly that of the association, was very much against the idea of insurance for engineering risks. Curious as it may seem today, a widely held attitude towards such insurance was

"that such a course would tend to increase rather than diminish accidents, as it would involve a carelessness which . . . should be punished rather than rewarded."

It is interesting to compare this attitude with the prevailing opinion about liability insurance generally in the nineteenth century (see **6.13**).

8.3 First insurers

Despite the feelings of some, there were individuals who recognised the value of engineering insurance. The Chief Inspector of the Manchester Steam Users' Association, which was set against insurance, was one of these. He left the association to form the pioneer boiler insurance company, the Steam Boiler Assurance Co., in 1858 (later to become known as the Vulcan Boiler and General Insurance Co. Ltd.). Another early insurer in this field was the National Boiler Insurance Co. Ltd. (now part of the Sun Alliance Group), formed in 1864.

8.4 Boiler Explosions Act 1882

As with some other classes of business, engineering insurance received great impetus from an Act of Parliament. The Boiler Explosions Act 1882 provided for inquiries into boiler explosions, with substantial penalties (and the high cost of the inquiry) where negligence was established. The owners of boilers found it cheaper to acquire the inspection services provided by insurers than to pay the cost of inquiries and any penalties imposed. The result was that business expanded considerably.

8.5 Other legislation

Particularly in the twentieth century, public concern over the maintenance and safety of machinery increased considerably. A host of statutes and regulations were passed, laying down very stringent technical and other requirements. These have further developed engineering insurance, a feature of which has always been the great emphasis placed on inspection services allied with the insurance protection. The most significant pieces of legislation are the various Factories Acts 1937–1961.

8.6 Scope of engineering insurance

The insurance of boilers and similar equipment has always been an important part of engineering insurance, but with the great advances in technology during the twentieth century, the scope of the business has widened considerably. The major sections of this class of insurance are as follows:

- (a) boilers and other pressure vessels;
- (b) cranes;
- (c) lifts;
- (d) engines (steam, gas or oil powered);
- (e) electrical plant (including refrigerators);
- (f) computers;
- (g) miscellaneous equipment and machinery.

8.7 Types of cover

The services provided by engineering insurers may be sub-divided into two classes:

(a) *Inspection services.* It is possible to acquire these services without actual insurance cover, but this is most commonly combined with (b) below.
(b) *Insurance cover.* This is often used as an adjunct to (a) above; the various types of insurance cover are studied below.

8.8 Forms of insurance available

Various combinations of cover are available, largely involving:

(a) damage to the actual equipment (including breakdown);
(b) damage to surrounding property (belonging to the insured);
(c) liability for death, injury or damage to third parties;
(d) consequential loss (similar to fire insurance: see **5.14**).

8.9 Associated action

As with other classes of business, engineering insurers found it useful to co-operate freely. This included the setting up of the Engineering Offices' Association in 1920 to administer the tariffs to which certain classes of engineering business are subject.

B. PROGRESS TEST 8

PART 1—SHORT ANSWERS (Answer in one or two sentences)

1. Why was engineering insurance originally opposed? **(8.2)**
2. What gave particular impetus to this class of business? **(8.4)**
3. Briefly outline the scope of engineering insurance. **(8.6)**
4. What are the two elements of cover under engineering policies? **(8.7)**
5. What combinations of cover are available with engineering insurance? **(8.9)**

PART 2—MULTIPLE CHOICE (Choose the most correct option)

1. The introduction of engineering insurance:
   (a) was obviously needed and gained immediate acceptance;
   (b) was originally opposed on moral grounds;
   (c) did not take place until the twentieth century;
   (d) was made possible by being made compulsory. **(8.2–8.3)**

2. Legislation in 1882 concerning boiler explosions:
   (a) was totally irrelevant to the development of engineering insurance;
   (b) made engineering insurance compulsory;
   (c) produced the first interest in engineering insurance;
   (d) paved the way for a great increase in engineering insurance. **(8.4)**
3. An inspection service for boilers and similar equipment:
   (a) can be provided by engineering insurers;
   (b) is quite unrelated to engineering insurance;
   (c) can only be obtained if insurance cover is also purchased;
   (d) had no part to play in developing engineering insurance. **(8.5–8.7)**
4. Public awareness of the dangers of engineering machinery:
   (a) played a great part in the development of engineering insurance;
   (b) was quite unrelated to the development of engineering insurance;
   (c) gave rise to legislation making engineering insurance compulsory;
   (d) did not begin until after the Second World War. **(8.4–8.5)**
5. Engineering insurance policies:
   (a) cover only damage to property owned by the insured;
   (b) cannot include the inspection service provided by insurers;
   (c) can cover both property damage and legal liabilities of the insured;
   (d) never cover consequential loss. **(8.8)**

(For multiple choice answers, see page 355.)

CHAPTER 9

AVIATION INSURANCE

A. THE DEVELOPMENT AND SCOPE OF AVIATION INSURANCE

9.1 Part of accident insurance

Whilst it is true that aviation business written by insurance companies was placed within the accident department, by its nature it has always been somewhat specialised and removed from the general run of other classes of accident business. Also, as indicated below, it owes much of its early development to underwriters at Lloyd's, who have always been among the leaders in marine insurance.

NOTE: It will be remembered that some of the earliest flying machines were called *airships*. With the close and vital involvement of Lloyd's underwriters, whose main expertise was in marine insurance, much of the terminology and practice of aviation insurance follows that class.

9.2 Beginnings

Aviation is a twentieth century phenomenon, and a few insurances were arranged before the First World War, covering the "crash" and third party risks. It was the military use of aircraft in the 1914–1918 war, however, that demonstrated the potential of aviation. The first regular civil aviation service commenced in 1919, but insurance companies were very cautious about this new form of transport, which from an insurance point of view presented hazards of which insurers had virtually no experience.

9.3 First important insurers

Because aviation was largely an uncharted area, the first real significant step in its insurance by companies was by a *group* or *pool* formed by the Union of Canton Insurance Company and the White Cross Insurance Company in 1923, under the name of the British Aviation Insurance Group. This tentative venture gained strength and the support of other insurers, being renamed the British Aviation Insurance Co. Ltd. in 1931. A similar pool of insurers formed the Aviation and General Insurance Co. Ltd. in 1936.

Lloyd's underwriters, true to their fine tradition as some of the leading insurers in the world, and much more flexible and entrepreneurial in their approach, were very closely involved in the pioneering of aviation insurance. Later, specialised syndicates of aviation underwriters were formed at Lloyd's during the 1930s.

9.4 The Second World War and after

It was in the Second World War that air power was shown to be a decisive military feature, and inevitably the speed and efficiency of air transport had an enormous impact once the war ended. Ever since the war there has been a great growth of air transport for goods, even though the cost is relatively high. But it is in the field of passenger transport that aviation has shown an increase of immense proportions. With the development of supersonic passenger planes, and ever larger aircraft able to carry hundreds of passengers, this growth with the corresponding demand for insurance has increased enormously in subsequent decades.

9.5 Government interest and control

With aviation assuming an ever-increasing importance, related insurance has become the subject of governmental interest and a measure of centralised control has been introduced. This has been achieved by:

(a) *The Insurance Companies Act 1958* (since replaced by Acts in 1967, 1974 and 1982). Under this Act, aviation insurance became one of the classes of business requiring special government returns and subject to particular statutory control.

(b) *The Civil Aviation Act 1949.* This Act prescribes compulsory third party insurance for aviation, but the requirements have not yet been made operative.

9.6 Scope of aviation insurance

Aviation insurance is a very specialised field, although several companies now have their own aviation departments to compete with the pools and Lloyd's underwriters . The main types of insurance available are:

(a) *Accidental damage* to the aircraft itself.

(b) *Liability* for death, injury or property damage to third parties (not passengers). Such cover is available for aircraft or airport owners.

(c) Similar liabilities towards *passengers.*

(d) *Cargo* insurance, which is usually on an "all risks" basis.

(e) Group *personal accident* insurance. Policies are arranged for aircraft crews and for travellers. The latter normally arrange insurance individually and the business is written within the accident department.

(f) *Products liability.* Such insurance is offered to aircraft manufacturers, covering the liability arising from faulty design or manufacture.

9.7 Associated action

In the early years there was very little competition (comparatively) in aviation insurance, as it was such a specialised branch that insurers acted with the closest co-operation. This was seen in the formation of *pools* to write the business at all (see **9.3**). The market became much more competitive, although the following central organisations still exist:

(a) The *Aviation Insurance Offices' Association* which was formed in 1949.
(b) The *Lloyd's Aviation Underwriters' Association*, which was formed rather earlier, in 1935.

B. PROGRESS TEST 9

PART 1—SHORT ANSWERS (Answer in one or two sentences)

1. Why does aviation insurance practice closely resemble marine insurance? **(9.1)**
2. How did insurance companies first transact aviation insurance? **(9.3)**
3. How did government show particular concern about aviation insurance? **(9.5)**
4. What different types of insurance are arranged? **(9.6)**
5. How did associated action of aviation insurers show itself? **(9.7)**

PART 2—MULTIPLE CHOICE (Choose the most correct option)

1. Aviation insurance largely followed marine insurance practice in part because:
   (a) it was subject to the same legislation as marine insurance;
   (b) only marine insurance companies wrote aviation business;
   (c) the early practice of aviation was mostly by Lloyd's underwriters;
   (d) it was totally different from fire and life insurances. **(9.1)**
2. The earliest company insurers in aviation business:
   (a) operated in groups or pools;
   (b) began such insurances long before Lloyd's underwriters did;
   (c) did not write such business until after the Second World War;
   (d) created a tariff to regulate the rates and policy terms. **(9.3)**
3. Government has become interested in aviation insurance:
   (a) by making it compulsory;

   (b) because of its considerable importance in modern society;
   (c) by nationalising this form of cover;
   (d) only in respect of the national airline. **(9.5)**

4. The cover under aviation insurance policies:
   (a) relates to both property and liability risks;
   (b) only relates to property risks;
   (c) only relates to liability risks;
   (d) will never include products liability. **(9.6)**

5. Associated action by aviation insurance companies:
   (a) was never a feature of this class of business;
   (b) is shown in that business is still only written by pools of insurers;
   (c) was particularly evident in the early days of the business;
   (d) has almost totally eliminated competition for this business. **(9.7)**

(For multiple choice answers, see page 355.)

CHAPTER 10

MORE RECENT DEVELOPMENTS

A. NEWER TYPES OF INSURANCE

10.1 Introduction

The previous chapters have reviewed the development of insurance largely from a U.K. perspective and a historical base. Looking back, there is a temptation to think that the established and ordered world of insurance evolved on a steady untroubled path. But this would be to misunderstand human nature and the nature of business. Competition and ingrained attitudes have meant that progress was at times anything but smooth. We can look at the current scene, and indeed to the future, with expectations of a similar picture emerging.

In a world of accelerating change, the insurance industry has demonstrated that it is a dynamic one, ready to meet new challenges. While not all the following types of insurance are new, perhaps they will give an indication of types of cover which have been created or developed in recent or relatively recent years to meet particular needs, sometimes with considerable controversy. The subject areas are not in any order of chronology or importance.

10.2 Kidnap and ransom insurance

"K and R" insurance was first offered in the 1930s, following the famous Lindbergh kidnapping, where a ransom of US$50,000 was demanded. As most will know, such criminal activity has become commonplace in parts of Europe and elsewhere. Sometimes the kidnap is political, sometimes merely for gain, but enormous sums, running into millions of pounds, have been demanded and paid.

Insurance to cover the risk is thought by some to be contrary to public policy and in some countries has been made illegal (e.g. Northern Ireland). It is widely practised, however, in many parts of the world. A strict condition of granting the cover is that its existence must never be disclosed, for obvious reasons. It also represents a classic case of "selection against the insurer" (i.e. only *target risks* are likely to insure). Nevertheless, this valuable form of cover to a specialised market has considerably grown in recent years.

Usually such policies are subject to a considerable *excess*, possibly 10 per cent of any ransom paid.

NOTE: A similar risk, perhaps more likely to affect "ordinary" people, is that of "hijack". While not as common as in the recent past, the danger of being hijacked still exists and many travel insurances now have this cover, with a fixed benefit of £100 or more a day with a limit of perhaps ten times that amount.

10.3 Legal expenses insurance

Increasing claims consciousness in society, coupled with high legal costs and relatively few people qualifying for legal aid, has created a demand for this type of cover, which is virtually self-explanatory. The market for this insurance is growing. Legal costs, incurred as claimant or defendant, can be covered for fairly low annual premiums. Legal costs and expenses are normally covered with conventional liability policies, but this type of cover is a valuable extra, especially where one is acting as claimant rather than defendant, for the costs of an unsuccessful action are very daunting.

10.4 Libel insurance

This form of cover has been in existence for some time and usually involves some selection against the insurer, but with high damages likely to be awarded in defamation cases, publishing and broadcasting organisations are keen to acquire such protection.

Cover is not likely to be granted lightly and the insured may well be responsible for a percentage of each claim, but in addition to any damages awarded policies will usually also cover such things as the cost of recalling and amending publications.

10.5 Nuclear insurances

Generally speaking, nuclear risks are considered to be fundamental risks and, as such, not normally insurable by commercial funds. Thus, virtually all property or liability policies, other than marine and aviation, have a standard exclusion regarding such risks. However, the Nuclear Installations Act 1965 requires site operators to effect liability insurance of up to £5 million, and this is arranged by a "pool" of insurers.

Most nuclear site owners in the United States, however, have participated in the formation of *captive insurance companies* (see **11.13**) to self-insure their property risks.

Isotopes and similar applications of the nuclear age are, however, commonly found in industry and are covered by conventional policies (e.g. employer's liability risks).

10.6 Political risk insurance

Such insurances give cover against the financial consequences of direct and indirect foreign government actions, which were formerly considered risks of a fundamental nature (and therefore uninsurable). The British Government has long provided this form of insurance for the benefit of exporters, through the Export Credits Guarantee Department. But with changing attitudes and the entrepreneurial wish to develop new lines of business, the commercial insurance world will now provide cover against such risks as:

(a) governments seizing or taking over insured property;
(b) imposition of confiscatory taxes, levies, custom duties, etc.;
(c) denying licences, permits or visas;
(d) establishing excessive prices, tariffs or monetary control;
(e) preventing the disposal of a covered financial interest;
(f) forcing the abandonment of covered property;
(g) denying access to essential products, raw materials or energy sources.

While not every insurer will provide this form of cover, the premiums (commensurate with the risks) are high and therefore attractive to the more adventurous underwriters.

10.7 Pollution insurance

This is basically a public liability risk, but has assumed great importance in recent years, following disasters like the *Amoco Cadiz* and more recently the *Exxon Valdez*. Governments are well aware of the problems and many international regulations have been made. In the United Kingdom, the Merchant Shipping (Oil Pollution) Act 1971 lays down certain compulsory requirements, for instance.

Pollution can arise by other than oil, of course, but the need for insurance on a massive scale is well appreciated. A form of cover gaining international recognition is the American EII (Environmental Impairment Insurance) policy, which basically covers liability for personal injury and death, property damage, loss of amenity and cleaning up and defence costs. Cover is likely to be measured in millions and may be subject to a very large excess (itself perhaps US$1 million or more).

10.8 Retroactive insurances

This extremely innovative form of insurance was developed, mostly in the United States, with liability cover being arranged *after an event* and backdated to apply to claims arising. The first notable example of this arose following a serious fire at a hotel in Las Vegas, resulting in claims approaching $300 million. The public liability insurance in existence was woefully inadequate, so about $170 million worth of cover was arranged and backdated to apply.

Those in favour of such covers argued that it was a natural development in *cash flow underwriting* (see NOTE: **28.5**). Claims arising would undoubtedly be exaggerated and the time value of money with claims notoriously slow in settlement would enable a mathematical premium to be quoted. Opponents argued that this was not insurance at all, but speculation on investment returns and thus not to be encouraged.

Not much is now heard of this innovation today. Reduced investment earnings and a system of class actions for numerous claimants would seem to have destroyed the basic arguments for this type of cover.

10.9 The St Christopher scheme

This proved controversial when introduced some years ago, some arguing that it was against public policy. Basically, the scheme provided a hired car and driver when the insured lost his driving licence because of a driving offence. Those in favour of the scheme maintained that it was only making available to the less well-off what has always been available to the rich.

10.10 Sonic boom insurance

The British Government announced in 1970 that it would pay compensation for sonic boom damage resulting from the test flights of the supersonic aircraft Concorde. Partly because of this and partly because of the great difficulty in investigating the validity of such claims, insurers have almost universally excluded such damage from virtually all property insurance.

10.11 Space satellite insurance

Space satellites have been insured since the mid-1960s. The claims history for this form of cover is somewhat chequered, at times showing losses running into hundreds of millions of US dollars. Conversely, the premiums are very large, usually tens of millions of US dollars: successful launches are therefore very profitable.

Cover, typically, will include malfunctioning of the space vehicle, failure to attain correct orbit, and a form of "life" cover on the satellite itself. The volatile nature of such risks might indicate total success or total loss within minutes or even seconds of launch, and it is not uncommon for there to be a refund of part of the premium if the launch proves successful.

This type of insurance is very specialised and many more traditional insurers are wary about covering such risks. The purist underwriter might argue that the very small number of exposure units entailed violates a basic criterion of insurance (see **2.4**). Those even more critical would look at the premium rates, which have been as high as 30 per cent or more of the value at risk, and say these represent gambling odds rather than insurance.

10.12 War and kindred risks

These are also fundamental risks, but war risks have been insurable with marine and aviation policies for a very long time. Apart from these classes, however, war and kindred risks are normally standard exclusions with property insurance.

During times of armed conflict, war damage is usually compensated for by government schemes. The special position in Northern Ireland during the "troubles" is also recognised by government compensation. Insurance of the person varies in its approach to such injuries. Life assurance does not normally exclude war risks, but personal accident insurance normally does. There is a form of "free" government insurance for injuries sustained as a result of criminal action.

10.13 Financial insurances

A modern development which is indicative of the process of narrowing the distinctions between insurance and other financial institutions is that of financial insurance. This is a novel concept, whereby the insured can remove risks from their own financial books, transferring them to an insurer, who will provide a *banking plan* (which is effectively a cash-flow arrangement) to fund anticipated losses.

With traditional insurance the premium is paid and the risk is transferred. If there are no or few claims the insurer makes a profit. With financial insurance the insured contracts to pay a number of annual premiums, which with interest will build up to the maximum cover, offered on an aggregate basis. Should claims not reach the insured amount during the period, there is a premium refund.

This explanation is rather simplistic, but it does indicate a new trend of insurers co-operating with insured clients to *fund* losses within a financial plan, rather than cover them by conventional insurance protection. This also marks a feature in the increasingly sophisticated risk management programmes of modern businesses.

B. PROGRESS TEST 10

PART 1—SHORT ANSWERS (Answer in one or two sentences)

1. Why is "K & R" likely to produce selection against the insurer? **(10.2)**
2. What kinds of losses might be covered by a political risks insurance? **(10.6)**

3. What is meant by "retroactive insurance"? **(10.8)**
4. Why do some underwriters disapprove of satellite launch insurance? **(10.11)**
5. How is financial insurance different from conventional insurance? **(10.13)**

PART 2—MULTIPLE CHOICE (Choose the most correct option)

1. Kidnap and ransom insurance:
   (a) is illegal in the United Kingdom;
   (b) is thought by some to be contrary to public policy;
   (c) was first offered in the very late twentieth century;
   (d) can only be provided by government insurance agencies. **(10.2)**
2. Legal costs and expenses insurance:
   (a) may cover the insured as plaintiff or defendant;
   (b) covers the insured only as defendant;
   (c) covers the insured only as plaintiff;
   (d) is a duplication of cover given in other policies. **(10.3)**
3. The St. Christopher scheme:
   (a) is contrary to public policy and illegal;
   (b) is a form of motor insurance for disabled drivers;
   (c) undertakes to pay for motoring fines;
   (d) provides alternative transport for disqualified drivers. **(10.9)**
4. Space satellite insurance is:
   (a) only possible at governmental level;
   (b) only available for military space programmes;
   (c) said by some to violate insurability criteria;
   (d) only intended to cover liability risks. **(10.11)**
5. The insurance of war and kindred risks:
   (a) is never provided by commercial insurances;
   (b) is freely offered with all types of insurance;
   (c) may be found with fire and motor policies;
   (d) may be found with marine and aviation policies. **(10.12)**

(For multiple choice answers, see page 355.)

PART TWO: OBJECTIVE TESTS (see Answers, page 356) and ASSIGNMENTS

2.1 State whether the following statements are *true* or *false*.

(a) Statutory authority for most marine insurance practices was given by the Marine Insurance Act 1906.

(b) One of the earliest commercial marine insurances was general average.

(c) Industrial life assurance was largely a product of the industrial revolution.

(d) Mortality tables are produced by life assurers to help determine premiums.

(e) Fire marks are used by forensic scientists to determine the cause of fires.

(f) Special perils are non-fire risks traditionally added to fire insurance policies.

(g) The Employers' Liability (Compulsory Insurance) Act 1969 made employers responsible for all injuries sustained by employees.

(h) "All risks" insurance covers every kind of loss.

(i) Credit insurance relates to a system of paying premiums by instalments.

(j) The Motor Insurers' Bureau is a central fund to compensate all people injured in motor accidents.

2.2 Select the *most correct* answer for the following questions.

(a) Lloyd's underwriters (i) have a monopoly of marine insurance; (ii) are an insignificant section of the insurance market; (iii) are mostly private individuals rather than limited companies.

(b) In marine insurance terminology freight (i) relates to the insurance of goods carried by vessels; (ii) is merged with cargo insurance if it is payable at destination; (iii) may be compared with postage and package charges on inland consignments.

(c) The Amicable Society is famous because (i) it was acquired by The Norwich Union Life; (ii) it was formed by royal charter in 1705; (iii) it survived unscientific underwriting practices and successfully adopted modern methods.

(d) A surrender value is paid by a life assurer (i) when the policyholder decides to terminate the policy; (ii) when the assurer decides to terminate the policy; (iii) when an endowment policy matures.

(e) The Tooley Street fire in 1861 (i) marked the beginning of fire insurance in this country; (ii) was the biggest fire ever recorded in the United Kingdom; (iii) was a major factor in revising underwriting methods.

(f) Consequential loss insurance (i) will pay all expenses and losses resulting from fire not paid by the fire policy; (ii) was originally considered contrary to public policy; (iii) is only practised by a few insurers.

(g) Fidelity guarantee insurance (i) is a specialist class of business which few insurers transact; (ii) can cover default by employees involving stock or money; (iii) can only insure the misappropriation of money by staff.

(h) Permanent health insurance is similar to life assurance because (i) it cannot be terminated by the insurer; (ii) it relates to insurance of the person; (iii) because insurers pay a surrender value on premature termination of the contract.

(i) The Road Traffic Act (i) was the origin of motor insurance in this country; (ii) greatly increased motor insurance because it made the motorist liable for any death or injury caused; (iii) was an attempt to ensure that innocent victims of road accidents received compensation for their injuries.

(j) Aviation insurance (i) was so hazardous that early company policies were insured through "pools" of insurers; (ii) was only possible in the early days through "pools" of insurers; (iii) relates to fundamental risks which are insured with government backing.

2.3 Assignments.

(a) Write an essay tracing the historical development of one major class of business, with your suggestions as to its likely future.

(b) Formulate a list of suggested types of insurance for a firm of your choice, calculate your own sums insured and make inquiries with local insurance firms to ascertain likely premium commitments.

(c) Bearing in mind recent developments in insurance, discuss these developments and suggest possible new types of insurance in existing or new fields.

PART THREE

THE INSURANCE MARKET

CHAPTER 11

INSURERS

A. INTRODUCTION

11.1 The concept of a market

A market is simply a term to describe the facilities for buying and selling to take place. The insurance market is no different, the commodity "sold" being security. As with any other market, that for insurance consists of (see Fig. 8):

(a) *Sellers*. These are insurers; the remainder of this chapter is concerned with the different kinds of insurer.
(b) *Buyers*. This includes just about everyone: individuals, corporations, clubs, societies, public bodies and the government. All require insurance to a greater or lesser extent, fulfilling the role of buyer in the insurance market. Even insurers themselves sometimes act as "buyers", as when they seek *reinsurance*: see Chapter 32.
(c) *Intermediaries*. These are the "middle-men", introducing buyers to sellers, and vice versa. They include insurance agents and brokers. Insurance intermediaries are studied in more detail in Chapter 13.

B. TYPES OF INSURERS

11.2 Summary

The different types of insurer in the insurance market may be summarised as follows:

(a) Lloyd's underwriters.
(b) Mutual companies.
(c) Proprietary companies.
(d) Mutual indemnity associations.
(e) Collecting friendly societies.
(f) Self-insurers: see below.

11.3 Insurers

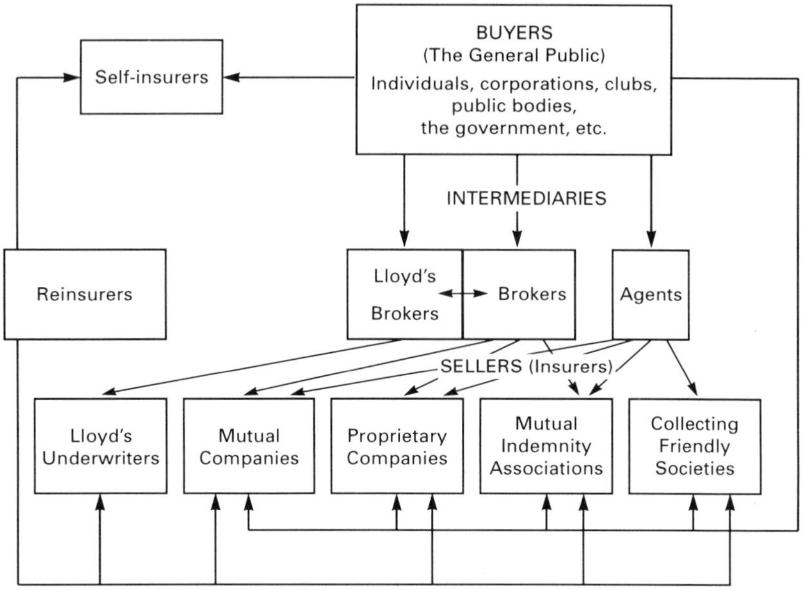

Fig. 8 The insurance market

11.3 Lloyd's underwriters

The majority of Lloyd's underwriters are individuals transacting insurance on their own behalf. Lloyd's itself is a corporation, but it merely provides facilities for its members to transact business and is not legally responsible for liabilities incurred by the underwriters. The public are not permitted to deal direct with Lloyd's underwriters, but only through a Lloyd's broker. A very important section of the insurance market, now transacting marine and non-marine business, Lloyd's underwriters and the corporation of Lloyd's are studied in more detail in Chapter 12.

11.4 Mutual companies

These are companies which have no shareholders, the owners being the policyholders, who share any profits made. Some mutual companies specialise in life assurance, but they compete freely with other insurers, dealing direct with (usually) all sections of the public. They are brought into being, or incorporated, by registration under the Companies Acts, or by the older form of a Deed of Settlement.

NOTE: It should not be assumed that the inclusion of the word "mutual" in an insurer's name necessarily means that the company is now constituted in the above form. Many insurers, originally so constituted, now transact business as *proprietary companies* (see **11.5**) while retaining the name.

11.5 Proprietary companies

A "proprietor" is an owner. Thus a proprietary company is one owned by its shareholders. They, after due provision for necessary expenses and reserves, are entitled to the profits made by the company.

The shareholders themselves have limited liability, limited to the extent of their shares' face value. The company, however, as a separate legal "person" is liable for any debts or liabilities it may incur. If the company's assets cannot meet its liabilities it must be liquidated.

Proprietary companies, with the attraction of limited liability for their members, are undoubtedly the most numerous type of insurers, and they may be incorporated by:

(a) *Royal charter.* This is a very rare privilege, enjoyed by only a few companies, e.g. the Royal Exchange Assurance.
(b) *Special Act of Parliament.* This again is fairly rare. An example of such a company is the Scottish Union & National.
(c) *Registration under the Companies Acts.* This is by far the most common form of incorporation. Again, some of the older companies were originally incorporated by Deed of Settlement, although many have since registered under the Companies Act.

Proprietary companies deal direct with the public and compete freely with all other insurers.

11.6 Mutual indemnity associations

For a full discussion of the meaning of the term "indemnity", see Chapter 19. For the moment, the word "compensation" may be substituted.

Mutual indemnity associations are quite different from mutual companies (see **11.4** above). The associations were originally formed as trade associations, as a kind of self-insurance club for the benefit of members within the trade only. Many such associations have since widened their scope and deal with the public generally.

These are common in marine insurance, where they are known as "Protection and Indemnity Associations" (or "Clubs") (see **3.15**). These "P & I" clubs insure liability risks on a mutual basis. The shipowners who are members of the club make contributions according to the tonnage of shipping in the scheme.

11.7 Collecting friendly societies

Springing directly from the social changes wrought by the industrial revolution, these societies operate almost exclusively in industrial life assurance.

11.8 Self-insurers

Self-insurance is not the same as non-insurance. With the former, the organisation has deliberately decided not to engage outside insurers but has set up its own insurance fund to meet possible losses. This is practised by a number of very large organisations, but the scheme has certain disadvantages: see a detailed consideration in **11.11–11.12**.

C. OTHER INSURER CLASSIFICATIONS

11.9 Tariff and non-tariff insurers

A more detailed examination of the implications of tariffs is given in **11.19–11.21**. For the purpose of insurer classification, tariff members belong to a voluntary association of competing insurers who agree to standardise policy wordings and certain other features. Non-tariff insurers, of course, do not subscribe to any such undertakings.

11.10 Specialist and composite insurers

The term *specialist insurer* used to denote an insurer who transacted only one type of insurance business (e.g. motor) and a *composite insurer* meant an insurer who transacted at least two different classes of insurance. In that previous sense, "specialist" insurers are still very much in evidence, particularly in life assurance, but the term "composite insurer" has come to have a rather different meaning.

A "composite insurer" now means an insurer transacting both life and general business (i.e both categories in the statutory classification (see **2.15**)). The Insurance Companies Act 1982 (see Chapter 33) forbids the creation of new composite insurers, although present composites control the major share of the overall U.K. insurance market.

D. REINSURERS

11.11 Reinsurers

Although not always a separate entity as in Fig. 8, reinsurers are important in the insurance market. (For detailed consideration of reinsurance, see Chapter

32). Reinsurers are the insurers of the insurers. All insurance companies practise reinsurance, reinsuring their own risks with other insurers and/or acting as reinsurers for other insurers. There are also a number of specialist reinsurers (who prefer to call themselves *professional reinsurers*).

E. ADVANTAGES AND DISADVANTAGES OF SELF-INSURANCE

11.12 Advantages

Self-insurance in whole or in part has become a much more common feature. The advantages of being one's own insurer may be summarised as follows:

(a) premiums (which may be substantial for large organisations) are retained, together with accrued interest thereon;
(b) the organisation is not penalised by higher premiums being charged because of the adverse claims experience of other firms;
(c) it may be possible for the insurance fund to qualify for at least partial tax relief;
(d) a direct incentive is given to care and safety, with no possible disagreement over the way claims are handled.

11.13 Disadvantages

The drawbacks of having one's own insurance fund are:

(a) heavy losses may occur before sufficient funds have accumulated, jeopardising the whole future of the scheme, and possibly of the company;
(b) catastrophic losses occasionally occur, which the accumulated funds of insurers and reinsurers can stand, but which may ruin or cripple a commercial undertaking;
(c) the capital in the fund has to be tied up in fairly short-term investments, earning lower interest rates, in case it is needed. The bulk of this (i.e. excluding premiums) could be better used if the firm were insured;
(d) it is difficult and expensive for staff to acquire the experience needed to administer the fund and deal with claims efficiently.
(e) a disproportionate number of staff would be required to administer the fund, the large-scale economies of an insurance company not being available;
(f) the technical advice of the insurer, with recommendations for risk improvement, would be lost.
(g) in the absence of detailed statistics, such as are possessed by insurers, it is difficult to assess a correct allotment to the fund. The past

experience of the company is almost certainly too narrow a basis on which to assess the future;

(h) if the fund enjoys a few successful years and accumulates a fair amount of capital, there is always the temptation to "borrow" from this for other purposes, so that future misfortunes find the fund unprepared;

(i) the whole principle and benefit of "spreading the risk" is lost.

F. CAPTIVE INSURANCE COMPANIES

11.14 Captive insurance companies

A very detailed study of this fascinating development in self-insurance is not possible within this book, but it has been and still is a significant part of insurance history. The concept of a "captive" (so called because it was not free to make its own decisions) is not new, but the movement mushroomed in recent decades. Essentially, the basic idea is a sophisticated form of self-insurance, whereby a non-insurance parent corporation forms its own insurance organisation to cover the risks of the parent.

11.15 Why are they formed?

There are many reasons for forming a captive, several covered by the advantages of self-insurance listed in **11.12**. Some particular reasons for the mushroom growth in recent years were:

(a) *Tax*. This was an early reason, and a prime reason for establishing the captive in an offshore domicile, but tightening fiscal regulations have made this less of a reason today.

(b) *Unavailable or unaffordable cover*. This was particularly true in the American market (most captives are U.S.-owned) for certain classes of business, e.g. products-liability and medical-malpractice business.

(c) *Cash-flow advantages*. Where substantial premiums are involved the immediate availability of retained money (particularly in *long-tail* business, where claim payments are spread over a long period) has an obvious appeal. In times of high interest rates the investment potential is also an attraction.

(d) *Excellent claims figures*. With a large premium volume and reliable statistics showing a consistent low loss-ratio, it makes sense to keep your money and pay your own claims. This has tended to apply more to property than to liability insurances.

(e) *Creation of a "profit centre"*. The basic idea of the parent concern was to diversify into insurance, transacting unrelated (the Americans call it "third party") business as well as its own. This did not always prove successful and some have gone into liquidation because of this development. As a consequence fewer captives actively seek unrelated business.

(f) *More accessible reinsurance*. Initially, the market attitude towards captives was more or less hostile. When it became obvious they were here to stay (and at a time when market conditions were becoming much less favourable to insurers) helping by way of reinsurance became much more commonplace.

11.16 Who forms them?

Nearly all large organisations will have given thought to forming a captive. There are probably over 2,000 captives in existence already (a large proportion of them domiciled in Bermuda). ICI in Britain (its captive is domiciled in the United Kingdom) and the Greyhound Bus Corporation in the USA are but two examples. In recent years, impetus in the growth of group or association captives (*multiple-parent ownership*) has been seen, and seems likely to continue.

11.17 Where are they located?

For tax and other reasons, their prime location has traditionally been offshore. Bermuda is by far the most favoured location, but there are several other domiciles, such as the Caymans, the Bahamas, the Channel Isles, etc. Some of the States within the USA have also become attractive as captive domiciles, e.g. Vermont.

11.18 How important are they?

With the disappointments experienced in the early 1980s, especially in unrelated or "third party" business results, some observers at that time felt that the best of the captive movement was over and that their significance would diminish. Others were more optimistic as to the future of the movement.

The most recent view seems clearly to point to the continuation and growth of captives and other forms of self-insurance. In the USA self-insurance has made heavy inroads into commercial insurances and there seems no reason to doubt that this will spread to other jurisdictions.

G. TARIFF ORGANISATIONS

11.19 What tariff organisations are

Essentially tariffs in insurance are associations of independent and competing insurers who agree to co-operate with one another in the following matters:

(a) standard minimum premium rates;

(b) standard policy wordings;
(c) standard commission rates;
(d) free exchange of statistical information.

11.20 Reasons for formation

In the developing years of insurance, studied in earlier chapters, insurer failures were experienced on account of lack of statistical knowledge and fierce rate-cutting "wars". This was not in anyone's long-term interests and inter-office co-operation was common in many classes of business, not least in the formation of tariffs.

11.21 Reasons for their decline

All the major tariffs in the United Kingdom are now defunct. The reasons for their disappearance include:

(a) insurers large enough to rely on their own statistics;
(b) competition from reputable non-tariff insurers;
(c) inability to innovate and react quickly to market needs;
(d) possible government and consumer apprehensions;
(e) tighter regulations providing the public with better security against insurer insolvencies.

H. PROGRESS TEST 11

PART 1—SHORT ANSWERS (Answer in one or two sentences)

1. Describe a typical insurance "market". **(11.1)**
2. Briefly describe the different types of insurer. **(11.2–11.9)**
3. What are the advantages of self-insurance? **(11.12)**
4. Why might a "captive" insurance company be formed? **(11.15)**
5. Why did tariff associations decline and largely disappear? **(11.21)**

PART 2—MULTIPLE CHOICE (Choose the most correct option)

1. Insurance markets:
   (a) are totally different from any other kind of market;
   (b) have buyers, sellers and intermediaries, like other markets;
   (c) consist only of insurers and intermediaries;
   (d) consist only of insurers and insured. **(11.1)**
2. Mutual insurance companies:
   (a) are legally owned by their policyholders;
   (b) are legally owned by their shareholders;

(c) transact only fire insurance business;
(d) only accept business insurance through brokers. **(11.4)**

3. Proprietary insurance companies:
   (a) are legally owned by their policyholders;
   (b) are legally owned by their shareholders;
   (c) accept business only through insurance brokers;
   (d) never accept business through insurance brokers. **(11.5)**
4. A strong argument against self-insurance is that:
   (a) it is illegal;
   (b) it will be impossible to obtain reinsurance;
   (c) an early large claim could seriously embarrass the fund;
   (d) there will be no incentive to earn premium discounts. **(11.13)**
5. Captive insurance companies are:
   (a) usually owned by a non-insurance parent organisation;
   (b) against the law in the United Kingdom;
   (c) mostly domiciled in the United Kingdom or the USA;
   (d) not able to obtain reinsurance cover. **(11.14–11.17)**

(For multiple choice answers, see page 355.)

CHAPTER 12

LLOYD'S

A. FORMATION AND STRUCTURE

12.1 Introduction

Lloyd's is such a world institution that it deserves a separate chapter, although its members are insurers (see **11.3**). With a great history spanning over three centuries, the term "Lloyd's of London" still has an impressive sound, despite at times a troubled past and, some say, an even more troubled present (mid-1990s).

12.2 Origins

Edward Lloyd, from whom the great modern Corporation of Lloyd's derives its name, owned a coffee house in London in the late seventeenth century. It was conveniently situated near the River Thames, so that merchants and others involved in marine ventures, including those offering and requiring insurance, frequently met there (see **3.9**). Lloyd himself did not transact insurance business, and to this extent the Corporation of Lloyd's has the same function. It provides facilities for transacting insurance, but is not itself responsible for any business so arranged.

12.3 Constitution and government

Lloyd's, as a corporation, does not write insurance business. This is all transacted by the individual *underwriting members*, who are personally liable for the business they write, to the full extent of their means (they are thus said to have "unlimited personal liability"). Lloyd's is a society incorporated by Act of Parliament in 1871 providing the premises and facilities for its members to conduct insurance business.

Fundamental changes in the society's constitution arose out of the Lloyd's Act 1982, a key result of which was the formation of an elected Council to assume disciplinary and rule-making functions. The Council has 21 members, consisting of eight "working members", five "external" (not actively engaged) members and eight nominated members approved by the Governor of the Bank of England and including the Chief Executive Officer and the Chairman of the Securities and Investment Board (SIB).

12.4 Syndicates

There are approximately 20,000 underwriting members of Lloyd's. Because of the numbers involved, and the complexity and size of modern insurance transactions, they have grouped into *syndicates*, consisting of from just a few to some hundreds of members, usually specialising in a particular class of business, although the great majority of members are not actively engaged in the market personally. Members are known as *Names* and are represented in syndicates by an underwriting agent, who may be one of their own members. Although underwriters operate in syndicates, the individual personal responsibility of each underwriter is unaffected, and Names have no responsibility for each other's losses.

12.5 Classes of business

Although Lloyd's began by being and is still very much involved with marine insurance, the main classes of business now underwritten by members are marine, non-marine (fire, etc.), aviation, motor, and short-term life.

There are about 400 syndicates active, but only a few underwrite life business. Long-term (life) business is not written directly. A separate company, Lloyd's Life Assurance Limited, was formed for this purpose.

12.6 Membership

As each underwriter takes upon himself or herself the onerous responsibility of *unlimited personal liability* for his share of losses, stringent requirements must be satisfied before becoming a member. These include:

(a) being recommended by other members;
(b) satisfying Council of their personal financial standing (e.g. at least £250,000 unencumbered assets are required);
(c) furnishing an approved security, varying according to the volume of business allowed to be transacted;
(d) paying all premiums received into Premium Trust Funds, from which only claims, expenses and ascertained profits may be paid;
(e) submitting to an annual audit, to confirm that underwriting assets will at least meet all liabilities.
(f) contributing a levy on premium income to a *Central Fund* which is intended for the protection of policyholders should any member be unable to meet his commitments. This fund is considerable but does

not replace the personal liabilities of underwriters. It is a form of extra security for policyholders.

12.7 Corporate "Names"

In 1994, limited liability corporate investors were admitted to Lloyd's. This was a historic change and may have considerable bearing upon future developments.

As with individual "Names", corporate members are required to make deposits and contribute to the Central Fund (see **12.6**). Corporate syndicates, comprising only one corporate member, are also permitted.

12.8 Lloyd's underwriting agents

These must be registered and their function is not only to underwrite on behalf of syndicate members, but also to take care of administration and comply with Lloyd's internal rules. The Lloyd's Act 1982 (see **12.3**), required Lloyd's brokers to divest themselves of any interest in any Lloyd's managing agents.

B. PLACING AN INSURANCE RISK AT LLOYD'S

12.9 "The Room"

The *underwriting room* (*"the Room"*) is where business is transacted. Marine, motor and aviation insurance is usually dealt with on the ground floor, non-marine on the gallery floor. Underwriting members sit, with one or two staff, in wooden "boxes".

12.10 Lloyd's brokers

The general public are denied access to the Room, and Lloyd's underwriters will only transact business through a recognised *Lloyd's broker*. A Lloyd's broker must also satisfy stringent requirements concerning his integrity and financial stability. He is a person with a very responsible position, as it is his duty to move among the underwriters in the Room, obtaining the best terms possible for his client. In practice, this duty is often performed by the broker's authorised clerk.

12.11 The "slip"

On being requested to place an insurance at Lloyd's, the broker will prepare a *slip*, which is quite literally a slip of paper containing brief details of the risk to be placed. He will then approach underwriters who specialise in that class of business, with a view to securing one of them as a *leader*, or *leading underwriter*. This means that the underwriter gives a lead, by quoting an appropriate rate of premium and accepting a certain percentage or proportion of the risk. He will then sign his name, or, more usually, just his or the syndicate's initials, below the details of the risk, indicating the rate and his proportion (hence the term "underwriter").

The broker is not bound to accept the proposed rate, but if it is thought suitable, he will circulate among other underwriters, requesting them to follow the lead by accepting similar or other proportions of the risk (at the same rate of premium), until 100 per cent has been placed.

NOTES: i. All risks placed at Lloyd's are dealt with on the basis of a broker's slip. This means that several insurers are simultaneously and quite independently involved with the insurance, i.e. by *co-insurance* (see **32.21**).

ii. By custom, a slip is used with nearly all marine insurers, whether at Lloyd's or elsewhere, especially in the London market.

iii. Risks incepting after 1 January 1996 should have full electronic versions on an electronic placing support system for all business placed at Lloyd's.

12.12 Policy signing office

The "slip" is quite sufficient evidence of agreement between the underwriters and brokers. However, a policy must be prepared for the policyholder. This is done in the broker's office but all policies issued at Lloyd's are checked and signed, and impressed with the formal seal, at *Lloyd's Policy Signing Office*. Although of ancient origin, this office is completely up to date, with modern electronic equipment to deal with literally millions of policies per year.

12.13 Claims

The Lloyd's broker is not merely important in the preliminary placing of the risk with underwriters, he also negotiates for his client in respect of claims.

The method of dealing with claims varies slightly according to the type of business concerned:

(a) *Marine*. Most marine claims to be settled in this country are dealt with in *Lloyd's Underwriters' Claims Office*, where settlements are negotiated with brokers. Claims settlement abroad is sometimes arranged with the local *Lloyd's agent*.

(b) *Non-marine*. Many non-marine claims are also settled in the Claims Office, but mostly they are negotiated by the brokers with the claims officials of the underwriters at the boxes in the Room (see **12.7**).

C. LINKS WITH THE PAST

12.14 Lloyd's traditions

Lloyd's is justly proud of its long history, and carefully preserves many historic links with traditions of its former years. Despite this, Lloyd's underwriters are keenly competitive in all types of insurance and they are completely up to date in their approach to business. Particular ways in which the present approach of Lloyd's has its roots in history are considered below.

12.15 Methods already considered

Some ways in which present practices of Lloyd's are directly linked with the past have already been mentioned, and are as follows:

(a) the organisation called Lloyd's is not responsible for business transacted on its premises (see **12.2–12.3**). The insurers concerned are individuals, not part of a company;
(b) underwriters sit in the Room, in "boxes", which are rather similar to the seating arrangements in the original Lloyd's coffee house (see **12.9**);
(c) Lloyd's brokers are extensively used, performing many more duties than do brokers not authorised to transact business with Lloyd's (see **12.10**);
(d) the use of a "slip" when negotiating new business (see **12.11**).

12.16 Policy forms

Until fairly recently, the document used for marine policies (the "SG" form) had essentially the same wording as was used in the eighteenth century, made more up to date by the attachment of appropriate clauses (see **3.13**).

12.17 "Waiters"

The uniformed staff of the Corporation of Lloyd's performing general duties still wear red gowns and are known as *waiters* much as in the times of the original coffee house.

12.18 Calling system

The proprietor of the original coffee house made available shipping and other intelligence, mostly announced by a boy (called the *Kidney*) who would report matters of importance from a pulpit. In principle, the same facility exists today in the *Caller's Rostrum* in the Room. Of course, the whole process has been modernised by the use of microphones, and there is an electronic dialling device which brokers can use to signify their whereabouts when they are called.

12.19 The Lutine Bell

This is the ship's bell of HMS *Lutine* (formerly a French vessel of that name), salvaged in 1859 from the vessel which had sunk in 1799. The bell hangs above the Caller's Rostrum in the Room, and is rung to call attention when very important announcements are to be made (not for every loss at sea). It is rung once for bad news, and twice for good. With improved methods of communication, the Lutine Bell now is only of historic and ceremonial importance.

12.20 The Casualty Book

In addition to insurance, Lloyd's has always been famous for shipping intelligence (see below). One of the aspects of this is the maintenance of a *Casualty Book*, which stands in the centre of the Room, and in which are entered the names of all vessels which have become, or seem certain to become, total losses. The entries in the book are still made in long-hand by the use of a quill pen. In addition, casualty sheets (yellow paper for marine, pink for non-marine and blue for aviation) are pinned on a *Casualty Board* near the entrance to the Room.

12.21 The Nelson Room

Lloyd's has always had the closest possible interest in maritime affairs. It still presents medals for acts of outstanding bravery and merit at sea. In memory of England's greatest sea hero, Lloyd's maintains the *Nelson Room*, which contains portraits, silver plate and other mementoes of Lord Nelson.

12.22 The Captain's Room

All members of Lloyd's have the right and privilege of dining in the *Captain's Room*, another indication of the strong connection between Lloyd's and the world of shipping.

D. SHIPPING INTELLIGENCE AND PUBLICATIONS

12.23 Shipping intelligence

Lloyd's has long been regarded as the world centre of shipping intelligence of all kinds. To maintain this position, an enormous volume of information is passed to Lloyd's daily, from a multitude of sources (including shipowners, coastal radio stations, and in particular *Lloyd's agents*: see below). This information requires constant processing and analysing, with the use of complicated equipment. Checking and collation of information for supply to the Room and other interested parties takes place in Lloyd's Intelligence Department.

12.24 Lloyd's agents

The vast amount of material needed to keep shipping intelligence up to date would not be possible without an extensive network of representatives, or correspondents, throughout the world. *Lloyd's agents* and *sub-agents*, fulfil this function, although they have many other duties as well. Their other duties include arranging for inspections and reports to be made in connection with reported losses, and sometimes actually negotiating settlement of claims on behalf of the underwriters concerned. They may be involved in non-marine duties, particularly with aviation and accident (usually travel) claims. At the present time there are over 1,500 Lloyd's agents and sub-agents throughout the world.

12.25 Publications

In conjunction with and forming part of the shipping intelligence provided, LLP, formerly a subsidiary of Lloyd's, produces various publications of particular value to the shipping and insurance world. These are:

(a) *Lloyd's List*. This is a daily publication, its full name being *Lloyd's List and Shipping Gazette*. It records shipping movements, with details of marine and aircraft casualties. It is London's oldest daily newspaper, first having appeared in 1734;
(b) *Lloyd's Shipping Index*. This is also published daily, and contains an alphabetical list of many thousands of ocean-going vessels, indicating various particulars, such as the owner, specifications, latest known position, etc.
(c) Various other technical publications, including *Lloyd's Law Reports*.

12.26 Lloyd's current troubles

While it is not appropriate for this book to dwell on the difficulties experienced at Lloyd's in recent years, mention must be made of them. Lloyd's has faced great challenges in its past, but the present problems are being widely discussed as perhaps bringing about the end of this great worldwide institution. The problems include bitter legal actions on behalf of hundreds of Names, who felt let down to the point of betrayal in enormous losses sustained in the late 1980s and early 1990s.

Much has been done to address the problems, including the publication of a business plan by Lloyd's in 1993 and the planned formation of a new reinsurance company called *Equitas* to take over liability for 1992 and prior year claims.

Everyone with a genuine concern for the insurance industry hopes that the present difficulties can be overcome and that the world-famous insurance market known as Lloyd's will be able to continue and uphold its finest traditions.

In closing these brief comments, it should be noted that in over 300 years no claimant with a genuine claim insured by Lloyd's has failed to receive payment and despite the present difficulties there remains great confidence all over the world in the security behind "Lloyd's of London".

E. PROGRESS TEST 12

PART 1—SHORT ANSWERS (Answer in one or two sentences)

1. Outline some requirements imposed by the Corporation of Lloyd's to ensure that members are both suitable and financially stable. **(12.6)**
2. What is the procedure for placing an insurance at Lloyd's? **(12.9, 12.12)**
3. Explain the following terms in the context of Lloyd's of London:

    (a) "Waiters"; **(12.17)**
    (b) The Lutine Bell; **(12.19)**
    (c) The Casualty Book. **(12.20)**
4. In what ways does history play an important role at Lloyd's? **(12.1–2, 12.14–22)**
5. Show how Lloyd's is involved in shipping intelligence. **(12.23–12.24)**

PART 2—MULTIPLE CHOICE (Choose the most correct option)

1. Syndicates at Lloyd's of London:
    (a) are associations of Lloyd's brokers;
    (b) are associations of underwriting Names;
    (c) have joint and several liability for all losses;
    (d) require each member to be active in the market. **(12.4)**
2. An underwriting member (Name) at Lloyd's;
    (a) must have professional qualifications in insurance;
    (b) must accept unlimited liability for losses;
    (c) need not show any significant financial assets;
    (d) is not required to pay anything to Lloyd's funds. **(12.6)**
3. Arranging an insurance at Lloyd's:
    (a) is usually done by the use of a "slip";

(b) is no different from the process with other insurers;
(c) can be done direct or through a broker;
(d) can be arranged by any insurance broker. **(12.9–12.11)**

4. Lloyd's has a long and distinguished history:
(a) but this has no part in present operations;
(b) which is remembered in many ways in the present Lloyd's;
(c) and owed its beginnings to the industrial revolution;
(d) stretching back for nearly one hundred years. **(12.14–12.22)**

5. Shipping intelligence supplied by Lloyd's:
(a) concerns only insurance matters;
(b) relates only to British shipping;
(c) is decentralised in several centres around the world;
(d) is gathered by a host of agents around the world. **(12.23)**

(For multiple choice answers, see page 355.)

CHAPTER 13

INSURANCE INTERMEDIARIES

A. GENERAL OBSERVATIONS

13.1 Intermediaries

The "middlemen" or intermediaries of the insurance market may be classified as insurance *brokers*, or insurance *agents*. While in the legal sense they are both agents, there are substantial differences between them (see **13.7**).

13.2 Intermediaries are not legally necessary

Although much insurance business is placed through an agent, and commercial organisations usually seek the assistance of professional insurance brokers, there is no legal necessity to act through a middleman. It is quite possible to approach an insurance company direct, and arrange insurance "at the counter" without the intervention of any intermediary. The words "insurance company" should be emphasised because by custom Lloyd's underwriters will not accept business direct from the public, or indeed from just any insurance agent or broker: see below.

NOTE: In the United Kingdom in recent years a new market phenomenon has emerged under the title *Direct Insurance*. More comment is made on this later (see **15.7**) but for the moment it can be understood as a concerted marketing drive by insurers, especially in personal insurances like motor and household, to eliminate the middleman and offer cheaper premiums.

13.3 Insurance with Lloyd's underwriters

Lloyd's underwriters, by custom, will only do business through a *Lloyd's broker*. He is a specially authorised broker, but will not necessarily deal exclusively with Lloyd's. Such a broker signifies that he is authorised to deal direct with Lloyd's by having the words "and at Lloyd's" printed on his stationery.

B. AGENTS AND BROKERS

13.4 Agents

The majority of insurance agents in this country are not primarily engaged in insurance. They are appointed agents on a part-time basis because from their own profession they are often in a position to introduce business to the insurer. Thus, it is extremely common for accountants, solicitors, garage proprietors, shopkeepers and the like to hold agency appointments, often with more than one company.

Because they are not professionals in insurance, they are not expected to have (nor do they need to have) detailed technical knowledge of the business. Their function is to introduce clients to their principal, the insurer. They receive advice and instructions about policies available from an official of the company, termed an *inspector of agents* (usually known as a *new business inspector*, or just an *inspector*, within the profession). He visits them periodically or on request.

13.5 Types of agents

According to the terms of their appointment, insurance agents may be:

(a) *Cash agents*. These have very limited powers indeed. They are in effect merely "conduit pipes" between the insurer and the insured, with no authority to bind the insurer in any way. As the name indicates, they are not allowed credit: transactions are for immediate payment.

(b) *Credit agents*. These have slightly wider powers and may within certain limits be authorised to commit the insurer. For example, a garage proprietor who is an agent for an insurer will usually have authority to issue cover notes (see **27.21**) in respect of motor insurance. Also, again as the name indicates, they are debited and credited in account for their transactions on behalf of the insurer.

(c) *"Own case" agents*. These are invariably credit agents (see (b) above), who merely introduce their own insurance to the insurer. As, like all agents, they are remunerated by commission, it may be argued that "own case" agencies are merely methods of obtaining cheaper premiums and as such should not be permitted. An answer to this is that such agencies are normally only granted to persons or organisations presenting a large amount of business to the insurer. (As such, they are termed *large* or *important connections*.) Commercial reality therefore prevails.

NOTE: An *industrial insurance agent* is usually quite different from the above, in that he is normally employed by the insurer or assurer. He is generally remunerated partly by commission on the business acquired and partly by salary. Being engaged in home service insurance (see **4.12–4.15**), such an agent calls at the homes of clients to collect premiums and seek further business.

13.6 Insurance brokers

Unlike insurance agents, insurance brokers profess to be experts in insurance. They are full-time specialists and offer advice and professional help in arranging insurance on behalf of their clients. Anyone may request an insurance broker to act for him, and the broker is required to seek the best terms possible for his client. As a professional, he or she may be liable in damages if the client can show that prejudice has been sustained because of the broker's professional negligence.

Formerly, anyone could operate as an insurance broker, but following the Insurance Brokers (Registration) Act 1977, it is necessary to be registered, after meeting the requirements of an Insurance Brokers' Registration Council. The criteria that must be satisfied for council registration include professional and financial standards, as well as the need for professional liability insurance. The Registration Council includes a strong representation of members from the professional insurance brokers' association (see **14.16**).

Rather strangely, although insurance brokers almost invariably act for the insured, they are not remunerated by their client but receive a commission from the insurer in much the same way as agents. Because of their professional standing and the responsibility borne, commission rates for brokers (termed *brokerage*) are generally higher than for agents in the United Kingdom market.

13.7 Comparison between agents and brokers

The distinctions between insurance agents and insurance brokers may be summarised as follows: see Fig. 9.

(a) *Insurance Agents*:
- (1) usually part-time only;
- (2) do not profess to be experts in insurance;
- (3) cannot be sued for professional negligence;
- (4) normally agents of the insurer;
- (5) remunerated by commission;
- (6) sometimes allowed limited powers, e.g. to issue cover notes;
- (7) special category: *"own case" agents* (see **13.5**(c));
- (8) need not be registered.

(b) *Insurance Brokers*:
- (1) full-time professionals;
- (2) profess to be experts;
- (3) can be so sued;
- (4) normally agents of the insured;

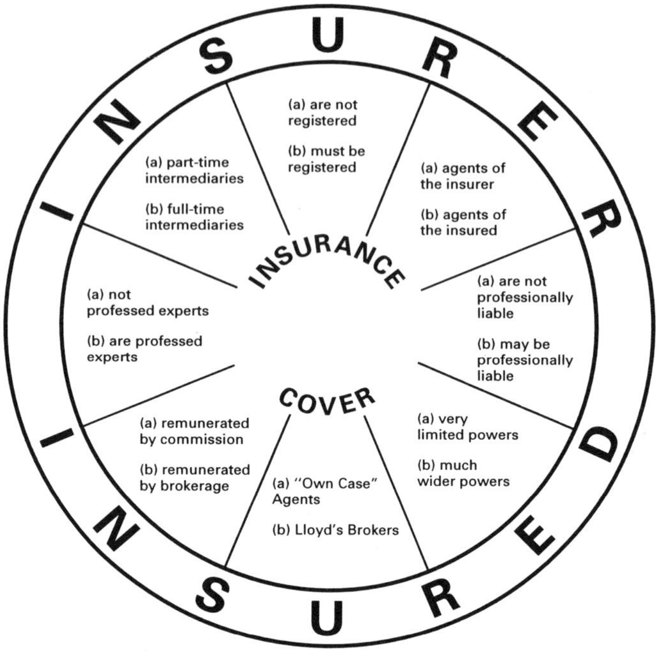

Fig. 9 Comparison between insurance agents and insurance brokers

(5) also remunerated by commission, but in the United Kingdom market this is usually at higher rates and termed brokerage;
(6) usually have wider powers, sometimes including authority to settle minor claims on behalf of the insurer;
(7) sometimes also Lloyd's brokers (see **13.3**);
(8) must be registered (see **13.6**).

C. LEGAL CONSIDERATIONS

13.8 Introduction

Although a detailed study of the law concerning agency is outside the scope of this book, it is necessary briefly to consider some legal aspects, as set out below.

13.9 Agents and brokers are both "agents"

Legally, an agent is one who is authorised to act for another, called his *principal*, in dealing with third parties. In this sense, both insurance agents and insurance brokers are *agents*. Further, there are several classes of persons who may not commonly be referred to as insurance agents, but who fulfil that role legally (see **13.11**).

13.10 Agent of whom?

The legal maxim applicable to agency generally is *qui facit per alium facit per se* (which means "he who acts through another is himself performing the act"). Thus, a duly appointed agent, acting within the scope of his authority, binds his principals by his actions just as though the principal has performed them personally.

Because of this it is particularly important in respect of any given action (e.g. completing insurance forms) to decide for whom the agent acted at the relevant time. It is quite possible for an agent of the insurer, as part-time agents usually are, to be legally regarded as agent of the insured for a given act, and vice versa.

EXAMPLE: In the case of *Newsholme Brothers* v. *Road Transport & General Insurance Company* (1929) an agent of the insurer completed a proposal form (see Chapter 26) on behalf of a prospective insured. Although the proposer gave correct information for certain questions on the form, the agent completed the form incorrectly. The proposer nevertheless signed the incorrectly completed form. The incorrect information was sufficient to enable the insurers to deny the contract and it was held that at the material time of completing the proposal form the agent was agent for the *insured*, not the insurer.

13.11 Agents of the insurers

As explained in **13.9**, the legal meaning of "agent" is wider than the normal usage of the term in insurance (see **13.4–13.5**). Agents of the insurer may be considered as follows:

(a) *Agents for a particular duty.* From time to time insurers employ firms or individuals to perform a specific task for them, usually of a specialised or technical nature. Examples are independent claims adjusters, solicitors, valuers and independent motor engineers. While acting for the insurers such individuals are their agents, but their authority is strictly limited to the instructions given.

(b) *Commission agents.* These are cash agents (see **13.5**(a)). They introduce business to the insurer, but usually have no other authority.

(c) *Agents with limited powers.* These include credit agents (see **13.5**(b) above). They have authority strictly within the terms of their appointment to grant temporary cover, to collect premiums and generally act on behalf of the insurer (their principal).

(d) *Agents with wide powers.* These, as the name suggests, are persons authorised to act on behalf of the insurer with considerable ability to enter into contracts and generally conduct business. They include the directors, executives, all levels of management and the general staff of the insurer. Of course, the degree of authority varies with each, according to their seniority. However, each may be considered under the title of *general agent*.

13.12 Authority of the agent

The general rule is that an agent is strictly limited by the terms of his appointment, which will usually outline the scope of his authority. However, it may be that an agent legally has *implied authority* to act beyond the apparent scope of the specific or *express authority* conferred upon him.

A classic legal case on this point is *Murfitt* v. *Royal Insurance Co. Ltd* (1922). In that case the agent gave temporary cover on behalf of the insurers, who refused to accept the insurance, not knowing a fire had occurred giving rise to a claim. The insurers pleaded that the agent had no authority to give cover for the class of business concerned, but it was shown that similar actions in the past by the agent for different types of insurance had been confirmed by them. It was therefore held that the agent had implied authority to issue the cover on behalf of the insurers, who thus had to meet the claim. (In legal terms the insurers were *estopped*, or prevented, from denying the claim because of their previous actions.)

13.13 Termination of an agency

An agency appointment will cease on the death of the agent or when the insurer ceases to exist. Also, the insurer has the right as principal to revoke an agent's authority at any time. Naturally any actions up to the time of revocation by the insurer remain valid. The insurer must also take reasonable steps to advise anyone who may deal with the agent thinking him still to be the insurer's representative. If these steps are not taken, the insurer may still be bound by the former agent's actions, provided the third parties have acted in good faith.

13.14 Rights and responsibilities

Insurance brokers and agents are both entitled to receive remuneration for their services. Normally this is a commission on the premiums paid by their policyholders. Brokers normally receive a higher rate of commission in the United Kingdom (see NOTE below). Also, it is not unknown for insurers to allow agents to claim limited sums for expenses.

The responsibilities of agents and brokers differ, as follows:

(a) *Agents.* They are not expected to be technical experts in insurance, but they must act in good faith and with the reasonable care that may be expected of them in complying with instructions. They are bound to inform their principal if unable to comply with instructions.

(b) *Brokers*. These may be termed "expert agents", and at law they are expected to exhibit professional skill on behalf of their clients. Any failure in this respect may make them liable for damages if their client is prejudiced.

NOTE: In some markets agents may be allowed higher commission than brokers. Where this happens it is likely to be more apparent than real. A common practice in some markets is for agents to share their commission with their clients, in varying degrees. Giving some premium back to the client is called *rebating commission*, which is generally frowned upon by insurers and in many cases is forbidden by agency contracts. Whatever the rules say, "informal arrangements" are part of human nature!

D. RECENT U.K. DEVELOPMENTS

13.15 The Insurance Brokers (Registration) Act 1977

This has already been mentioned (see **13.6**). The Act required registration for all who wished to call themselves "insurance broker". However, those intermediaries who did not wish or were otherwise unable to register could avoid regulation by using other titles (e.g. "adviser", "consultant", etc.). This was rather anomalous, but to a large extent the unsatisfactory situation was taken care of by:

(a) The Financial Services Act, 1986; and
(b) The ABI Code of Practice for Selling of General Insurance: see below.

13.16 The Financial Services Act 1986

Under this Act life assurance and other investment business can be handled by only two classes of intermediary:

(a) *Company representatives*: these are limited to one assurer, who must accept full responsibility for the intermediary's actions.
(b) *Independent intermediaries*: they must be truly independent and have access to many insurers and investment vehicle providers. They must be authorised by the Securities and Investment Board (SIB), the Personal Investment Authority (PIA) or a Recognised Professional Body (RPB).

Both types of intermediary must give their clients "best advice" (respectively, either the best product from the company they represent, or the best on the market).

13.17 The Association of British Insurers (ABI) Code of Practice

In consultation with the government a self-regulatory code was issued regarding non-broker intermediaries dealing with non-life insurances. Under the code, all such intermediaries must become either:

(a) *an independent intermediary*, accepting responsibility for all services rendered; or
(b) *a company agent*, who may act for a maximum of six insurers. Those insurers must accept responsibility for the agent's activities (on a joint basis where applicable).

13.18 Insurance consultants

Intermediaries and advisers not wishing to be categorised as above may still provide consultancy services and term themselves "insurance consultants". They like many market interests have their own representative body, the Institute of Insurance Consultants (see Chapter 14).

E. PROGRESS TEST 13

PART 1—SHORT ANSWERS (Answer in one or two sentences)

1. Is it essential to engage the help of an intermediary in arranging insurance? **(13.2)**
2. What different types of agents exist:
   (a) in normal insurance terminology; **(13.5)**
   (b) in the wider legal sense? **(13.11)**
3. Distinguish between insurance agents and insurance brokers. **(13.7)**
4. What are the rights and duties of insurance agents and brokers? **(13.14)**
5. What is meant by "rebating commission"? **(13.14)**

PART 2—MULTIPLE CHOICE (Choose the most correct option)

1. A private citizen arranging a personal insurance contract:
   (a) may do it direct with any insurer;
   (b) must always use an insurance broker;
   (c) with an insurance company may act direct or through an agent;
   (d) must always use an insurance agent. **(13.2–13.3)**
2. An "own case" agent:
   (a) is found only in insurances with Lloyd's underwriters;
   (b) receives a higher rate of commission than other agents;
   (c) is illegal in the United Kingdom;
   (d) effectively receives a discount on his premiums. **(13.5)**

3. An insurance broker:
   (a) must be duly authorised and registered;
   (b) is not an agent in the legal sense;
   (c) is only a matter of terminology, which anyone can use;
   (d) usually receives his commission from the insured. **(13.6)**
4. The Insurance Brokers (Registration) Act 1977:
   (a) totally regulated all intermediaries;
   (b) required registration for all insurance consultants;
   (c) exempted Lloyd's brokers from its regulations;
   (d) required registration of insurance brokers. **(13.15)**
5. The ABI Code of Practice for Selling General Insurance:
   (a) specifies two types of such agents;
   (b) requires all agents to be registered;
   (c) regulates agents selling all kinds of insurance;
   (d) has statutory authority. **(13.17)**

(For multiple choice answers, see page 355.)

CHAPTER 14

U.K. INSURANCE MARKET ASSOCIATIONS

14.1 Introduction

As with all professions and commercial enterprises, it has been found desirable to have various central and professional associations within the insurance industry. The variety of such organisations is wide, but all will have in common the objectives of maintaining and fostering the interests of their members or those they seek to serve.

It will not be feasible to mention all market associations, but omission of any in no way detracts from its importance to its own members.

A. THE CHARTERED INSURANCE INSTITUTE (CII)

14.2 Membership and aims

All employed or engaged in insurance work are eligible for membership. First formed in Manchester in 1893, incorporated by royal charter in 1912, and now operating through over 80 local institutes, with several affiliated institutes overseas, the CII thus serves the whole industry. Its aims are:

(a) *Educational.* This is its leading purpose, the primary object being to prepare its members for its own qualifying examinations, which are recognised and esteemed worldwide. Tuition for these is provided by postal courses from the central body, or orally, arranged through the local institutes. In addition, the central body organises many conferences on important issues affecting insurance, and there is a College of Insurance providing instruction at all levels of insurance work;

(b) *Benevolent and social.* This work is largely arranged through local institutes, although there are central *insurance charities* which "implement" much of the benevolent work among insurance members and their families.

B. THE ASSOCIATION OF BRITISH INSURERS (ABI)

14.3 Membership

The ABI is the leading insurance industry association. Formed in 1985 from an amalgamation of the previous British Insurance Association (BIA) and a number of associations dealing with specialised insurances, it represents insurance companies carrying on business in the United Kingdom.

14.4 Councils and Committees

The ABI operates through two Councils:

(a) The General Insurance Council; and
(b) The Life Insurance Council.

Each has specialised committees.

14.5 Objectives

The declared objectives of the ABI are:

(a) to protect and promote the interests of members;
(b) to take "concerted measures" in relation to the interests of members in connection with government action;
(c) to co-operate with others having similar objectives.

C. LLOYD'S

14.6 Various associations

The ABI (see above) is primarily intended to represent insurance companies only. Comparable organisations representing the interests of underwriters and others connected with Lloyd's include:

(a) Lloyd's Aviation Underwriters' Association;
(b) Lloyd's Motor Underwriters' Association;
(c) Lloyd's Underwriters' Association (marine insurance);
(d) Lloyd's Non-Marine Underwriters' Association;
(e) Lloyd's Insurance Brokers Committee (LIBC);
(f) Association of Lloyd's Members (ALM);
(g) Lloyd's Underwriting Agents' Association.

D. BRITISH INSURERS' INTERNATIONAL COMMITTEE (BIIC)

14.7 Membership and activities

All British insurers, including Lloyd's and P & I Clubs, may become members and the great majority are. The BIIC acts as a liaison body with many European and wider international organisations, including the E.U., the OECD, UNCTAD and the WTO.

E. OTHER INSURER ORGANISATIONS

14.8 London Insurance Market Strategy Committee

Including representatives from various market associations (ABI, ILU, LIRMA, Lloyd's and LIBC—see above and below), this committee actively seeks to promote the interests of the London insurance market, which is still probably the world's leading insurance centre. Specifically, the committee's concerns include information technology, taxation and competitiveness.

14.9 London Insurance and Reinsurance Market Association (LIRMA)

Full members consist of those authorised to do business in the United Kingdom. Others are termed Associate Members. Replacing the former *Reinsurance Offices Association* (*ROA*) and the *Policy Signing and Accounting Centre* (*PSAC*), LIRMA now works in close liaison with the ILU (see below), particularly through the *London Processing Centre* (*LPC*). The LPC forms a centralised policy preparation, accounts and claims processing centre for both ILU and LIRMA, whose accounting bureaux have merged.

As its name suggests LIRMA represents reinsurers and London market direct insurance companies. It is greatly involved in reinsurance treaty wordings, research and statistics. It also played a leading role in the formation of the *London Insurance Market Network* (*LIMNET*) (see **15.18**).

14.10 Institute of London Underwriters (ILU)

Primarily concerned with marine, aviation and transport business, the ILU is famous for the formation and review of *institute clauses* (see **3.13**). It is not restricted to United Kingdom members and its interests are worldwide.

Another important role of the ILU is that of Secretary to the Joint Committees of Lloyd's and Non-Lloyd's marine insurers, with others involved in marine and related business. A newer development is the close association with LIRMA and the LPC (see above).

14.11 Mutual Insurance Companies Association

This represents a small number of mutual insurers transacting non-life business, mainly employers' liability. Membership, however, does not include P & I Clubs.

14.12 Aviation Insurance Offices' Association

This represents non-Lloyd's aviation insurers and included within its scope is consultation on standardised policy wordings where appropriate.

F. LIFE AND RELATED ASSURANCE ORGANISATIONS

14.13 Association of Scottish Life Offices (ASLO)

Based in Edinburgh, its name clearly indicates its primary areas of interest and activity.

14.14 The Life Insurance Marketing and Research Association Ltd. (LIMRA)

The aims and objectives of LIMRA speak for themselves, with great concentration on research and service in the field of life assurance.

14.15 The Life Insurance Association (LIA)

With over 10,000 members (about half of whom are in sales and the rest intermediaries) the LIA is much involved with life assurance education and conferences for financial advisers.

14.16 The Institute of Pension Consultants

Once more the name indicates the activities and concerns of this organisation.

G. OTHER INTERMEDIARY ORGANISATIONS

14.17 The British Insurance and Investment Brokers Association (BIIBA)

This fulfils a similar role for insurance brokers as does the ABI (see **14.3**) for insurance companies. BIIBA is a national body, with representation throughout the United Kingdom. As the name suggests, it represents registered brokers and authorised independent financial advisers.

Mainly, BIIBA operates through a number of specialist interest committees and is much involved in education and training work among insurance brokers.

14.18 The Institute of Insurance Consultants

Originally formed to represent the interests of those intermediaries who for different reasons did not register as insurance brokers, this institute mainly serves small organisations. Some of its members, however, are now registered insurance brokers.

14.19 Other intermediary and consultant organisations

In alphabetical order, these include:

(a) The Corporation of Insurance and Financial Advisers;
(b) The Independent Financial Advisers Association;
(c) The Institute of Insurance Brokers.

14.20 The United Kingdom Insurance Brokers International Committee

This fulfils a similar role for insurance brokers as does the BIIC (see **14.7**) for insurers.

H. RISK MANAGEMENT

14.21 The Institute of Risk Management (IRM)

Risk management is a growing discipline (see **1.14**) and the IRM is much involved with promoting qualifications and education in this field.

14.22 The Association of Insurance and Risk Managers in Industry and Commerce (AIRMIC)

The self-explanatory title indicates its sphere of interest. Originally consisting of individual members only, it now also has corporate membership.

I. CLAIMS AND SURVEYING ORGANISATIONS

14.23 The Association of Average Adjusters

These are concerned with marine *average* claims, especially *general average apportionments* (see **31.3**).

14.24 U.K. Insurance Market Associations

14.24 Chartered Institute of Loss Adjusters

These are independent professional claims assessors, engaged in virtually all classes of insurance, but particularly in fire and accident.

14.25 Insurance surveying organisations

The following organisations should be noted:

(a) The Institute of Automobile Assessors;
(b) The Association of Burglary Insurance Surveyors;
(c) The Association of Fire Insurance Surveyors.

J. EDUCATIONAL AND CHARITABLE

14.26 The Worshipful Company of Insurers

A London livery company, this honoured body operates through two trusts. One trust is dedicated to education in the world-wide insurance industry. The other gives donations to London City and national charitable appeals.

NOTE: In view of the straightforward factual nature of information in this chapter, we shall not have a Progress Test 14.

CHAPTER 15

THE LATE TWENTIETH CENTURY

A. MISCELLANEOUS OBSERVATIONS

15.1 Introduction

The author can look back over more than 40 years' experience in the insurance industry, during which time great changes have taken place. But the truth is that changes are *always* taking place, so this should be no big surprise. It may be helpful, however, to note recent developments and market features, perhaps with appropriate comment, as possible pointers towards the future picture of insurance.

As with earlier notes (see Chapter 10) the following are not in order of importance or chronology. They are, however, factors to be taken into account in understanding the dynamic and complex world of insurance.

B. PRODUCT AND OTHER INNOVATIONS

15.2 General observations

In a competitive business world, there will always be striving to produce new products. Often this is more a case of redesigning and re-presenting existing or former ideas, although there will be occasions where technology presents a completely new challenge that will test the ingenuity (e.g. aviation and nuclear risks: perhaps also the completely new world of computers).

The following represent some of the thoughts and ideas exercising the minds of forward-looking insurers as the new millennium approaches.

15.3 Risk management (see 1.14)

The sophistication of this process is seen in a number of ways which we have mentioned before, e.g.:

(a) creation of risk managers (see **1.13**);
(b) financial insurances (see **10.3**);

(c) captive insurance companies (see **11.13**).

Some insurers in the past have been guilty of treating risk management as if it consisted solely of risk reduction or avoidance, in the form of improved safety and physical loss containment measures. This is an important element in risk management, but the science is much wider. As stated earlier (see **1.16**), far from risk management being a part of insurance, the opposite is the truth.

15.4 Risk retention and self-insurance

Closely linked with the above, commercial organisations are increasingly questioning to what extent they need conventional insurers. Large companies have realised their own financial capabilities and especially in the USA the practice of retaining risks rather than transferring them, in whole or in part, has greatly increased. It seems certain that conventional insurance will continue, but for commercial risks the larger units may well insist upon some of the benefits of partnership rather than remain mere policyholders.

15.5 Pollution/environmental impairment insurance

Undoubtedly an extremely "hot" and sensitive political issue today, pollution represents a major threat to liability insurers both in the future and in respect of liabilities already incurred. The figures involved in such types of loss are so enormous that earlier underwriters would have had no hesitation in declaring these fundamental risks (see **1.8**) which should be entirely the responsibility of governments. To some extent this still pertains, but governments are becoming less ready to assume responsibilities which they can pass to the private sector.

It seems therefore that a commercial insurance solution is needed. It has been suggested that perhaps some risk-financing mechanisms can be set up, probably having safeguards for the insurer such as:

(a) *claims-made* cover: this implies that the cover ceases on the expiry date of the policy, not only for future claims but also for those not yet reported. The more traditional cover for liability risks is on a *claims occurring* basis. This means that incidents arising during the period of insurance are covered even if the claim is made after the expiry date of the policy;
(b) *aggregate cover*: this means that there will be a limit of cover for the whole period of insurance, rather than for each claim that arises;
(c) *pooling arrangements*: not new to insurance (see **9.3**), pools are a well tried answer to unknown or excessive risk. It could be that European or totally international pools will need to be developed.

This is for the worldwide industry to resolve, but the problem is great and it is urgent.

15.6 Directors' and Officers' insurance

This is a fairly new form of professional indemnity insurance (see **6.18**). The latter traditionally covered the organisation against public liability claims. Individual directors and other officers were not usually claimed against in their personal capacity, but this has changed and in many jurisdictions it is not possible for the individual to hide behind what is sometimes called the "corporate veil" (separate legal existence of the company).

Such insurance has become much in demand and seems likely to increase in the future. The cover granted is likely to exclude bodily injury and property damage claims, dishonesty and fraud. The primary intention of the cover is to deal with claims arising from breach of duty, neglect, etc. of the individual(s) concerned.

15.7 Direct insurance (see 13.2)

The major thrust of insurance marketing in the past may have been directed more towards commercial insurances. The aggregate importance of personal insurances, particularly motor and household policies, is now appreciated. Following a lead from "Direct Line" (a subsidiary of the Royal Bank of Scotland) in 1984, the growth of *direct insurance* has been considerable, with several insurers following the idea. This eliminates the intermediary and cover is arranged by telephone. It has proved extremely successful. By the end of 1995 it was estimated that over half of the private motor insurance market in the United Kingdom was through the direct system. It has now been introduced to life assurance. Offering cheaper premiums, direct insurance seems certain to grow further.

C. OTHER MARKET FEATURES IN THE UNITED KINGDOM

15.8 General observations

Economic, weather and other features have combined to produce some significant developments in the United Kingdom insurance market in the past ten years or so. Again with no attempt to establish their relative importance, the following should be noted.

15.9 Life assurance

The economic depression of recent years, coupled with much lower interest rates, has had a significant impact on the practice of life assurance. For example with profits endowment assurances (see **4.19**), which owed much of their attraction to significant bonus earnings, have become very much less popular.

Also, there has developed a significant market in "second-hand" life policies, known as "TEPS" (Traded Endowment Policy Sales). This means that the policy is sold to a person totally unconnected with the life assured, because the latter wishes to terminate the insurance and the surrender values (see **4.34**) being offered by insurers are disappointingly low. "Selling" life policies is perfectly legal and the financial sections of United Kingdom papers invariably carry two or three advertisements for companies offering to purchase them. A "TEP" is now a recognised investment option.

15.10 Mortgage guarantee insurances

During the property market boom of the 1980s very significant amounts of business were generated with building societies, covering the risk of default of borrowers and potential loss to the building society should the property have to be sold at a loss. With property prices seemingly on an unending spiral upwards the business was eagerly sought by many insurers. The subsequent collapse of property prices, coincident with economic recession and times of redundancy and high unemployment, produced disastrous losses. The situation in the mid-1990s is not yet resolved.

15.11 Climatic influences

A popular view is that global warming is having a dramatic effect on weather patterns for the United Kingdom. What is certainly true is that there have been some dramatic weather-related series of claims seriously affecting the United Kingdom market in recent times. These include:

(a) *hurricanes*: it was thought that the United Kingdom was likely to see hurricane force winds only once in 100 years, but at least three such phenomena were experienced in almost as many years in the late 1980s/early 1990s. The impact on household and other property insurance classes was very serious;

(b) *subsidence and heave*: the former relates to the collapse of ground level, whilst the latter (hardly in anyone's normal vocabulary before) means the upsurge of the ground level. Both can cause serious damage to buildings and each was experienced after water levels shrank during successive abnormally hot summers, followed by heavy rains later. Again, the household and fire insurance accounts were hit very hard;

(c) *earthquake*: another risk thought alien to the United Kingdom had to be reconsidered, with a number of tremors being experienced. None was of disaster proportions, but fire underwriters seriously reconsidered their cover (earthquake was often included in fire policies without extra premium). As with the hurricane risk, the United Kingdom is now likely to be classified in various zones for rating purposes.

D. GENERAL MARKET FEATURES

15.12 The insurance "cycle"

Traditional insurance wisdom maintained that insurance profitability could be charted on graphs showing a cyclical variation. The variations would be between *soft market* and *hard market* conditions. Respectively, these terms imply:

(a) *soft market conditions*: these are times when the supply of insurance cover is high in relation to demand. Consequently times are easy, or "soft" for the insured, who can easily obtain cover and favourable terms. Such conditions would lead to reduced profits or losses being made, thus tending to reduce the availability of insurance (or *capacity*), leading to:

(b) *hard market conditions*: when the opposite situation prevails, leading to difficulty in obtaining cover, with correspondingly high premiums and stricter terms.

The standard philosophy reasoned that the "cycle" was likely to take four to five years. It is now quite obvious that modern communications and attitudes, with much less central market influence (e.g. the collapse of tariffs: see **11.21**), have resulted in the cycle being much more volatile and much less predictable. Clearly the underlying logic of supply and demand does not change, but the modern scene lends itself to much more rapid developments. (It is often said, for instance, that the expected exclusive lifespan of a new product is now only about three months! By then competitors will have adopted and/or adapted it.)

15.13 Reduced capacity

In some areas it is clear that insurance capacity (in the sense of the availability of cover) has been reduced. This is an obvious if, it is hoped, a temporary phenomenon with Lloyd's of London, which has seen a dramatic reduction in the number of Names (see **12.4**) over the past decade. Other areas where there has been a similar experience include:

(a) *terrorism in the United Kingdom*: compensation for damage caused by IRA activities in Northern Ireland during "the troubles" is provided by the British Government, but fire and similar policies gave this cover on the mainland. Following the terrorist explosions in London in 1992, international reinsurers and consequently direct insurers said they were no longer able to provide unlimited cover for such claims. This created something of a crisis, only solved by the British Government acting as "reinsurer of the last resort" and the creation of a new company, *Pool Reinsurance Company Limited* (*"Pool Re"*) in March 1993.

15.13 The Late Twentieth Century

NOTE: These developments provide an interesting example of the use of "pools" for high-risk situations (compare **9.3**, for example). They also reflect a *particular risk* becoming something of a *fundamental risk* (see **1.8–1.9**).

(b) *reinsurance cover*: there had been a great growth in the number of reinsurers in recent decades, but this process was reversed in the late 1980s. The resulting shrinking of reinsurance capacity was not serious, as there had been very "soft" market conditions. However, a particular feature that occurred in some countries following the United Kingdom system of unlimited compulsory insurance requirements (see **7.12**) was that reinsurers said they were no longer prepared to back unlimited liability. In at least one jurisdiction this led to a change of compulsory insurance law, introducing a minimum limit in place of the unlimited requirement.

15.14 Government "interference"

It is a little impertinent to use that word, when governments are perfectly entitled to introduce laws and controls which they deem in the best interests of their society. What is intended, however, is to point out an increasing trend of governments across the world to become ever more closely involved with the operation of insurance. This topic will be considered later (see Chapter 33), but two random examples will illustrate the point:

(a) the Australian government introduced far-reaching laws changing many of the long-standing principles and practices of insurance (e.g. insurable interest requirements and policy cancellation conditions);
(b) the Insurance Commissioner of the State of Oklahoma was reported as saying he would not allow insurers to deny any claims related to the Oklahoma City bomb outrage in 1995 even if their policies contained specific exclusions relating to such forms of loss.

The United Kingdom Government has traditionally preferred a more persuasive approach, but consumer interest and consumer power is now strong. It is therefore vital for the insurance industry to have adequate self-regulation if litigation and government decree contrary to their wishes is to be avoided.

15.15 Demutualisation?

Great concern was caused by the collapse of two non-life mutual insurers, the *National Employers Mutual* and the *Municipal Mutual*, by the start of the 1990s. Although some new mutual indemnity associations have been formed (e.g. dealing with professional and other specialised liability risks, some would say that the somewhat "cosy world" of mutual insurance is under threat. Note has been made of many former mutual insurers becoming proprietary (see **11.4**).

In 1995, one of the top ten insurance groups in the United Kingdom announced possible plans to change its mutual status. This will give greater flexibility in raising capital for instance, but the cut and thrust sometimes associated with the existence of shareholders could indicate more important market changes.

15.16 The welfare state?

Following the election of a socialist government in 1945 the nation largely became accustomed to look to the State for medical care, education and old age care. This in turn led to a reduced demand for certain private insurances. For example, the introduction of *national insurance* abolished workmen's compensation insurance (see **6.15**). Also, the National Health Service, which commenced in 1948, much reduced the need for private medical insurance.

In more recent years, especially during long years of conservative rule, the trend has been towards the encouragement of more private insurance, as:

(a) long delays in obtaining non-essential hospital treatment under the NHS could be avoided by *private medical insurance* schemes (often arranged on a group basis through employers) such as BUPA;
(b) educational grants have been cut. With a marked preference for private schools on the part of parents, and the great majority of young people going on to further or higher education, the market for *school fees insurance* or similar intended life assurance savings plans has developed considerably;
(c) full-time care for the aged in nursing homes and the like has become very expensive. Such fees are not payable by the State unless the person concerned has relatively modest means (as from 1996 this is only £16,000, well under one year's costs for many nursing homes). As a result new types of insurance have been developed to provide for this expense. The premium is usually a single payment and is not cheap. With an ageing population, however, the State has encouraged such insurances, not least by making all benefits and income from such schemes tax-free.

15.17 Bancassurance

When the forerunner to this book was first published, some 25 years ago, it was being prophesied widely that by the end of the century there might only be "financial supermarkets", replacing conventional bank and insurance company structures.

While this has not yet occurred, the involvement of banks, building societies and similar institutions in insurance has grown considerably (see, for example, **15.7**). This is especially so in mainland Europe, where the term *bancassurance* was invented.

15.18 Information Technology (IT)

What might be described as the first phase of IT, when it was a very specialist area, and all practitioners were programmers and very knowledgeable about the "mechanics" of the new science, has long passed. The modern scene has jokingly been referred to as "PCs (personal computers) and all that", with management and staff so familiar with the new technology that any future insurance officer who is not computer-literate is likely to be a "professional cripple".

There is nothing exclusive to insurance in this, of course. All sections of the community, but perhaps particularly the "white-collar" areas, have been affected by the electronic revolution. In insurance, as in other financial areas, the revolution has not taken place without resistance.

The new technology has not been embraced by all with equal enthusiasm, challenging as it does the systems and practices of the ages. Moreover, the fiercely competing, and usually non-compatible, different systems have added to the problems. The transition has been neither easy nor complete to date.

Direct Insurance (see **15.7**) is one obvious application of the new technology and electronic trading is now an established, if not totally comfortable, fact today. The potential applications, ranging from near immediate document preparation to complex underwriting, seem endless and there can be no doubt that the change is here to stay. It is not possible in these few brief comments to present a comprehensive picture of a huge subject, but some other applications or organisations set up directly or indirectly as a consequence of IT's influence can be noted, as follows:

(a) networks and systems especially found on the London market:
   (i) LIMNET (London Insurance Market Network);
   (ii) RINET (Reinsurance and Insurance Network);
   (iii) EPS (Electronic Placing Support);
   (iv) LUCID (London Underwriting Centre Information Database)

(b) *Commercial Lines Market Initiative* (*CLMI*) is an organisation formed by insurers and brokers.

(c) *Polaris United Kingdom* is an organisation set up originally by a consortium of seven leading United Kingdom insurers to "ensure viability and prosperity of the personal lines insurance intermediary channel". Co-operation between CLMI and Polaris should be enhanced, as at the time of writing they are to share the same building in the City of London.

(d) *World Insurance Network* (*WIN*) is an organisation formed in late 1995 (to operate in 1996) by six leading international insurance brokers. Insurers will be allowed to join as Associates.

It is tempting, looking at the last two organisations, to make the pun that IT seems to have the worldwide insurance market at "sixes and sevens". That may be unkind and inaccurate. However, much has yet to be agreed and doubtless many "battles" are yet to be fought, but the way has to be forward.

15.19 The economy and the insurance profession

The insurance profession, like banking, was traditionally thought of as a safe, if dull, line of work where new entrants could rest secure, knowing that they would have employment until they retired. Times have changed. Of course, this is not only for insurance and banking. In the United Kingdom at the present time it is said that no job is safe. Certainly, there has been massive "restructuring", "re-engineering", "rationalisation" (or whatever euphemism is used) to reduce the number of employees, as an economy measure.

One obvious consequence of this is the voluntary or compulsory early retirement of very large numbers of older staff, usually in middle management positions. One leading insurance group in the United Kingdom is said to have only four or five employees aged over 55 in a staff of many thousands. It is too soon to say how this may affect things, but unease has been expressed about this great loss of experience. One view (not exclusive to insurance) is that standards and flexibility are bound to suffer. Certainly, great disappointment and stress are being experienced, with much uncertainty and apprehensions among many of the staff who have been retained.

It is ironic that one of the classic functions of insurance is to remove fear and establish confidence (see **1.21**), when at least in the short term many of the staff within the industry itself are experiencing the opposite emotions. It must again be said that this is not unique to insurance, but clearly the insurance industry's need to react to change in society generally now also applies within itself. As one chief executive said "if management (and staff) cannot adjust to change, we must change the management!"

It is sincerely to be hoped that the present traumas are temporary, but in this transitional stage of reshaping of corporate structures there will be many who would have empathy with the alleged old Chinese curse, "May you live in interesting times!"

E. PROGRESS TEST 15

PART 1—SHORT ANSWERS (Answer in one or two sentences)

1. What is meant by "claims-made" cover? **(15.5)**
2. Why has D & O cover become more popular? **(15.6)**
3. What is generally understood by mortgage guarantee insurance? **(15.10)**
4. What is understood by "subsidence and heave" claims ? **(15.11)**
5. Differentiate between "hard" and "soft" market conditions. **(15.12)**

PART 2—MULTIPLE CHOICE (Choose the most correct option)

1. The practice of risk management:
   - (a) has no implications for insurers;
   - (b) has very profound implications for insurers;
   - (c) will always mean the client effects more insurance;
   - (d) is part of insurance. **(15.3–15.4)**
2. Pollution and environmental pollution insurance in the future:
   - (a) will have to be totally provided by governments;
   - (b) will not present any serious problems;
   - (c) is likely to have certain safeguards for the insurer;
   - (d) will probably be eagerly desired by all insurers. **(15.5)**
3. Mortgage guarantee insurance:
   - (a) produced great losses for insurers in the recent past;
   - (b) produced great profits for insurers in the recent past;
   - (c) is issued to borrowers in order to pay off mortgage loans;
   - (d) pays the mortgage loan if the mortgagor dies. **(15.10)**
4. The insurance "cycle":
   - (a) refers to alternating "hard" and "soft" markets;
   - (b) relates to the popularity of certain types of insurance;
   - (c) is talking about fluctuations in premium volumes;
   - (d) refers to the loss and gain of particular accounts. **(15.12)**
5. "Bancassurance":
   - (a) relates to the increasing involvement of banks in insurance;
   - (b) relates to specialised insurances arranged for banks;
   - (c) is a mainland Europe term which has no relevance to the United Kingdom;
   - (d) is another term for financial guarantees. **(15.17)**

(*For multiple choice answers, see page 355.*)

PART THREE: OBJECTIVE TESTS (see Answers, page 356) and ASSIGNMENTS

3.1 State whether the following statements are *true* or *false*:

(a) All British insurers are subject to the regulations of the various Companies Acts.

(b) A captive insurance company is so called because the first such companies were not free to transact business with the general public.

(c) A Lloyd's broker can only transact business with Lloyd's.

(d) Tariff insurers must all charge the same premium for a given risk.

(e) A person wishing to be known as an insurance broker in the United Kingdom must now register as such.

(f) Mutual insurance companies are not found in life assurance.

(g) The only people allowed in "the Room" at Lloyd's are Lloyd's underwriters and their staff.

(h) The Lutine Bell is rung once for good news and twice for bad.

(i) One great advantage of self-insurance is that one does not have to pay increased premiums because of the claims experience of others.

(j) With a greater accumulation of experience, it has become progressively easier to predict the movements in the insurance "cycle".

3.2 Select the *most correct* answer to the following questions:

(a) A mutual insurance company (i) is only permitted to transact one class of business; (ii) has no shareholders; (iii) is intended to be a non-profit-making enterprise.

(b) Insurance agents acting with express authority (i) are normally insurance brokers; (ii) are acting in accordance with specific instructions; (iii) legally bind their principals.

(c) A self-insurance fund is a bad thing for a commercial firm to undertake because (i) insurance companies will retaliate by charging for such risks as have to be insured by them; (ii) the money in the fund can only be invested at low rates of interest; (iii) a major loss could threaten both the fund and the firm.

(d) An "own case" agent (i) introduces only his own business to the insurers; (ii) receives higher commission on his own business than on that of others he introduces; (iii) has wide powers, enabling him to deal with his own claims.

(e) Membership of the Association of British Insurers (ABI) is open to (i) all persons or firms engaged in insurance; (ii) any individual or organisation which wishes to join and is accepted by the Committee; (iii) insurance companies carrying on business in the United Kingdom.

(f) The British Insurance and Investment Brokers' Association (BIIBA) (i) represents all insurance intermediaries in the United Kingdom; (ii) is the professional body that authorises the registration of insurance brokers; (iii) fulfils a role for insurance brokers similar to that of the ABI for insurance companies.

(g) Lloyd's underwriters now operate in syndicates (i) but retain unlimited personal responsibility for their percentage of losses; (ii) in order to gain the benefit of limited liability; (iii) so that there can be more space in "the Room".

(h) A Lloyd's agent (i) reports frequently to Lloyd's on such matters as shipping intelligence; (ii) is paid commission on business introduced to underwriters; (iii) is an employee of the Corporation of Lloyd's sent abroad to report back on local happenings.

(i) Under the Financial Services Act 1986 life insurance intermediaries (i) must all be accredited to Lloyd's; (ii) have to belong to a recognised body of intermediaries; (iii) must be company representatives or independent intermediaries.

(j) Direct insurance in the United Kingdom (i) is mostly arranged by telephone; (ii) is only conducted via reputable Lloyd's underwriters; (iii) is largely concerned with commercial insurances.

3.3 Assignments.

(a) Write an essay on the general structure of the British insurance market, with your opinion on likely changes in the next decade.

(b) Discuss the relative merits of continuing or abolishing (i) "own case" agents, and (ii) commission for brokers being paid by insurers (this would envisage clients paying a separate fee, as with virtually all other professional consultants).

(c) Arrange visits to Lloyd's and/or a major insurance company head office and report back on the administrative structure with suggested possible improvements.

PART FOUR

BASIC PRINCIPLES

CHAPTER 16

THE INSURANCE CONTRACT

A. GENERAL OBSERVATIONS

16.1 Meaning of "contract"

A contract is a legally binding agreement between two or more parties. Provided an agreement complies with certain basic essentials (see **16.5–16.11** below), a failure on the part of one party to fulfil his obligations enables the other party to seek enforcement through the courts and/or might give rise to an action for damages. This is true of all contracts, including those of insurance.

16.2 The policy is not the contract

From the definition given above, it follows that the policy is not the contract in insurance. The contract is the *invisible agreement* between the contracting parties. The policy is merely *evidence of the contract.* A simple example will illustrate the difference.

EXAMPLE: Suppose a life assurance contract were negotiated with a sum assured of £10,000, but owing to an undetected typist's error the policy document was issued showing a sum assured of £100,000. The contract would be for £10,000 only, as this represented the intention or agreement between the parties. In the event of the policyholder's death (assuming that the intention of the parties could be proved by reference to a proposal form or by other means), the legal personal representative would not be able to obtain a court judgment for £100,000.

16.3 Simple and speciality contracts

As far as insurance is concerned, there are two basic types of contract:

(a) *Simple (or parol) contracts.* These constitute the great majority of insurance contracts. They do not have to be expressed in writing and they are issued *under hand,* not *under seal.* They are considered in more detail in **16.5–16.11**.

(b) *Speciality contracts* (or *deeds*). These are very formal agreements, that must be *signed, sealed and delivered.* Although not common in insurance, they are found in fidelity guarantee insurance, with various types of bonds (see **6.7**).

16.4 Writing is not legally necessary for most insurance contracts

As most insurance contracts are simple contracts, there is no necessity for them to be evidenced in writing. However, great practical difficulties arise in ascertaining the precise terms of the contract without a written instrument. Accordingly, it is rare for an insurance contract not to be evidenced in writing. Moreover, there are certain instances, where statutory requirements demand writing (this of course includes printing); for example:

(a) *Statute of Frauds 1677* (as amended by a 1954 Act). Contracts of guarantee (which include fidelity guarantees), among others, are required to have written evidence by this statute.
(b) *Marine Insurance Act 1906* (see **3.10**). Section 22 of this Act requires marine insurance contracts to be in writing.

B. SIMPLE CONTRACTS

16.5 Essentials of a simple contract

There are six essentials to every simple contract, as follows (see Fig. 10):

(a) intention to create legal obligations;
(b) unrevoked offer;
(c) unqualified acceptance;
(d) consideration;
(e) legality;
(f) capacity of the parties to contract: see below.

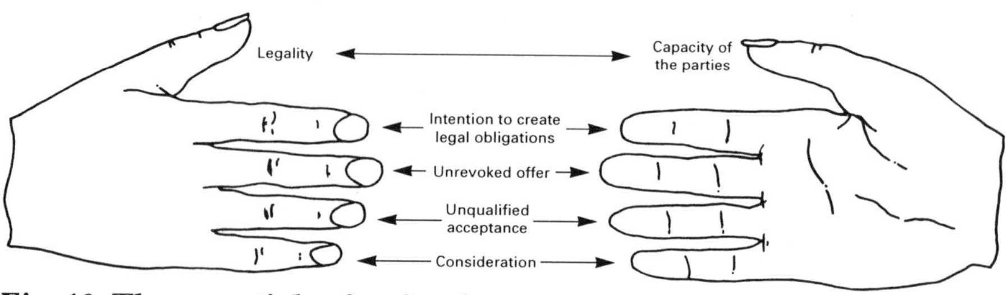

Fig. 10 The essentials of a simple contract

NOTE: A "simple" contract does not imply that it is easy to understand. Some policy wordings are very complex. Rather, it implies that it is easily arranged, without many legal formalities (hence Fig.10 indicates a mere handshake).

16.6 Intention to create legal obligations

With many informal and social agreements (such as an arrangement to give a friend in lift in one's car) there is never any intention of legal consequences should the agreement for some reason not be carried out. Such intention must be present in any legal contract. This point seldom gives rise to any difficulty in insurance, where it is usually quite evident that the parties intend the agreement to be legally binding.

16.7 Unrevoked offer

Such an offer may be in writing or made verbally. In insurance, both methods are found. When the offer is in writing, it is usually in a duly completed proposal form (see Chapter 26), completed by the prospective insured. With insurances at Lloyd's, it is contained in the written details on the "slip" shown to underwriters (see **12.9**). A verbal offer may be made on behalf of clients by brokers, or by the applicant himself in *direct insurance* (see **15.7**), over the telephone, but frequently such offers are followed up by obtaining a completed proposal form, if only to confirm the verbal understanding.

NOTE: The issuing of a blank proposal form (also known as an *application*) by an insurer does not in itself constitute the offer in an insurance contract, even if premium rates are quoted on the form. It is rather similar to the legal position of an article marked with a price ticket in a shop window, where the ticket merely indicates the likely acceptance figure if a customer offers to buy the article. The blank proposal form is similarly only an invitation to a prospective insured to offer an insurance, which the insurer may accept or reject (in law called an "invitation to treat").

16.8 Unqualified acceptance

An offer must be accepted in precisely the terms submitted for a binding contract to be formed. Giving a qualified acceptance indicates a refusal of the offer and the making of a counter-offer, which will technically relate to a different contract. Acceptance may also be verbal or in writing, not necessarily in the same form as the offer.

Once the above essentials have been satisfied, the parties are said to be in *consensus ad idem* (of one mind), which is a fundamental requirement of any agreement that is to be legally enforceable.

16.9 Consideration

Guarantees do not necessarily require consideration from both parties, but this is a vital ingredient of all simple contracts. In insurance, both parties provide consideration, as follows:

(a) *Consideration from the insured to the insurer.* This is the premium.

(b) *Consideration from the insurer to the insured.* This is the promise to compensate the insured or to make certain payments in the event of specified happenings taking place. This promise is applicable whether a claim arises during the period of insurance or not. Thus, an insured cannot ask for his money back on the grounds of lack of consideration by the insurer in a claim-free year.

NOTE: It may not be necessary for the insured actually to have paid the premium for the contract to be binding. Sometimes this is a prerequisite, but many policies are issued (giving evidence of the contract) on the basis that the insured "has paid or has agreed to pay" the premium.

16.10 Legality

Any contract which is contrary to the laws of this country (such as a marine cargo insurance on goods being traded with an enemy national in time of war) is *void* (see **16.13**). A contract with an overseas person, infringing the laws of the foreign country but not those of this country, may well also be considered invalid, on the grounds of being contrary to public policy (see **2.10**).

16.11 Capacity of the parties to contract

Most persons have full contractual capacity, but certain individuals such as minors (formerly *infants* at law) and persons of unsound mind have limited powers. A full consideration of these limitations is outside the scope of this book. It is sufficient to say that a binding contract can only be made when both parties have the legal capacity to make such an agreement.

NOTE: "Capacity" in the context of contract law will have a different meaning from that considered earlier, where it implied the availability of insurance cover (see **15.13** for example).

C. SPECIALITY CONTRACTS

16.12 "Signed, sealed and delivered"

The most important features about speciality contracts in insurance are that they must be:

(a) in *writing*;
(b) issued *under seal*.

Although consideration from both parties is not an essential element with guarantees, insurers will always require a premium (sometimes called a *fee*) with this type of contract. This may be a single payment, even though the contract lasts for many years.

D. CONTRACTS WHICH ARE DEFECTIVE

16.13 Void contracts

A void contract is one which legally does not exist. It is therefore somewhat of a contradiction in terms. Nevertheless, the expression is used to describe an apparent agreement, but one which is completely destitute of legal effect. Such a "contract" arises where some essential feature is missing (see, for example, **16.5–16.11**).

16.14 Voidable contracts

This, quite literally, means a contract that is "able to be voided (made void)". Thus, where either party is in breach of a vital contractual term the other party has a right to consider the contract void. On the other hand, the aggrieved party may decide to overlook the breach (or to *waive* the breach, as it is called), in which event the contract is unaffected and remains in full force.

It may be said that "voidable" is a temporary situation. The aggrieved party must make a decision whether to void the contract or waive the breach within a reasonable time (to be determined by the court if necessary). If he does not, he will be deemed in law to have waived the breach.

16.15 Unenforceable contracts

An unenforceable contract is one which is neither void nor voidable, but which cannot be enforced through the courts. This will arise when a contract is lacking some required formality: for example, if a marine insurance contract is not evidenced by the issue of a policy, as required by the Marine Insurance Act 1906 (see: **3.10**); also, if stamp duty has not been paid on a document requiring such duty (see below). Thus, it may be said that unenforceable contracts are quite valid but the contracting parties are deprived of the ultimate remedy of enforcement through the courts. (Usually, however, the defect is easily remedied, by issuing a policy or paying the required duty.)

E. STAMP DUTY

16.16 Legal provisions

Introduced under the Stamp Act 1891, stamp duty is now payable only on life policies and certain fidelity bonds. Special rates are applicable to the latter, but life contracts are subject to duty on a sliding scale.

F. SUBJECT MATTER OF THE INSURANCE, AND OF THE CONTRACT

16.17 Differentiation

It is necessary to distinguish between the *subject matter of the insurance* and the *subject matter of the contract*. These will be considered below.

16.18 Subject matter of the insurance

This, in simple terms, is the thing or possible liability insured (i.e. in which the insured has an *insurable interest*: see Chapter 17). Some examples are:

(a) *marine insurance*: the actual vessel or cargo;
(b) *life assurance*: the life assured;
(c) *fire insurance*: the building insured;
(d) *motor insurance*: the actual vehicle, or liability arising from its use.

16.19 Subject matter of the contract

An insurance contract cannot guarantee the restoration of goods or the cancelling of liability. It can, however, guarantee that the insured will be protected from financial loss within the terms of the insurance. Thus, the subject matter of the *contract* is the policyholder's *interest* or financial involvement in the subject matter of the insurance.

NOTE: The distinction was drawn in the leading case of *Castellain* v. *Preston* (1883), in which it was said: "What is it that is insured in a fire policy? Not the bricks and materials used in building the house, but the interest of the insured in the subject matter of the insurance."

G. PROGRESS TEST 16

PART 1—SHORT ANSWERS (Answer in one or two sentences)

1. Explain how the policy is not the contract of insurance. **(16.2)**
2. What types of contract are found in insurance? **(16.3)**
3. What are the essentials of a simple contract? **(16.5–16.11)**
4. Distinguish between *void*, *voidable* and *unenforceable contracts*. **(16.13–16.15)**
5. Differentiate between the *subject matter of the insurance* and the *subject matter of the contract*. **(16.17–16.19)**

PART 2—MULTIPLE CHOICE (Choose the most correct option)

1. If the sum insured shown in the policy can be proved to be wrong:
   (a) the insurer is nevertheless bound by the printed figure;
   (b) the matter must be referred to arbitration;
   (c) the courts will order a compromised settlement of any claim;
   (d) the insurer is liable for the correct figure only. **(16.2)**
2. An implication of a "specialty contract" in insurance is that it:
   (a) applies only to highly specialised classes of business;
   (b) does not necessarily have to be in writing;
   (c) must be issued under seal;
   (d) is legally unenforceable. **(16.3)**
3. The implication of a "simple contract" in insurance is that it:
   (a) may be arranged easily with minimum legal formality;
   (b) has a policy written in simple language;
   (c) applies only to uncomplicated risks;
   (d) only deals with small sums insured. **(16.5)**
4. The premium payable by the insured in an insurance contract:
   (a) constitutes his consideration;
   (b) must always be paid before cover is operative;
   (c) is refunded if no claim arises during the policy year;
   (d) is no longer payable if a claim arises before payment. **(16.9)**
5. If a contract is said to be "unenforceable", this means that:
   (a) the premium has not been paid;
   (b) the insured does not have the money to take a dispute to court;
   (c) it is probably lacking in some legal formality;
   (d) it is illegal. **(16.15)**

(*For multiple choice answers, see page 355.*)

CHAPTER 17

INSURABLE INTEREST

A. GENERAL OBSERVATIONS

17.1 Meaning generally

When we say that someone has an "interest" in several companies, we usually imply that they have more than a mere mental attraction towards them. We mean that they have a financial involvement with them. This is also the sense in which the term is used in *insurable interest*. Thus, insurable interest may be defined quite literally as "financial involvement which is able to be insured".

17.2 A prerequisite for insurance

An alternative definition of insurable interest to that above is "the legal right to insure". This definition is an important one, because common law has always regarded possession of an insurable interest to be a necessary prerequisite for insurance. For a closer study of the law applicable to this important principle of insurance see **17.4–17.9**.

Without insurable interest any apparent insurance contract would be nothing more than a wager, which may not necessarily be illegal, but it is not an enforceable agreement. Thus, the necessity for insurable interest constitutes perhaps the greatest difference between insurance and wagering (see Chapter 23).

17.3 What constitutes insurable interest?

It must be remembered that when considering insurance as a whole, the subject matter of the insurance may consist of material goods, a human person, liability or financial rights. Any general definition should take this into account. Thus, the *essentials of insurable interest* are as follows (see Fig. 11):

(a) there must be life or limb, property, potential liability, rights or financial interest capable of being covered;
(b) such life or limb etc. in (a) above must be the subject matter of the insurance;

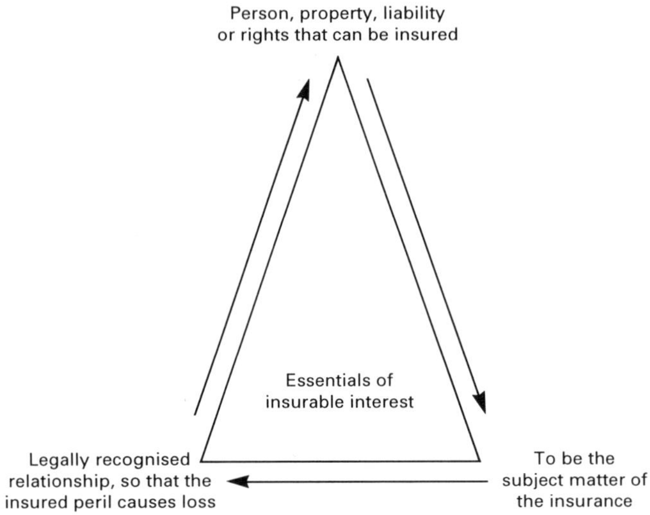

Fig. 11 The essentials of insurable interest

(c) the insured must be in a legally recognised relationship to the subject matter of the insurance, whereby he benefits from its continued safety or the absence of liability and is prejudiced by its damage or destruction, or the creation of liability.

B. INSURABLE INTEREST AND THE LAW

17.4 Common law and statute law

In the sixteenth and seventeenth centuries it was not unusual in the United Kingdom for wagers and gambling agreements to be considered binding and legally enforceable. Insurance contracts, however, were considered to be somewhat different, it being thought contrary to public policy to enforce such contracts in the absence of insurable interest. Nevertheless, this common law position became relaxed during the late seventeenth and early eighteenth centuries, with the result that insurance policies without insurable interest were often issued and enforced.

To remedy this situation, and to clarify other aspects surrounding this principle, legislation was enacted at different times: see below.

17.5 The Marine Insurance Act 1745

The formative years of insurance were concerned almost exclusively with marine or life business. It is not surprising therefore that the legislation outlining this basic principle of insurance should largely be centred on these major classes.

The Marine Insurance Act 1745 rendered illegal insurances on British ships and goods laden or to be laden on them unless insurable interest existed.

17.6 The Life Assurance Act 1774 (see **4.9**)

Sometimes called the *Gambling Act*, the Life Assurance Act 1774 was intended to put an end to the scandal of "gambling policies", often effected on the lives of notorious criminals or on military men. The following points about this important Act should be noted:

(a) Policies effected on the lives of persons in which the policyholder had no insurable interest, or by way of wagering, were illegal.

(b) The Act was not limited to life assurance, but specifically excluded reference to insurance of *"ships, goods and merchandises"*. This meant that the legislation about "wagering insurances" to date only covered lives, British ships and goods on or for them (see **17.5**).

(c) The Act provided that the amount to be recovered under the assurance should not exceed the amount of insurable interest in the life or lives assured. While this is quite logical, it is ambiguous. The two possible interpretations of this are:

   (i) the amount recoverable should not exceed the insurable interest *at the time the claim arose*. In *Godsall* v. *Boldero* (1807) this was effectively the position, when it was held that insurable interest must exist at the time a claim arose under the policy;

   (ii) the amount recoverable should not exceed the insurable interest *at the commencement of the insurance*. This is the currently accepted position, and has been accepted since it was decided in *Dalby* v. *The India and London Life Assurance Co.* (1854) that *Godsall* v. *Boldero* (above) should be overruled. Thus, while insurable interest is necessary at the inception of life assurances, it need not exist at the time any claim arises. (This is of great importance, as will be considered later.)

17.7 The Marine Insurance Act 1788

Insurance contracts on goods, other than those on or for ships, could still be effected without insurable interest. The Marine Insurance Act 1788 remedied the position by rendering illegal insurances without insurable interest on "any ship or *any goods, merchandises, effects or other property whatsoever*".

17.8 The Gaming Act 1845

It would seem that the legislation outlined above had effectively prohibited speculation with insurances. However, ingenious persons have frequently managed to evade the spirit of the law, while adhering to its letter. Since the previous legislation all dealt with *policies of insurance*, straight *gaming contracts* were therefore outside its scope and could still be arranged. To close this remaining gap, the Gaming Act 1845 rendered all wagering and gaming contracts void. Since any insurance arranged without insurable interest is nothing more than a wager, such "contracts" became completely useless and unenforceable.

17.9 Additional legislation

Basically, the present legal position is as outlined above, but the following additional Acts of Parliament were passed in connection with marine insurance:

(a) *Marine Insurance Act 1906* (see **3.10**). This was a codifying statute and embodies virtually the whole law relating to marine insurance. As such it repealed (but replaced with similar requirements) the earlier Acts of 1745 and 1788.

(b) *Marine Insurance (Gambling Policies) Act 1909*. This Act made it a criminal offence to effect a marine insurance without an insurable interest or a genuine expectation of acquiring such an interest. To date there has never been a prosecution under the Act, which has therefore been totally successful or completely unenforceable. (The Act also referred to so-called *PPI policies*, which are dealt with in **17.13**.)

C. HOW INSURABLE INTEREST ARISES

17.10 Insurance of the person

Insurable interest in life assurance and personal accident insurance presents few problems, as the person insured is usually the policyholder himself. Everyone has an unlimited insurable interest in himself. Thus, legally, there is no limit to the amount of life assurance or personal accident insurance that one can effect on one's own life. In practice, the ability to pay the premiums required restricts the total amount insured, and in personal accident insurance insurers usually try to limit the amount insured to a figure roughly commensurate with the policyholder's position and income.

17.11 Insurance of other people

It is sometimes legal to assure the life of another person. This situation arises in the following cases:

(a) *Husband and wife.* Stemming from the ancient concept that man and wife are one person, a husband and wife have a mutual unlimited insurable interest in each other. In addition to the common law position, a wife is given specific statutory ability to assure her husband under the Married Women's Property Act 1882.

(b) *Creditors and debtors.* A creditor stands to lose if his debtor dies without paying the debt. Thus he has a right to assure the debtor, but only to the extent of the loan (plus reasonable interest) at the time of effecting the assurance.

(c) *Partners.* The death of a partner could well cause financial loss to the survivor(s), who therefore have a right to assure him. This could arise with a professional firm or perhaps with theatrical performers. The amount of insurable interest may be difficult to ascertain, but legally it is limited to the financial involvement in the person assured.

(d) *In industrial life assurance.* Under the Industrial Assurance and Friendly Societies Act 1948 (with the 1958 Amendment Act), one may assure up to a sum of £30 the life of one's parent, step-parent or grandparent.

NOTE: i. The right to assure does not arise automatically from mere family relationship. Thus, a father has no right to assure his son, parents, etc. unless some direct financial loss is likely to arise from their death. The examples given in (d) above are statutory exceptions to the general rule of law on this point.

ii. Not every jurisdiction follows this rule. Family relationships are quite sufficient to justify insurance for example in the USA and now in Australia (see **15.14**).

17.12 Insurance of property

Insurable interest in property may arise as follows:

(a) *Ownership.* This is the most common and most obvious form, but in addition to full ownership, part or joint-ownership gives the right to insure. With part ownership, the insurable interest is strictly limited to the financial involvement, but a part owner may insure the property for the full value, as he will be deemed to be acting as agent for the other co-owners. Any amount he receives from the insurance over and above his own interest is to be held in trust for the co-owners.

(b) *Agents.* Provided the principal possesses an insurable interest, an agent may effect an insurance on his behalf. Legally this is reckoned to be the position where a householder effects a policy which extends to cover the belongings of members of his family. Another example is with private car insurance, which normally extends to cover the liability of other drivers using the vehicle with the insured's permission.

(c) *Administrators, executors and trustees.* These are all persons entrusted with the estate and affairs of others (usually called the *legal personal representatives*). They have a right to insure the property for which they are responsible. Where they acquire responsibility for goods by the operation of a will or by law, any existing insurance on the property usually automatically extends to cover their interest.

(d) *Bailees.* These are persons legally in possession of goods belonging to others, for example launderers, dry-cleaners, pawnbrokers, etc. Whether the bailee is legally responsible for losses to goods in his custody may depend on whether he is a *bailee for reward* or a *gratuitous bailee*. In either case, however, it is permissible for him to insure the goods, if only in the capacity of agent for the owner.

(e) *Husband and wife.* As with each other's lives (see **17.11**(a)) a husband and wife have a mutual insurable interest in each other's property.

(f) *In mortgages.* A *mortgagor* (the borrower) has an insurable interest as owner of the property, the *mortgagee* (the lender) has such an interest to the extent of the loan made. In practice, the lender (often a building society) usually places a clause in the mortgage contract requiring the mortgagor to insure the property, at least against fire. (An exception to this was in *mortgage guarantee insurances* effected by building societies to cover possible loss in repossession and sale of mortgaged property: see **15.10**).

17.13 PPI policies

In addition to the examples of insurable interest shown above, policies are issued in marine insurance on a completely different basis. There are many commercial interests, particularly in the flexible world of maritime affairs, where it may be difficult to establish insurable interest at any given time. Nevertheless, unless such interest can be established any insurances are of no legal value. In marine insurance, therefore, it became customary to issue policies where there was no need to establish insurable interest. Such policies are termed *PPI* (*Policy Proof of Interest*) policies, and are distinguished by a PPI clause attached to the policy document.

Since insurable interest has not been established, PPI policies are legally void. It is for this reason that they are sometimes termed *honour policies*, since payment under them is dependent upon the honour of the insurer. Such policies are peculiar to marine insurance.

NOTE: i. It was held in *Edwards* v. *Motor Union* (1922) that a void policy cannot subsequently be made valid. Thus a PPI policy cannot be made valid merely by removing the PPI clause from it.

ii. The Marine Insurance (Gambling Policies) Act 1909 (see **17.9**(b) above) made it a criminal offence for any person in the employment of a shipowner to effect a PPI policy on the vessel. The Act in effect further required that PPI policies should not be taken out unless an insurable interested existed or could be reasonably anticipated.

17.14 Insurance of liability

Insurance of liability seldom gives rise to any difficulty over the existence of insurable interest. A person clearly has an interest in any potential liability he may incur. Certain considerations arise, however, as follows:

(a) *Criminal acts.* It is quite permissible to insure against the *civil* consequences of a criminal act, such as a claim for damages from the victim of a road accident where the motorist is being charged with dangerous driving. However, it is not possible to insure against any fines imposed (see **2.10**). Nor is it possible for a criminal to obtain direct financial gain from the result of his crime, such as a murderer collecting the proceeds of a life policy on the life of his victim.

(b) *Liability of others.* An insured can effect a policy which extends to protect the interests of another, such as a private car policy which allows others to use the vehicle and be covered by the insurance.

17.15 Insurance of rights or interest

Insurable interest is usually quite obvious in insurance of rights or interest. An employer clearly has a financial involvement in the dishonesty of his staff (as in fidelity guarantee insurance), and a shopkeeper has an obvious interest in defaults on the part of credit customers, for example.

D. INSURABLE INTEREST AFFECTED BY STATUTE

17.16 Insurable interest created by statute

Some Acts of Parliament confer an insurable interest which would not exist without the legislation. Examples are as follows:

(a) *Repair of Benefice Buildings Measure 1972.* This requires diocesan boards of finance or their parsonage boards to insure any buildings for which they are responsible.

(b) *Married Women's Property Act 1882.* A woman was always considered under common law to have an insurable interest in her husband. However, she herself was regarded at law to be little more than a chattel of her husband. The 1882 Act gave her the right to be considered a separate person in her own right, and thus entitled to effect an assurance on herself.

(c) *Settled Land Act 1925.* This required a life tenant in property falling within the scope of the Act to effect fire insurance as prescribed.

(d) *The Industrial Assurance and Friendly Societies Acts* (see **17.11**(d)) created a limited insurable interest in parents.

17.17 Insurable interest modified by statute

Common law imposes strict liability, unlimited in amount, upon certain persons in charge of property belonging to others. Various statutes have been enacted, however, which in some circumstances limit the liability of the persons concerned. Where such circumstances pertain, the insurable interest is affected accordingly. Examples are as follows:

(a) *Carriage of Goods by Sea Act 1924.* The Act enables a shipowner to limit his liability to £100 per packet on goods his vessel carries. (The legal limit was extended to £200 by gentleman's agreement.)
(b) *Carriers Act 1830.* A common carrier is exempted from all liability in respect of certain valuable articles worth over £10, unless special arrangements were made for their carriage.
(c) *Hotel Proprietors Act 1956.* Provided he complies with the requirements of the Act, a hotel proprietor may restrict his otherwise unlimited liability towards guests to £50 per article and £100 per guest.

E. MISCELLANEOUS LEGAL FEATURES

17.18 Mere expectation is not insurable interest

A beneficiary under the will of an aged insane person has every reason to suppose that he will in due course enter into his inheritance. At law, however, this is no more than an expectancy, which does not give the right to insure. (This was an illustration given in the case of *Lucena v. Crauford* (1806)). The sophistication of the law is, however, demonstrated in the following:

(a) *Loss of profits insurance* (see **5.14**). There is no certainty that profits would have been made if there had not been a fire. Nevertheless, such assumed profit can be insured. This is because there is an *expectancy founded on legal rights* (of ownership of the property damaged by fire).
(b) *A legal right dependent on an expectancy* also constitutes insurable interest. This arises rarely, but if the beneficiary above agreed to sell in advance certain property that he seemed certain to inherit, the purchase money to be returned by him should he in fact not obtain ownership, the purchaser would have the right to effect assurance on the beneficiary's life, to the extent of the purchase price.

17.19 Insurable interest is limited to the financial involvement

The owners of property frequently have an emotional or sentimental attachment to it that makes the property worth far more to them than the intrinsic or market value. Their interest in such goods, however, is strictly limited to the *financial* involvement in the subject matter of the insurance (i.e. the intrinsic or market value).

17.20 The insurable interest need not be shown in the policy

The policy evidencing the contract of insurance need not mention the exact insurable interest. This is sometimes done, but it is not legally necessary. An exception arises under the Life Assurance Act 1774 (see **17.6**), where the person who is to benefit from the assurance must be mentioned by name in the policy document.

17.21 An equitable interest is sufficient

An equitable interest is sufficient to give a right to insure. Such interest, arising under the old law of equity, can occur, for instance, in respect of property held in trust.

F. WHEN INSURABLE INTEREST MUST EXIST

17.22 In marine insurance

The Marine Insurance Act 1906 specifically provides that insurable interest must exist *at the time of the loss* but need not exist when the insurance is effected.

17.23 In life assurance

The case of *Dalby* v. *The India and London Life Assurance Co.* (1854) (see **17.6**) established that in life assurance insurable interest must exist *when the contract was effected* but need not exist at the time of the loss. Thus, as long as insurable interest is satisfied at the outset it does not matter if the interest has diminished or even ceased at the time of a claim.

17.24 In all other insurances

The general rule with other than marine and life insurances is that insurable interest must exist *both* at the inception of the insurance *and* at the time of the loss. This rule has scarcely ever been challenged, but it is generally felt that the existence of insurable interest at the time of the loss would probably be considered adequate if it could be established that the insurance was effected in good faith. This is not the strict law on the point, although it has been established that insurances may be effected to commence at some date in the future (e.g. holiday insurances).

G. THE TRANSFER OF INSURABLE INTEREST (ASSIGNMENT)

17.25 The two meanings of "assignment"

The basic meaning of *assignment* is "transfer", but the term is used in two different contexts in insurance:

(a) *assignment of the proceeds of the policy.* This arises when the policyholder gives instructions to the insurer to pay any money due under the insurance to another person. In this sense, unless the contract specifically provides to the contrary, all policies are freely assignable. It is of little importance to the insurer who receives the money they must pay, and apart from any clause in the contract they must comply with the instructions given;

(b) *assignment of the policy.* This is the normal meaning of *assignment*, and means a "change of interest", i.e. somebody else is substituted for the original insured in the contract, which otherwise remains in force covering the same subject matter. All policies can be so assigned, but depending on the type of insurance the insurer's prior consent may be essential.

17.26 Personal contracts

The insurer's prior consent to *assignment of the policy* is required where the insurance is a *personal contract.* A contract of insurance is always personal, in the sense that some human element is invariably involved, but a *personal contract*, in the technical sense, is one where the insurer's decision to enter the contract depends on the personal qualities of the insured and the insurer's confidence in him. In simpler terms, it may be said that a *personal contract* is one where it matters to the insurer who the insured is. Under this technical description:

(a) *fire and accident* policies are "personal contracts;

(b) *life and marine* policies are not considered "personal contracts".

NOTE: It must be remembered that with assignment of the policy, the policyholder changes but the subject matter of the insurance remains the same. Thus, an assigned life policy still covers the original life assured, not the assignee.

17.27 Application to the various classes of insurance

The particular application of assignment to the different classes of insurance varies, and is considered below.

17.28 Assignment of marine policies

Under the Marine Insurance Act 1906, all marine policies are freely assignable, but this rule may be varied by special provision in the contract. In practice, the following usually applies:

(a) *Hull insurances.* The insurance of the vessel itself has something of the nature of a *personal contract* (see **17.26**) and the contract usually provides that the insurers must give their prior consent to an assignment.
(b) *Cargo insurances.* These policies are freely assignable, so that the insurance is virtually transferred with the sale of the goods. However, assignment or the agreement to assign the policy must be made before or when the assured parts with his interest.
(c) *Other insurances.* These are generally freely assignable.

17.29 Assignment of life policies

Life policies are not *personal contracts* (see **17.26** above), but are treated in law as *reversionary interests*, which can be freely assigned. Certain legal aspects of life policy assignments should be noted:

(a) Assignment must be for consideration.
(b) Unless the contract so provides, notice of assignment to the assurer is not obligatory, but the Policies of Assurance Act 1867 states that such notice should be given.
(c) Life assurance is unique in that the assignee *need not possess insurable interest.* Sometimes industrial life assurances restrict assignments to persons having such an interest, the clause being originally introduced to prevent the speculation in life assurance and to prevent exploitation of the less educated working classes.

NOTE: The current market in "second-hand" life policies in the United Kingdom (see **15.9**) is quite legal because of the above. It would not be so with motor or most other classes of insurance.

17.30 Nominations under life policies

The primary intention of life policies is to provide for dependants. This overriding purpose is protected by the ability to arrange life policies so that when payment is due the policy moneys are considered separate from the assured's estate. The moneys are then available for the dependants and not for any creditors. In addition, certain tax obligations may be avoided in respect of the proceeds of policies so arranged.

The procedure for such policies is for the assured to *nominate a beneficiary* (or *nominee*) when effecting the assurance. Such beneficiary, who need not be the legal representative of the assured, alone has the right to enforce any claim in due course. The regulating legislation for nominations consists of:

(a) *The Married Women's Property Act 1882*, with the earlier Married Women's Policies of Assurance (Scotland) Act 1880.
(b) *The Friendly Societies Act 1955*, which limited the total amount for nominations to £200.

NOTE: Nomination is really assignment of the proceeds of the policy as distinct from assignment of the policy itself (see **17.25**).

17.31 Assignment of "personal contracts"

Since, with *personal contracts*, the qualities, experience and record of the insured are of vital importance to the insurers, no assignment of such policies is valid without their prior approval. The insurers have the right to question and investigate the proposed assignee, and vary the terms of the contract, before accepting an assignment.

If an assignment does take place, this is sometimes termed a *novation*. (This term comes from the root word meaning "new", since the assignment effectively creates a new contract with the assignee.)

H. PROGRESS TEST 17

PART 1—SHORT ANSWERS (Answer in one or two sentences)

1. What are the essentials of insurable interest? **(17.3)**
2. Outline the legislation requiring insurable interest. **(17.4–17.9)**
3. Do the following have an insurable interest (give reasons)?
   (a) A farmer wishing to insure his haystacks against fire. **(17.12)**
   (b) A father wishing to effect a life policy on his daughter's life. **(17.11)**
   (c) A thief wishing to insure his "swag" against loss. **(17.3)**
   (d) A moneylender wishing to insure a client's life. **(17.11)**
   (e) A young woman wishing to insure her father's life because he has promised to give her £1,000 when she gets married. **(17.18)**
4. What are PPI policies ? **(17.13)**
5. Give two examples of how insurable interest has been
   (a) created;
   (b) modified by statute. **(17.16–17.17)**

PART 2—MULTIPLE CHOICE (Choose the most correct option)

1. Which of the following statements is correct?
   (a) insurable interest was only required after the Marine Insurance Act 1906;

(b) it is always necessary for an assignee to have insurable interest;
(c) at some time insurable interest is needed with all insurances;
(d) insurable interest relates to bonuses on life assurances. **(17)**

2. Which of the following statements is correct?
   (a) insurable interest is not possible in the life of another;
   (b) bailees have an insurable interest in the property of their bailors;
   (c) liability policies can only cover the named insured;
   (d) a creditor cannot insure the life of his debtor. **(17.10–17.12)**
3. With which of the following is there a valid insurable interest?
   (a) man wishes to insure his wife;
   (b) man wishes to insurer his brother;
   (c) company wishes to insure counterfeit computer software;
   (d) smugglers wish to insure goods against seizure by customs.
4. Insurable interest is needed at policy inception and at time of loss with:
   (a) every class of insurance;
   (b) motor insurance;
   (c) marine insurance;
   (d) life assurance. **(17.22–17.24)**
5. A "personal contract" in the context of policy assignment means:
   (a) one which cannot be assigned without the insurer's prior consent;
   (b) one which can be insured without the insurer's prior consent;
   (c) a contract covering an individual rather than a company;
   (d) a life or personal accident insurance. **(17.26)**

(For multiple choice answers, see page 355.)

CHAPTER 18

UTMOST GOOD FAITH

A. GENERAL OBSERVATIONS

18.1 Ordinary commercial contracts

All contracts are subject to *good faith*, since the law cannot support fraud. However, under ordinary commercial contracts the contracting parties are not required to reveal all they know about the proposed agreement. Certain protections are available to purchasers, following the Sale of Goods Act 1893, and subsequent legislation, but the common law principle applicable to most commercial contracts is still *caveat emptor* (let the buyer beware). In contracts for the sale of an article, for example, the seller must not misrepresent the article or deceive the buyer, but he need not point out all the defects and disadvantages. The buyer must satisfy himself that the contract is a reasonable one. He has no legal redress if he makes a bad bargain.

18.2 Insurance contracts

Insurance contracts are based upon mutual trust and confidence between the insurer and the insured. Because of the fiduciary nature of insurance, it is not possible for the doctrine of *caveat emptor* to apply. The information necessary for the parties adequately to assess the contract cannot be ascertained as with contracts of sale, for instance. The common law duty applicable to insurance contracts, therefore, is the much more stringent one of *uberrima fides* (utmost good faith), or, in the genitive case, *uberrimae fidei* (of the utmost good faith).

18.3 Meaning of utmost good faith

In simple terms, utmost good faith in insurance means that each party to a proposed contract is legally obliged to reveal to the other all information which would influence the other's decision to enter the contract, whether such information is requested or not.

It has been said that utmost good faith requires each party to tell the other "the truth, the whole truth and nothing but the truth" about the proposed contract. It is important to note that, unlike the situation in the law courts, such an obligation is not applicable merely to any questions asked. Failure to reveal vital information, even if not asked about it, gives the aggrieved party the right to regard the contract as void.

18.4 Duty applies to insured and insurer

Inevitably, the duty of utmost good faith rests more heavily on the prospective insured, since he alone knows, or should know, the great bulk of information vital to consideration of the contract. Nevertheless, the duty applies to the insurer also. The insurer, for instance, cannot withhold information in his private possession to the detriment of the prospective insured. This occurred in a marine case, where the insurer knew that the vessel proposed for insurance had in fact already sunk, unknown to the owner. Withholding this information was held to be a breach of utmost good faith.

B. UTMOST GOOD FAITH AND THE LAW

18.5 Legislation

Very little exists in connection with utmost good faith, as this has always been accepted as applicable to insurance contracts. However, the common law principle is endorsed by the Marine Insurance Act 1906, section 17 of which reads:

> A contract of marine insurance is a contract based upon the utmost good faith, and, if the utmost good faith is not observed by either party, the contract may be avoided by the other party.

18.6 Case law

Many disputes have arisen under insurance contracts, where the principle of utmost good faith has been considered by the courts. Some examples of this are:

(a) *Carter* v. *Boehm* (1766). This case is a very early confirmation of the principle. Lord Mansfield, in his summary, said: "Good faith forbids either party, by concealing what he privately knows, to draw the other into a bargain, from his ignorance of that fact, and his believing the contrary." (The reference was to *utmost good faith*.)

(b) *London General Omnibus Co. Ltd* v. *Holloway* (1911–13). In this rather more recent case, Kennedy L.J. observed: "No class of case occurs, to my mind, in which our law regards mere non-disclosure as a ground for invalidating the contract, except in the case of insurance. That is an exception which the law has wisely made in deference to the plain exigencies of this particular and most important class of transaction."

(c) *Rozanes* v. *Bowen* (1928). In this case, the following was said: "It has been for centuries in England the law in connection with insurance . . . that . . . it is the duty of the assured . . . to make a full disclosure to the underwriters without being asked of all the material circumstances. . . . That is expressed by saying that it is a contract of the utmost good faith."

C. MATERIAL FACTS

18.7 Definition of a material fact

A *material fact* has been defined as a fact that influences the mind of a prudent underwriter in assessing a risk. The principle of utmost good faith places each party to the contract under a duty to disclose all material facts to the other.

18.8 Examples of material facts

What is *material* in the technical sense cannot be left to the judgement of the person required to disclose it. In every case it is a matter of fact, to be decided by the courts if necessary. Certain facts, however, are quite obviously material to an insurance contract. For example:

(a) *Marine insurance*: that a vessel proposed for insurance has unrepaired damage affecting its handling.
(b) *Life assurance*: that a person has a known lung infection.
(c) *Fire insurance*: that a building is of wooden construction.
(d) *Theft insurance*: that premises had been burgled several times before.
(e) *Motor insurance*: that a standard model car has a specially tuned engine.

NOTE: Other examples will easily come to mind, but it should be remembered that the duty to disclose material facts is a *common law* one. While considering the matter in principle, it is better to ignore the complication of proposal forms, which in some jurisdictions may vary the common law position: see **18.23** below.

18.9 Qualification on the duty of disclosure

At *common law* a person cannot be penalised for not revealing facts which he does not know and which he cannot reasonably be expected to know. If, for instance, a person is unknowingly afflicted with a brain tumour, which kills him shortly after effecting a life policy, the underwriters cannot avoid liability on the ground that the existence of the tumour was not disclosed. (On the other hand, if it can be proved that a reasonable man should and could have ascertained this serious situation, the underwriters would be able to avoid the policy.)

18.10 Known facts which need not be disclosed

Quite obviously, there are many facts concerning any proposed insurance contract which are not of vital consideration to the parties involved. Basically, the duty of utmost good faith exists to prevent the parties being drawn into a contract in ignorance of detrimental information. Accordingly, the following types of facts need not be revealed, even if they are material within the definition in **18.7** above:

(a) *facts which improve the risk*, e.g. the existence of a sprinkler system in premises proposed for fire insurance;

(b) *facts which the insurer may be presumed to know.* The insurer knows, or is presumed to know, matters of *common knowledge* such as the existence of a state of war, and matters which fall within his *professional knowledge*, for example, that jewellery is much more attractive to thieves than timber stocks. (Obviously, the examples are extreme to illustrate the point. More sophisticated examples may have to be decided by a court of law);

(c) *matters of law.* Insurers are deemed to know legal requirements, such as the contents of the various Factories Acts (highly relevant to employer's liability insurance).

(d) *facts capable of discovery by the insurer from information supplied.* If, in connection with an inquiry for further insurance, an existing policyholder states that his claims history can be ascertained from the underwriters' records, and the insurers do not pursue the point, they cannot later complain if the claims record was unsatisfactory.

(e) *facts which the insurer's representative fails to notice on a survey.* It often happens that an insurer will require a survey of premises before accepting insurance in theft or fire insurance. Provided necessary details are not withheld or concealed by the prospective insured, he will not be penalised for any failure on the part of the insurer to note hazardous features.

(f) *facts which are unnecessary to disclose because of policy conditions.* Policies are sometimes made subject to conditions, or warranties (see **18.16–18.19**), which make certain requirements, e.g. that a certain form of padlock be fitted to doors (with theft insurance). It is thus superfluous to disclose that the particular locks are fitted.

D. DUTY OF DISCLOSURE

18.11 Duration of the duty

At common law the duty of disclosure remains in force throughout all negotiations leading up to the formation of the contract. Once the contract is in force, the contract is subject only to ordinary good faith. However, this position may be amended by specific provisions in the contract.

EXAMPLE: At common law, a person arranging a personal accident insurance would not be obliged to tell the insurer if he changes to a more hazardous occupation during the policy year. Personal accident policies, however, normally contain a condition requiring the insured to advise the insurer of any such change in the risk, which must be agreed by the insurer if the policy is to continue.

18.12 Revival of the duty

Where an alteration is to be made to an existing contract, the duty of disclosure revives in respect of the proposed alteration. The duty also revives at renewal, although the position with renewals is a little complicated, in that it has never been finally decided whether renewal constitutes a fresh contract or is merely the continuance of an existing one. The legal position seems to be that renewal is generally regarded as a fresh contract, except with policies which are arranged on a long-term basis.

18.13 Disclosure by an agent

It very frequently happens that the information supplied to an insurer about a proposed insurance is given by the insured's agent. In addition to the requirement that the prospective insured supplies all material facts through his representative, the agent is under a duty to disclose all material facts which he knows or ought to know about the risk.

E. REPRESENTATIONS

18.14 Representations

A prospective insured will supply statements, perhaps through an agent, bearing upon the proposed risk. These statements may be verbal or in writing. In either event they are termed *representations* (i.e. they represent to the insurer the proposed risk).

18.15 Common law duty regarding representations

Representations need not necessarily involve material facts (see **18.7**). Where they do, however, they must be *substantially true*. This means that they must be true to the best knowledge and belief of the prospective insured. Where the representations concern matters of belief, expectation or intention, the expectation, etc. need not be realised.

EXAMPLE: A person requiring a life assurance may state that it is not his intention to reside in tropical areas. After effecting the policy, his circumstances may change and he may indeed take up residence in the tropics. His assurance will not be prejudiced because of the alteration in his plans. However, it should again be emphasised that this represents the *common law* position. This could be amended by contract provisions (see **18.23**).

F. WARRANTIES

18.16 Warranties in insurance

A warranty in ordinary commercial contracts is a guarantee. For example, the warranty with a new car means that any defect will be remedied by the seller, but the contract of sale still stands. The buyer cannot return the car and demand his money back if there is a problem. With insurance warranties, however, any breach of them *goes to the root of the contract*, giving the aggrieved party the right to avoid the whole contract. The particular terms of the contract will determine whether a breach of a warranty gives the right to repudiate *ab initio* (from the beginning) or from the date of the breach.

18.17 Definition of insurance warranties

A statutory definition of a warranty is found in the Marine Insurance Act 1906. The Act describes a warranty as something "by which the assured undertakes that some particular thing shall or shall not be done, or that some condition shall be fulfilled, or whereby he affirms or negatives the existence of a particular state of facts".

18.18 Effect of a warranty

Warranties must be complied with strictly and literally. It makes no difference whether they bear upon material facts or not, nor whether any breach is innocent or fraudulent. Any breach whatsoever is sufficient to enable the insurer to avoid the policy.

An insurer may waive a breach of warranty. Also, where changes in circumstances render a warranty inapplicable or illegal, a breach is excused.

18.19 Types of warranty

There are two types of warranty:

(a) *Express warranties*. These are warranties which are *expressed* in the policy document, either specifically or by reference. Some examples of express warranties are:
   (i) *Marine insurance*: warranted leaving Arctic ports by a certain date.
   (ii) *Life assurance*: warranted not to live in the tropics without the insurer's consent and payment of extra premium.
   (iii) *Fire insurance*: warranted all cinema ashtrays be emptied after each day's final performance.
   (iv) *Accident insurance*: warranted that iron bars be fitted over windows (theft insurance).

(b) *Implied warranties*. These are found in marine insurance. They are warranties which are automatically applicable, although they do not appear in the policy document. An example is the warranty that a vessel is seaworthy.

G. DISTINCTION BETWEEN REPRESENTATIONS AND WARRANTIES

18.20 De Hahn v. Hartley (1786)

An important observation on the differences between warranties and representations was made in the case of *De Hahn* v. *Hartley*, in which it was said:

> There is a material distinction between a warranty and a representation. A representation may be equitably and substantially answered, but a warranty must be strictly complied with. . . . A warranty in a contract of insurance is a condition or a contingency, and unless that be performed there is no contract.

18.21 Comparison between representations and warranties

A comparison may be made as follows:

(a) *Representations*:
   (i) need only be substantially correct, even when material;
   (ii) breach must relate to a material matter before the right to repudiate arises;
   (iii) do not appear in the policy.

(b) *Warranties*:
   (i) must be strictly and literally complied with;
   (ii) any breach gives the right to repudiate;
   (iii) must appear, directly or by reference (except implied warranties).

H. THE INHERENT AND CONTRACTUAL DUTIES OF UTMOST GOOD FAITH

18.22 The inherent duty of utmost good faith

The inherent or common law duty of utmost good faith is outlined in **18.3–18.13**. It is fulfilled by the prospective insured making *representations* to the insurer: see **18.14–18.15**.

18.23 The contractual duty of utmost good faith

This is the duty of utmost good faith as expressed in the insurance contract. Since insurance contracts are negotiated agreements, this may vary, but in several classes of business the insurer obtains information about a proposed risk by the use of a *proposal form* (see Chapter 26). Where such forms are used, they are completed by or on behalf of the prospective insured and at the foot of the form there used to be a *declaration* which was worded as a *warranty* (see **18.16**). The wording of the declaration varied, but it used to be that the proposer warranted his answers to be true and complete, and that the proposal form was to form the basis of the contract. The effect of this was to change all the *representations* on the form into *warranties* (see **18.21**).

18.24 Powerful position of insurers

The declaration at the foot of a proposal form which was worded in the form of a warranty placed the insurer in a powerful legal position. Any inaccuracy on the form, whether material or not, innocent or fraudulent, enabled the insurer to avoid the contract. Thus the person suffering from an unknown tumour (see **18.9**) would have been in breach of a warranty if he had disclosed that he was in good health.

This practice of extending the common law duty of utmost good faith into a more stringent contractual duty of utmost good faith has been discontinued by nearly all insurers, in accordance with a "Statement of Insurance Practice" issued by the British Insurance Association and another by the Life Offices Association, following the Unfair Contract Terms Act 1977 (see **18.30**).

I. BREACHES OF UTMOST GOOD FAITH

18.25 Classification of breaches of utmost good faith (see Fig. 12)

The breaches of utmost good faith may be classified in the following way:

(a) *Non-disclosure*. This is the failure to disclose a material fact, either by accident or because the fact was not considered to be important.

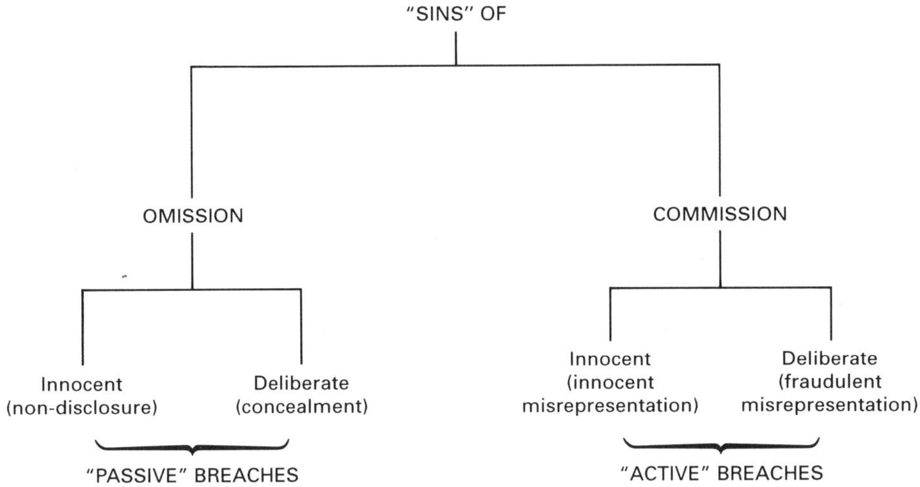

Fig. 12 Breaches of utmost good faith

(b) *Concealment.* This is the wilful failure to disclose a material fact.

(c) *Fraudulent misrepresentation.* This speaks for itself, and consists of the deliberate giving of false or intentionally misleading information on a material matter.

(d) *Innocent misrepresentation.* This occurs when incorrect information is given about a material matter, but where the error is unintentional.

NOTE: Basically, there are two sub-divisions of breaches of utmost good faith. One, sometimes called *passive breaches*, involves the failure to supply material information. The other, sometimes called *active breaches*, involves the supply of incorrect material information. With each the breach may be accidental (or innocent) or deliberate (or fraudulent).

18.26 Effect of a breach of utmost good faith

Breach of utmost good faith gives the aggrieved party the right to avoid the contract. The contract is not automatically void, but the aggrieved party must decide on his course of action within a reasonable time. The options open to him are as follows:

(a) *To consider the contract void.* This requires notification to the offending party. It is virtually unknown for a breach to be committed by the insurer, who is therefore almost invariably the aggrieved party. The insurer will state that he is coming off risk. If the policy has already matured (e.g. in life assurance) no payment will be made.

(b) *To sue for damages.* If the breach were fraudulent, the insured would be guilty of the tort of deceit, which could give rise to an action for damages. Such an action, however, is virtually unknown, since the trouble and expense are normally not worthwhile. This action is additional to (a) above.

(c) *To waive the breach.* The insurer may overlook the breach if he so desires, in which case the breach legally never occurred. If the insurer takes no action within a reasonable time, he will be deemed to have taken this course.

J. EFFECT OF LEGISLATION

18.27 Generally

In recent decades our society has become increasingly consumer conscious, with a great deal of social legislation to protect the seemingly weak. It is not surprising, therefore, that the practical effects of utmost good faith, which often appeared to favour the insurer, have to some extent been modified by statute. Some examples can be seen below.

18.28 The Rehabilitation of Offenders Act 1974

Under this Act certain criminal convictions are to be regarded as "spent offences" (i.e. legally cleared from the record) after stipulated periods. Although such facts might well previously have been considered material facts (see **18.7**) by insurers, they may no longer be so regarded, because legally they did not happen.

18.29 The Unfair Contract Terms Act 1977

While insurance is exempted from this Act, to allay any apprehensions in society about the exemption the "Statement of Insurance Practice" was issued by the British Insurance Association and the Life Offices Association. Some particular applications to utmost good faith included the following:

(a) declarations on proposal forms would only be made according to the proposer's knowledge and belief (i.e. the common law duty of utmost good faith would not be extended to a contractual one (see: **18.23**). Strictly, this application is to private individuals only, but insurers for the most part apply this to all proposal forms);

(b) material matters would normally be the subject of specific questions on proposal forms;

(c) the common law duty of disclosure and the consequences of not observing this would be clearly indicated on proposal forms;

(d) claims would not be refused because of a breach of warranty (see **18.18**) if the breach was irrelevant to the claim.

K. LAW REFORM AND CASE LAW

18.30 Law Reform Committee recommendations

The provisions of the statement of practice are not ultimately binding in law. This has caused disquiet in some circles and the Law Reform Committee cites four particular causes of concern in relation to utmost good faith:

(a) the duty of disclosure is thought to be too stringent;
(b) this duty can operate harshly upon the insured;
(c) material relevance of breach of warranty is legally not vital in avoiding claims thus affected;
(d) making extended declarations on proposal forms the basis of the contract exacerbates the problem in (c).

As a consequence, recommendations were made to reform the law so that it was more in favour of policyholders in these respects. A particular recommendation was that a "material fact" should be so decided in the context of a "reasonable insured".

18.31 Lambert v. Co-operative Insurance Society Ltd (1975)

The strength of feeling of at least some judges against the present position on utmost good faith can be seen in this case, where judgment was given for the insurance company. On renewal of a policy covering jewellery, Mrs Lambert failed to reveal that her husband had a recent conviction. Jewellery was lost and a claim filed. The policy was denied on a breach of utmost good faith. In somewhat scathing language, MacKenna J., after finding for the insurer, said, "The defendant company would act decently if, having established the point of principle, they were to pay her."

This case was a classic example of what might be called the sovereignty of statute, and why the Marine Insurance Act 1906 remains such an important influence on insurance law (see **3.10**). Central to the arguments and judgments in this case was the definition of what constituted a *material fact*. Section 18 of the MIA 1906 makes the profound, if now controversial, statement:

> every circumstance (fact) is material which would influence the judgement of a prudent insurer in fixing the premium, or determining whether he will take the risk.

This is statute law and although MacKenna J. was obviously unhappy about its implications in this case, he was obliged to defer to it. As a fellow judge on the same case, Lawton L.J., remarked: "Such injustices as there are must now be dealt with by Parliament, if they are to be got rid of at all." So far, statutory revision has not taken place and the MIA definition remains.

18.32 The "Oceanus" and other "material fact" cases

The above MIA definition of a material fact caused considerable argument in recent years. Unless a statute gives its own interpretations (which the MIA does not in this instance) it is left to the judges to apply the meaning they feel correct (compare, for example, the debate over the time when insurable interest is needed under the Life Assurance Act 1774: see **17.6**).

For generations, insurance claims staff would interpret the phrase "influence the judgement of a prudent insurer" as an indication that the piece of information in question would positively make a difference, either to the acceptance or to the terms of a proposed insurance. In the more litigious environment of company liquidations and reinsurance disputes, this apparently sensible and logical understanding was given new connotations.

The complexity of law reveals itself in this connection with no fewer than three possible meanings for "influence the judgement". These are that the "fact" in question would:

(a) indeed make a significant difference to the underwriter's decision: this became known as "*the decisive influence*" test;
(b) increase the risk, but not necessarily cause the underwriter to make any different decision: known as "*the increased risk*" test;
(c) be information the underwriter would like to know, but would not necessarily increase the risk or change his decision in any way: known as "*the mere influence*" test.

The three cases bearing upon this issue were:

(a) *Container Transport International Ltd* v. *Oceanus Mutual Underwriting Assn.* (1982, and in the Court of Appeal in 1984). There, to some surprise and consternation, the Court of Appeal overturned the "decisive influence" test and effectively rendered "mere influence" the criterion. This seemed to be contrary to the feelings of the judiciary in the *Lambert* case (see **18.31**) and appeared to confirm a very strong position for insurers in such disputes.

(b) *Pan Atlantic Insurance Co. Ltd* v. *Pine Top Insurance Co. Ltd* (1993), where the argument resumed. By a three to two majority the House of Lords rejected the "decisive influence" test, apparently confirming the "mere influence" criterion but not, as will be evident from the narrow margin, with unchallenged authority.

(c) *St Paul Fire & Marine Company (U.K.) Ltd* v. *McConnell Dowell Constructors Ltd* (1995). While not confirming the "increased risk" test, the judgment clearly indicated that Court of Appeal judges considered it significant that the fact in question was of great importance to the underwriters (and not merely of passing interest).

18.33 So where are we?

The layman may well pose such a question. What is clear is that the MIA definition of a material fact remains the authoritative one. What is also clear is that the insurance industry has taken note of the judges' comments in the *Lambert* case (see **18.31**). With personal insurance disputes, therefore, it seems likely that the "decisive influence" test is more likely to be the guideline for insurers (especially bearing in mind the background presence of the Insurance Ombudsman: see **30.27**). With liquidations and reinsurance disputes (in what might be described as "the battles of the financial Titans") it could be that there will be further expensive arguments, unless and until statutory revisions occur.

L. PROGRESS TEST 18

PART 1—SHORT ANSWERS (Answer in one or two sentences)

1. Why does utmost good faith apply in insurance? **(18.2)**
2. Define a material fact and give examples. **(18.7–18.8)**
3. Must a proposer reveal all facts about the proposed insurance? **(18.9–18.10)**
4. Outline the different breaches of utmost good faith. **(18.14–18.21)**
5. In what areas do the Law Reform Committee suggest amendments to the present legal position with utmost good faith? **(18.30)**

PART 2—MULTIPLE CHOICE (Choose the most correct option)

1. The duty of utmost good faith applies:
   (a) to both the proposer and the insurer;
   (b) only to the proposer;
   (c) only to the insurer;
   (d) only in the first year of the insurance policy. **(18.4)**
2. A material fact is one:
   (a) that the reasonable policyholder would think to be important;
   (b) which would influence the mind of a prudent underwriter;
   (c) that has to be disclosed only if a specific question is asked;
   (d) which will only affect property insurances. **(18.7)**
3. Which of the following facts must be disclosed?
   (a) matters of common knowledge;
   (b) facts which increase the risk beyond normal;
   (c) facts which decrease the risk below normal;
   (d) matters covered by a policy warranty. **(18.10)**
4. A warranty in insurance:
   (a) is very different from an ordinary commercial warranty;

   (b) must always appear in writing;
   (c) does not go to the root of the contract;
   (d) need not be strictly complied with. **(18.16–18.21)**

5. The contractual duty of utmost good faith:
   (a) does not change common law rules;
   (b) is less stringent than that at common law;
   (c) is more stringent than that at common law;
   (d) puts the insurer in a weaker position. **(18.23–18.24)**

(For multiple choice answers, see page 355.)

CHAPTER 19

INDEMNITY

A. GENERAL OBSERVATIONS

19.1 Meaning

Indemnity restores the insured to the same financial position after a loss as he enjoyed immediately prior to the loss. This is in accordance with the basic concept of insurance, which is to compensate the unfortunate for the loss they have sustained, but which is not intended to provide profit from misfortune.

More simply, indemnity may be defined as an *exact financial compensation.*

19.2 Cannot apply to all classes of insurance

From the above definition, it is immediately apparent that indemnity cannot apply to every class of business. With virtually all *life* and *personal accident* contracts it is impossible to provide exact financial compensation since life, limbs and health cannot be precisely measured in financial terms. Life and personal accident contracts are therefore sometimes termed *benefit policies,* in the sense that they cannot indemnify but only pay a certain benefit if the insured event happens.

19.3 Linked with insurable interest

There is a direct link between indemnity and insurable interest (see Chapter 17). In the event of the total loss of an insured article, the indemnity payable is equal to the insurable interest at the time of the loss. Where there is a measurable insurable interest, therefore, any insurance will be subject to indemnity. With life and personal accident policies, there is normally an unlimited interest, which means that an indemnity can never be given.

NOTE: With some life and personal accident policies the insurable interest is not unlimited. For example, in personal accident insurance an employer may insure his staff in respect of wages he continues to pay them when they are away ill, or a policy may cover medical expenses. Should a claim arise in these circumstances the policyholder can be indemnified in respect of any loss.

19.4 The position with non-indemnity policies

Even with those policies not normally subject to indemnity, the principle is not entirely overlooked, in the sense that the financial benefits are kept roughly in line with the policyholder's likely financial requirements and commitments. This is achieved by:

(a) *Ability to afford the premiums.* While in theory life and personal accident policies can have an unlimited sum insured, in practice the sum insured tends to be restricted by the ability or willingness of the policyholder to pay the premium required.

(b) *Direct action by insurers.* A sum insured which on the face of it seems to be well in excess of customary amounts, bearing in mind the occupation and age of the insured, may well put insurers on inquiry. Also, in personal accident insurances in particular, insurers will want to know of any existing insurances, so that aggregation of policies will not provide a benefit which is out of all proportion to the insured's likely needs. Policies giving weekly benefits far in excess of the insured's normal earnings, for instance, could lead to a temptation to malinger when claims arise. Policy conditions may also require notice of any additional insurance of that type arranged subsequently.

19.5 Legal position

Indemnity has always been considered a fundamental principle of insurance. Unfortunately, this has not always been appreciated by the general public, however. Many policyholders in the past have considered themselves victims of sharp practice on the part of insurers when they have been paid less than they thought insurance should provide. Perhaps insurers have not always made it clear to policyholders exactly what insurance means, but the legal position is quite plain. So clear is it, in fact, that there is no evidence that the principle has ever seriously been challenged in the courts. In the leading case of *Castellain* v. *Preston* (1883) the position was emphasised in the following words:

> The very foundation, in my opinion, of every rule which has been applied to insurance law is this, namely, that the contract of insurance contained in a marine or fire policy is a contract of indemnity, and of indemnity only. That is the fundamental principle of insurance.

NOTE: The comment, although applied specifically to marine and fire policies, applies equally to all but life and personal accident insurances.

19.6 Policy position

While the fundamental principle of most insurances is indemnity, the terms of the policy may prevent an indemnity being provided. For example:

(a) *Sum insured*. The *maximum liability* of the insurer is always the *sum insured*, even though this may not represent a full indemnity. Policies covering liabilities usually pay for legal costs in addition to the stipulated limit of cover, but normally the insurer cannot be compelled to pay more than the sum insured.

(b) *Inadequate sum insured*. If the insurance is based on the understanding that the sum insured represents the full value at risk, it may be made *subject to (pro rata) average*. This is considered fully later (see **31.8**), but briefly it means that in the event of *partial loss* the amount otherwise payable by the insurer will be reduced proportionately to the under-insurance.

(c) *Policy excess* (also known as a *deductible*). If a policy is subject to an *excess* of say £50, this means that the policyholder is responsible for the first £50 of each and every claim. Such an excess may be compulsorily applied by the insurer, or the insured may voluntarily agree to the provision, in which event a certain reduction in premium is allowed.

(d) *Policy franchise*. A *franchise* is similar to an excess, in that it is designed to eliminate trivial claims. However, with a £50 franchise, for example, the insured would be responsible for any claims not exceeding that amount, but, if the cost exceeded £50, the insurer would pay in *full*. Such a provision is rather rare these days, but it may be useful, for instance, in "all risks" insurance, where an insured has a record of numerous trivial losses.

NOTE: i. Sometimes a *time franchise* is found in personal accident insurance (not subject to indemnity, of course). It may be, for instance, that the weekly sickness benefit under such policies is not payable for incapacity of less than one week's duration but full compensation is payable for the whole of any longer period.

ii. The principle of indemnity may be deceptively easy to understand. What could be more obvious than that a person should recover only what they had lost? As stated, however, the principle is not always appreciated by the general public. The Court of Appeal decision in *Leppard* v. *Excess Insurance Co. Ltd* (1979) does little to reassure the layman's mind about indemnity.

Mr Leppard had insured for £8,694 an empty cottage he owned and was trying to sell. The proposal form required a declaration as to an insured value of not less than the present replacement cost. Both sides agreed that £8,694 represented the latter figure. A total loss claim arose and insurers contended that only the *actual loss* (indemnity) was payable. Since the market value (in 1974) was £4,500 and this included a site value of £1,500, the court awarded only £3,000.

It would be quite wrong to make sweeping assumptions from individual cases. In formal disputes, each case will be decided strictly on its individual merits. But this case does present an interesting example of problems which can arise with this principle, where discovering the true measure of loss may not be simple.

B. HOW INDEMNITY IS ASSESSED

19.7 Normal methods

The contract itself may contain specific provisions regarding the amount to be paid by the insurer: see below. A normal indemnity, however, would be calculated in the following ways:

(a) *With property insurance*. The indemnity will equal the intrinsic value of the article immediately prior to the loss or damage, with total losses. This would have to take into account any appreciation or depreciation on the original cost, and insurers are liable only up to the sum insured. With partial losses, the cost of necessary repairs or assessed reduction in value of the article provides indemnity.

(b) *With liability insurance*. Indemnity here is much more easily measured, in that it simply consists of the amount of damages awarded to (or negotiated with) the third party, plus any legal costs involved.

(c) *With pecuniary insurance*. Again, indemnity is fairly easily ascertained. It consists of the financial loss involved with the infringement of rights or prejudice of financial interest, such as by default by a cashier insured under a fidelity guarantee policy.

(d) *With insurance of the person*. Normally indemnity does not arise (see **19.2**). Where it does, however, it concerns the strict financial involvement.

19.8 Salvage

With property insurance, it often happens that the remains of the subject matter has some salvage value, even though the article is a total loss from an insurance point of view. For example, a motor car may be damaged beyond economic repair, but still have some scrap value. Such value should be taken into account. Usually the full assessed value is paid to the insured with total loss claims and the insurer takes over the salvage. He then obtains any salvage moneys, to reduce the net cost of the claim. Sometimes, however, the insured may wish to retain the salvage, in which case an appropriate sum should be deducted from the claim payment.

19.9 Abandonment

This is a term usually found in marine insurance and means that in certain circumstances the policyholder has the right to abandon the subject matter of the insurance to the insurer and claim the policy moneys. This is sometimes referred to as making a *constructive total loss* of the subject matter. It might arise, for instance, where a vessel is stranded on rocks and where it is impossible to salvage her. Technically, a claim for total loss could not be made until the vessel breaks up, but the right of *abandonment* enables the assured to have the policy moneys immediately. The vessel automatically becomes the property of the insurer.

The right of abandonment is not legally restricted to marine insurance. In non-marine classes, however, a policy condition usually specifically prohibits the insured from abandoning the property to the insurer and claiming as for a total loss.

19.10 Moneys recovered on salvage and after abandonment

Legally, there is a difference with regard to moneys recovered on salvage and after abandonment:

(a) *Salvage moneys*. It is said that recoveries on salvage are "limited to 100p in the pound". In practice this is seldom of any importance, but if a freak circumstance arose whereby the salvage price acquired a value higher than the claim payment, the insurer would be legally obliged to return to the insured the balance over and above the amount paid.

(b) *Recoveries after abandonment*. When the policyholder abandons the property to the insurer, he surrenders all title to it. Thus, any moneys that the insurer realises on the property belong exclusively to the insurer. In the example in **19.9** above, it could happen that after abandonment an abnormally high tide lifted the vessel clear of the rocks. The insurer could then sell it, possibly at a price higher than the total loss payment, and the assured would not benefit.

19.11 Rights of recovery against third parties

It often happens that the insured has a right to claim under his policy and against a third party for damage to property. The insurer cannot say that the insured must first claim against the third party, but he may acquire the rights of recovery if he makes a payment. This is concerned with the principle of *subrogation*: see Chapter 20.

C. METHODS OF PROVIDING AN INDEMNITY

19.12 Different methods available

There are four basic methods of providing an indemnity, as follows (see Fig. 13):

(a) *Cash*. This is the most obvious, and in some ways the most suitable,

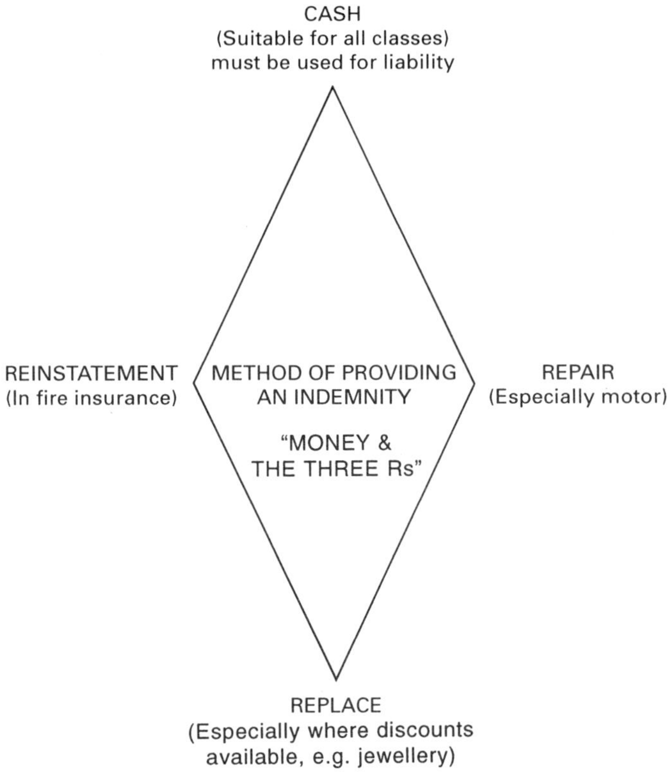

Fig. 13 Methods of providing an indemnity

method of settling claims. Indeed, with liability claims this is the only practical method available, if payment is made to the policyholder in reimbursement of outlays to third parties.

(b) *Replacement.* It is sometimes advantageous for the insurer to replace an article rather than to pay cash. With a very new item, or with such things as jewellery and furs, depreciation is likely to be negligible and the insured may well be content with a new replacement, which might possibly be acquired at a discount from the appropriate dealer. Because of speed, this is also the usual method of dealing with glass claims.

(c) *Repair.* An adequate repair constitutes an indemnity. This form of settlement is particularly common in motor insurance, where the insurer settles the repair bill direct with the garage concerned.

(d) *Reinstatement.* This is a term usually found in fire insurance and concerns the restoration or rebuilding of premises (not necessarily on the same site) to their former condition. This can give rise to difficulties, if the insured is not happy about the standard of work, but in some circumstances the insurer may be required to pay towards reinstatement. This arises under the Fires Prevention (Metropolis) Act 1774, where reinstatement can be insisted upon by any interested party or where fraud or arson is suspected. (Reinstatement in the latter instances would frustrate any illegal efforts to obtain the policy moneys, although any claim could of course be refused if fraud or arson could actually be proved.)

19.13 Who has the option in the method of indemnity?

The choice of method whereby indemnity will be provided is normally given to the insurer by policy conditions. However, the insurer will usually try to meet the insured's wishes, unless there are very strong reasons to do otherwise. Clearly, little is to be gained by insisting on one's legal rights against a customer acting in good faith, but the legal terms of the policy are a useful guide, particularly where an insurer may have suspicions about a claim.

NOTE: An insurer is always very reluctant to accuse a policyholder of fraud. If fraud cannot be proved, not only will the claim have to be met but the insurer may also be faced with an action for defamation of character.

D. REINSTATEMENT OF THE SUM INSURED

9.14 How the need may arise

When a total loss payment is made, or the total sum insured is paid under a policy, the insurer's obligations under the contract are clearly extinguished. Where a payment is made in respect of a partial loss, however, the position varies in respect of the amount of cover available during the remainder of the period of insurance. With some classes of business, a partial loss payment reduces the sum insured by the amount paid, and extra premium is required to reinstate the amount of cover available for the rest of the policy's term.

19.15 Marine insurance

Partial loss payments do not reduce the subsequent amount of cover. Thus, successive partial loss settlements may in aggregate exceed the sum insured, or an insurer can be liable for a total loss after payment of a partial loss, in the same period of insurance. A total loss after earlier unrepaired damage is subject to the following considerations:

(a) *If in the same period of insurance.* The insured would receive payment only in respect of the total loss.
(b) *If in successive periods of insurance.* In marine insurance, the periods of insurance are regarded as quite separate. Thus, unrepaired damage

in an earlier period can be claimed *in addition* to a total loss in a subsequent period. This seems quite anomalous, but is a well-established principle in this class of business.

19.16 Fire insurance

In fire insurance, the sum insured is automatically reduced by any amounts paid in respect of claims, and the insurer is not liable in aggregate for more than the sum insured during the policy term. If full cover is required after a partial loss payment, therefore, an additional premium must be paid, on a *pro rata* (exactly proportionate) basis, to reinstate the sum insured.

19.17 Life assurance

Obviously, reinstatement of the sum assured does not arise, since a claim payment automatically concludes the contract.

19.18 Accident insurance

Accident insurance involves different types of contract, for which different considerations arise, as follows:

(a) *Insurance of the person* (personal accident). Reinstatement of the sum insured does not arise. If a capital sum is paid, in respect of death or major injury, the policy is automatically terminated. With weekly benefits, there is no reduction of cover after claim payments, except that the policy limits the cover to a specified number of weeks' benefit for any one claim and if that limit is reached the policy cover is exhausted.

(b) *Insurance of property.* Normally, the sum insured stands reduced by any payments made, as with fire insurance, but there are some exceptions. *Glass* policies have no sum insured, and so reinstatement does not arise. *Livestock* policies provide benefits for the death of animals only; thus any claim concludes the contract. (Motor insurance is considered below.)

(c) *Insurance of liability.* Reinstatement of the sum insured, as such, does not arise, except where the extent of cover is limited to an aggregate sum in any one year. Any payment under such policies obviously reduces the available cover for the remainder of the policy term, unless extra premium is paid.

(d) *Insurance of pecuniary interest.* The amount of cover is normally limited in aggregate to the sum insured, but often such contracts provide for termination once a claim is paid. It would not be possible, for instance, to continue an individual fidelity guarantee insurance on a cashier who has defaulted.

19.19 Motor insurance

The insurance of liabilities and any personal accident benefits under motor policies is subject to the same considerations as with accident insurance generally: see above. Property insurance, however, is different, in that partial loss payments do not reduce the sum insured. In this respect motor insurance is similar to marine insurance (without the concession over partial and total losses in different periods of insurance: see **19.15**).

E. POLICIES WHICH MODIFY INDEMNITY

19.20 Reinstatement policies

In fire insurance, it is sometimes possible to arrange policies on buildings or machinery which will pay the cost of reinstating or replacing damaged premises and machines, without making any allowance for wear and tear, depreciation, etc. This "new for old" concession modifies the fundamental principle. Nevertheless, policies on this basis will only expend moneys on reinstatement or replacements; the insured is never paid cash on replacement values.

NOTE: Also in fire insurance, policies can be made subject to a *local authorities clause* which will provide more than a strict indemnity, in that any extra costs incurred as a result of modified reinstatement, owing to national or local requirements (such as structural improvements) after a fire, are covered.

19.21 "New for old" policies

An innovation in household contents insurance in recent years has been to offer cover on a replacement rather than an indemnity basis. This has proved highly popular, but the policyholder pays a higher rate of premium and should insure for full replacement value of the contents. Most insurers now offer this facility, although some restrict the "new for old" benefit to articles less than say three years old. Many policies revert to strict indemnity if the sum insured is not adequate.

19.22 Valued policies

Valued policies are virtually the norm in marine insurances. This is considered in **19.26**. In principle it is the same in marine insurance as with other classes of business, where it means that in the event of *total loss*, the sum insured is paid irrespective of the value of the article. In non-marine insurance such policies are usually called *agreed value* policies, and they are only issued in respect of articles of stable or increasing value, such as jewellery, works of art and furs. At the inception of such policies an independent expert's valuation is obtained, constituting the sum insured. It is now common for private car comprehensive policies to replace with a new vehicle any insured car which is a total loss in its first year of insurance.

With marine valued policies, *partial losses* are settled proportionately to the sum insured, and a legal case held that the same should apply to fire insurance on an agreed value basis. Now, however, non-marine valued insurances have a provision requiring partial losses to be settled on a strict indemnity basis.

19.23 Policies based on an inventory and valuation

These policies are not to be confused with valued policies (see above) although they are also based on an independent expert's valuation. An inventory is a list of articles, and this is precisely what is meant with policies based on an *inventory and valuation*. Such insurances are not common now, but where found they normally cover household goods and personal effects. A list of articles is drawn up by the insured and a professional valuer, who states the sum to be insured under each item.

The main difference between this form of policy and a valued policy is shown at the time of a loss. With these policies the sum insured is accepted as the original value at policy inception, but the amount payable takes into account wear and tear and depreciation, i.e. it provides an indemnity.

A benefit of such policies is that proof of original value does not have to be provided at the time of a claim, as is the position with normal indemnity policies. Such proof has already been provided in the valuation. An inventory also helps to ensure that all articles are covered. However, this system does have the drawback that the list has continually to be kept under review as items are acquired or disposed of.

19.24 Comparison of valued policies and policies based on an inventory and valuation

Both types of policy have in common an initial valuation by an independent expert. The differences may be tabulated as follows:

- (a) *Valued policies*:
  - (i) usually cover articles of stable or increasing value, e.g. jewellery, paintings, works of art;
  - (ii) expert's valuation constitutes the sum insured, which is automatically payable in the event of a total loss (partial losses normally subject to indemnity, i.e. cost of repair, etc.);
  - (iii) revaluation by an expert is usually required at policy renewal.
- (b) *Inventory and valuation policies*:
  - (i) usually cover household goods and personal effects;
  - (ii) expert's valuation only accepted as the value at policy inception;

normal indemnity is applied at the time of any loss;
(iii) inventory must be kept under close review (with valuation for new items) if cover is to be adequate.

19.25 Justification of valued policies

It has sometimes been said that valued policies ought not to be issued, since they may provide more than an indemnity and thus violate a fundamental principle of insurance. This argument can be countered with the following points:

(a) The valuation (i.e. the sum insured) is made by an independent expert.
(b) Such policies are normally issued only in respect of articles which are unlikely to depreciate.
(c) Partial losses are dealt with on the basis of strict indemnity.
(d) It is possible to argue that these are policies of indemnity, but that the indemnity is fixed at policy inception and not at the time of the loss.
(e) Such policies have statutory authority, in the MIA 1906.
(f) It may be fairer, bearing in mind the type of article involved, to determine the value in advance. Many articles so insured are incapable of being valued accurately after a loss as they are often unique.

NOTE: Valued policies are not *indisputable* policies in the sense that the sum insured is inevitably paid with a total loss. No payment is made where fraud or breach of other policy condition occurs.

F. SPECIAL CONSIDERATIONS IN MARINE INSURANCE

19.26 "In manner and to the extent agreed"

By virtue of long-standing maritime practice, as confirmed by section 1 of the MIA 1906, it is usual for marine policies to promise to indemnify "in manner and to the extent agreed". In other words, it is usual for the policy to provide a *commercial indemnity* rather than a strict common law indemnity. In practice, the following position usually obtains:

(a) *Hull policies.* These are normally *agreed value* policies (see **19.22**), the amount insured normally being fixed at a level rather above the current market value.
(b) *Cargo policies.* In addition to the value of the goods, such policies normally include in the sum insured an amount for certain charges and for profit. Again, these policies are usually on an *agreed value* basis.
(c) *Freight and other policies.* These are not normally on a valued basis.

19.27 Agreed value and unvalued policies

The MIA 1906 allows both valued and unvalued policies in marine insurance. Separate considerations arise:

(a) *Agreed value policies.* Basically, these are as outlined in **19.22**, except that the valuation is not made by an independent person. It is agreed between the assured and the insurer, and proportionate payments are made in respect of partial loss of goods. This means, for instance, that the destruction of one quarter of insured cargo would involve a payment of one quarter the agreed value, irrespective of the cost of replacing the goods. (Partial damage to ships is indemnified by the payment of the repair costs.)

(b) *Unvalued policies.* Where unvalued policies are issued, the insurable value (i.e. the insurable interest) must be computed in accordance with section 16 of the Act.

G. PROGRESS TEST 19

PART 1—SHORT ANSWERS (Answer in one or two sentences)

1. What is indemnity and why is it not universally applicable? **(19.1–19.2)**
2. In what circumstances may a policy normally subject to indemnity not provide a full compensation to the insured? **(19.6)**
3. What is "abandonment" and how do recoveries after it have different considerations from those with ordinary salvage? **(19.9–19.10)**
4. In what ways may indemnity be provided ? **(19.12)**
5. When is reinstatement of the sum insured necessary? **(19.14–19.19)**

PART 2—MULTIPLE CHOICE (Choose the most correct option)

1. Indemnity is a principle that:
   (a) is unrelated to insurable interest;
   (b) promises to pay the sum insured with all total losses;
   (c) settles partial losses on a proportional basis;
   (d) seeks to give an exact financial compensation. **(19.1–19.3)**
2. A policy franchise:
   (a) will pay larger claims in full;
   (b) will deduct the stated amount from every claim;
   (c) is exactly the same as a policy excess;
   (d) is another name for a policy deductible. **(19.6)**
3. The term "abandonment" in insurance indicates that the:
   (a) insured gives up a claim that the insurer refuses;
   (b) insurer will not contest a third party claim;

(c) subject matter becomes the property of the insurer;
(d) the policy has lapsed. **(19.9)**

4. Reinstatement of the sum insured implies that:
   (a) a partial loss has been settled and more cover purchased;
   (b) a total loss has occurred and a new insurance is arranged;
   (c) the insured wishes to increase his sum insured;
   (d) the policy has lapsed and is to be revived. **(19.14)**
5. "In manner and to the extent agreed" is a term:
   (a) found particularly in marine insurance;
   (b) found particularly in non-marine insurance;
   (c) that always means only a common law indemnity is payable;
   (d) that always means more than indemnity is payable. **(19.26)**

(*For multiple choice answers, see page 355.*)

CHAPTER 20

SUBROGATION

A. GENERAL OBSERVATIONS

20.1 Meaning

Subrogation means the exercise for one's own benefit of rights or remedies possessed by another against third parties. If the rights or remedies have already been exercised, subrogation entitles one to the proceeds therefrom. Subrogation rights are acquired by insurers once they have provided their insured with an indemnity (see Chapter 19), and at common law any actions to recover from third parties must be conducted in the name of the insured.

NOTE: The term is derived from two Latin words: *sub*, meaning "under", and *rogare*, meaning "to ask". Thus, *subrogation* means "asking (for a payment) under another's name".

20.2 A corollary of indemnity

A corollary is a natural consequence of an established principle. Subrogation is a corollary of indemnity, in that an insured, who possesses rights under his policy and against third parties in respect of the same loss, would receive more than indemnity if he retained the proceeds of claims under both headings.

20.3 A common example of subrogation

A very common example of subrogation rights arising is in motor insurance. A motorist insured under a comprehensive policy has two sources of compensation if another motorist negligently damages his vehicle: from his insurers and from the negligent motorist. If he decides to claim under his own policy, his insurers are in due course *subrogated* to his rights against the third party. They can thus recover any money paid under their policy, and the insured is not paid twice for the same damage.

NOTE: It is not technically correct, however, to say that subrogation prevents an insured from claiming for damages from two sources. The motor case of *Morley* v. *Moore* (1936) established that having rights under an insurance contract did not prevent the insured from claiming against a negligent third party as well. However, the proceeds of the claim against the third party were to be passed to the insurers, to the extent of any payment under their policy.

20.4 Only applicable to contracts of indemnity

Since the common law principle of subrogation provides that such rights are only acquired after an indemnity has been provided, it follows that the principle can only apply where indemnity applies. As a corollary of indemnity, subrogation only arises in conjunction with the parent principle. Therefore, subrogation does not normally arise with *life* and *personal accident* policies (see **19.2–19.3**).

EXAMPLE: A life assurer has no subrogation rights against a negligent motorist who knocks down and kills his policyholder. The deceased's estate can claim under the policy and at common law against the motorist.

20.5 Legal position

As with its parent principle indemnity, the basic tenet has long been accepted at law. It is, after all, common sense that a person should not be compensated twice for the same loss. Two important legal cases where the doctrine was confirmed are:

(a) *Castellain* v. *Preston* (1883). In this famous case the following words were said:

> A person who wishes to recover for, and is paid by the insurers as for, a total loss cannot take with both hands. If he has a means of diminishing the loss, the result of the use of these means belongs to the insurers.

(b) *Burnand v. Rodocanachi* (1882). In this slightly earlier case, Lord Blackburn said in relation to a marine policy:

> If the indemnifier has already paid it, then, if anything which diminishes the loss comes into the hands of the person to whom he has paid it, it becomes an equity that the person who has already paid the full indemnity is entitled to be recouped by having that amount back.

B. HOW SUBROGATION RIGHTS ARISE

20.6 Four main ways

The main ways in which subrogation rights may arise are as follows (see Fig. 14):

(a) in tort;

(b) by contract;
(c) under statute;
(d) with salvage: see below.

20.7 Subrogation arising out of tort

A tort is a civil wrong, the most common types of tort being negligence and nuisance. The former is the most frequent cause of subrogation rights arising in connection with an insurance contract. An example is given in **20.3**. A further example, in fire insurance, would arise if a painter failed to take adequate care when using a blowlamp and set fire to the insured's premises. Other examples will readily spring to mind with all classes of business subject to indemnity.

NOTE: Examples from motor insurance are often modified in practice by inter-company agreements. The knock-for-knock agreement (see **20.13**), for instance, effectively states that any insurer party to such agreement will waive its subrogation rights against another subscribing insurer.

20.8 Subrogation arising out of contract

It may be that a third party is bound by contract to make good any loss sustained by the insured, irrespective of any fault on his part. The insurer is equally subrogated to any contractual rights possessed by the insured which will diminish or extinguish the loss. Examples of subrogation arising under contract are:

(a) *Goods damaged while in the custody of a common carrier.* The contract of carriage will automatically involve the carrier in some liability for damage to goods in his custody, irrespective of negligence.
(b) *Tenancy agreement.* It sometimes happens that a contract of tenancy contains a covenant, or binding agreement, that the tenant will make good any damage however caused. Such was the situation in *Darrell v. Tibbitts* (1880), where the owner recovered cash from his fire insurers and had the same damage repaired by the tenant. It was held that the insurers were entitled to have their money back.
(c) *Rental agreement.* It is quite common for hiring contracts, TV rentals for example, to stipulate that the hirer is responsible for any loss or damage to the appliance, however arising.

20.9 Subrogation arising from statute

In a few cases, Acts of Parliament give subrogation rights which might not otherwise exist. Examples are:

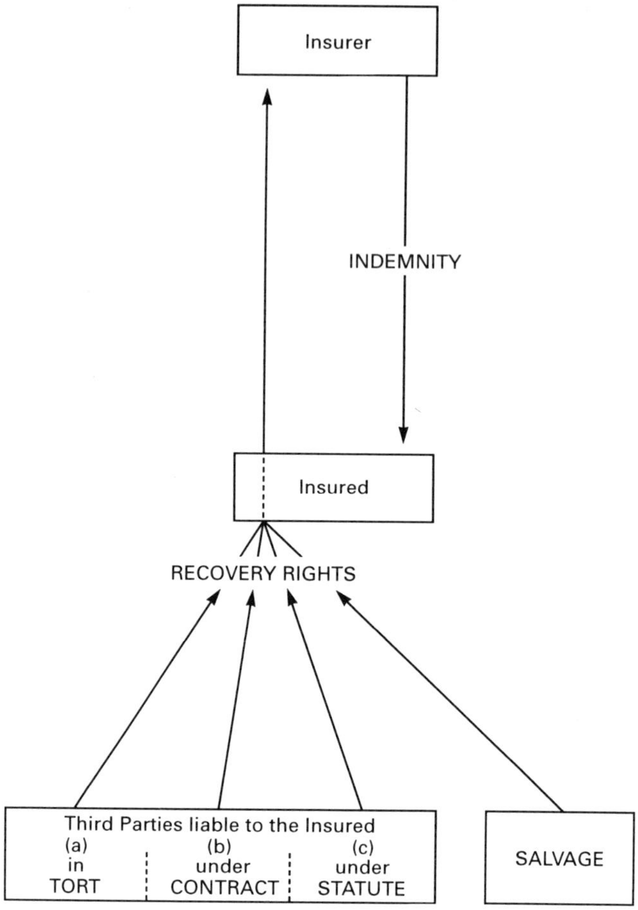

Fig. 14 How subrogation arises

(a) *The Riot (Damages) Act 1886.* The local police authorities are responsible for peace and order within their jurisdiction. Where riot damage has been caused within the scope of the Act, an insurer who makes payment in respect of such damage has a right of recovery against the police. The position is unique, in that the insurer may proceed against the police authorities *in his own name.*

(b) *The Railway Fires Act (1905) Amendment Act 1923.* Acting under statutory powers, railways were not responsible for damage caused by flying sparks and hot cinders. This Act removed the defence in respect of damage to agricultural land and crops. In the absence of negligence, however, liability was limited to £200. British Rail voluntarily increased this limit to £400.

20.10 Subrogation arising out of salvage

It is arguable whether salvage and the proceeds therefrom should be considered as a factor in assessing indemnity (see **19.8**) or as a source of subrogation rights. Where the insured is paid as for a total loss without any account being made of the monetary value of the remains of the property insured, it may be said that subrogation rights arise out of the subject matter of the insurance.

The most obvious example of such subrogation rights is perhaps a wrecked motor vehicle, but other instances include fire damaged materials such as paper which probably has a salvage value as pulp, or stranded ships which have considerable value as scrap metal.

C. HOW THE COMMON LAW POSITION IS SOMETIMES MODIFIED

20.11 The common law position

At common law subrogation rights are not acquired by the insurer until he provides an indemnity to his insured.

20.12 How common law is sometimes modified

In those policies which are subject to subrogation (not marine), it is quite common for a policy condition to amend the common law position, so that subrogation rights are acquired *before* the insurer has provided an indemnity. This immediate acquisition of recovery rights is very useful, in that the insurer may institute proceedings (in the insured's name), against any third party at once. Otherwise, delays could jeopardise recovery chances. In motor insurance, the immediate acquisition of subrogation rights would enable an insurer to approach a negligent third party before repairs to the insured's vehicle had been put in hand, to obtain his agreement to discharge the repair bill in due course. This would save considerable administration expense for the insurer.

With *marine insurance* the common law position is not usually modified.

D. WHEN SUBROGATION RIGHTS ARE SOMETIMES WAIVED

20.13 Inter-company agreement

It frequently happens that the exercise of subrogation rights involves a payment by another insurer. Sometimes the insurers involved are parties to an agreement whereby all subrogation rights against member insurers are waived. This saves considerable time and expense in arguing over liabilities of the respective insured. The "swings and roundabouts" theory ensures that an insurer with a substantial portfolio will not be unduly prejudiced by this arrangement, in that the rights he forsakes are likely to be balanced by claims not pursued against him. In the long run, such agreements are to the customers' benefit, since they cut down costs.

Examples of this type of agreement (which may involve Lloyd's underwriters as well as companies) are particularly found in motor insurance. Two examples are:

(a) *Knock-for-knock agreements.* These are frequently misunderstood by the general public and often regarded with a certain amount of suspicion. The basic principle, however, is that no insurer will exercise subrogation rights against another insurer with whom he has such an agreement. This agreement is strictly an inter-insurer agreement and should in no way benefit or prejudice the position of the respective insured. They still possess their full common law rights and may proceed with claims against the other motorist or any other party they consider at fault.

(b) *Third party claim sharing agreements.* Where two motorists are involved in an accident and third parties are injured (perhaps pedestrians, or passengers in the respective vehicles), within the scope of their policies the insurers will ignore the question of blame for the accident and settle any third party claims on an equal sharing basis. Such agreements usually have an upper limit.

20.14 In employer's liability insurance

Although an employer may be vicariously liable for acts of negligence by employees causing injury to fellow employees, the negligent person remains primarily liable at law. Employer's liability insurers have generally agreed, however, that subrogation rights against the negligent employee will not be exercised, unless there is suspicion of collusion between him and the claimant. (It is not unknown for a negligent workman causing an injury to a colleague to promote a claim against the employer, with a view to sharing the proceeds with the victim.)

E. MISCELLANEOUS LEGAL CONSIDERATIONS

20.15 Subrogation is limited to 100p in the £

By the exercise of subrogation rights the insurer is not permitted to make a profit on a claim. (This was considered under *salvage* in **19.10**.) The position was amply demonstrated in the case of *Yorkshire Insurance Co. Ltd* v. *Nisbet Shipping Co. Ltd* (1962). In that case, the marine insurers had subrogation rights in a claim of £72,000 against the owners of another vessel, in fact the Canadian government. The shipowners' claim was successful and the Canadian Government paid in dollars, which, owing to the 1949 devaluation of the pound sterling, realised almost £127,000. The shipowners were held to be entitled to keep the balance of £55,000. As stated by Diplock J.:

> The simple principle which I apply is that the insurer cannot recover under the doctrine of subrogation . . . anything more than he has paid.

NOTE: The position above would have been quite different had the vessel been the subject of an abandonment to the insurers (see **19.10**).

20.16 *Ex gratia* payments

An *ex gratia* payment is one made "out of grace (favour)". That is, it is a payment made where no legal obligation to pay exists. As such, it has the nature of a gift, which acquires no legal rights. Therefore, any such payments will not give the insurer subrogation rights.

Case law has concerned this general understanding, for example with payments under PPI policies (see **17.13**). Being policies which are binding *in honour* only, there is no legal obligation to make payments under them, and any such payments will therefore be *ex gratia*. It was held in *John Edwards & Co.* v. *Motor Union Insurance Co. Ltd* (1922) that no subrogation rights arose.

F. PROGRESS TEST 20

PART 1—SHORT ANSWERS (Answer in one or two sentences)

1. Show how subrogation is linked with indemnity. Give an example. **(20.1–20.3)**
2. In what ways may subrogation rights arise? **(20.6–20.10)**
3. How do policy conditions sometimes modify subrogation rights? **(20.11–20.12)**
4. Give some examples in which insurers waive subrogation rights. **(20.13–20.14)**
5. Explain the statement that "subrogation is limited to 100p in the £". **(20.15)**

PART 2—MULTIPLE CHOICE (Choose the most correct option)

1. The principle of subrogation:
   (a) is a corollary of the principle of indemnity;
   (b) is unconnected with the principle of indemnity;
   (c) allows the insured to recover more than he has lost;
   (d) can apply to all insurance claims. **(20.2)**
2. Subrogation rights arising out of contract:
   (a) are not passed to the insurer providing an indemnity;
   (b) are passed to the insurer providing an indemnity;

(c) belong to the insurer only if the contract specifically says so;
(d) will not apply with rental or hiring contracts. **(20.8)**

3. The common law position with subrogation rights:
   (a) cannot be changed by insurance policy conditions;
   (b) is always changed by insurance policy conditions;
   (c) means that rights may be exercised before an indemnity is given;
   (d) requires an indemnity to be provided first. **(20.12)**
4. Inter-company agreements:
   (a) may modify or waive subrogation rights;
   (b) will never waive subrogation rights;
   (c) may mean that an insured will lose his rights against a third party;
   (d) can never be in the interests of policyholders. **(20.13)**
5. An "ex gratia" payment, as under a PPI policy:
   (a) does not affect any subrogation rights;
   (b) does not acquire any subrogation rights;
   (c) will only acquire subrogation rights if the insured consents;
   (d) is illegal and therefore not subject to subrogation. **(20.16)**

(*For multiple choice answers, see page 355.*)

CHAPTER 21

CONTRIBUTION

A. GENERAL OBSERVATIONS

21.1 Meaning

Contribution is the doctrine which enables an insurer to call upon other insurers similarly (but not necessarily equally) liable to the same insured to share the cost of an indemnity payment. It arises where there is an "overlap" of insurances, so that an insured is covered more than once in respect of the same loss. (The MIA 1906, for instance refers to it as *double insurance*.)

21.2 A corollary of indemnity

Contribution, with subrogation (see Chapter 20), is one of the "twin corollaries of indemnity". It follows naturally from the parent principle, in that an insured would be more than indemnified if he could receive full compensation under more than one policy for the same loss.

It is important to understand the difference between contribution and subrogation. Subrogation is concerned with rights or recovery against third parties or elsewhere in respect of payment of an indemnity, and need not involve any other insurance, although it frequently does. Contribution necessarily involves more than one insurance, each covering the interest of the same insured.

21.3 Usually arises by accident rather than design

Since contribution is "double insurance", it seldom arises other than by chance. Indeed, if an insured deliberately arranged polices which duplicated cover, this might be indicative of an intent to defraud. However, because of desire for full insurance protection and the fact that many policies offer various extensions to their basic cover, contribution can arise in quite innocent circumstances. For example, a person might insure his camera under an "all risks" policy. If the camera is stolen from his car, there could be contribution with his comprehensive motor policy, which has a section covering personal effects stolen from the vehicle.

It is quite possible for double insurance to be arranged by mistake. It could happen that a husband and wife separately arranged insurance of jewellery he bought her, each not realising that the other had effected a policy. There would be no suggestion of fraud, but clearly any loss would not be paid twice, and contribution would exist between the two insurers.

21.4 Only applies to contracts of indemnity

Being a corollary of indemnity, contribution will only apply where indemnity applies. Thus, it will not normally apply to *life* and *personal accident* policies: see **19.2**.

A situation that may often occur is when airline travellers effect temporary personal accident insurance covering their death or injury in the event of an air crash. If they also hold ordinary personal accident (or life) policies, there is no contribution between the insurances in the event of a claim. The insured's estate is entitled to the full proceeds of each insurance.

21.5 Legal position

Common law demands that an insured should not make a profit from a loss by being over-compensated. Contribution, therefore, like indemnity and subrogation, has always been accepted as a fundamental legal principle of most insurances. A very important case, described in more detail in **21.13**, *North British & Mercantile* v. *London, Liverpool & Globe* (1877), confirmed the principle. During the course of the case, the following was said:

> Contribution exists where the thing is done by the same person against the same loss, and to prevent a man first of all recovering more than the whole loss, or, if he recovers the whole loss from one which he could have recovered from the other, then to make the parties contribute rateably. But that only applies where there is the same person insuring the same interest with more than one office.

B. THE OPERATION OF CONTRIBUTION

21.6 Essentials of contribution

Contribution only applies where the following conditions are fulfilled (see Fig. 15):

(a) Two or more policies of indemnity exist.
(b) Each must cover the same peril giving rise to the loss.
(c) Each must protect the same interest of the same insured.
(d) Each must relate to the same subject matter.

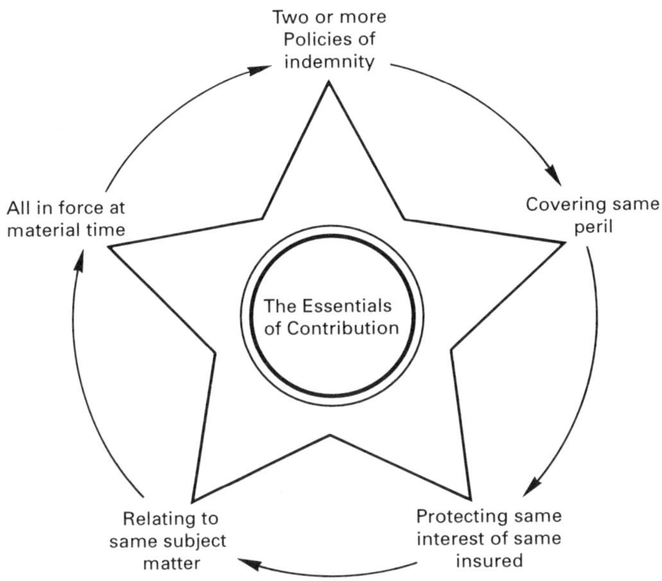

Fig. 15 The essentials of contribution

(e) Each must have been in force at the relative time (i.e. valid and not subject to a non-contribution clause: see **21.9**).

21.7 Basis of contribution

At the time of a claim, insurers usually inquire whether any other insurances exist covering the loss. Where other insurances do exist and each policy is subject to a valid claim, contribution will apply so that the respective insurers share the loss *rateably*. This term allows two constructions, both of which are found in insurance:

(a) *Contribution according to independent liability.* This means that the amount payable by each insurer is assessed as if the other insurances do not exist. If the aggregate of the amounts so calculated exceeds the loss, each insurer's contribution is scaled down proportionately, so that an indemnity is provided. This method is usually found where for some reason, e.g. pro rata average (see **31.8**), one or more of the policies will not cover the loss in full. This happens particularly in many fire policy contributions, or *apportionments*.

NOTE: Contribution on the basis of independent liability is becoming more widely accepted. In *Commercial Union* v. *Hayden* (1977), for instance, it was held that this should be the basis with liability policies where each policy states that the insurer should not be liable for more than its rateable share of each claim.

(b) *Contribution according to the sums insured.* This is another method of contribution. Insurers will pay proportionately to the cover they have provided, in accordance with the following formula:

$$\frac{\text{Sum insured with the particular insurer}}{\text{Total sums insured with all insurers}} \times \text{Loss}$$

EXAMPLE
Office "A" covers stock for £400,000
Office "B" covers stock for £200,000
By the above formula:

$$\text{Office “A” pays } \frac{£400{,}000}{£600{,}000} \times 120{,}000 = £\,80{,}000$$

$$\text{Office “B” pays } \frac{£200{,}000}{£600{,}000} \times 120{,}000 = £\,40{,}000$$

Total £120,000

C. MODIFICATIONS OF THE BASIC PRINCIPLE

21.8 Policy modification of common law

At common law, an insured entitled to recover under more than one policy can claim an indemnity from one insurer only, if he wishes. That insurer then has contribution rights against the other insurers, but he has to incur the trouble and expense of collecting the rateable proportions.

Marine policies do not amend this position, but other policies subject to contribution normally have a policy condition to the effect that, where contribution exists the insurer will never be liable for more than his rateable share of the loss. This means that if the insured wishes to obtain full indemnity, he must claim against all insurers for their respective shares of the loss.

NOTE: It is sometimes said that policy conditions require the insured to claim against all insurers, where contribution exists. Insurers do not insert such a condition in their policies. The condition merely says that the insurer is not liable for more than his rateable share. It is left to the insured to decide whether he will claim the balance from the other insurers.

21.9 Policy exclusion of contribution

It sometimes happens that policies will contain terms specifically intended to exclude the possibility of contribution. Examples are as follows:

(a) *More specific insurance.* Householder's policies, for instance, will not grant cover for articles more specifically insured. Thus, there would be no contribution between a householder's policy covering unspecified personal effects and an "all risks" policy specifically insuring, say, a particular camera.

The camera insurance is more specific, and therefore pays any claim for the camera. (Should the more specific insurance be inadequate, perhaps because of a limited sum insured, the householder's policy would probably provide any balance of cover required.)

(b) *Any other insurance.* Some policies will not operate if other insurances exist covering the same risk. An unusual situation arose in motor insurance, where two policies had a similar exclusion and the effect seemed to be that there was no cover at all. The situation is best seen in an example:

EXAMPLE: "A" has a motor policy, which covers him while driving other vehicles, *provided no other insurance exists.* "B" has a motor policy, which covers other drivers using the vehicle, *provided no other insurance exists.* "B" allows "A" to use his vehicle and an accident occurs. Both insurers deny liability on the cover under their respective policies, "B" was covered under none. The court, quite rightly, decided that such a situation was absurd, ordering each insurer to pay half the claim. Policy wordings have since been amended to prevent this situation recurring.

21.10 Inter-insurer agreements

Insurers have found that implementing contribution rights is not always satisfactory, for various reasons. Thus agreements have been made to modify application of the principle, e.g. the *common law agreement*, whereby an employer's liability insurer will not seek contribution from a motor insurer if both policies apply in respect of injuries to employees in or on motor vehicles.

Previously, legislation allowed motor insurers to exclude liability towards employees, and policies normally did that. This will no longer be permitted, in view of the Third EC Motor Insurance Directive (see **7.14**), so the common law agreement seems likely to have renewed application.

There is a market agreement between some insurers to avoid contribution between motor policies and (for example) "all risks" policies, with small claims. This avoids expense and complications over *no claim discounts.*

21.11 *Ex gratia* payments

Ex gratia payments (see **21.16**) are, in effect, gifts and would not give rise to contribution rights to the insurer. In practice, however, it is unlikely that an *ex gratia* payment would be made if some other insurance applied.

D. CONTRIBUTION NOT APPLICABLE WHERE DIFFERENT INTERESTS EXIST

21.12 Same loss can legally be paid twice

Where different interests are involved it is legally possible for different payments to be made in respect of the same loss. Such unusual circumstances arose in the following example:

EXAMPLE: A building society loaned money on the security of a building, which it insured against fire. The owner of the building effected a second mortgage with another building society, which also insured the property against fire. A fire occurred and the first building society was paid cash. It was held that the second building society was also entitled to claim a similar sum from its insurers. There was no contribution, since the interests were different (see **21.6**(c) above).

(This was a case where settlement by reinstatement, with both insurers paying towards the cost, would have been such more satisfactory (see **19.12**(d)).

21.13 The King and Queen granaries case

This was the name given to the case of *North British & Mercantile* v. *London, Liverpool & Globe* (1877) (see **21.5**). The case was a friendly action between offices which were seeking to clarify a point of law, i.e. to decide whether contribution applied or not. As has often proved the case, the legal definition of a principle was established in an action where the principle was held not to apply.

Briefly, the facts of this case were that a firm of merchants, named Rodocanachi, insured grain in the possession of a wharfinger, Barnett. Barnett had also insured the grain in accordance with trade custom, being grain for which he was responsible. Fire damaged the grain, and it was held that contribution would not apply as the interests involved were different. Subrogation arose instead, and the insurer of the wharfinger paid the whole loss.

NOTE: The decision in this case prompted an agreement among many fire insurers that for certain types of risk they would apply contribution in circumstances similar to the recorded case, even though different interests were involved. This agreement in no way prejudices the respective insureds' positions, but it does mean that no one insurer has to pay the whole loss in such circumstances.

21.14 An everyday example where different interests are involved

Motor insurance gives perhaps the commonest example of situations where contribution will not apply, even though two insurances cover the same loss.

EXAMPLES: Assume "A" has a comprehensive policy, which will cover, amongst other things, damage to the insured vehicle. "B" also has a motor policy, which includes cover for his liabilities to third parties. If "B" negligently damages "A"'s car, both policies will be involved with the damage sustained. However, there is no contribution between the policies as there are different interests involved. "A"'s interest in the damage is as owner of the vehicle, "B"'s interest in the damage is in his common law liability in causing it. (The principle involved therefore would be subrogation not contribution.)

E. DIFFERENT MEANING OF "CONTRIBUTION" IN INSURANCE

21.15 Normal English usage

The term "contribution" is sometimes used in insurance in the standard, non-technical, sense of a part-payment by the insured. For example, it may be that repairs to a car will leave the vehicle in a better condition than before the accident occurs. New replacement tyres, batteries, and complete paint resprays might well have this effect. In such circumstances it is customary to require the insured to contribute towards the betterment involved with the repair/replacements.

In this sense, the payment by the insured is connected with indemnity rather than the technical principle of contribution.

F. PROGRESS TEST 21

PART 1—SHORT ANSWERS (Answer in one or two sentences)

1. How is the principle of contribution connected with indemnity? **(21.1–21.2)**
2. In what circumstances does the right to contribution arise? **(21.6)**
3. (a) What is the usual method of assessing the amount of contribution to be paid by respective insurers?
   (b) What amounts are payable by the respective insurers in the following circumstances:
   Office "A" insures the premises for £100,000
   Office "B" insures the premises for £50,000
   A loss of £15,000 occurs. (Ignore any under-insurance.) **(21.7)**
4. How may policies modify the common law with contribution? **(21.8)**
5. A motorist negligently causes his car to crash through a shop window. The shopkeeper has a plate glass insurance which covers the damage. State, with reasons, whether contribution would arise between the glass and motor insurers. **(21.13–21.14)**

PART 2—MULTIPLE CHOICE (Choose the most correct option)

1. The principle of contribution:
   (a) is a corollary of the principle of indemnity;
   (b) has no relationship with the principle of indemnity;
   (c) is where the insured and a third party policy each cover a loss;
   (d) relates to situations involving under-insurance. **(21.2)**
2. If the principle of indemnity does not apply:
   (a) the principle of contribution will also not apply;

(b) the principle of contribution may still apply;
(c) insurers may agree to waive contribution;
(d) contribution will always be on a 50/50 basis. **(21.4)**

3. Contribution according to independent liability means that:
(a) no contribution will in fact take place;
(b) calculations are based upon aggregate sums insured;
(c) separate legal actions will be needed to determine liabilities;
(d) initial calculations are made ignoring other insurances. **(21.7)**

4. Policy conditions relating to the principle of contribution:
(a) never exclude contribution altogether;
(b) usually insist upon 50/50 settlements;
(c) often limit liability to a "rateable share";
(d) never modify the common law position. **(21.9)**

5. The term "contribution" in insurance:
(a) sometimes does not relate to two insurers sharing a loss;
(b) always relates to two insurers sharing a loss;
(c) has the same meaning as "subrogation";
(d) means that the policy bears an excess. **(21.15)**

(For multiple choice answers, see page 355.)

CHAPTER 22

PROXIMATE CAUSE

A. GENERAL OBSERVATIONS

22.1 Meaning

The classic definition of proximate cause was given in *Pawsey* v. *Scottish Union & National* (1908):

> Proximate cause means the active, efficient cause that sets in motion a train of events which brings about a result, without the intervention of any force started and working actively from a new and independent source.

Examination students would do well to memorise this definition, as it can always be used with relevance in the answer to any question on this topic.

22.2 The need to discover the cause of loss

It is obvious that the cause of loss must be reasonably established before insurers are considered liable. A peril of some kind will have caused the loss, but not all perils are insured. In fact, there are three basic types of peril:

(a) *Insured perils.* These are plainly understood, such as fire under a fire policy and burglary under a theft policy.
(b) *Excepted perils.* These are perils which are specifically excluded from the insurance cover, either because they are not practicable to insure at all or because they cannot be insured at the premium applicable to the policy. Examples are suicide under a personal accident policy, or spontaneous combustion under a standard fire policy.
(c) *Uninsured perils.* These are perils which are not mentioned in the policy document and are outside the scope of cover, such as fire damage under a theft policy and death from natural causes under a personal accident policy.

22.3 The effective cause must be regarded

There may be a number of causes, of greater or lesser importance, which have combined to produce a certain result. As has been said, however, "the law cannot concern itself with trifles", which means that the dominant, effective cause must be singled out and regarded as the one which produced the result. The legal maxim is *cause proxima non remota spectator* (the immediate, or *proximate*, not the remote, cause must be regarded).

The insurer is not liable for any loss unless the proximate cause was an insured peril.

B. LEGAL CONSIDERATIONS

22.4 General

In theory, the doctrine of proximate cause is very straightforward. The loss must arise directly from an insured peril, or be the result of a direct chain of events initiated by an insured peril. In practice, most claims are quite clearly covered or not covered, because the proximate cause is very evident. However, the chain of events giving rise to a loss can be complicated by the occurrence of excepted or uninsured perils. In such circumstances determining whether or to what extent the insurer is liable can become difficult.

The general rules of interpretation are studied in **22.10–22.16**.

22.5 Proximate in efficiency, not time

The term *proximate* comes from the Latin root meaning "next" or "nearest". However, the proximate cause of loss is that cause which is nearest in effectiveness, not necessarily in time. This point was illustrated in the case of *Leyland Shipping Co. Ltd* v. *Norwich Union Fire Insurance Co. Ltd* (1918), when a ship belonging to the plaintiffs was sunk during a storm some time after being damaged by a torpedo. It was held that the torpedo (a war risk, which was excluded) was the proximate cause of the loss, and not the storm. The following words from the judgment should be noted:

> to treat proximate cause as if it was the cause which is proximate in time is out of the question. The cause which is truly proximate is that which is proximate in efficiency.

22.6 Common sense standards to be applied

As with many aspects of the law, the determination of proximate cause is based upon the standards of the reasonable man. Thus, although a scientist or a theologian might advance different arguments in determining proximate cause, the legal standards were outlined in *Yorkshire Dale S.S. Co.* v. *Minister of War Transport* (1942): the

> choice of the real or efficient cause ... must be made by applying commonsense standards. Causation is to be understood as the man in the street, and not as either the scientist or the metaphysician, would understand it.

22.7 Practical complexities

The sophistication of the law and the practical difficulties sometimes encountered in determining proximate cause can be seen in the following two similar cases:

(a) *Johnston* v. *West of Scotland Insurance Co.* (1828). A fire left a wall in a dangerous state and the local authority ordered the wall to be demolished. Before this order was carried out, the wall collapsed on neighbouring property. It was held that the damage to the neighbouring property was proximately caused by fire.

(b) *Gaskarth* v. *Law Union* (1876). Again, a fire left a wall standing in a dangerous state. Some days later, a gale caused the wall to fall and damage other property. It was held that fire was only the remote cause; the proximate cause was the failure of the owner to demolish or support the wall. (In other words, a new intervening cause occurred, breaking the direct chain of events.)

22.8 Another example

A further case which illustrates the importance of determining the proximate cause of loss is *Marsden* v. *City & County Assurance Co.* (1865). This involved a plate glass insurance which covered breakages from any cause *except* fire. A fire broke out in a neighbouring building and a mob broke the plate glass of the insured's premises to carry out looting. It was held that the insurers were not entitled to avoid liability, as fire was only the remote cause of the damage. The proximate cause was the unlawful action of the mob.

22.9 Additional losses reasonably incurred

It frequently happens that the occurrence of an insured peril results not only in financial loss as a direct result of the peril, but also in respect of additional expenditure or consequential loss. For example, a fire may well result in loss of profits for a business while the premises are out of action during reinstatement, or a motorist may need to hire another vehicle while his car is being repaired after an accident. Unless the policy has specifically been extended to cover this contingency, such consequential loss is normally excluded.

Some types of additional losses, necessarily resulting or reasonably incurred from an insured peril, however, are covered. Some common examples are:

(a) *Fire-fighting damage.* Water used in extinguishing fires sometimes causes as much damage as the actual flames. Also, firemen and others on occasions have to cause damage, such as the destruction of windows, etc., to get at the fire or to check its progress. All such damage is considered to be within the cover of the fire policy.
(b) *Damage caused by thieves.* In addition to the items stolen, damage to the premises caused by theft or attempted theft is normally covered by policies covering theft risks.
(c) *Legal costs* incurred in dealing with third party claims are normally covered in addition to any damages awarded in all types of liability insurance.

C. GENERAL RULES OF APPLICATION (See Fig. 16)

22.10 Single cause

Where a loss occurs as the result of a single cause, such as a roof being damaged by lightning, proximate cause presents no problems. Either the damage is covered by the policy or it is not (i.e. whether lightning is an insured peril is easily ascertained from the policy).

22.11 Chain of events

It frequently happens that a loss arises following or during a chain of events rather than from a single cause. The application of proximate cause can be complicated in such cases, which basically consist of two distinct types:

(a) *Unbroken sequence.* This means that each event is caused by and necessarily follows from the previous one.
(b) *Broken sequence.* This arises where a new and independent cause intervenes, so that the end result is not the inevitable consequence of the first event.

Both types are considered below.

22.12 Unbroken sequence, no excepted peril involved

Where a chain of events is in unbroken sequence and contains an insured peril but no excepted peril (see **22.2**), all losses caused by and following the insured peril are recoverable.

A case which particularly illustrates this type of situation was *Re Etherington*

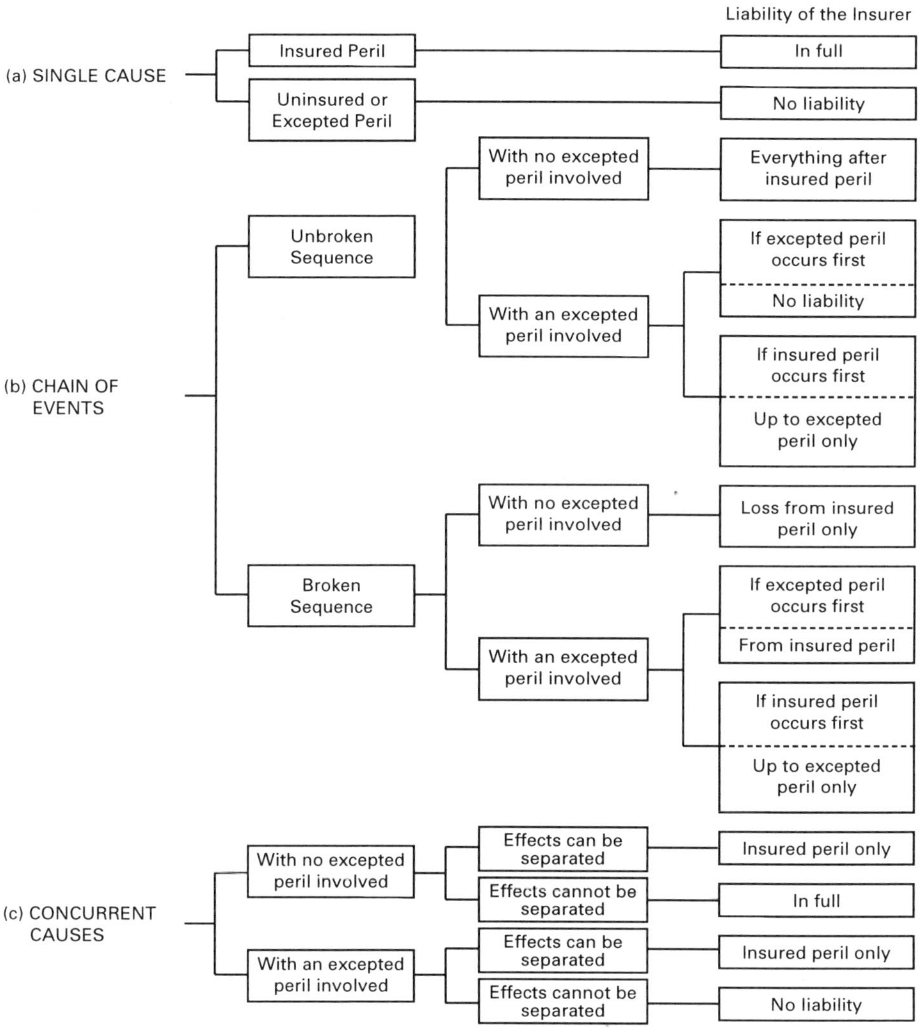

Fig. 16 The application of proximate cause

and the Lancashire & Yorkshire Accident Insurance Co. (1909). This case involved a policy which provided a death benefit for accidents, but not for sickness. The insured fell heavily from his horse, and although he was not badly injured physically, he suffered from shock and a severe wetting, which resulted in his contracting pneumonia, which caused his death. Being an illness, pneumonia was merely an *uninsured peril*, but since the proximate cause of the death was the original accident, the insurers were held liable to pay under their policy. The following comments made in the case make the position very clear:

There is no pretence for treating the death as less due to the injury because one step in the train of circumstances which followed was that the insured caught cold.

22.13 Unbroken sequence, with excepted peril involved

Where an excepted peril occurs in an unbroken chain of events, the insurer's liability will depend on whether the excepted peril occurred before or after the insured peril:

(a) *Where an excepted peril precedes an insured peril.* Any natural consequences of an excepted peril, even if they include an insured peril, are outside the scope of the policy. Thus, in *Tootal Broadhurst Lee Co.* v. *London & Lancashire Fire Insurance Co.* (1908), the insurers were successful in maintaining that a fire which was started in another building by earthquake (an excepted peril under their policy) and spread to their insured's premises by natural means did not involve them in liability towards their insured.

(b) *Where an excepted peril follows an insured peril.* Where this arises and the damage from insured and excepted perils can be distinguished, the insurer is liable for the damage caused by and following the insured peril, up to the happening of the excepted peril, only. Thus a fire policy which excludes explosion would pay for any fire damage but not for any concussion damage in any explosion the fire might cause. Theoretically, if the damage caused by insured and uninsured perils cannot be distinguished, the insurers are not liable at all. However, in practice, a compromise settlement would always be made.

22.14 Broken sequence, no excepted peril involved

Where no excepted peril is involved and a chain of events takes place, but not as an inevitable result of each other, the insurer will only be liable for losses arising directly from the insured peril.

EXAMPLE: A personal accident policy, which does not include any sickness cover. If the insured is injured by an accident, but dies from a disease which is contracted quite independently of the injury during his period of convalescence, the insurer is not liable to pay the death benefit. Death from disease is an uninsured peril, which was not proximately caused by an insured peril. The insurer is only liable for any weekly benefit, payable up to the time of death.

22.15 Broken sequence, with excepted peril involved

Where a chain of events is interrupted by a new and independent cause, and one of the events is an excepted peril, the insurer's position depends on when the excepted peril occurred:

(a) *Where an excepted peril precedes an insured peril.* If an insured peril, as an independent cause, breaks a chain of events started by an excepted peril, the insurer is liable. This was precisely the position in *Marsden* v. *City & County Assurance Co.* (1866) (see **22.8**).
(b) *Where an excepted peril follows an insured peril.* Where an excepted peril intervenes, as an independent cause, the insurer is liable only up to the time of the intervention.

In the example quoted in **22.14**, if the insured had committed suicide (which would have been an excepted peril), the insurer would only be liable for the weekly benefits up to the time of death.

22.16 Concurrent causes

It sometimes happens that two or more causes operate at the same time (concurrently) to produce a result. The procedure for determining the insurer's liability in such cases is as follows:

(a) *If no excepted peril is involved.* Strictly the insurer is only liable for losses from an insured peril, but where the effects of insured and uninsured perils cannot be separated, the insurer is liable in full.
(b) *Where an excepted peril is involved.* If the effects of insured and excepted perils can be separated, there will be liability for the former but not the latter. If the effects cannot be separated, the insurer is not liable at all.

NOTE: Where complicated cases such as the above arise, the strict legal position is seldom invoked. Normally, such cases are resolved by a compromise settlement, and usually insurers will try to give a generous interpretation of the facts.

D. AMENDMENT OF THE POSITION BY POLICY CONDITION

22.17 General

As with most basic principles applicable to insurance, it is quite possible for the common law position to be modified by policy conditions, provided the contract remains legal. Two examples where the doctrine of proximate causes are modified are considered below.

22.18 Standard fire policy

Under the old standard fire policy (still used in some overseas jurisdictions), the contract is so worded that proximate cause is modified in respect of losses following explosion. This is seen as follows:

22.18 Proximate Cause

(a) Fire damage is covered *whether resulting from explosion or not*. Thus, even though the proximate cause may be explosion, the policy exclusion relating to explosion is overridden in respect of subsequent fire.

(b) Most types of explosion damage are excluded *whether resulting from fire or otherwise*. This means that the intention to exclude all explosion damage is preserved, even though the insured peril of fire was the proximate cause.

22.19 Exclusions "directly or indirectly arising from . . ."

Where a policy exclusion is worded in very wide terms, such as "directly or indirectly arising or resulting from", or "proximately or remotely connected with", the legal view is that such an exclusion profoundly affects proximate cause.

In *Coxe* v. *Employers' Liability Assurance Corporation* (1916) a serviceman was accidentally killed by a train during the course of his military duties. His personal accident policy excluded death "directly or indirectly caused by, arising from, or traceable to ... war". Because of blackout regulations and other factors, including the fact that the insured was at the place during the course of military duties, it was held that death was indirectly the result of war. The train was undoubtedly the proximate cause of the loss, but proximate cause had been modified by the wide wording of the exclusion.

NOTE: It is rare to find exclusions so widely worded in the United Kingdom today. With increasing consumer awareness, the judiciary and Insurance Ombudsman (see **30.27**) tend to be very critical of such restrictions. The phrase "directly or indirectly" does still appear in some personal accident policy exclusions. However, the extent to which an insurer would seek to apply this seems doubtful.

E. PROGRESS TEST 22

PART 1—SHORT ANSWERS (Answer in one or two sentences)

1. Define proximate cause. **(22.1)**
2. Why is it necessary to discover the proximate cause of a loss? **(22.2)**
3. "Proximate cause is proximate in efficiency, not necessarily in time." Explain this statement. **(22.5)**
4. A motorist has personal accident insurance covering death from accident but not disease. He crashes on an isolated road in icy weather, and although only slightly hurt he is trapped in the wrecked car. Owing to the weather conditions he contracts pneumonia, from which he later dies. Is there a valid claim under his personal accident policy? Give your reasons. **(22.12)**

5. How is proximate cause applied where concurrent causes result in a loss? **(22.16)**

PART 2—MULTIPLE CHOICE (Choose the most correct option)

1. The doctrine of proximate cause:
   (a) determines whether a particular risk is insurable;
   (b) determines whether or not the insured has committed fraud;
   (c) is trying to find out the primary reason for a loss;
   (d) is trying to discover the final cause of a loss. **(22.1–22.3)**
2. An excepted peril, in the context of proximate cause:
   (a) can never be deleted and therefore covered by the policy;
   (b) means the same as an uninsured peril;
   (c) has a different meaning from an uninsured peril;
   (d) is one which is specifically insured by the policy. **(22.2)**
3. The proximate cause for a given loss:
   (a) is not necessarily the cause immediately before the loss arises;
   (b) is always the cause nearest the loss in time;
   (c) may only have an indirect bearing upon the loss;
   (d) must not arise from an excepted peril. **(22.5)**
4. In the context of proximate cause, an unbroken chain of events means:
   (a) the last cause will always be considered the proximate one;
   (b) the first cause will always be considered the proximate one;
   (c) the final result will always be insured by the policy;
   (d) the final result will never be insured by the policy. **(22.11)**
5. The common law rules for the application of proximate cause:
   (a) are sometimes varied by policy conditions;
   (b) are never varied by policy conditions;
   (c) will not always require an insured peril;
   (d) will ignore any uninsured perils. **(22.18)**

(*For multiple choice answers, see page 355.*)

CHAPTER 23

INSURANCE AND WAGERING

A. INSURANCE AND WAGERING IN THE PAST

23.1 Historical position in the United Kingdom

There is no doubt that for the past 200 years or so the public view of gambling was that it was a social evil that was not to be encouraged. This view was scarcely shared by perhaps the majority in private, since betting and wagering have always held an attraction for human nature. Publicly, however, gambling contracts at least were not to be given recognition at law (see the Gaming Act 1845, **17.8**). Specifically in insurance, gambling or gaming contracts were rendered void by legislation (see for example the Life Assurance Act 1774 (see **17.6**) and the Marine Insurance (Gambling Policies) Act 1909: see **17.9**).

23.2 The more modern view

Without making a heavy social comment on the development, it is now quite evident that society in the United Kingdom is much more willing to perceive gambling as part of the acceptable social scene. Perfectly legal betting shops abound in high streets and the national lottery was welcomed with fervour by millions in 1994. In this environment it could be that this chapter has become redundant over the years. However, the legislation mentioned above is still extant and there is little evidence that the United Kingdom is ready to return to the "anything goes" attitude with speculation under the guise of insurance (see **17.4**).

B. SIMILARITIES BETWEEN INSURANCE AND GAMBLING

23.3 General

Despite the remarks immediately above, it is probably true that the majority of the population, who are generally not well versed in the basic principles of insurance, consider that there is very little if any difference between insurance and gambling. Certainly, it is frequently found in practice that the general public neither understands nor immediately accepts the legal principles on which insurance is based.

Whatever the professional insurance purist might say, it would be quite unrealistic to suggest that there are no similarities between, say, the bookmaker and the insurer. Some similarities are shown below.

23.4 Both assess risks

The bookmaker and the insurer will both calculate the possibilities of a certain event occurring and will indicate a certain rate at which they will be prepared to assume the risk. With the bookmaker, this rate is the "odds" quoted. With the insurer, it is the premium.

23.5 Both seek to minimise heavy individual losses

Neither the bookmaker nor the insurer wishes to incur heavy losses with individual transactions. Both seek to "spread the risk" of potentially heavy commitments.

The bookmaker does this by "laying off" part of the bet with other bookmakers (i.e. he wagers in the same way as his client, but for a lower sum, so that if his original wager is lost he will recoup at least some of his outlay). In principle, the insurer does exactly the same thing when he insures again (or reinsures, see Chapter 33) with other insurers part of the risk he has assumed.

C. DIFFERENCES BETWEEN INSURANCE AND GAMBLING

23.6 General

If only from the evidence of the previous chapters in this section, it should be obvious that there are several very important differences between insurance and wagering. Some of these differences are considered below.

23.7 Insurance contracts are legally enforceable

Insurance contracts are legally binding agreements that can be enforced through the courts if necessary (see **16.1**), whereas most wagers are destitute of legal effect, and unenforceable (see **17.8**).

23.8 Insurance requires insurable interest

With insurance contracts the insured or prospective insured must possess an insurable interest (see **17.2**). This is not necessary with a wager.

NOTE: Another way of expressing the above point is to say that insurance covers an existing risk whereas wagering in fact creates the risk.

23.9 Insurance requires utmost good faith

Both parties to an insurance contract must exercise utmost good faith (see **18.2–18.4**). Neither party in a wager need disclose any material information he possesses about the proposed agreement. Indeed, in the majority of bets if one party has secret information of importance about the proposed bet, he will almost certainly not reveal it.

23.10 Many insurances are subject to indemnity

All insurances, except most life and personal accident policies, are subject to indemnity. This restricts the amount recoverable to the exact financial consequences of an insured event (see **19.1**). With a wager, the winner will certainly make a profit on the transaction.

Insurances subject to indemnity are also subject to subrogation and contribution, where these principles may arise (see Chapters 20–21). Wagers are not.

23.11 Most insured events are only possibilities

With the exception of most life policies, insurance contracts are intended to deal with events which are possibilities and not certainties (see **2.7**). Wagers on the other hand normally involve a definite future event, such as a horse race.

23.12 Most insured events are not desired by either party

With the possible exception of the maturity of life endowment policies (see **4.19**), neither the insured nor the insurer desires the occurrence of an insured event. With wagers, the loser may change his mind later, but initially both parties want the event to take place.

23.13 Most insurances can involve degrees of loss

With many insurance contracts, claims can involve varying degrees of loss. (A motor policy, for example, can be the subject of a claim for minor damage, or for hundreds of thousands of pounds' worth of liabilities.) With wagers, the amount payable to the winner is normally known in advance.

23.14 Insurance is encouraged by the State

Insurance has the general approval of society. This may be seen as follows:

(a) *Compulsory insurances.* Although the State has not intervened in the affairs of insurers to any great extent, a measure of compulsory insurance has been introduced, for example, with motor and national insurance.

(b) *Certain tax concessions.* The premiums for most insurances effected by commercial firms are considered legitimate business expenses and thus allowable against profits for tax purposes. Policyholders of life assurances effected before March 1984 are usually entitled to some tax relief on premiums.

Wagering is not made compulsory or encouraged by similar concessions. Indeed, the heavy taxation on betting was partly imposed as a deterrent. It has to be conceded, however, that the argument of State disapproval is much less valid today.

23.15 Insurance losses do not involve the return of premium

If an insured event occurs, the insured in due course receives any money due under the policy, but he is not thereby entitled to the return of his premium. In wagering, the equivalent of the insurance premium would be the stake money, which if he wins is often returned to the one who bets, in addition to the prize money.

23.16 Insurance and immunity from loss

If it is accepted that the payment of an insurance premium is not a loss, in the sense that it is a contribution to a central fund, two further differences between insurance and wagering appear:

(a) *One party is immune from loss.* Provided the insurance is properly arranged, only the insurer can lose if the insured event happens. Either party may win or lose a wager.

(b) *It is known who is immune from loss.* Again, with properly arranged insurance, it is known from the outset that the insured cannot lose. The winner or loser of a wager can only be ascertained after the event occurs.

NOTE: If it is insisted that an insurance premium and wagering stake money are essentially the same, as in **23.2**, this last argument is not valid. Further, it must again be said that the "high moral" stand differentiating insurance and wagering may well appear "quaint" in the present state of public opinion (compare the changes in *public policy – see* **2.10**).

D. PROGRESS TEST 23

NOTE: this topic is hardly of sufficient weight to merit a full progress test, but the following questions and exercises might usefully be attempted:

1. What similarities are there between insurance and wagering? **(23.4–23.5)**
2. "After all, insurers are only more respectable bookmakers!" Discuss this statement. **(23)**

PART FOUR: OBJECTIVE TESTS (see Answers, page 356) and ASSIGNMENTS

4.1 State whether the following statements are *true* or *false*:
   (a) All insurance contracts must be evidenced in writing.
   (b) You cannot effect any insurance before you have an insurable interest.
   (c) A personal contract is one where assignment of the policy is subject to the insurer's agreement.
   (d) At common law material information must be revealed whether asked for or not.
   (e) A breach of an insurance warranty must be relevant to the circumstances of a claim before insurers can deny liability.
   (f) Indemnity never applies to insurance of the person.
   (g) In subrogation an insurer must always claim under the name of the insured.
   (h) Contribution would apply to an indemnity contract whether the policy contained such a condition or not.
   (i) Where concurrent causes produce a loss and only one cause is insured the insurer does not have to pay anything.
   (j) A major difference between insurance and wagering is that the latter is always illegal.

4.2 Select the *most correct* answer for the following:
   (a) A void insurance contract (i) is one that is illegal; (ii) is of no effect legally; (iii) is one lacking insurable interest.
   (b) It is perfectly legal to insure another person's life (i) as long as one has an insurable interest at policy inception; (ii) as long as one loses financially at the time of their death; (iii) provided the other person agrees.
   (c) A policy proof of interest (PPI) policy is called an honour policy because (i) it is based on utmost good faith; (ii) payment is dependent upon the honour of the insurer; (iii) genuine claims will be honoured by insurance companies.
   (d) Insurance contracts are subject to utmost good faith because (i) there would not otherwise be adequate protection for insurers; (ii) each party must agree to the proposed insurance; (iii) it is not possible to learn all information unless the other party reveals it.
   (e) A breach of utmost good faith (i) invalidates the insurance; (ii) renders the policy voidable by the aggrieved party; (iii) renders the policy void and the premium forfeit.
   (f) Reinstatement of the sum insured (i) is not necessary with all types of policies; (ii) is compulsory with fire policies; (iii) is needed only when a total loss payment has been made.
   (g) The common law principle of subrogation is sometimes modified by policy condition (i) in life policies; (ii) by inter-company agreement; (iii) to acquire subrogation rights before payment.

(h) Contribution is a common law principle (i) which arises as a corollary of indemnity; (ii) which seeks to ensure that insurers are aware of double insurance; (iii) requiring a policyholder to pay towards a loss for which he is under-insured.

(i) When determining proximate cause the difference between an uninsured peril and an excepted peril (i) is not very important; (ii) is not important if the loss was caused by a single peril; (iii) is that the insurers may sometimes pay for the latter.

(j) An insurer is unlike a bookmaker when (i) he arranges reinsurance; (ii) he calculates the probabilities of having to make a payment; (iii) he refuses payment in respect of a breach of utmost good faith.

4.3 Assignments:

(a) Write an essay on the basic legal principles behind insurance, with reasons for their existence and examples of how the common law position is often modified in practice.

(b) Discuss the suggestion that people should be free to arrange such contracts as both parties will agree to, without the law raising "complications", and that insurable interest and indemnity, for example, are therefore a restriction on personal liberty.

(c) Research local insurers and brokers and draft a report on the way the insurance market (i) is prepared to grant more than indemnity; (ii) copes with the effect of inflation on sums insured; (iii) calculates allowances for wear and tear or depreciation with strict indemnity settlements.

PART FIVE

INSURANCE IN PRACTICE

CHAPTER 24

UNDERWRITING

A. SOME BASIC OBSERVATIONS

24.1 "Underwriter" and "underwriting"

We previously studied these terms in the context of marine insurance (see **3.5**). Underwriting may be defined briefly as the process of assessing risks and deciding the terms on which they may be insurable, or not as the case may be. The underwriter in most modern usages of the term is the person carrying out that process on behalf of the insurer.

24.2 Ancient and modern applications

In the early days, before the benefit of accumulated experience, the underwriter had great personal input as to the insurability or individual terms of a proposed insurance contract. As such, a broker for instance could exercise considerable influence in the outcome of his client's application, in knowing who to approach and how to make representations.

There is still truth in the remark that insurance is a "people business", so personal contacts can be very important, especially at executive level. But it has to be said that the vast accumulation of experience and the sophisticated equipment now available to process data have produced *underwriting guides* and *rating manuals* giving comprehensive instructions to staff on all normal risk applications. As a consequence, for the great majority of individual insurance proposals the underwriting is relatively simple, often delegated to quite junior staff.

24.3 An obsolete process?

From the above it must not be assumed that underwriting was a process that was necessary in the past, but that the job has been done definitively. Change, trends and new developments are always with us. There is also the ever-present "threat" of competitors. It is therefore impossible to conclude that underwriting guides are immutable. Moreover, there will always be large numbers of risks which do not conform to the standard perceptions envisaged by rating manuals and the like. The day of the technical underwriter is far from over.

24.4 An "art" or a "science"?

Argument has raged over perhaps centuries whether insurance underwriters are "born not made". The truth probably is that underwriting is both an "art" and a "science". Individual, sometimes difficult to explain, personal inclinations of the underwriter (colloquially referred to as "gut-feelings" or "hunches"), often based on long and wide experience, still have a part to play in the overall picture. The use of statistical analysis and professional instruction, however, has at least as important a role.

24.5 "Risk prone" or "risk averse"?

These are American terms which succinctly express possible underwriting attitudes. The former relates to the adventurous, entrepreneurial attitude (well expressed by a famous British underwriter at Lloyd's as the "why not?" approach). The latter implies a very conservative and reluctant approach, especially with any unusual or new risks.

It would be impertinent to suggest which is the correct approach. In the United Kingdom there is a free market, allowing insurers and underwriters to form their own criteria and attitudes. Since insurance exists to give confidence and stability, there is a case for treating the unusual with caution. On the other hand, insurance is there to offer cover for risk and if the underwriter always says "no", he and his colleagues will soon be out of a job!

B. STEPS IN UNDERWRITING

24.6 In general

While individual types of insurance will call for very different underwriting expertise, the basic concepts are the same throughout insurance. Although perhaps simplistic, the process may be summarised as consisting of two basic questions:

(a) *Is the risk insurable at all?* If the answer is "no", we need not ask the second question.
(b) *On what terms is it to be insured?* There can be no simple answer to this. Rather, we may think of various questions the underwriter will consciously or subconsciously ask himself (or herself). These will include those considered below.

24.7 What premium should be charged?

The possible options available to the underwriter in deciding a premium include:

(a) *Standard (or book or manual) premium.* This is self-explanatory, referring to the normal premium charged for this type and class of risk.
(b) *Higher than standard premium.* This is sometimes called *premium loading*, and will occur when the proposed risk presents extra hazard or where "hard market" (see **15.2**) conditions prevail, allowing an upward adjustment of rates generally.
(c) *Lower than standard premium.* These may have to be given generally in "soft market" conditions (see **15.2**). Alternatively, the specific risk proposed may have especially low hazard features, or emanate from an important "connection" (usually an insured or broker offering large amounts of business).
(d) *Individually rated risk.* Some risks, owing to their novelty, size or complexity, require individual premium assessment. It is here that the skill and "inspired guesswork" of the professional underwriter is particularly valuable.

NOTE: In many cases the underwriter will be asked to quote a *premium rate* rather than a specified amount. This is usually on a "per cent" (per £100) or per mille (per £1,000) of the sum insured. For further consideration of premiums, see Chapter 28.

24.8 What other contract terms should apply?

Contrary to wide public opinion and the apparent sole criterion of mass marketing, the premium is not the only factor to be taken into account with an insurance. It may be ponderous and a cliché to say so, but the old saying that "you tend to get what you pay for" is still worth remembering by the insuring public. From the more professional approach of the underwriter, a risk needs rather more sophistication than the price alone, whatever marketing pressures may arise. As far as the policy terms are concerned, the main options for the underwriter will be:

(a) *Standard policy wordings.* With the abolition of tariffs (see **15.20**) and the absence of government prescribed wordings (in the United Kingdom) there is great flexibility in the provision of contract terms. However, companies normally have standard policy wordings which will apply to all normal risks of the type concerned.
(b) *Modification of standard wordings.* Because of particular features, an underwriter may insist upon additional clauses or warranties (see **18.16**) to limit or otherwise modify the standard cover. These will be added to any standard policy wording by means of *endorsements* (see **27.24**).

(c) *Individual contract terms.* Just as the premium may have to be individually calculated, so the precise terms of the contract may have to be individually "tailored" to the needs of the insured, especially with very large or complicated risks (e.g. airport construction).

24.9 What proportion of the risk to accept?

The *capacity* of an insurer (see **15.12–15.13**) will depend upon several factors, including the financial strength of the insurer himself, the attitude towards risks (see **24.5** above) and the availability of reinsurance. Considering all these and perhaps other factors, an underwriter will have the following options for risks that he does not reject:

(a) *Accept the risk fully.* This is self-explanatory, indicating that the whole risk is "assumed", although it may in some measure be reinsured.

(b) *Accept only part of the risk.* It may be that a risk is of such magnitude that a total loss possibility would present an undue strain on the insurer's resources. If reinsurance for whatever reason is not the answer, the underwriter may offer to accept only part of the risk. This is quite normal practice at Lloyd's (see **12.9**). Where it occurs elsewhere (and indeed with the Lloyd's practice) this gives rise to *co-insurance* by more than one direct insurer (see **32.21**).

24.10 EML (or PML) considerations?

Especially bearing in mind reinsurance arrangements, an underwriter considering property insurance risks will usually consider the *estimated maximum loss* or *probable maximum loss* (EML/PML). This is a sophisticated process whereby the reinsurance arrangements will be made on the assumption that a total loss is for practical purposes impossible (unless the EML/PML is 100 per cent). The calculation of this is rather complex and not without controversy, but for the moment we should note that the percentage EML/PML could influence the underwriter in deciding the amount of risk he is prepared to assume.

C. FEATURES TO BE CONSIDERED BY THE UNDERWRITER

24.11 General

Primarily, the underwriter must make a technical assessment of the merits of the risk and make his professional recommendations or decisions accordingly. As with all commercial enterprise, however, he will not "operate in a vacuum". That is, he will not be able to ignore other factors which may even have a decisive influence on the final decision. Technical and some other features we consider below.

24.12 "Technical" features

These may be described as the "intrinsic merits" of the risk from the professional insurer's standpoint. To arrive at a decision on these features the underwriter will consider:

(a) *the physical features*: these will relate to the objective dangers and likelihood of a claim arising and/or the extent of such a claim from the very nature of the subject matter and objective features related thereto (more usually referred to as the *physical hazard*);

(b) *the human element*: this relates to the lifestyle, attitudes and behavioural patterns of the insured or other people likely to affect or be associated with the risk (more usually referred to as the *moral hazard*).

NOTE: Physical hazard and moral hazard are studied in more detail in the next chapter (Chapter 25).

24.13 Other possible features

Other features which could have an influence upon the underwriter's judgement include the following:

(a) *state of the market*: the existence of "hard" or "soft" market conditions (see **15.2**) is clearly likely to suggest an appropriate reaction from the underwriter when considering new or renewal business;

(b) *company strategy*: the current philosophy and instructions from senior management cannot be ignored. If the declared aims are for expansion and increase in market share for the business concerned, clearly an underwriter may have to be more accommodating. If opposite philosophies pertain, of course he/she will react accordingly;

(c) *important "connections"*: clearly, well-connected people or risks representing considerable financial "clout" (influence) are unlikely to be treated in a completely objective manner;

(d) *personal goals*: senior underwriters will probably have considerable autonomy in their decision-making. They may well also be given "targets" to achieve in a given time period. Towards the end of a "target period" decisions seem certain to be influenced if achievements to date are behind schedule;

(e) *reinsurance*: the availability of quality reinsurance is bound to have an important influence, especially when considering large or hazardous risks. The absence of such reinsurance could mean that risks are declined, or less than total acceptances of business offered.

D. UNDERWRITING REMEDIES

24.14 Sub-standard risks

Applications for insurance will not always present ideal or even normal risks. Additionally, there may be market or other considerations to bear in mind when making an underwriting decision (see above). However, not all sub-standard, or below-average, risks need to be declined or refused by the underwriter. An American expression is that judicious underwriting measures might "normalize" a sub-standard application, or at least make it insurable.

The field of underwriting in the various classes of insurance is too wide to consider every line of business, but the arsenal of "weapons" available to the underwriter in reacting to sub-standard risks will include the options shown below.

24.15 Extreme options

The two extremes in the underwriter's reaction to sub-standard risks are as follows:

(a) *Declinature*: clearly some risks will be unacceptable for insurance under any terms. An example might be a high-powered sports car owned by an irresponsible young person, for motor insurance.
(b) *Normal acceptance*: this ignores the "defect" and provides standard terms. Such might arise, for instance, if commercial reasons (e.g. large "connection", or very soft market conditions) prevail.

24.16 Other options

In between the two extremes a number of other possibilities arise. It should also be remembered that more than one of the following could be possible in a given case. The other options (with just one example for each) would include:

(a) *premium loading*: a heavily overweight person might be charged a higher premium in life assurance;
(b) *a policy excess or deductible* (see **19.6**) (this would be additional to any standard excess in that class of business, and to any voluntary excess requested by the insured): a motorist having a series of small claims might merit this penalty;
(c) *a policy franchise* (see **19.6**): several small losses with an "all risks" policy might warrant the imposition of such a provision, perhaps at policy renewal;
(d) *a policy warranty* (see **18.16**): an example could be that in time of international tensions a marine policy covering war risks could be

subject to a warranty that the ship concerned only travelled in a convoy of other vessels in specified areas;

(e) *a policy exclusion*: in addition to the standard exclusions on, say, a personal accident and sickness policy, there might be a specified exclusion added relating to a particular medical problem, e.g. "slipped disc";

(f) *policy cover reduced*: again with a personal accident and sickness insurance, a particular person may have an unhappy sickness record but be perfectly acceptable for "accidents only" cover;

(g) *reduce sum insured*: not a common remedy but, where found, it is likely to concern benefit policies (life or personal accident), so an example once more from personal accident business could arise if the policy were a group one covering young children, when a lower than standard death benefit might suffice.

(h) *require physical improvements*: found with property insurances, an example could be that in theft insurance for a jeweller's shop the insurer would require additional or enhanced physical protection for the premises;

(i) *limit persons covered*: with motor insurance the knowledge that the insured had a son or daughter with a poor driving record might mean that the policy restricted driving to the insured and spouse only (without any premium reduction);

(j) *require a counter-guarantee*: with some specialised classes of business offering guarantee-type cover, e.g. fidelity guarantee and construction bonds, the insurer may require a counter-guarantee to safeguard his position;

(k) *defer a decision*: with insurances of people, e.g. life and personal accident insurances, a temporary medical condition (such as pregnancy or recent injuries) may mean that the underwriter prefers to wait until a more normal medical condition returns before offering cover.

NOTE: It should be understood that this is not a technical underwriting book, as such, and there will be other more specific options available to the underwriter in the respective classes of business concerned.

E. UNDERWRITING IN THE DIFFERENT CLASSES

24.17 Long-term and other insurances

Long-term insurances are those classes of business where the contract is intended to last for a number of years (often until death) and the insurer does not have the right of cancellation. This arises primarily in life insurance, of course, but also in permanent health (permanent sickness) insurance.

24.17 Underwriting

It will be immediately obvious that the underwriting of such business has greater significance. With other classes the policy is normally on an annual basis, so underwriting can be reviewed or totally re-done at renewal. Also, there is likely to be a cancellation clause to enable the insurer to come off risk if necessary. With long-term insurances underwriting can only be done once. In view of this, it is not unusual with life and similar business for underwriting to be centralised, perhaps at Head Office. Certainly, with these classes of business more senior staff are likely to be entrusted with the responsibility of making underwriting decisions.

F. PROGRESS TEST 24

PART 1—SHORT ANSWERS (Answer in one or two sentences)

1. Is underwriting an art or a science? **(24.4)**
2. What two basic questions arise in underwriting a specific risk? **(26.6)**
3. Is the premium the only consideration in underwriting? **(24.8)**
4. What is meant by the EML (or PML) of a risk? **(24.10)**
5. What are the "extreme" options when considering a sub-standard risk? **(24.15)**

PART 2—MULTIPLE CHOICE (Choose the most correct option)

1. With the publication of rating manuals and underwriting guides:
   (a) individual risk underwriting is no longer necessary;
   (b) only the most senior staff can underwrite risks;
   (c) the majority of risks are much easier to underwrite;
   (d) underwriting has completely lost its flexibility. **(24.2–24.3)**
2. If an underwriter is said to be "risk prone", it means that he:
   (a) is unlikely to be enthusiastic about accepting new risks;
   (b) is likely to be enthusiastic about accepting new risks;
   (c) always seems to be making mistakes;
   (d) will always have a profitable account. **(24.5)**
3. Premium loading:
   (a) means that a higher than standard risk is to be charged;
   (b) cannot be done now that underwriting manuals exist;
   (c) means the volume of business that an underwriter must achieve;
   (d) is not possible because the business will be lost. **(24.7)**
4. If a proposed risk presents an abnormally high potential loss figure:
   (a) the underwriter will never accept it;
   (b) the excess risk can always be reinsured;
   (c) the underwriter must accept or reject the whole risk;
   (d) co-insurance may be a possible answer. **(24.9)**
5. "Hard" or "soft" market conditions:

(a) will frequently affect the underwriter's judgement;
(b) will never affect the underwriter's judgement;
(c) must be ignored, as the underwriter's job is purely technical;
(d) will only affect premiums, not policy terms. **(24.13)**

(For multiple choice answers, see page 355.)

CHAPTER 25

PHYSICAL AND MORAL HAZARD

A. INTRODUCTION

25.1 The assessment of risk

Since the underwriter is continually assuming the risks of others for a consideration, it is vital for him or her to become proficient at the assessment of risks offered. The technical assessment will be based on the consideration of:

(a) *physical hazard*: this may briefly be described as the material aspects surrounding the risk;
(b) *moral hazard*: this is concerned with any human element involved with the risk (see **24.12**).

NOTE: As noted in Chapter 24 the underwriter will also be influenced by other matters in deciding whether and on what terms to accept a proposed insurance.

B. PHYSICAL HAZARD

25.2 Definition

Physical hazard may be defined as the risk arising from the physical nature of the subject matter of the insurance and inherent factors related thereto.

Another description might be "the risk arising from the natural qualities of the subject matter, in relation to the likelihood and extent of claims". Thus, for example, cash presents a much worse physical hazard in theft insurance than does heavy machinery, since it is much more attractive to thieves, being easily taken away and immediately usable by them.

25.3 Need of a qualifying adjective

It is technically meaningless merely to say that physical hazard exists with a particular risk. It always exists, in the sense that the term virtually means "physical nature". Thus, physical hazard is a neutral expression that needs to be qualified by a preceding adjective, such as "good" or "bad", as the case may be.

Similarly, the adjective should denote quality, not quantity. That is, it is wrong to say that a particular risk has a "large physical hazard", or that "the physical hazard is small". Increasingly, this type of expression is being found, but technically this is a misuse, showing a misunderstanding of the term.

25.4 Reasonably evident and ascertainable

Although the risk presented by a particular insurance may be somewhat specialised, as for instance with certain trade processes, generally speaking physical hazard can be ascertained. The actual construction or composition of material property is quite easy to discover. Similarly, the likelihood of an insured peril occurring is very often a matter of common sense. Thus, given full details of a proposed risk or the opportunity to carry out a survey, an insurer can make a fairly accurate assessment of the physical hazard presented.

25.5 Examples of physical hazard

Physical features which render a proposed risk good or bad from the insurer's point of view can easily come to mind. Some examples on the major classes of business are as follows:

(a) *Marine insurance*: the type of power used to propel the vessel; the type of goods comprising the cargo; the geographical area and season involved for the voyage.
(b) *Life assurance*: the health of the proposed assured; the family medical history; the age of the proposer.
(c) *Fire insurance*: the construction of the premises; the proximity of fire brigades; the trade processes involved in the insured premises.
(d) *Accident insurance*: the occupation of the insured (personal accident); the type of machinery used (employer's liability); the system of check and supervision (fidelity guarantee).

C. UNDERWRITING REMEDIES FOR BAD PHYSICAL HAZARD

25.6 General

Where bad physical hazard exists, this is usually evident at the time the insurance is proposed, and the underwriter can often make suitable adjustments to compensate for the adverse features present. Where suitable underwriting measures will not counteract the adverse features, the only prudent option is to decline the risk altogether.

25.7 Remedies available

The remedies available to combat physical hazard have already been considered under the general heading of underwriting (see **24.15–24.16**). The use of these will be a value judgement on the part of the underwriter.

D. MORAL HAZARD

25.8 Definition

Moral hazard is the risk arising from the nature and behaviour of human beings connected with the subject matter of the insurance.

The term is a little misleading in that it is not concerned exclusively with the morals of the insured. Indeed, in the normally accepted sense, these may have no bearing on any insurance considerations. Obviously, dishonesty on the part of the insured is likely to have a great bearing on the insurer's assessment of the risk, but moral hazard is of wider meaning (see **25.12**).

25.9 The character of not only the insured involved

Any personal element involved with the subject matter of the insurance has a bearing on moral hazard. Thus, the behaviour of the insured's employees and of third parties is to be considered in addition to that of the policyholder himself.

25.10 Also needs qualifying

As with physical hazard (see **25.3**), moral hazard needs a qualifying adjective. It has become very common for expressions like "there is considerable moral hazard with the risk" to be used, when the intention is to signify the existence of very bad moral hazard. Care should be exercised when using the term, for moral hazard can be very good, for example with a firm which is well disciplined and safety conscious (when considering employer's liability insurance).

25.11 Very difficult to ascertain

Moral hazard is far more difficult to measure and observe than physical hazard. Impressions can be gained of the carefulness, honesty and general integrity of an insured when conducting interviews or by surveyors when visiting the insured's or proposer's premises. Nevertheless, it frequently happens that impressions are misleading. Furthermore, bad moral hazard may not become evident until a claim arises, by which time it is too late to take any underwriting measures, at least in respect of that particular claim.

E. ADVERSE MORAL HAZARD AND ITS REMEDIES

25.12 Four basic categories

First-class moral hazard is present when the insured is basically honest, is careful in the handling of his property, is reasonable in his demands, and where any others likely to be connected with the subject matter are similarly unlikely to give rise to an insured peril. On the other hand, bad moral hazard may arise from:

(a) fraud;
(b) carelessness;
(c) unreasonableness;
(d) trend of events: see below.

NOTE: The U.S. insurance market makes a useful distinction between *moral hazard* (implying dishonesty of the insured) and *morale hazard* (indicating carelessness or other non-dishonest unsatisfactory features).

25.13 Fraud

Quite obviously, fraud is the worst form of moral hazard. Examples may be as dramatic as the deliberate "staging" of a loss, which never really occurred, or in the form of inflating the amount claimed in respect of genuine losses. Both constitute fraud, which can never satisfactorily be countered by underwriting remedies. The only suitable course of action where a record of fraud exists is to decline the proposed risk. Certainly, increasing the premium is worse than useless, since the fraudulent claim will just be that much higher to account for the greater initial outlay, and the mere fact of increased terms may well precipitate a claim earlier.

25.14 Carelessness

In extreme examples, carelessness could be nearly as unsatisfactory as fraud, and the same remedy of declinature may have to be adopted. However, various other underwriting measures may be adopted according to the circumstances. Some examples are as follows:

(a) *Where the insured personally is careless.* In an "all risks" insurance on personal effects, repeated minor losses through carelessness may be eliminated by a suitable excess or franchise.
(b) *Where the insured's employees are careless.* Carelessness has been the cause of many serious claims. Warranties in the policy requiring certain precautions, such as sweeping away shavings at the end of work, may be useful.
(c) *Where third parties are careless.* Usually such carelessness is completely outside the control of the insured. In certain isolated premises, for instance, vagrants and children have often caused fire damage by leaving cigarettes or other burning substances. This is difficult to

combat, but sometimes physical adjustments to the premises, such as fencing certain areas or covering pavement grilles, will help.

25.15 Unreasonableness

This is a form of bad moral hazard that seldom comes to light until a claim arises. It is shown by the insured who is basically honest, but will only accept his own interpretation of any situation. Every experienced claims official will have met at least one such individual, who usually manages to cause considerable unpleasantness, delay and expense in his dealings with the insurer.

Flexibility and a generous interpretation of policy conditions are the standard qualities of responsible insurers, but quite obviously a line must be drawn somewhere. When an insured's attitude goes beyond reasonableness, this must be regarded as bad moral hazard, which will probably mean refusal to offer renewal terms, or even policy cancellation in extreme cases. A possible alternative in motor insurance would be to reduce cover to third party only, so that the insured personally will not benefit from any claims; this might arise where considerable difficulty had arisen over claims for damage to the insured's own vehicle. With third party only cover the insurer would largely be dealing direct with third parties in any claims.

25.16 Trend of events

This is a rather nebulous term, but it applies to the behaviour of society in general. This will vary from time to time, and from place to place. Some areas in the world, for instance, have a far worse record of petty crime than others. Also, the general state of the economy can have a bearing on the rate of burglaries and fires. In times of great distress, such as periods of economic depression, unsuccessful businessmen may well have been tempted to "arrange" fires to realise the capital tied up in stocks which they could not sell. In times of affluence, too, the great quantities of consumer goods encourage organised crime on a large scale. Political unrest, especially in some areas, could well have a serious effect on insurance claims.

If business is to be written under such circumstances, a general rise in premium rates may be called for. In addition, policy exclusions regarding riot and civil commotion may well be applied. Generally, however the insurer will watch results and trends very carefully, possibly declining the less attractive business altogether.

25.17 Sometimes difficult to differentiate

It is sometimes difficult to say whether a particular consideration arising with a risk is related to the moral or physical hazard. There is a certain overlap of ideas, but quite obviously the underwriter is not concerned to make academic distinctions. He is concerned with assessing the risk as a whole and the composite picture on which he will base his technical assessment will be composed of an accurate appraisal of both physical and moral hazards.

F. PROGRESS TEST 25

PART 1—SHORT ANSWERS (Answer in one or two sentences)

1. What is understood by the term "physical hazard"? **(25.1)**
2. Why is it incorrect to say "physical hazard exists with this risk"? **(25.3)**
3. Explain the difference between physical hazard and moral hazard. **(25.1–25.8)**
4. Why is moral hazard difficult to ascertain? **(25.11)**
5. How might an underwriter react to bad moral hazard? **(25.12–12.17)**

PART 2—MULTIPLE CHOICE (Choose the most correct option)

1. The technical assessment of a risk:
   (a) will only involve consideration of physical factors;
   (b) is only concerned with the human element involved;
   (c) involves both physical and moral hazards;
   (d) can be made from consulting the rating book. **(25.1)**
2. Physical hazard:
   (a) is much easier to assess than moral hazard;
   (b) is more difficult to assess than moral hazard;
   (c) exclusively concerns the health of the proposer;
   (d) exclusively concerns statistically measurable factors. **(25.4)**
3. The underwriting remedies for physical hazard:
   (a) can never make a sub-standard risk acceptable;
   (b) can be implemented at any time with all classes of business;
   (c) are a guarantee that the policy will not be subject to a claim;
   (d) normally make a sub-standard risk insurable. **(25.7)**
4. Adverse moral hazard would indicate that:
   (a) the insured is dishonest;
   (b) the physical features of the risk are sub-standard;
   (c) the human element with the risk is sub-standard;
   (d) the insured has a criminal record. **(25.8)**
5. Unreasonableness on the part of the insured:
   (a) will constitute adverse moral hazard;
   (b) will constitute adverse physical hazard;
   (c) means that the insurer should be difficult with claims;
   (d) means that the risk is uninsurable. **(25.15)**

(*For multiple choice answers, see page 355.*)

CHAPTER 26

PROPOSAL FORMS

A. GENERAL OBSERVATIONS

26.1 What proposal forms are

The average individual who has effected any insurances, perhaps on his home, his belongings, or his life, will almost certainly have been required to complete a proposal form issued by the insurers. It must not be assumed, however, that such forms are a legal necessity, nor that they are invariably used with every class of business.

Where proposal forms are used, they consist, basically, of a series of questions drawn up by the insurers, requesting certain information which will enable them to assess the proposed risk (i.e. the answers to the questions will shed light on the physical and perhaps moral hazard involved: see Chapter 25).

NOTE: The answers to questions on a proposal form will not necessarily discharge the duty upon a prospective insured to disclose all material information (see **18.3**). However, the courts would probably require strong evidence that information not covered by the questions on the form was of material consequence to the insurers.

26.2 Why proposal forms are used

Although the issue and completion of a proposal form are not legally required, in practice such forms are used with most types of insurance.

The reasons they are used are as follows:

(a) *Convenience*. Since the questions are framed by the insurers, the production of a standard type of form is likely to produce the required information most speedily, and in a sequence that can readily be checked and considered.

(b) *Advertising*. Well-produced forms can have an advertising value in their own right. Also, notice of other types of insurance can be given on any spare space on the forms. Many proposal forms contain prospectuses of different types of cover available from the insurer concerned.

(c) *Basis of the contract*. The issue of a blank proposal form by the insurer does not in itself constitute the offer in the contract (see **16.7**). The offer normally consists of the completed form, which usually includes a declaration. The declaration is extremely important and, *inter alia*, usually provides that the completed proposal form is the basis on which the contract is formed (see **26.17**).

NOTE: The American term for a proposal form is an *application*, which is exactly what it is. This application may be filled in on the applicant's behalf, but he remains responsible for the answers given.

B. USE IN THE MAJOR CLASSES OF BUSINESS

26.3 Marine insurance

Except for minor risks, such as the insurance of small pleasure craft, proposal forms are not normally used in marine insurance. Instead, details of a proposed risk are submitted to the insurer on a "slip".

This practice is followed by insurance companies as well as Lloyd's underwriters, although the latter originated such methods in the early days of marine insurance. (Lloyd's underwriters, in fact, retain the same system for non-marine risks also: see **12.9**.)

26.4 Life assurance

Proposal forms are invariably used in life assurance. The importance of the answers is emphasised by the normal type of declaration incorporating the proposal form into, and making it the basis of, the contract.

Many life policies are also subject to satisfactory medical examination of the prospective assured. Where such medicals are arranged, the findings and comments of the medical experts are considered part of the proposal for the assurance.

26.5 Fire insurance

Only the smaller risks, such as household insurances, are made subject to a completed proposal form. The larger risks are almost invariably subject to an inspection and report on the premises, often by a surveyor on the insurer's staff. A survey is necessary because of the complexity of building structures and trade processes, all of which may have a profound effect on the fire risk and which cannot adequately be described merely by answering questions on a form.

26.6 Accident insurance

This is similar to life assurance, in so far as proposal forms are invariably obtained. They also contain the normal type of declaration, incorporating the proposal into, and making it the basis of, the contract.

For some minor risks, usually of short duration, such as travel policies or cover for an event such as a garden fête (perhaps against excessive rainfall), proposals may be waived.

26.7 Motor, engineering and aviation insurance

The practice in these classes of business tends to follow that of other accident insurance. With motor insurance, particularly, the completed proposal form is of great importance. It will often be referred to in the event of a claim, if only to check information given on the claim form regarding previous accidents and any driving convictions.

With engineering and some aviation risks, a proposal is sometimes not necessary, in that an inspection is made on behalf of the insurers.

C. STRUCTURE OF MOST PROPOSAL FORMS

26.8 Different types of form

It would be quite impossible to outline a comprehensive collection of proposal forms, in view of the multiplicity of forms used by the different insurers in the many different classes of business. The student is recommended to make comparisons with forms from different insurers.

26.9 Questions common to most forms

Although there is a great variety of proposal forms in current use, there are certain basic questions which will be found on practically every form, as follows:

- (a) proposer's name;
- (b) proposer's address;
- (c) proposer's occupation;
- (d) insurance history;
- (e) losses history: see below.

26.10 Proposer's name

Clearly, the proposer's name is vital for identification and communication purposes. In addition, however, the name could give an insight into the physical or even moral hazard. For example, the name of a public celebrity proposing for theft insurance would inform the underwriter of an adverse physical hazard, since the proposer's movements would be public knowledge and often the homes of celebrities are "target risks" as far as burglaries are concerned.

The moral hazard could be influenced by a foreign name proposing for insurance in an area where there is general local resentment against foreigners of that nationality. (It is arguable that this involves the physical hazard, rather than the moral, but in any event the detail could be of importance.) A more obvious issue involving moral hazard is where a name arises which is known to the insurer as being of doubtful integrity, perhaps from past dealings with him.

26.11 Proposer's address

Again, there is an obvious requirement for this, for communication purposes. The address is also of considerable importance to many classes of business. For example, in motor insurance the address where the vehicle is normally garaged (which is usually at least in the district where the proposer lives) is frequently a vital factor in rating the policy. In theft insurance, also, the address can be of significance, if it is in an area where burglaries are very common.

26.12 Proposer's occupation

The type of work the proposer does can have a tremendous importance to the risk presented. Obvious examples arise in life and personal accident insurance. With both, a hazardous occupation, such as that of a deep-sea diver, could have a profound effect on the premium quoted or even whether the risk is accepted at all.

The occupation of the insured is also of great significance in many other classes of business, such as fire, motor, employer's liability, etc. Examples will readily come to mind illustrating how different occupations in these classes of business greatly affect the physical hazard involved.

26.13 Insurance history

There are usually questions on proposal forms requesting details of any existing or previous insurances for the particular class of business. This is quite separate from details of any claims or previous losses (see **26.14**).

The reasons for such a question are basically twofold:

(a) *Possible insight into moral hazard.* A frequent change of insurer may indicate a degree of adverse moral hazard, in that the person may be difficult to deal with. Insurers may be willing to co-operate with each other, if requested to give confidential information about their impressions of a particular insured.

(b) *Upholding indemnity.* In a contract subject to indemnity this will present little difficulty, as contribution will account for any "double insurance". With life and personal accident policies, however, the insurer likes to know of any other similar policies, so that any income benefits are kept approximately in line with the proposer's financial requirements (see **19.4**).

26.14 Losses history

It should be noted that questions on this topic usually request information about *losses*, whether or not they formed the basis of an insurance claim. Usually, the proposal form will only require details of losses during the previous three or five years.

In motor insurance, the history of losses has considerable importance, particularly since most insurers allow a discount off their premium rates for previous claim-free years of insurance (*"no claims discount" or "bonus"*). A series of losses, however, might indicate bad physical or moral hazard in almost any class of business.

26.15 Other questions frequently found

The following questions are often found in proposal forms:

(a) *Sum insured.* Frequently, in policies of all kinds, the proposer may select his own sum insured, which will represent the maximum liability of the insurer and is usually a factor in the premium to be charged. Sometimes, however, the sum insured or limit of liability is a standard one, shown on the proposal form; no question is therefore necessary in such circumstances.

(b) *Age of proposer.* This is of greatest importance with life assurance, but can also be significant with young (or very old) drivers in motor insurance. Outside a wide age band (say 16–65), very young or very old persons may not be insurable for personal accident insurance.

(c) *Subject matter.* One of the prerequisites of an insurance contract is that the subject matter of the insurance is capable of identification (see **27.15**). Thus, with most policies there is provision for an adequate description to be given. With some policies (e.g. life) there is no need for a specific question.

26.16 Signature and date

The proposal form should always be signed by the proposer or his duly authorised representative, since the form normally represents the offer in the contract. For obvious reasons, the date should also be inserted.

26.17 Declaration

Before the various Statements of Insurance Practice issued by the insurance industry, it was common for proposal forms to have a suitably worded declaration at the foot of them which had the effect of a warranty (see **18.16–18.18**). This warranty changed the common law duty of utmost good faith into a contractual duty (see **18.23**). This will no longer take place (see **18.29**).

Often the declaration would be very detailed, covering many issues, including:

(a) warranting the truth and completeness of answers;
(b) warranting that the sum insured represents the full value;
(c) incorporating the proposal into, and making it the basis of, the contract;
(d) providing for any adjustment of premium;
(e) (in personal accident insurance) warranting that the insured would not participate in certain sports, etc.

D. PROGRESS TEST 26

PART 1—SHORT ANSWERS **(Answer in one or two sentences)**

1. Why are proposal forms so frequently used? **(26.2)**
2. When are proposal forms not normally used? **(26.3–26.7)**
3. What questions are common to most types of proposal forms? **(26.9)**
4. Why is it necessary to ask separate questions in proposal forms about past insurances and past losses? **(26.13–26.14)**
5. Give examples of how the following can be important in considering various risks proposed for insurance:
    (a) proposer's address; **(26.11)**
    (b) proposer's occupation; **(26.12)**
    (c) proposer's age. **(26.15)**

PART 2—MULTIPLE CHOICE **(Choose the most correct option)**

1. In insurance a proposal form is used:
    (a) when completing a survey of property to be insured;
    (b) by the insurer when he wishes to quote for a risk;
    (c) by a broker to summarise details of an intended insurance;
    (d) to help the intending insured to present information. **(26.2)**
2. Proposal forms are used for nearly all risks in:
    (a) marine insurance;
    (b) life assurance;

(c) engineering insurance;
(d) fire insurance. **(26.3–26.7)**

3. The proposer's name on a proposal form:
   (a) could be important with moral or physical hazard assessment;
   (b) is only ever of significance for identification purposes;
   (c) will be an important factor in the premium to be charged;
   (d) is not really needed by the insurer. **(26.10)**
4. The proposer's occupation on the proposal form:
   (a) sometimes has an important bearing on the premium;
   (b) is never of any real importance to the insurer;
   (c) has an important bearing on moral hazard;
   (d) is of no importance in fire assurance. **(26.12)**
5. The declaration at the foot of a proposal form:
   (a) is a formality, of no real importance;
   (b) always changes the common law duty of utmost good faith;
   (c) is now unlikely to affect the duty of utmost good faith;
   (d) is always very short. **(26.17)**

(*For multiple choice answers, see page 355.*)

CHAPTER 27

POLICY FORMS

A. GENERAL OBSERVATIONS

27.1 Evidence of the contract

It should be remembered that the policy is not the contract, but merely the written evidence of it (see **16.2**). Nevertheless, the courts will require strong evidence to contradict the plain statements made by the policy, which will be taken to represent the intention of the parties in the absence of proof to the contrary. In practice, therefore, it is essential for the policy document to be prepared with the greatest care.

27.2 Policy prepared by the insurers

The policy is a document produced by the insurers, setting out the terms of the contract. Since they are putting forward the document, any reasonable ambiguity in its phraseology will be construed in favour of the insured. This is in accord with the long-standing legal maxim, briefly known as the *contra proferentem* rule, that the person drawing up a legal document is responsible for any defects in it and cannot profit from such defects.

27.3 Basic policy styles

There is very little standardisation of either the presentation or the cover provided by policies of similar type issued by different insurers. However, competition and other factors have meant that the basic terms of policies within the same class of business tend to be very similar. The basic policy styles, in ascending order of market prominence, are:

(a) narrative-style policies;
(b) "modern-language" style policies;
(c) scheduled policies: see below.

27.4 Narrative and modern-language style policy forms

A *narrative* policy is written in continuous prose, with little or no attempt to sub-divide into paragraphs or clear-cut divisions. (Hence the name, in that the policy document *narrates* the cover provided.) The earliest policies were written in this style, but it is now virtually obsolete. Even the "SG" policy (see **3.13**), which was presented in this style, has now passed into history.

Laudable attempts have been made in recent years by some insurers to present policy wording in simpler English, at times supplementing the text with pictorial representations to assist understanding. Changing the style of contract wordings is not without its dangers as regards legal interpretation, but undoubtedly the general public would approve the attempt to make policies more comprehensible to the average insured.

27.5 Scheduled policies

The somewhat antiquated narrative form of policy became replaced by a *scheduled* form. A schedule is a list or catalogue, and this conveys the idea of a scheduled form of policy. All parts of the policy are in clearly defined sections, which for the same insurer will be identical within a class of business, except the "schedule". This will contain all the information peculiar to that individual policy (see **27.10**).

These forms are much easier to administer and understand. From an administrative point of view, for example, the insurers need keep only a copy of each individual schedule (with any individual variations on the standard policy wording), and one specimen copy of the policy form, to have a complete record. There is no need to have a separate copy of the whole policy document for each insured.

Because of the many advantages, the great majority of non-marine policies are now issued on a scheduled basis.

B. STRUCTURE OF A SCHEDULED POLICY FORM

27.6 Heading

It is usual to find a heading to each policy document. This heading will indicate the name and address of the insurer, and may give other details such as the assets of the particular company.

The heading is there for identification and perhaps advertising or information purposes.

27.7 Recital clause

This part of the policy is sometimes termed the *preamble*, and it is basically the introduction to the contract.

The clause, as it were, recites in general terms some basic particulars about the contract, as follows:

(a) *The parties involved.* The parties will not be named (this information is given elsewhere in the policy: the insurer is named in the heading, the insured is named in the schedule). They will merely be referred to as "the insured" and "the insurer".
(b) *Reference is made to the schedule,* as the section of the policy making the contract apply individually to the named insured.
(c) *Reference is made to the signed proposal form,* as being incorporated in the contract and forming the basis of it.

EXAMPLE: The recital clause of policies invariably starts with the word "whereas", and a typical example is as follows:

> Whereas the Insured named in the Schedule has by a signed proposal and declaration which proposal and declaration the Insured has agreed shall be the basis of this Contract and be held as incorporated herein applied to the Company named in the Schedule (hereinafter called the Company) for insurance against the Contingencies specified herein.

NOTE: Sometimes the recital clause will also make general reference to the insured's promise to pay the premium, and to any renewal provisions. Practice varies amongst insurers: the above example makes no such references.

27.8 Operative clause

This section is sometimes termed the *insuring clause,* in that it specifies the extent of the insurance. Perhaps an easier way of remembering the function of the operative clause is to regard it as the clause *which sets out the circumstances in which the insurance is operative* (i.e. it outlines the insured perils for which the insured or his legal representatives are indemnified, or for which the policy benefits are payable).

The operative clause usually starts with the words "Now this policy witnesseth" and then goes on to describe the insurer's undertakings. The clause may be quite a short one, as with a life policy, or it may be very long, as with a comprehensive motor car insurance. The former need say little beyond the fact that the assurer is liable for the policy benefit in the event of the assured's death, whereas the latter must outline several different aspects of cover provided (see **7.9**).

27.9 Exceptions

Whereas the operative clause outlines the cover provided by the policy (see above), the *exceptions* will indicate any restrictions on the scope of the insurance. It is virtually impossible to have a policy with no exceptions, as there are always causes of loss which must be excluded if the premium is to be economically acceptable and the contract is to conform with public policy.

Where the operative clause consists of different sections, as with most motor policies, it is quite common for exceptions peculiar to individual sections to be inserted against the part to which they apply, with a separate policy division for "*general exceptions*". (These exceptions are "general" in the sense that they apply to the whole of the policy and not just to individual sections.)

Some typical examples of policy exceptions would be:

(a) *suicide*: with a personal accident policy;
(b) *earthquake*: with a standard fire policy;
(c) *radioactive losses*: nearly every insurance policy has a standard exception relating to losses caused by radioactivity.

27.10 Schedule

It is this part of the policy from which the term "scheduled" policy arises. This section of the document contains all particulars which make the policy different from any other in that class of business. The information that is found within the schedule, therefore, will include most or all of the following:

(a) Insured's name.
(b) Insured's address.
(c) Insured's profession, business or occupation.
(d) Period of insurance (i.e. inception and termination, or renewal, date).
(e) Premium. (Possibly indicating a renewal premium if the first premium is likely to be different. This could happen if it were intended that the policy operate annually, from perhaps a quarter-day, and the first period of insurance was a so-called "odd-time" until the quarter-day.)
(f) Policy number.
(g) Sum insured, or limit of indemnity.
(h) Description of the subject matter of the insurance.
(i) Any particular warranties applied to that policy.

27.11 Signature clause

This makes provision for the insurer to affirm the conditions of the contract as set out in the policy. For this reason the clause is sometimes termed the *attestation clause*, in that the insurer thereby "attests", or gives formal verification of his undertaking.

As the policy represents an undertaking by the insurer, the insured is not required to sign the policy document. In a sense the insured has already given his signature on the proposal form, which is incorporated within the contract.

An insurer's internal rules may regulate the manner of signing policy documents, but usually there is the printed signature of a director of the company, with provision for a further signature, or initialling, by a duly authorised lesser official. The wording of a typical signature clause is as follows:

"In witness whereof I, being a Director and Authorised Officer of the said Company, have hereunto subscribed my name on the date mentioned in the Schedule."

27.12 Conditions

Every insurance policy is subject to conditions, because even if none is specifically mentioned in the document common law insists that certain *implied conditions* are always read into the contract (see **27.15**).

In practice, virtually every scheduled policy will have written conditions, which regulate the cover provided. These conditions may vary considerably between classes of business and between individual insurers, but their basic intentions may be summarised as follows:

(a) *To remind the insured of common law provisions.* An example in motor insurance is a condition requiring the insured to keep the vehicle in good order and to take all reasonable steps to avoid losses. Such conditions are not really necessary, in that they apply automatically, but they do tend to emphasise the position.
(b) *To restrict the cover provided.* Foreign travel and residence may be so restricted by a condition in a life policy. These conditions have similar functions to exceptions.
(c) *To grant privileges.* Mostly found in life assurance, examples of such conditions would be those granting surrender value rights (see **4.34**).
(d) *To outline certain procedures.* There will invariably be policy conditions to define what constitutes formal notice to the company, and the procedure to be adopted in the event of a claim. Other examples are considered in **27.14** below.

C. CLASSIFICATIONS OF POLICY CONDITIONS

27.13 Two classifications

Remembering that a classification involves the sub-division of the whole subject into categories (see **2.11**), policy conditions may be classified in two main ways (see Fig. 17):

(a) *By whether they appear in the policy document or not*, i.e. whether they are *express* or *implied* conditions: see below.
(b) *By the time when they need to be fulfilled* (see **27.16–27.18**).

27.14 Express conditions

These are conditions which actually appear (or are "expressed") within the policy document. There is no standard set of policy conditions, but examples of express conditions frequently found in fire and accident policies are:

(a) *What constitutes notice to the insurer.* The appropriate condition might well require notice to be in writing, to the head office of the company or to the branch office which issued the policy.
(b) *Claims procedure.* Details of any time limit for giving notice of claims, together with any particulars of substantiating evidence required, would be given in this condition. With liability policies, the condition would give the insurer the right to take over the complete handling of all third party claims, with the right to decide whether any offer or compromise arrangements should be made in settlement.
(c) *Cancellation.* In the absence of a specific condition, termination of a contract in mid-term can only be done by mutual consent. The condition may give the right to the insurer and/or the insured to end the contract prematurely. The amount of premium to be refunded may be *pro rata*, if cancellation is by the insurer, or rather less than *pro rata*, if the insured cancels (see *short-period premium rates*, **28.11**).
(d) *Contribution.* The condition usually modifies the common law position, so that the insurer is only liable to pay his rateable share of any loss (see **21.8**).
(e) *Arbitration.* This condition provides for the settlement of certain disputes by a means other than through the courts (see **30.20**).
(f) *Adjustment of premium.* Certain policies are rated on factors which cannot be precisely known at the inception of the policy. For example, if the premium on cash in transit insurance is based on the annual amount of cash carried, the exact figures cannot be known until the end of the year. This condition gives the appropriate requirements regarding the adjustment procedure.

NOTE: Marine policies normally have no express conditions.

27.15 Implied conditions

These are conditions which the law will read into any contract of insurance, but which do not appear in the policy document. There are four such conditions:

(a) *Insurable interest.* The insured must be legally entitled to effect the

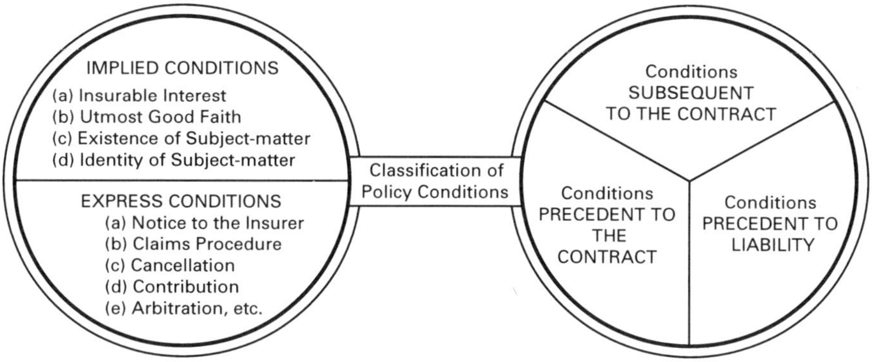

Fig. 17 Classification of policy conditions

policy (see **17.2**).

(b) *Utmost good faith.* The insured (and the insurer) must exercise utmost good faith in the negotiations leading up to the formation of the contract (see Chapter 18).

(c) *Existence of the subject matter.* The subject matter of the insurance must be in existence for a valid contract to be made.

(d) *Identity of the subject matter.* The subject matter of the insurance must be capable of being identified.

27.16 Conditions precedent to the policy (or contract)

Sometimes merely called "conditions precedent", these are conditions which must be fulfilled before the contract can become valid. An example is the implied condition of utmost good faith.

27.17 Conditions subsequent to the policy (or contract)

Conditions subsequent are conditions which must be fulfilled if the contract is to continue once it has become binding. An example is the express condition often found in personal accident policies requiring the insured to notify any change of occupation to the insurer.

27.18 Conditions precedent to liability

These are conditions which must be fulfilled before the insured is legally entitled to recover under the contract. For example, the claims condition may require notification to the company within a certain specified time limit.

27.19 Comparison between the above conditions

All policy conditions, whether express or implied, will be within the three categories. A breach of a condition precedent or a condition subsequent is said to *go to the root of the contract* This means that the contract is thus void or voidable, so that it can in effect be destroyed either *ab initio* (*right from the beginning*), in the case of the former, or from the date of the breach in the case of the latter.

A breach of a condition precedent to liability does not destroy the contract, which remains in full force. However, the insurer is not legally obliged to meet any claim to which the breach of condition applies. (Another way of expressing this is to say that the contract is made voidable in respect of the particular claim only.)

NOTE: Those familiar with other branches of law will know that in many cases the word "express" has a different connotation. In insurance, as seen above, it indicates a *visible contract provision*, whereas in the law of agency, for example, "express authority" would mean *definite (perhaps oral) authority.*

D. RECTIFICATION

27.20 Policy must represent the intention of the parties

The policy, as evidence of the contract, should represent the intention of the parties. Where it does not, owing to a mistake in its preparation, the document can be rectified:

(a) *by mutual consent*: where there is an obvious mistake, such as a mis-typing of the amount insured, it frequently happens that the insured will merely return the document to the insurer for the appropriate correction to be made. (The insured is always requested to read the policy carefully and to return it to the insurers at once should any error be found therein);

(b) *by application to the court*: where the policy does not represent the intention of the parties, but one party refuses to have the policy document amended, the other can make application to the court to have the rectification made. Naturally, the court would require proof as to the intention of the parties, but where this is established rectification can be ordered.

NOTE: The contract is the agreement between the parties. Where this is established, it will be legally enforceable whatever the policy document says.

E. COVER NOTES AND CERTIFICATES

27.21 Temporary policies

It frequently happens that there is some delay between the time the contract becomes binding and the issue of a policy. This may be because of administrative difficulties or because the insurer agrees to give temporary cover until such time as full particulars have been investigated and a final decision can be given. Where this occurs, it is quite common for the insured to be given proof of the existence of insurance by the issue of *cover notes*, which are slips of paper in effect constituting temporary policies.

Cover notes are used extensively in several classes of business such as motor, fire, theft, etc. They are of particular importance in motor insurance, since they provide evidence to the police that the bearer complies with statutory insurance requirements until such time as the policy and insurance certificates are to hand (see **27.24**).

27.22 Effect of cover notes

Cover notes are usually issued for a limited period, say 15 days or a month. Even where they represent only provisional acceptance of the risk, however, they bind the insurer exactly as if a full policy had been issued. For example, if a cover note is issued for motor insurance and it subsequently transpires that the insurer wishes to refuse the risk, he is still liable for any claim that may arise in the period before the cover note expires or is cancelled.

27.23 Form of cover notes

Cover notes may be in printed form, as in motor insurance, with provision for particular details of the risk and future policy to be issued. On the other hand, a brief typed or handwritten slip is sometimes used. There is no uniformity of practice or design with cover notes.

27.24 Certificates

Apart from providing evidence of compulsory insurance in motor and employer's liability insurance (see **27.21**), certificates are also found, for example, in marine cargo insurances, giving evidence of individual shipments covered under a master policy.

F. ENDORSEMENTS

27.25 Meaning and application

An endorsement is merely an *alteration* to the existing policy terms. This may be relatively trivial, such as the correction of a misprint or changing the address of the insured. Alternatively, it can be of great importance, such as the removal of a policy exclusion or in some other way profoundly affecting the cover provided.

Endorsements should be attached to the policy schedule (see **27.10**), since they constitute or relate to information peculiar to the particular policy. They are often in standard format and will frequently start with a phrase such as "Notwithstanding anything contained herein to the contrary" and conclude with a phrase like "Subject otherwise to the terms and conditions of this insurance". Thus, they will clearly identify with all other terms of the contract.

G. PROGRESS TEST 27

PART 1—SHORT ANSWERS (Answer in one or two sentences)

1. In whose favour will ambiguity in the policy document be construed? **(27.2)**
2. What is meant by narrative and scheduled policies? **(27.4–27.5)**
3. Briefly describe the structure of a scheduled policy form. **(27.6–27.12)**
4. Give two alternative classifications of policy conditions. **(27.13–27.19)**
5. What is meant by policy rectification? How may it come about? **(27.20)**

PART 2—MULTIPLE CHOICE (Choose the most correct option)

1. The insurance policy is not the insurance contract because:
   (a) it is issued by the insurer and not jointly;
   (b) it may be incorrectly prepared;
   (c) the contract is the invisible agreement between the parties;
   (d) the contract is the completed proposal form. **(27.1)**
2. The narrative style of policy is:
   (a) not in writing or printing;
   (b) no longer legal;
   (c) written in modern English;
   (d) now obsolete. **(27.4)**
3. The "Schedule" in a scheduled policy form:
   (a) contains all information peculiar to that particular policy;
   (b) contains information common to all policies in that class;
   (c) consists of the conditions and exceptions to the contract;
   (d) indicates the types of risks that are covered. **(27.10)**

4. Express conditions are so named in insurance policies because they are:
   (a) very important;
   (b) "expressed" or written in the policy document;
   (c) agreed verbally with the insured and are not in the policy document;
   (d) terms requiring urgent action by the policyholder. **(27.14)**
5. Cover notes and certificates in insurance:
   (a) fulfil exactly the same function;
   (b) are parts of the policy document;
   (c) are only required in compulsory insurance classes;
   (d) both indicate cover of some kind. **(27.21–27.24)**

(*For multiple choice answers, see page 355.*)

CHAPTER 28

PREMIUMS

A. GENERAL OBSERVATIONS

28.1 What the premium is

The premium is the monetary consideration passing from the insured to the insurer. As such it is a necessary element in the formation of the insurance contract (see **16.9**).

28.2 When the premium is payable

Strictly, the premium is due at the inception of the contract, but frequently policies are issued before payment. Indeed, legally, the payment of the premium is ancillary to the basic agreement between the parties. Sometimes, policies will state that the insurer is not bound under the contract until the premium has been paid, but in the absence of this provision the insured may sue for a loss covered by the policy even though he has not yet paid the insurer. In those circumstances, the insurer has a separate right to sue for the premium, if necessary.

28.3 The premium represents a full payment by the insured

Except in the case of policies with an adjustable premium, e.g. stock declaration policies (see **5.15**), the insurer is not entitled to ask for additional payment from the insured in any circumstances. The payment of the premium by the insured discharges his financial obligations for the period of the insurance. Of course, the insurer may vary the terms of the insurance for any subsequent period of insurance (except with life policies, which involve level premiums (see **4.33**)).

28.4 How the premium is payable

The premium is payable in cash, in advance. The fact that payment is due at the beginning rather than at the end of the policy term has an important bearing on the rate of premium, since interest earnings can be taken into account in keeping the premiums as low as possible.

The manner of payment is usually annually, although arrangements are increasingly being made for payment by monthly or other instalments (usually involving slight extra cost). With industrial life assurance the whole basis of premium payments is quite different, they being collected from the insured's home at weekly, fortnightly or monthly intervals (see **4.15**).

28.5 What the premium must cover

The calculation of the premium must be carried out as accurately as possible, as it has to cover the following:

(a) *Claims.* If there were never any claims, there would be no insurance. It is on the claims service of an insurer that his reputation most depends. Clearly, therefore, premiums must be adequate at least to cover the cost of all claims, since this is the very foundation and function of insurance.

(b) *Catastrophe risk.* In addition to the claims actually made during any given year, with most classes of insurance there is the possibility of a particularly disastrous claim or series of claims, which will threaten the stability of the insurance fund. Obvious examples are the earthquake risk in fire insurance, and other major losses such as hurricanes, oil-rig disasters etc. Since payments for such major losses must also be made from premium income, an element in the premium calculation should be the catastrophe risk.

(c) *Commission.* Forming part of the acquisition costs, commission to brokers or other producers of business is important (except in "direct" insurances).

(d) *Administration costs.* No business organisation can function without incurring expenses. Staff salaries, cost of buildings, printing costs, transport requirements and many other examples combine to produce a considerable *expense ratio* for insurers. This ratio could well be in the region of 30–40 per cent, or even more, and this must be provided for in the premium calculations.

(e) *Reserves.* In addition to the provision for unexpectedly large claims, all prudent insurers will set aside reserves. These also must come from premiums, and are considered in more detail in **27.17–27.18**.

(f) *Profit.* It must always be remembered that commercial insurance is a business and not a philanthropic institution. It is true that insurance provides immense help to people in various kinds of difficulties, but the commercial insurer is in business for profit. Where a proprietary limited liability company is concerned the shareholders will expect a dividend on their investments. Ultimately, profit must be derived from premiums received.

NOTE: *"Cash flow" underwriting.* This is a term that was commonly used until recently. It refers to the practice of taking investment earnings of premiums into account when calculating basic rates. Obviously, this has always been an integral part of life assurance rating, but it was far less overt in other classes. Making an allowance for what is sometimes called "the time value of money" became popular in a business environment of fierce competition, at times of high investment earnings. This was not without its dangers, especially if investment rates became more volatile, and some insurers had unhappy experiences as a result. The purists would demand that investment earnings should not be a feature of non-life premium calculations.

B. HOW PREMIUMS ARE CALCULATED

28.6 General

Rating a risk (i.e. assessing the appropriate premium) cannot be a haphazard process, if sound and equitable underwriting results are to be produced. Basically, mathematics must be applied to produce the individual premium that a particular risk demands, bearing in mind the fact that the premium has to provide for all the aspects outlined above.

In theory at least, rating should not be based on the "swings and roundabouts" principle (i.e. that losses in one type of risk will be balanced by profits in another). The basic principle of premium rating is that over a period the results for a particular type of risk will show neither excessive losses, nor excessive profits. This is in accord with the fundamental idea of an insurance fund. The classic position of insurers is that it is wrong for contributions into a fire insurance fund to make up deficiencies in, say, a theft insurance fund. Taking the point further, fire insurance premiums on warehouses should not be used to offset continual losses on those for rubber factories, and so on.

Of course, in practice the insurers have to take an overall view in any given year, but in principle the rating should be directly related to the actual risk presented.

28.7 Life assurance

The calculation of life assurance premiums is the most scientific of all, partly because it has certain constant factors:

(a) *A claim is certain.* With the majority of life policies it is known that a claim must ultimately arise. Either the policyholder will die, or the policy will mature after the expiry of the stipulated period. With all other classes of business, claims are not certain with individual policies. A motor policy may never be subject to a claim, for example.

(b) *The amount of the claim is known.* In the event of a claim, the amount payable is known in advance (i.e. the sum assured, plus any accrued "profits"). With other classes of business (apart from minor exceptions, such as personal accident death benefits), claims may vary in size from just a few to many millions of pounds.

(c) *Statistical knowledge.* Mortality tables, and the collated experience of the different life offices, are available to life assurers. These, with a sufficiently large spread of risks, give relatively accurate indications as to the likely time when claims will arise (on an average basis).

The above factors mean that life premiums can be calculated with a considerable degree of accuracy. "Net premiums" in life assurance means the premiums necessary solely to meet the eventual cost of claims. To these must be added an appropriate sum for expenses and profit, with an additional amount if the policies are to be "with profits".

NOTE: Since life policies are long-term contracts, an important consideration in assessing their premium is the rate of interest likely to be earned on past years' contributions. While still a factor, this is of less significance in other classes of business, where policies are generally on an annual basis.

28.8 Marine insurance

The premiums charged for marine insurance depend very much on the past experience of the assured. Detailed statistics are kept by individual insurers, and a slightly different approach is given to hull and cargo insurances:

(a) *Hull insurances.* All British insurers are party to the *Joint Hull Agreement*, whereby the premium for hull insurance is based on the claims experience of the shipowner during the previous three years. Special assessed premiums are quoted for new shipowners.

(b) *Cargo insurances.* Rates are based on the underwriting results of the assured's account in the past. Thus, again, the personal record of the policyholder is of vital consideration, rather than results in the class of business as a whole.

28.9 Fire insurance

Rating in fire insurance has developed into a highly sophisticated and technical process, compared with the early days, when a rather rudimentary rating structure was employed (see **5.4**). To enable an equitable premium to be charged for an individual risk, the following considerations arise:

(a) *Classification.* This is the process of allocating the general type of risk to a specific category, which will have a basic rate applicable. With the increasing diversification of business and trade processes, new classifications are continually being made to keep pace with a developing technology.

(b) *Discrimination.* Once the classification has been assessed for a given risk, its individual features, for good or ill, will be taken into account, so that the basic premium can be modified by reductions or increases, as the case may be.

EXAMPLE: A particular risk might be placed in a classification which has a basic rate of £0.50 per cent, i.e. 50p premium is charged for each £100 worth of cover. This basic rate may be increased by a further £0.05 per cent because the premises are situated in a rather inaccessible place. The gross rate thus produced, namely £0.55 per cent, may be reduced by, say, £0.10 per cent because a suitable type of fire extinguishing apparatus has been installed, thus producing a rate of £0.45 per cent for that particular risk.

28.10 Other classes of business

With accident and other types of insurance, rating tends to be on the mathematical basis of previous years' experience for the class of business or type of risk as a whole, rather than being closely tied to the record of the individual policyholder. However, there are exceptions to this generalisation. For example, motor insurance is increasingly paying considerable attention to the past experience of the insured, in allowing sometimes a very substantial *no claims discount* on the subsequent year's premium.

The general rate for particular types of risk is assessed on a year-to-year basis, but it is not common for rates to fluctuate rapidly. When dealing with statistical matters, the result of a single year is a very unreliable guide. If results are bad, it could be that the particular year gave freak results; if they are good, similar considerations apply. In any event due provision must be made for a future year when a catastrophe is likely to occur. Thus, rates are likely to be changed only when a definite trend can be established over a reasonable period.

Of course, the above comments represent the ideal. Competition and alarming economic developments may have a disruptive influence on rating.

C. SHORT-PERIOD PREMIUM SCALES

28.11 Meaning

It sometimes happens that policies are issued for a period of less than one year in a class of business where policies are normally on an annual basis. Where this happens, the premium charged is rather more than the *pro rata* annual one. For example, a motor policy for a period of three months may be charged at 50 per cent of the premium that would have been charged for an annual policy. Such a premium is said to be charged on *short-period rates.*

28.12 Justification of short-period rates

There are a number of reasons why "short-period" policies should be charged higher than *pro rata* premiums:

(a) *Identical expenses.* The cost of producing a short-term policy, such as printing costs, stamp duty, expert's time in assessing the risk, etc., is the same as for an annual contract. Thus, the expenses involved represent a proportionately higher percentage of the premium, which should be increased accordingly.

(b) *Possible seasonal factor.* It can happen that the particular period for which the insurance is required is selected against the insurer, i.e. the period selected is the most hazardous period, for example the summer months with a passenger-coach risk. It would be inequitable for the period of the year presenting the greatest hazard to receive only a *pro rata* premium assessment.

(c) *Could amount to annual premium by instalments.* If policies could be effected for a period of less than one year at strictly proportionate premiums, it would be possible to have continuous cover by effectively paying premiums in instalments. While such arrangements may be possible, payment by instalments usually involves a higher annual cost.

D. RETURNS OF PREMIUMS

28.13 General

The general position about returns of premium is summed up in the maxim "once the risk has attached, the premium is considered fully earned". This means that the insured is not entitled to any return of premium once the contract has become binding. (This position can be amended by specific provision in the contract, or by an extraordinary legal situation: see Fig. 18 and **28.15–28.16**.)

In practice, insurers generally give sympathetic consideration to at least a partial refund of premium where, for instance, the subject matter is destroyed by an uninsured peril. Strictly, however, no such entitlement would arise.

28.14 Understanding the legal position

It may be thought inequitable that an insured is not entitled to any premium back if, for example, he disposes of the subject matter before the end of the policy year. (There may be a cancellation condition which amends this position, but at common law no rights of refund arise.) This thought would arise from the apparently logical argument that if, say, £120 is paid for a whole year's insurance, £30 ought to be returned if the insured article is sold by the insured after nine months. However, this is a misunderstanding of the legal nature of an insurance contract.

The contract is in effect saying that in return for a certain consideration (the premium) the insurer will make certain payments should certain events occur within a specified period. Legally, such an undertaking by the insurer is always conditional upon the insured fulfilling all legal requirements, such as possessing insurable interest, complying with any policy conditions, etc. Such a contract is firmly binding upon both parties and, unless the terms of the contract so provide, neither the insured nor the insurer is entitled to withdraw part or all of his consideration unilaterally.

28.15 Total returns of premium

Where a binding contract exists (i.e. where the insurer has borne the risk for at least some period of time) there can never be a legal entitlement to a full refund of premium. However, there are some circumstances where a contract appears to exist, but where the insurer has never legally been on risk. This means that there has been a *failure of consideration* on the part of the insurer, which entitles the insured to a full repayment of any premium advanced. These circumstances are as follows:

(a) *No agreement between parties.* It sometimes happens that a policy is issued when there has been a misunderstanding about the basic intention of the contract. Since the very foundation of the contract rests upon the fact that the parties are of one mind (*ad idem*) as to the agreement, the absence of genuine agreement means that the contract has never existed and any premium paid must be returned in full.

Naturally, the courts will not entertain frivolous submissions under this heading. Reasonable proof of the situation must be supplied, should the matter be disputed by the other party.

(b) *Breach of a condition precedent.* Conditions precedent to the contract (see **27.16**) must be fulfilled before any contract becomes binding. Therefore, any breach of such a condition, such as a breach of utmost good faith, or absence of insurable interest, might mean that the contract was void *ab initio*.

The premium would not have to be returned if the breach constituted fraud or wilful deception on the part of the insured.

(c) *Illegal contract.* If the insured realises that a proposed contract is

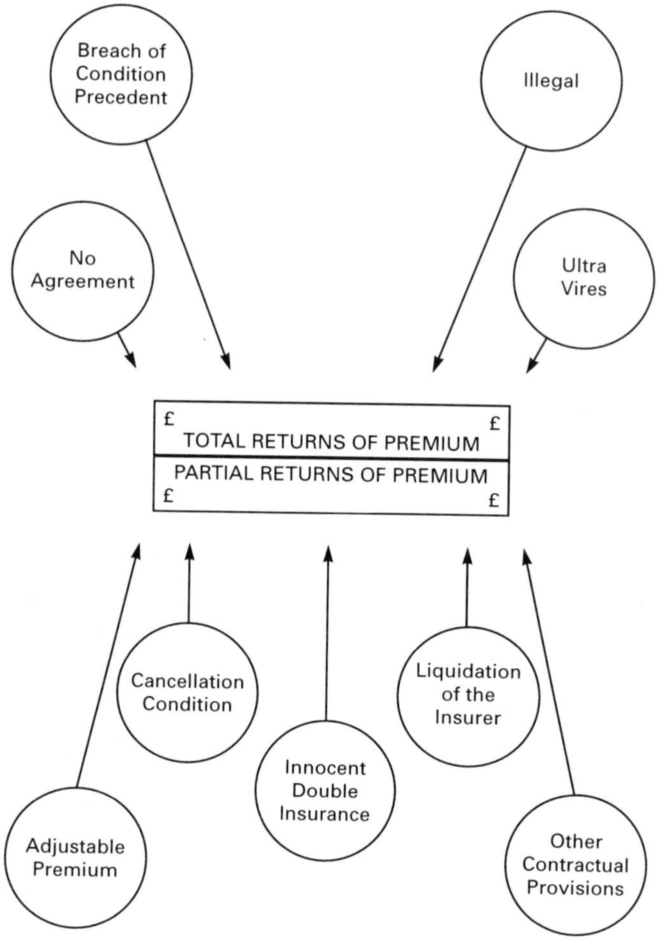

Fig. 18 Returns of premiums

in fact illegal, he is entitled to claim a full refund of any premiums advanced, provided he claims *before the risk attaches.* If he does not claim until afterwards, the right to a refund will depend on whether he knew, or ought to have known, that the contract was illegal.

(d) *Ultra vires.* A limited liability insurance company is restricted in the scope of its business transactions by the terms of its constitution (Memorandum of Association). If such a company issues a policy for a class of business that it is not authorised to transact, such a policy is said to be *ultra vires* (literally, "beyond its powers") and any premium paid is returnable in full.

28.16 Partial returns of premium

Policy provisions, or legal circumstances, may give the insured a right to a partial refund of premium. Some examples are as follows:

(a) *Under adjustable premiums.* Where the initial premium is recognised to be of a provisional nature, with a view to adjustment at the end of the policy year, a refund is made if the initial premium turns out to be higher than required.
(b) *Under a cancellation condition.* Some policies give the insurer and/or the insured the right to terminate the contract mid-term, with an appropriate part refund of premium. The refund may be on a *pro rata* basis, but in motor insurance when the insured cancels he may receive back the balance of the whole premium after being charged short-period rates (see **28.11**) for the time on risk. (Practice varies with insurers on this point.)
(c) *Innocent double insurance.* Where there has been no attempt to defraud, but double insurance has been arranged possibly by mistake, a refund of premium is usually made by a suitable adjustment agreed between the insurers involved.
(d) *Liquidation of the insurer.* Recent decades have seen the liquidation of several insurers. Their policyholders had a legal right to claim a *pro rata* refund of premium for the unexpired period of their policies. The Policyholders Protection Act 1975 (see **33.24**) would then apply, if necessary.
(e) *Other contractual provisions.* The contract may make specific provisions for part repayment of premium in certain circumstances.

A no claims discount, in motor insurance, usually does not mean a refund of premium as such, but a reduction on the next year's premium. However, it sometimes happens that a discount is suspended pending the outcome of a possible third party claim. The insured then pays the renewal premium as though the discount had not been earned. If the discount is subsequently allowed, the appropriate refund is claimable. (In practice, the amount may well be held in credit for the future.)

E. RESERVES

28.17 Reserves generally

Reserves may be considered as the holding back of money that would otherwise constitute profit as a safeguard against future known or anticipated needs. The need for reserves in insurance will be obvious, but as an item in a company's annual accounts (shown as a *liability*) it will have mixed implications. On the one hand, it will reduce the net profit and thus avoid tax, or at least defer it.

On the other, by reducing net profit it will not be to the immediate liking of shareholders, whose prime concern may be the dividend on their shares. The resulting "political" or "tactical" temptations thus arising are therefore a matter of prime concern for the regulatory authorities and others interested in a company and the manner and extent of (particularly loss or claims) reserving deserves the closest attention.

28.18 Specific (or technical) reserves

There will be specific funds for internal purposes, such as staff pension funds, etc., but for other particular known or anticipated liabilities the following reserves are likely to be held:

(a) *Unsettled reported claims.* At the end of any given period of account there will obviously be claims notified and likely to involve payments yet to be made. Settlement may have been agreed, or the claims are still under investigation or awaiting developments. In each case, the accounts should reflect a liability.

(b) *Incurred but not reported claims* (IBNR). These reserves are now extremely important in both insurance and reinsurance. The basic concept is that claims will be "in the pipeline", i.e. occurrences will have taken place in times past but the resulting claims have not yet been notified. Reserving for such contingencies, which may confidently be expected to arise (especially in reinsurance and "long-tail" business, where a considerable time-delay factor exists) has assumed a great significance, and with some companies a crucial one.

(c) *Unearned premium reserves.* With the great majority of policies, there will still be time to run when the end of the accounting period is considered. Thus premiums received during the accounting period cannot be considered fully earned. Further claims may arise during the period yet to run. Policies may be cancelled and refunds payable to insured. There are varying methods of calculating these reserves (as with the claims reserves mentioned above). Some companies reserve 40 per cent of the gross annual premiums as unearned premium. Others use a more sophisticated mathematical process. Whichever method is used, the reserves held back this year must be brought forward as income in the next account period.

(d) *Life fund.* With known liabilities for future claims (in most cases) the great majority of life premiums are reserved to form the *life fund*). This results in massive accumulations of money, but it must be remembered that virtually every policy will result in a claim and there are accordingly also enormous potential liabilities.

NOTE: With very bad results experienced in many classes of business in the recent past there arose real doubts as to the ability of reinsurers to meet liabilities, in some instances. Some insurers, particularly in the United States, therefore established reserves against *uncollectable reinsurance*. Not all regulatory authorities will accept these reserves as tax deductible.

28.19 Unexpired risk reserve

In former years this title was applied to what is now called *unearned premium reserves*, see above. There was logic in this title, but the term has changed over the years and now implies an additional reserve set amongst other liabilities in the accounts in case of real doubts as to the adequacy of other reserves. This is particularly valuable during a trend of worsening results and is accepted by the authorities as tax deductible.

28.20 Uncommitted (or free) reserves

Sometimes held in a *general* or *contingency* fund, these reserves are self-explanatory and a useful extra security measure to the technical reserves above.

F. TERMINOLOGY OF PREMIUMS

28.21 Glossary

It may be helpful to indicate various terms used in connection with premiums. Many have already been considered in this chapter. The terms include:

(a) *Gross premium*: the full premium payable by the policyholder.
(b) *Net premium*: this term may be used to represent either the premium *net of commission* or the premium *net of reinsurance*.
(c) *Written premium*: the same as gross premium (i.e. it is the premium "written" by the underwriter).
(d) *Earned premium*: the proportion of the gross premium relating to the period of cover that is past, at the time of accounting.
(e) *Provisional premium*: the premium paid at the start of the year with a policy subject to an adjustable premium. At the end of the year an adjustment is made.
(f) *Refund (or return) premium*: part of the provisional premium refunded if the adjustment (see above) indicates that too much premium was paid. May also be made if the policy is cancelled, etc. (see **28.16**)
(g) *Pro rata premium*: an exact proportion of the annual premium for a period of cover for less than a year. (May also relate to a *pro rata refund premium*: see above.)
(h) *Short-period premium*: a more than *pro rata* annual premium charged for a period of cover for less than one year. (May also relate to a short-

period refund premium: see above.)

(i) *Minimum premium*: the lowest premium charged in a particular type of insurance (especially important with personal insurances on very small sums insured). May also be applied with adjustable premiums, effectively reducing the maximum refund (see above).

(j) *Instalment premium*: (usually) monthly payments of an annual premium, normally subject to a loading or higher rate.

(k) *True monthly premium*: premium paid at monthly intervals, as above, but representing cover purchased for one month at a time (not on an annual basis). This is important in life assurance: under an annual premium policy paid by instalments, the U.K. system requires the rest of the year's premiums to be paid if death occurs. With a true monthly premium this does not apply.

(l) *First premium*: the premium paid for the first period of cover with the policy (may be more or less than a year, for example to allow the policy renewal to coincide with other policy dates or a quarter-day).

G. RATIOS

28.22 Claims, expenses and combined ratios

Although not exclusively related to premiums, it may be useful to mention insurance ratios in this chapter. The customary ones are:

(a) *Claims ratio*: this is the percentage produced by comparing the cost of claims with *earned premiums* during the same accounting period.

(b) *Expense ratio*: this is the percentage produced by comparing the cost of expenses with *written premiums* during the same accounting period.

(c) *Combined ratio*: the combination of (a) and (b) above. Although not a true percentage (earned and written premiums are on different bases), it is often so expressed, and used by management as an indication of profitability or otherwise.

28.23 Underwriting ratio

It has long been recognised that with non-life insurance there is a ratio between premium income and available assets that cannot be exceeded with safety. Massive premium growth may give short-term satisfaction, but in a competitive market this is unlikely to be achieved without considerable risk.

Obviously, what is "safe" will be a matter of dispute and personal opinion, but a typical ratio widely adopted in the U.K. will be that premiums (normally measured *net of reinsurance*) should not be more than three times more than available assets. In some hazardous classes of business in the U.S., cautious underwriters and observers would recommend no more than a 1:1 ratio. (In at least one Eastern European country, the regulators insist on a ratio not greater than 5:1.)

H. PROGRESS TEST 28

PART 1—SHORT ANSWERS (Answer in one or two sentences)

1. What must an insurance premium provide for? **(28.5)**
2. Why are life premiums said to be the most mathematical? **(28.7)**
3. What basic considerations arise in rating fire insurance? **(28.9)**
4. An insurance on a luxury coach for three months from May is quoted a premium of two-thirds the annual amount required. How would you justify this to the owner? **(28.11–28.12)**
5. What reserves should be held by a composite insurance office? **(28.17–28.20)**

PART 2—MULTIPLE CHOICE (Choose the most correct option)

1. Once the insured has paid the full annual premium:
   (a) he is not liable for any additional premium;
   (b) he may have to pay extra premium if the insurer's results are bad;
   (c) under no circumstances can any refund be made;
   (d) he will never be able to obtain a full refund. **(28.3)**
2. In calculating premium rates in the United Kingdom the underwriter:
   (a) must follow those set by the government;
   (b) cannot charge more than is being charged by competitors;
   (c) should relate the premium level to the risk;
   (d) can ignore market trends entirely. **(28.6)**
3. Life assurance premiums are said to be the most calculable, because:
   (a) it has been in existence for centuries;
   (b) there are certain constants, allowing considerable relative accuracy;
   (c) it is known exactly when any one individual will die;
   (d) of the volume of business transacted. **(28.7)**
4. Short-period scales of premium:
   (a) apply with travel and similar short-term insurances;
   (b) cannot be justified;
   (c) are at a lower than *pro rata* rate;
   (d) are at a higher than *pro rata* rate. **(28.11)**
5. An unearned premium reserve relates to:
   (a) a policy on which there have been no claims;
   (b) the period of cover that has elapsed at the accounting date;

(c) the period of cover that has not elapsed at the accounting date;
(d) projected premiums for the coming year. **(28.18)**

(*For multiple choice answers, see page 355.*)

CHAPTER 29

RENEWALS

A. GENERAL OBSERVATIONS

29.1 Meaning

The renewal of an insurance policy is self-explanatory, consisting of the continuance of the contract for a further period from the expiry date of the current term.

Except with those contracts which are intended to be of a long-term nature, renewals are not automatic. They must be invited or negotiated as though they constituted new contracts. The legal position about whether a renewal is a new contract or merely the continuance of an existing one has not been finally resolved.

NOTE: Although renewals must be negotiated, the inquiries are nowhere near as searching as with the original contract. Nevertheless, the duty of utmost good faith revives at renewal and the insured is obliged to disclose any material alterations in the risk (see **18.12**).

29.2 Renewals not obligatory

Apart from life assurances and long-term agreements (see **29.6**), there is no legal obligation on either party to seek or invite renewal. The contract is for a certain period, usually one year, and neither insured nor insurer is obliged to continue for a further period.

Normally, unless the experience with the individual risk has been particularly bad, the insurer will invite renewal. That is why he is in business.

B. UNDERWRITING CONSIDERATIONS ARISING AT RENEWAL

29.3 General

Even if renewal is invited, there is no obligation to offer terms on exactly the same basis as for the previous year. Indeed, many considerations may arise which will mean that the terms should be varied, either in favour of the insured or in favour of the insurer, as the case may be. It is the underwriter's duty to make a fresh appraisal of the contract at renewal, or preferably a short time before, to see whether any amendment of terms is necessary.

29.4 Life assurance

Life policies and permanent health personal accident policies (see **6.12**) are arranged on the basis that the insurer is not permitted to come off risk, or impose different terms, at the policy anniversary date, even though the risk may have deteriorated substantially. Provided the policyholder continues to pay the premiums and complies with any policy requirements, the renewal must go through on the terms originally arranged.

This is an exception to the general rule, and applies because the nature of the contracts is long-term. It would be quite inequitable for the position to be otherwise, and naturally the premiums are calculated to take this aspect into account.

29.5 Other classes of business

With virtually every other type of insurance contract, circumstances can arise where the insurer will wish to vary the terms if the contract is to be renewed. Sometimes, renewal will not be invited at all. (It is incorrect to say in such circumstances that the policy is *cancelled at renewal*. The contract is simply not renewed and the policy *lapses*.) Some examples of underwriting considerations leading to an amendment of renewal terms are:

(a) *No claims discount entitlement*. A claim-free year in motor, and in a few other types of policy, means a reduction in the renewal premium.
(b) *Bad claims record*. If the claims record is unsatisfactory, but not sufficiently bad to warrant declinature, terms may be imposed, such as:
    (i) increased premiums;
    (ii) reduction in cover (e.g. from comprehensive to third party in motor insurance);
    (iii) imposition of a policy excess or franchise;
    (iv) imposition of restrictive warranties.
(c) *Age of insured*. It may be that a restriction of the cover provided (e.g. from accidents and all sickness to accidents only in personal accident insurance) is called for, because of the insured's advancing age.
(d) *Sums insured*. The responsibility for estimating the sum insured is upon the insured. Often, however, this is not understood or is overlooked, and serious problems of under-insurance have arisen, particularly with property insurance in times of rapid inflation. Insurers try to help by forcefully reminding policyholders in renewal documents. Some policies are subject to an automatic increase in sum insured and premium, either on a fixed scale, or index-linked in

some way (to cost of living, or average building costs, for example). Inadequate sums insured remain a problem, however, and the insurance industry has yet to find a perfect solution.

29.6 Long-term agreements (LTAs)

It is quite common with some types of fire risks (especially churches) for the insurer to give a discount on premium in return for a binding commitment by the insured to offer the business for renewal, for a period of three, five or seven years. The insurer remains free to refuse the renewal. He may also suggest revised terms, but in this event the insured is released from his obligation to insure with that office. Should the policyholder fail to offer the business for renewal, strictly speaking the insurer is entitled to claim back the discount allowed in previous years.

C. GENERAL RENEWAL PROCEDURE

29.7 Long-term undertakings (LTUs)

In a bid to retain business and an attempt to stabilise rates, some companies have introduced *long-term undertakings*. These involve a mutual commitment for a period of three or more years, with an agreed annual premium rate. The practice cannot be said to be widespread yet, but at least one example involves a premium fixed for five years, related to a buildings and contents insurance. Time will tell whether this proves a successful counter to rate volatility and frequent change of insurer at renewal.

29.8 Before the policy expiry date

Some four to six weeks before the normal expiry date of an annual policy, the insurer will review the experience of the particular insurance and prepare the necessary renewal papers. The nature and content of these varies between insurers and the classes of business, but the general purpose is to advise the policyholder that the insurance for the current period is drawing to a close and to indicate the terms on which renewal is to be invited.

The renewal papers are prepared and issued well in advance to give the insured a reasonable period in which to remit the renewal premium. It also allows time for him to arrange alternative cover if the terms quoted are not satisfactory.

29.9 Days of grace

The renewal premium should be paid before the expiry date, if cover is to be continuous, but with many types of insurance a concession, known as *days of grace* (or *grace period*) is allowed. The term relates to a period, perhaps 14 days or one month, after the normal expiry date of the policy, during which the renewal premium may be paid and cover kept continuous. Thus, for example, the renewal premium for a policy having 14 days of grace may be paid, say ten days after the expiry date and a loss arising one week earlier than the payment would be recoverable.

29.10 The concession may be forfeited

Days of grace are allowed as a customary concession with most classes of business, but their benefit can be lost if the insured indicates before the expiry date that he does not intend to renew the policy. Further, the premium must actually be received by the insurer within the period allowed. If an insured sustains a loss within the days of grace and reports the loss, but fails to pay the renewal premium within the time allowed, the insurer can refuse to meet the subsequent claim. (In practice, of course, the insurer is unlikely to adopt this attitude, unless there are other elements in the case rendering the position unsatisfactory.)

NOTE: Often renewals are handled through brokers or agents who may have credit facilities with the insurer. Payment to such a broker or agent would usually be accepted by the insurers as being made to themselves, even though this point might be legally arguable (i.e. at law, the agent might be regarded as agent of the insured not the insurer).

29.11 Where days of grace are not applicable

Days of grace are not available with the following types of policy:

(a) *Marine policies.* Through long-standing custom, renewal premiums are expected on or before the due date.
(b) *Motor policies.* The renewal of motor policies requires special consideration, owing to the terms of the Road Traffic Acts (see **29.13**).
(c) *Livestock policies.* The benefit under such policies is only payable if the animal dies within the policy dates. An injury sustained within the policy period, but resulting in death after expiry date, would not give rise to a valid claim under many livestock insurances (unlike a similar position with humans insured under a personal accident policy). Partly for this reason, days of grace are not allowed under livestock policies.
(d) *Short-period insurances.* These are not normally renewed, but even if they are, no entitlement to days of grace arises.

29.12 Where premium is not paid within days of grace

It used to be customary for the insurer to send a reminder to the policyholder in these circumstances. However, this remains the practice with only certain types of business, e.g. fire, and then probably with only selected policies. The volume of business and common practice of changing insurer at renewal, especially in motor insurance, has made the practice obsolete. If the business is highly desirable, however, attempts may be made to revive the insurance, but the policy has lapsed and even if further premium is received there is technically a gap in cover.

Practice varies among insurers about policies which are revived. The following solutions have been applied:

(a) To consider the cover continuous from the normal expiry date, but to obtain an undertaking from the insured that no claim will arise for the period between expiry date and the time the premium was paid.
(b) To allow a full period of 12 months' cover from the date the premium is paid (i.e. leaving a "gap" in cover and amending the new expiry date).
(c) To leave a "gap" in cover, up to the time of the premium payment, and to insist upon the normal expiry date for the renewed insurance. In effect, this means that the insured is paying a full year's premium for less than a year's cover, but this can be justified by the extra expense incurred in securing the renewal. (This attitude is not likely to be taken up often, as it is the insurer who is seeking the business.)

NOTE: Life assurance policies have their own contractual provisions to deal with the above situation. They are subject to a *revival* (or *reinstatement*) clause, allowing the policy to be kept continuous. The concession is allowed for a period (perhaps up to five years) and is subject to certain safeguards, such as payment of back premiums and other measures.

29.13 Position with motor renewals

It is an offence under the Road Traffic Acts to grant cover retrospectively for compulsory insurance. This means that a certificate of insurance (or cover note) cannot be back-dated, or given earlier than the time of actual issue. Since the allowance of days of grace is doing this in effect, motor policies do not have this concession. Instead, the renewal papers incorporate a cover note providing Road Traffic Act cover only (see **7.12**) for a period of 15 days from the expiry date.

This allows the insured at least not to infringe the law if he omits to pay the renewal premium before the expiry date and uses his vehicle. In view of such limited cover, however, the renewal should be completed in advance by early payment.

D. PROGRESS TEST 29

PART 1—SHORT ANSWERS (Answer in one or two sentences)

1. Is the insurer obliged to offer renewal of every insurance contract? **(29.2–29.3)**
2. Why may an underwriter vary the existing terms on renewal? **(29.5)**
3. Explain what is meant by days of grace. **(29.9)**
4. With what types of policy are days of grace not allowed, and why? **(29.11)**
5. Outline the general procedure for the renewal of most policies. **(29.8–29.12)**

PART 2—MULTIPLE CHOICE (Choose the most correct option)

1. The renewal of a non-life insurance policy:
   (a) must be offered by the insurer;
   (b) need not be offered by the insurer;
   (c) must be on the same terms as the existing insurance;
   (d) is only granted if the insured requests it. **(29.1–29.2)**
2. A long-term agreement (LTA):
   (a) applies only to life assurance policies;
   (b) binds the insured to offer but the insurer need not accept;
   (c) binds the insurer to offer but the insured need not accept;
   (d) commits the insured to existing terms for the whole period. **(29.6)**
3. Days of grace:
   (a) are of value only if the premium is paid by the end of them;
   (b) give a free extra period of insurance;
   (c) will be lost if a claim arises before the premium is paid;
   (d) apply to all insurance contracts. **(29.9–29.13)**
4. The "revival" or "reinstatement" of a life assurance:
   (a) concerns a policy which had been cancelled by the assured;
   (b) occurs when the premium is paid during the days of grace;
   (c) is not possible;
   (d) is permitted within a specified period. **(29.12)**
5. The renewal of motor policies in the United Kingdom:
   (a) needs special treatment with regard to days of grace;
   (b) is no different from any other class of business;
   (c) needs no special underwriting consideration;
   (d) is guaranteed because cover is compulsory. **(29.5, 29.13)**

(For multiple choice answers, see page 355.)

CHAPTER 30

CLAIMS AND DISPUTES

A. CLAIMS GENERALLY

30.1 The "acid test"

Possibly the greatest single feature of an insurer's reputation as far as the customer is concerned is the claims service provided. However promptly and well the issue of policies, collection of premiums and notices for renewals are handled, the whole effect can be ruined by an inefficient or apparently inequitable claims service. If payments are delayed or withheld without satisfactory reasons, policyholders will quite rightly lose confidence in the insurer concerned. Thus, the handling of claims becomes perhaps the most important aspect of the insurer's advertising.

30.2 Who may act for the insurers

The insured may submit his claim personally, or through a duly authorised agent acting on his behalf, such as a solicitor or his insurance broker. Similarly, different persons may act on behalf of the insurer, as follows:

(a) *The insurer's employees.* Most insurers have their own full-time claims staff, who will negotiate settlement of the insured's claim. Such negotiation may be completed by inside staff, by correspondence, or by outside staff, such as claims inspectors, calling upon the insured.

(b) *Loss adjusters.* These are independent professional claims investigators. They are often appointed by insurers, especially in connection with marine, fire and large claims in other classes of business. They must act strictly within their scope of authority, and in the first instance their duty is usually merely to report the circumstances and approximate extent of the loss to the insurer.

(c) *Other agents.* Occasionally, insurers will authorise other agents, such as solicitors, or, with certain minor claims, brokers, to agree settlement on their behalf.

30.3 Most claims are settled amicably

Some people have the suspicion that insurers generally are unwilling to settle claims, and that payments are always delayed, with a degree of unpleasantness. This is a gross distortion of the true position. The vast majority of claims are settled quite amicably, within a reasonable time. For reasons stated in **30.1**, it is in the insurer's interests to complete on this basis. It has been estimated that of the millions of claims handled by British insurers fewer than 1 per cent have to be resolved by the courts.

B. CLAIMS PROCEDURE

30.4 Notification

It is important that the insurer should be notified of claims as soon as possible. This includes all events which could give rise to a claim later. The obvious reasons for this are that investigations may have to be made to verify the loss, which may be prejudiced by delay. Chances of recovery from any negligent party are also reduced if inquiries are not put in hand with reasonable despatch.

Nearly every insurance policy will require the policyholder, or his legal personal representative, to notify the insurer of a possible claim within some stipulated period. But for this requirement, the position would be governed by the Limitation Acts 1939–1975, which broadly allow three years for starting a court action in connection with a claim involving death or injury, and six years for other claims. Clearly, this period is too long for insurers with claims from their own policyholders.

NOTE: The legal limitation periods will apply to third parties wishing to claim against insured persons. Such third parties cannot be bound by the terms of the policy, and provided the insured has given notice as required under his contract he will be indemnified against third party claims arising.

30.5 Particulars and proof of loss

The duty of providing full particulars and proof of loss rests squarely upon the insured. He must prove to the insurer that a loss has been sustained by an insured peril.

In practice, this may sometimes be difficult, such as providing proof of a burglary. However, all reputable insurers allow a liberal interpretation of what constitutes proof, and unless there are reasons for suspecting the integrity of the insured the insurer will virtually never stand on technicalities.

30.6 Investigations should be thorough

Although it is the insurer's intention to give a good claims service, speed in payments should not be obtained at the expense of thorough investigation. In a sense, the insurer is holding the insurance fund on behalf of all policyholders. Payments, therefore, should be completely warranted. This requires careful investigation and reasonable proof, both of the insurer's liability and of the amount involved.

30.7 Payments should not be unduly delayed

The guiding principle in claims work is that there should be careful attention to detail and thorough investigation, but when liability is established payment should be made forthwith. Once the claim is found to be valid, nothing is to be achieved by delaying settlement. The only result of delay will be loss of goodwill and possible future loss of business. A prompt and fair claim payment has great advertising value to the insurer.

30.8 Method of settlement

There are four basic ways in which claims may be settled:

(a) cash;
(b) replacement;
(c) repair;
(d) reinstatement: see **19.12**.

C. *EX GRATIA* CLAIM PAYMENTS

30.9 Meaning and general considerations

An *ex gratia* claim payment is a payment, either in full or in part, where there was no legal obligation on the insurer to make such a payment. It is a payment, therefore, *out of grace* (or *favour*) and not out of obligation.

Ex gratia payments should only be made in exceptional circumstances, because the insurer has a duty to the other policyholders, who would in effect be contributing to such a payment. Nevertheless, there are occasions where a payment cannot legally be demanded but where the insurer feels that there are good sympathetic or commercial grounds upon which the legal position can be waived. Some points for and against *ex gratia* payments may be summarised as follows:

30.10 Claims and Disputes

(a) *For*:
   (i) A technical breach of a warranty or policy condition would give the insurer the right to refuse any claim payment, but this may be a little harsh.
   (ii) A liberal interpretation of claims is a good advertisement and a comfort to other policyholders who may become similarly placed.
   (iii) Refusal to make at least some sort of payment could mean a substantial loss of business, weakening the whole fund.

(b) *Against*:
   (i) Cover has been provided within certain limitations. The premium takes these limitations into account. Anything outside the limitations should therefore be refused.
   (ii) Payments without obligation ultimately mean higher premiums.
   (iii) Too ready a payment could set an unfortunate precedent, and make all policyholders over-demanding even with clearly invalid claims.

30.11 Naturally more sympathy for policyholders

Although every reputable insurer seeks to be scrupulously fair in its dealings with all claimants, there will inevitably be greater sympathy for policyholders than for third parties over borderline issues. Where a claimant is a third party (i.e. not the policyholder) insurers are far more likely to require substantial proof of the claim, and far less likely to consider *ex gratia* payments. This is natural, since the insurer depends upon his policyholders for his income, and satisfied customers are likely to remain with him.

This is not to say that the insurer adopts an uncompromising and harshly legalistic attitude towards third parties. On the contrary, many insurers have secured substantial business from persons introduced to them in the capacity of third party claimants, because the claims have been dealt with well and fairly.

D. CLAIMS IN THE MAJOR CLASSES OF BUSINESS

30.12 Marine insurance

Apart from the comparatively trivial losses, marine claims are handled by independent adjusters (termed average adjusters: see **14.22**). This is so because marine claims are usually of a technical nature and may be difficult to evaluate correctly, particularly in view of the fact that there are frequently many insurers involved.

30.13 Life assurance

Life policies will mostly be sure to result in a claim, as the policyholder will die or the stipulated period of years will expire. In the former case, the legal personal representative will have to provide proof of death. In every case, the policy will be surrendered and checks must be made to see that the policy has not been assigned (see **17.29**) or otherwise subject to any charge upon it.

30.14 Fire insurance

As with marine insurance, all but the minor claims are dealt with by independent loss adjusters. This, again, is partly due to the fact that many insurers are likely to be involved, and partly because the loss may be of great complexity, requiring specialised technical knowledge.

30.15 Accident insurance

Accident claims are usually dealt with by the insurers' own staff. Adjusters are sometimes appointed for the larger theft claims, and occasionally for other classes of business. Also, when negotiations in any class of business seem unlikely to produce an out-of-court settlement, solicitors are frequently instructed. They will endeavour to complete the matter amicably, or represent the insurers in court if necessary.

30.16 Motor claims

Most large insurers now have their own motor engineers to assist them with the technical assessment of damage to vehicles. Otherwise, the procedure for claims handling is much as with accident business generally: see above.

30.17 Engineering and aviation insurance

Both these classes are highly technical in nature, and independent experts are frequently instructed to assist with claims. As far as possible, however, the insurer's own staff deal with negotiations and payments.

E. DISPUTES OVER CLAIMS

30.18 Two basic causes

Disputes causing delay in the settlement of claims will fall under one or both of the following headings:

(a) *Liability*: i.e. if the claimant is a third party, the insurers may maintain that the insured (and therefore they) have no liability towards him, or the insurer may deny to the third party, or the insured, that there is any liability under the policy.

(b) *Quantum*: i.e. the amount payable by the insurers is under dispute.

30.19 How disputes are resolved

Disputes may be resolved in the following different ways:

(a) *Negotiation.* A disagreement may be settled by discussion between the parties concerned, resulting in one party's point of view prevailing or an amicable compromise being reached.

(b) *Litigation.* If the dispute cannot be resolved by discussion between the parties, court proceedings may be necessary. This is normally regarded by insurers as a last resort, entered into only when a substantial amount is involved or when an important point of principle is at stake.

(c) *Arbitration.* An alternative to litigation, but still involving a decision by a person not involved in the dispute, is the process termed *arbitration.* This involves a party, or parties, accepted by both sides, hearing both sides of the argument and giving a decision. The hearing, however, is not conducted in a court of law, and the person giving the decision is often not a judge. Arbitration is considered in more detail below.

F. ARBITRATION AND MEDIATION

30.20 Effect of arbitration

Settling disputes over civil matters is a duly authorised procedure, by virtue of the Arbitration Act 1950. Technically, it does not supplant the authority of the court, as a dispute can be heard in court after an arbitration award has been made. However, the judge in any subsequent court action will not set aside the arbitration award if the arbitration has been properly conducted in complete impartiality and provided the arbitrator has not erred on a point of law. For practical purposes, therefore, the decision of an arbitrator is binding.

30.21 Arbitration procedure

Policies containing an arbitration condition may merely state that the procedure to be adopted is to be in accordance with the current Arbitration Act. Alternatively, the condition may stipulate that *one* arbitrator be mutually appointed by the disputing parties. If the parties cannot agree on a single arbitrator, each may appoint one and the two arbitrators must appoint an *umpire.* The umpire sits in on the hearing, but has only a casting vote.

Technical experts, who have particular knowledge of the matter under dispute, are usually appointed as arbitrators, and the costs of the hearing are awarded at the discretion of the arbitrator or umpire.

30.22 Only applicable to claims on quantum

In the years 1957–1958 the central associations representing virtually every British insurer gave an undertaking to the Law Reform Committee, representing the government, that their policies would not contain arbitration conditions except in so far as disputes concerning *quantum* were concerned. This means that an insured in dispute with his insurer over a claim has every right to have the dispute aired in open court, except where the dispute is not over liability, but over the amount of claim only. In that case any arbitration condition will apply.

NOTE: i. Arbitration cannot be insisted upon by an insurer unless the policy contains an arbitration condition.

ii. The insurer cannot insist on arbitration with a claim from a third party. The third party is not bound by the terms of the contract, and has every right to proceed to litigation even if the dispute concerns quantum only.

30.23 Not every policy has an arbitration condition

Because arbitration can only be insisted upon for disputes over amount (see **30.22**), insurers do not usually have an arbitration condition in policies only insuring against legal liabilities of the insured (since claims are from third parties, who are not bound by policy conditions). Nor do they have such a condition in personal accident insurances, since the amount payable is not so often under dispute. Once liability is established the policy benefit is payable.

30.24 Advantages of arbitration

The advantages of arbitration as opposed to litigation, as far as the insurer is concerned, are as follows:

(a) *Speed*: it is usually possible to arrange an arbitration hearing much more quickly than one in court.
(b) *Privacy*: the fact that proceedings are not conducted in open court is of considerable value to the insurer. Having one's name in court is never a good advertisement, even if the case is won. Reports on court hearings can often be misleading and damaging.
(c) *May be cheaper*: it does not necessarily follow that arbitration will be cheaper than litigation, but this is sometimes the case.
(d) *Protection from "difficult insured"*. There are certain individuals who will use the threat of court action virtually to "blackmail" the insurer

into a higher payment, rather than the adverse publicity of litigation. An arbitration hearing removes this threat.

30.25 Mediation

A relatively new development in attempts to resolve claims disputes is called *mediation*. Similar to arbitration, in that it avoids the formality of litigation, it is in fact even less formal than arbitration. The function of the mediator is to try to get the parties to resolve their differences and to reach a settlement. To do this, the mediator is likely to have private meetings with each of the contending parties and to act as a "go-between" carrying offers, counter-offers and the like.

The arbitrator will have the more formal role of hearing evidence with both parties present and giving a ruling. Mediation is likely to be less expensive than arbitration and hard bargaining can take place in the more informal environment. It seems likely to grow.

G. INSURERS' ARBITRATION SERVICES

30.26 Two voluntary schemes

Partly in response to public disquiet over insurance claims disputes, some insurers instituted two voluntary schemes in 1981:

(a) The Insurance Ombudsman Bureau;
(b) The Personal Insurance Arbitration Service: see below.

30.27 The Insurance Ombudsman Bureau (IOB)

Set up in 1981, there are now over 300 insurer members of the scheme, including the Corporation of Lloyd's. The Council of the Bureau has a majority of members representing consumer interests. The Ombudsman was appointed to deal with disputes relating to policies (only for natural persons, not companies, etc., and only within the United Kingdom, Channel Isles, etc.). No dispute can be referred to the Ombudsman until a final decision is given by the senior management of the insurer involved in the dispute. It must then be referred to IOB within six months.

The IOB is an independent unlimited company and within his terms of reference the Ombudsman has the right to award up to £100,000 against member companies. This award is binding on the member, but the policyholder still has the right to proceed legally if he is dissatisfied. There is no charge to the policyholder for this service.

30.28 The Personal Insurance Arbitration Service (PIAS)

Not all insurers were happy with the IOB (above) and so an alternative organisation was formed in conjunction with the Chartered Institute of Arbitrators. The PIAS does not apply to life assurances or any insurances effected by an employer on behalf of his employees.

The only costs falling upon the policyholder are for the preparation and submission of documents and for attending any hearing. Even these costs may be awarded against the insurer at the discretion of the arbitrator.

Both voluntary schemes mark a positive attempt by insurers to improve public relations in the field of insurance policy disputes. One major difference between PIAS and IOB is that with the former the decision of the PIAS arbitrator is legally binding.

30.29 Strictly inter-insurer arrangements

For convenience and economy of administration, many insurers have arranged inter-insurer agreements to facilitate the settlement of claims, largely ignoring the common law position. Examples of this occur particularly in motor insurance (see **20.13**), but they are also found in employer's liability insurance (see **20.14**, **21.10**) and are not unknown in fire insurance.

These agreements, which usually involve the forsaking of recovery rights or an arrangement to share certain claims on a fixed basis, do not infringe the rights of the respective insured in any way. They are not party to such agreements, and they should neither benefit nor be prejudiced by the operation of the agreements.

H. FRAUDULENT CLAIMS

30.30 Traditional "double standards"

It is sadly true that large numbers of people have double standards when dealing with insurance claims. While they rightly expect the insurer to act with total integrity and fairness, many see no wrong in exaggerating claims beyond reasonable optimism and being very "economical with the truth" at times during claim discussions.

It is probably true that only a small minority of policyholders will deliberately fake a loss, or otherwise seek to perpetrate a "complete fraud". Nevertheless, when a genuine claim arises, there are many who do not hesitate to include damage not sustained in the particular accident, with motor insurance claims, claim for things not stolen or to give knowingly false values (higher of course) for other property insurance claims, and so on. There is nothing new or exclusive in this. People frequently exhibit the same qualities with expense accounts, income tax declarations and the like. Human nature is always tempted towards opportunism (looting at scenes of fires, or during social unrest is commonplace, for example). As with theft from supermarkets, up to a point this can be catered for in the pricing of the product.

30.31 "Complete frauds"

Any knowing dishonesty or intent to cheat is fraud, but the term "complete fraud" may be understood as a deliberate staging of a loss (arson, etc.) or a total fabrication of a "loss" that never occurred (alleged theft, etc.) or even a faked "death" (life assurance). These have always been factors with insurances. With the high degree of trust implicit in such contracts, fraud is not difficult. Where suspected, however, insurers go to great lengths to investigate and generally make life difficult for the suspected fraudster.

There is a danger in this, because by the nature of things suspected fraud is often subjective and the insurer must take care before alleging dishonesty. The laws of defamation are rightly strict, so it is rare that fraud will be alleged, unless very substantial evidence exists to support the allegation.

On the other hand, the burden of proof in civil cases (including claims under insurance policies) is only on a "balance of probabilities". The insurer does not have to prove his case "beyond a reasonable doubt", as in a criminal court. Cases of suspected fraudulent fire claims, for example, have been won by insurers contesting the matters in the civil courts.

I. CLAIMS RESULTS

30.32 Claims and other ratios

We considered ratios earlier (see **28.22**). Quite obviously, the largest expenditure insurers have concerns claim payments. It is therefore necessary to keep good control over claims. This must not be at the expense of equity, but in the United Kingdom especially there has been a great deal of effort to detect and track down fraud.

Also, as we have seen (see **15.17**), considerable efforts have been made to cut down on costs by reducing staff numbers.

30.33 The "bottom line"

This colloquial expression looks at the final analysis of a situation. The final analysis of a commercial company looks for a profit to be made. (Indeed, its very survival may depend upon it.) Managements and insurance financial analysts consider two types of profit:

(a) *underwriting profit*: this is achieved when income from premiums alone (ignoring investment and other income) exceeds claims and expenses (i.e. the *combined ratio* (see **28.22**) is less than 100 per cent);

(b) *operating profit*: this is achieved when all income (premiums, investment, etc.) exceeds the combined ratio.

Very detailed study of these matters does not really belong to this book, but the importance of claims in the financial results of insurers cannot be ignored.

J. PROGRESS TEST 30

PART 1—SHORT ANSWERS (Answer in one or two sentences)

1. By whom may claims negotiations be conducted? **(30.2)**
2. Why is it essential to investigate claims thoroughly? **(30.6)**
3. What are the arguments for and against *ex gratia* payments? **(30.10)**
4. Under what basic headings may disputes arise over claims? **(30.18)**
5. Why is arbitration preferable to litigation? **(30.24)**

PART 2—MULTIPLE CHOICE (Choose the most correct option)

1. Formal action must be started with property damage claims:
   (a) within three weeks of the damage being caused;
   (b) within three years of the damage being caused;
   (c) within six months of the damage;
   (d) within six years of the damage. **(30.4)**
2. Once liability and the amount of a valid claim have been determined:
   (a) payment should be delayed to earn interest for the insurer;
   (b) payment should be delayed to negotiate a smaller amount;
   (c) settlement should be made as quickly as possible;
   (d) payment is required by law immediately. **(30.7)**
3. *Ex gratia* claim settlements:
   (a) should not be made without careful thought;
   (b) should always be made if a court action is started;
   (c) are contrary to public policy;
   (d) are illegal. **(30.10)**
4. The two basic elements in all insurance claim disputes concern:
   (a) arbitration and litigation;
   (b) liability and quantum;
   (c) the insured and third parties;
   (d) when and to whom the money is payable. **(30.18)**
5. A major difference between arbitration and mediation is that:
   (a) mediation is likely to be more expensive;
   (b) mediation takes place in a court, before a judge;

(c) arbitration is less formal;
(d) arbitration is more formal. **(30.20–30.25)**

(*For multiple choice answers, see page 355.*)

CHAPTER 31

AVERAGE

31.1 Different meaning in insurance

When used in connection with insurance, the word "average" has a technical meaning quite different from the ordinary English usage. Moreover, it has different meanings when used in the various classes of insurance business.

A. AVERAGE IN MARINE INSURANCE

31.2 Meaning

When used in marine insurance, average means *partial loss*. Understanding this technical meaning will help to clarify the following terms which are commonly used in marine insurance.

31.3 Particular average

This refers to partial loss affecting one particular interest involved with the marine venture. Therefore, it can refer to loss or damage to the ship itself, i.e. "average" which is "particular" to the hull interest, or to partial loss or damage to cargo, i.e. "particular" to that interest.

31.4 General average

This is not strictly an insurance term, but relates to a practice of ancient origin and which is very similar to insurance in its intention (see **3.2**). Marine policies usually provide cover for general average contributions.

General average retains the meaning of partial loss, but it refers to a loss that is "general", i.e. that is to be shared by all interests involved in the marine venture, and not merely to rest upon the owner of the damaged or lost goods. (The student should compare the use of the word "general" in this context with, for example, "general election", which implies that every constituency needs to elect its member of parliament.)

31.4 Average

Before general average arises, or rather "is declared", the following conditions must be fulfilled:

(a) *The loss must have been sustained voluntarily.* For example, deck cargo may have to be thrown overboard during a heavy storm for the safety of the ship.
(b) *The sacrifice must save the whole venture.* In the above example, general average will not be declared if the ship sinks despite the measures taken.

Where general average is declared, all interested parties (and this would include the owner of the sacrificed goods) bear a share of the loss, so that the owner of the goods sacrificed is not unfairly prejudiced.

B. AVERAGE IN FIRE INSURANCE

31.5 Meaning

In fire insurance, the term "average" refers to a practice used to combat under-insurance.

Where under-insurance exists, the whole principle of insurance is being undermined, in the sense that the insured is not paying a fair premium into the common fund for the risk presented. Thus, full compensation paid in the event of a loss would be inequitable to other policyholders.

NOTE: The element of unfairness would not arise if all claims involved total losses, since the sum insured would be the maximum amount payable and under-insurance would automatically be penalised. The great majority of claims, however, do not involve total losses. In these cases it is surely right that any under-insurance should receive some penalty.

31.6 Application

There are different types of average found in fire insurance. Basically, they all have this in common: where under-insurance exists and average applies, the insured who makes a claim under the policy is paid less than the amount he would have received if the insurance had been properly arranged, i.e. for a full sum insured.

31.7 Three main types of average

In fire insurance the three types of average are:

(a) the *pro rata* condition of average;
(b) the special condition of average;
(c) the two conditions of average: see below.

31.8 The *pro rata* condition of average

The term *"pro rata"* means *exactly proportionate* and this is the meaning here. By the condition inserted in the policy, an insured is penalised exactly proportionately to the degree of under-insurance that exists. If, for instance, he insures for only 75 per cent of the value of the property covered, when he should have insured for the full value, he will receive payment of only 75 per cent of any loss sustained.

This is fair, in that premium rates are based on the assumption of full values being insured. The policyholder has paid only 75 per cent of the premium he should have done (in the above example); he receives only 75 per cent of the payment he would have received.

NOTE: i. The more formal application of the condition in a fire policy states that the insured is to be considered a co-insurer where under-insurance exists. This has the same practical effect as outlined above, and a specimen wording of such a policy condition reads:

> "Whenever a sum insured is declared to be subject to average, if the property covered thereby shall at the breaking out of any fire or at the commencement of any destruction of or damage to such property by any other peril hereby insured against be collectively of greater value than such sum insured, then the insured shall be considered as being his own insurer for the difference and shall bear a rateable share of the loss accordingly."

ii. The amount payable under a policy subject to this condition is calculated from the following formula:

$$\frac{\text{Sum insured}}{\text{Value at risk}} \times \text{Loss sustained}$$

The above means that the sum insured is only payable in the event of total loss.

31.9 The special condition of average

The adjustment of claims under this condition of average is identical with the *pro rata* condition. The only difference is that under the special condition of average under-insurance is not penalised unless the sum insured represents less than 75 per cent of the value at risk. Thus, a certain degree of under-insurance is permitted, and this concession may be found with policies insuring agricultural produce.

For obvious reasons, this is sometimes known *as the 75 per cent condition of average* (an *80 per cent condition of average*, on similar lines, is not unknown).

31.10 The two conditions of average

This type of average is employed sometimes with warehouse insurances. The system comprises:

(a) The normal *pro rata* condition of average as Condition 1.

(b) An exclusion of property more specifically insured (except to the extent that the other insurance may be inadequate) as Condition 2.

This type of average was developed to cope with situations which might otherwise involve *contribution* (see **31.21**) between two or more insurances. It was found that there was frequently double insurance of warehouses, so this clause was devised.

NOTE: It may be helpful to understanding to think of the two conditions of average first as a *non-contribution clause* (see **21.9**) with other insurances and then applying the normal *pro rata average* condition to any claim under the present policy. The two conditions may therefore be considered to be "applied in reverse order". If there is a more specific policy, it deals with the loss. If not (or it does not deal with the loss in full) this policy is subject to *pro rata* average.

31.11 Average is not automatically applicable

Average is not an implied condition in every contract of insurance (see **27.15**). It does not apply unless the contract specifically so provides. Where it is applicable, it is usually incorporated in the policy as one of the policy conditions. If average is not specifically included and under-insurance exists the insurer is liable up to the full sum insured for any loss sustained.

NOTE: An exception to the above comment may arise where the policy is subject to a proposal form and declaration, where the declaration incorporates a warranty of full value. If under-insurance exists in those circumstances, and average is not a condition of the policy, the insurer's remedy is to decline liability under the policy altogether. In practice, such claims are often dealt with on an *ex gratia* basis, as though average applied.

31.12 Present position

For many years persistent under-insurance by policyholders has forced insurers to make virtually all property insurances subject to average. The major exceptions are household policies (which are subject to a full value declaration and warranty) and church insurances. The latter were traditionally free from average, but even here the leading insurer in this field has been forced to introduce a form of average.

31.13 The American term for *pro rata* average

In the USA *pro rata* average is more usually called *co-insurance*. In the United Kingdom "co-insurance" refers to a situation where more than one insurer is covering the given risk (see **32.21**). But the American term is no less correct, since with *pro rata* average the insured is made to bear a rateable share of the loss, i.e. made a *co-insurer* (see NOTE i, **31.8**).

The practical outworking of the U.S. system (increasingly also being used in other countries) is rather kinder to the insured. The application is usually with household insurances, where the prospective insured may choose a premium rate based upon "80 per cent (or some other percentage) co-insurance". This means that claims will be paid in full up to the sum insured as long as the amount insured represents at least 80 per cent (etc.) of the value at risk.

This allows a measure of under-insurance without penalty, as with the U.K. *special condition of average* (see **31.9**). The big difference between the two systems is what happens when the sum insured does not meet the minimum requirement. Under the special condition of average the situation reverts to the *pro rata* condition of average formula (see NOTE ii, **31.9**). With the American system it may be said that the formula becomes:

$$\frac{\text{Sum insured}}{\text{80\% (etc.) Value at risk}} \times \text{Loss sustained}$$

which, as stated, is kinder to the insured (user-friendly!).

C. AVERAGE IN ACCIDENT INSURANCE

31.14 Meaning as in fire insurance

Where it is found in accident insurance, the term "average" has the same meaning as in fire insurance. The application is also similar, except that the special condition of average (see **31.9**) is rarely if ever found, and the two conditions of average (see **31.10**) are unknown.

The *pro rata* condition of average is particularly found with theft and "all risks" insurance on commercial properties, although a schedule of individual items specified under "all risks" cover might not be subject to average.

31.15 "First-loss" policies

Although the general rule is that premiums should be based on a full sum insured, it sometimes happens that this rule is waived. *First-loss policies* are issued where both parties know and accept that the sum insured represents less than the value at risk, but normal *pro rata* average is not applicable.

These are found in commercial theft insurance. They are justified in respect of some risks, where the possibility of a total loss is extremely remote, such as the contents of a very large department store. To steal the complete contents of a place like Selfridges, for instance, is a practical impossibility. With this type of risk, therefore, it is permitted to insure for a proportion of the actual value. The premium would have to be specially calculated, on rather more than a *pro rata* basis.

NOTE: i. "First-loss" policies are also found in fire insurance, but there they are rather more rare. Total losses from fire are much more likely with every kind of risk.

ii. *Pro rata* average in its customary form (see **31.9**) is applied to first-loss policies if the "declared value" (total sum declared to be at risk) is less than the actual sum at risk in the event of a loss.

D. AVERAGE IN LIFE ASSURANCE

31.15 Not used

Average, in the technical sense described above, is not applicable to life assurance. This is immediately evident when one remembers that life assurance (and personal accident) concerns insured "benefits" rather than values at risk.

The reference to an "under-average" life would have the normal English meaning of "average", in the sense that the health of the life considered or some feature relating to it was sub-normal in some respect. This might require special underwriting considerations, but has no relevance at the time of a claim.

E. PROGRESS TEST 31

PART 1—SHORT ANSWERS (Answer in one or two sentences)

1. What is meant by particular average in marine insurance? **(31.3)**
2. When would general average be declared on any loss at sea? **(31.4)**
3. How would you justify *pro rata* average? **(31.8)**
4. What is meant by "the two conditions of average"? **(31.10)**
5. What are "first-loss" policies? **(31.15)**

PART 2—MULTIPLE CHOICE (Choose the most correct option)

1. The term "particular average" is:
   (a) found in marine insurance and refers to a non-total loss;
   (b) found in fire insurance and concerns under-insurance;
   (c) a statistical term used in premium calculations;
   (d) commonly used in all classes of insurance. **(31.3)**
2. Pro rata average, as found in fire insurance:
   (a) is a system of compromising claims during arbitration;
   (b) can never be justified;
   (c) calculates the average sum at risk with stock declaration policies;
   (d) is used to penalise under-insurance. **(31.8)**
3. The special condition of average:
   (a) differs from *pro rata* average in the formula used in its application;
   (b) is used for all unusual types of property insurance;
   (c) is no different from *pro rata* average;
   (d) allows a measure of under-insurance without penalty. **(31.9)**

4. The U.S. equivalent of *pro rata* average, "co-insurance" is:
   (a) kinder to the insured if serious under-insurance exists;
   (b) less kind to the insured in its application;
   (c) exactly the same as *pro rata* average in its application;
   (d) nothing like any U.K. system of average. **(31.13)**
5. Penalising under-insurance with *pro rata* average does not apply in life assurance because:
   (a) life assurance concerns "benefits" not values at risk;
   (b) most people are under-insured;
   (c) it would not be fair on the dependants;
   (d) all claims are total losses. **(31.15)**

(For multiple choice answers, see page 355.)

CHAPTER 32

REINSURANCE

A. GENERAL OBSERVATIONS

32.1 Meaning of reinsurance

As with many words containing the prefix "re", there is the implication that something is repeated. Thus "reinsurance" means the insuring again (by the insurer) of a risk already insured.

32.2 The effect of reinsurance

These can be summarised as follows:

(a) it continues the basic principle of insurance by spreading the risk over an even wider field;
(b) it protects the insurance fund of the original insurer, thus giving additional security to the insured and all other policyholders;
(c) apart from the indirect ways mentioned in (a) and (b) above, *the insured is in no way involved.* There is no contractual or other relationship between the insured and the insurer. Thus:
  (i) the insured can only claim from the insurer. If the insurer fails, the insured has no access to the reinsurers (they would have to meet any contractual liabilities to the insurer, but moneys paid would not be payable direct to the insured);
  (ii) if a reinsurer fails, the insured is in no way prejudiced. Any resultant loss falls upon the insurer.

32.3 Reasons for reinsurance

The overriding result of reinsurance is the reduction of the net cost of claims to the insurer. There are, however, a number of reasons why reinsurance is purchased. These reasons include the following five headings:

(a) *Capacity.* The ability to accept large risks is severely curtailed if each acceptance is for the insurer's net account.

(b) *Catastrophe.* Some reinsurances (see **32.12–32.13**) pay claims in excess of a stated figure. This greatly helps in catastrophe situations, reducing the net cost to acceptable levels.
(c) *Control.* Some reinsurances (see **32.10–32.11**) share risks and claims. This ensures greater stabilisation of results.
(d) *Consultation.* Especially with highly technical and unusual risks the reinsurer's expertise and advice is invaluable.
(e) *Corporate strategy.* An insurer's accounts show assets and liabilities net of reinsurance. Judiciously arranged reinsurances can therefore substantially affect the net financial position.

32.4 By whom reinsurance is practised

Virtually all insurers seek reinsurance, on at least the larger risks. With the great increase of large groups of insurers, and the consequent increase in resources and stability, the amount retained by insurers has tended to increase. Further, reinsurance is often arranged between companies within a group organisation.

32.5 What reinsurance consists of

Reinsurance consists of:

(a) *specialised* (or *professional*) *reinsurers*, who transact no direct insurance;
(b) *virtually all other insurers.* Nearly all insurers act in the capacity of reinsurers for other insurers. Frequently reciprocal arrangements are made in respect of their own risks.

32.6 Definitions

The following should be clearly understood:

(a) *Ceding office* (or *cedant*, can be spelt *cedent*): the original insurer.
(b) *Cession*: this is the amount ceded by the insurer to the reinsurer. (Note that the entry on the lists, or *bordereaux*, showing details of re-insurance transactions would be allocated an identifying *cession number*.)
(c) *Commission*: the standard meaning is "a percentage of the premium concerned". In reinsurance contracts the amount (paid by the reinsurer to the insurer) is larger than for direct business, one reason being that all the underwriting considerations have been dealt with.
    Commission is normally only paid with "sharing" reinsurances

(quota share and surplus) not with excess of loss arrangements. The commission paid for the business, regardless of results, is termed *ceding commission*. It is also common with "sharing" treaties for *profit commission* to be payable in addition, if results warrant it.

(d) *Deductible*: the more usual name given to the *retention* (see below) in excess of loss reinsurance. Also known as the *threshold* or *underlying retention*, or *attachment point*.
(e) *Guarantee*: an alternative term, formerly much used in fire insurance, for reinsurance.
(f) *Line*: a term that is synonymous with retention. A "ten line treaty" therefore indicates a treaty whose capacity is ten times the amount of the insurer's retention (see **32.11**). Reinsurers usually base their acceptance of the risk on a fraction (or multiple) of the insurer's line.
(g) *Reciprocity*: the mutual exchange of business by way of reinsurance. In the past this was often used to "spread the risk" further. More likely today it will be used in order to gain entry to other markets.
(h) *Retention*: the amount of the risk retained by the original insurer, i.e. the maximum net loss that can be sustained on that risk by the ceding office. More usually applied to "sharing" rather than excess of loss reinsurance.
(i) *Retrocession*: The reinsurance of a reinsurance. The party obtaining such cover is known as the *retrocedant* and the party giving the cover is the *retrocessionnaire*.
(j) *Security*: the confidence that a cedent (insurer) may have in the value and "collectability" of reinsurance effected. This would embrace not only the financial security offered by the reinsurer, but also its integrity and honour. Before the recent reduction in reinsurance capacity, the great growth in the number of reinsurers led to considerable (often very justified) fears over the security of the reinsurance offered.

B. TYPES OF REINSURANCE

32.7 Three main types

These are as follows:

(a) Facultative reinsurance;
(b) Treaty reinsurance;
(c) Reinsurance pools: see **32.8–32.14** below.

32.8 Facultative reinsurance

This is the oldest form of reinsurance. One dictionary meaning of "faculty" is "special permission", and this conveys the connotation of facultative reinsurance. The insurer has to make specific inquiry of the reinsurer for individual risks, and the insurer may accept or decline the offer. Because of this, the system has the following drawbacks:

(a) It is *cumbersome*. The paperwork and inquiries are much the same as with the original insurance.
(b) It is *uncertain*. The insurer has no guarantee that reinsurance will be available. The reinsurer may decline the risk offered.

32.9 Treaty reinsurance

A treaty is a formal, legally binding agreement. So with treaty reinsurance the insurer makes a legal contract with the reinsurer(s), who agree to accept reinsurance automatically within the terms and scope of the treaty. It is of considerable importance for the insurer to know that reinsurance protection is immediately available.

There are several different kinds of treaty reinsurance: see below.

32.10 Quota share (or fixed share) treaty

As the name suggests, the reinsurer(s) takes a certain proportion of all risks written by the insurer. He receives the agreed proportion of all premiums and refunds that proportion of all claims. While simple to operate, this system was rarely used except with new or small insurers who needed the substantial protection afforded. However, with the increasing awareness of the necessity to restrict administrative costs, the economy of operation presented by this system has led to its being more widely adopted.

32.11 Surplus treaty

The insurer fixes a maximum retention, which is agreed with the reinsurers. If the sum insured for a given risk exceeds the insurer's desired retention (subject to the agreed maximum), reinsurance is necessary, and the *surplus exposure* over and above the retention, up to the sum insured, is ceded to the treaty. Treaties are normally arranged on the basis of so many *lines*. An example will illustrate:

EXAMPLE: Suppose the insurer's retention is £100,000 and he has arranged a ten-line treaty. Reinsurance on a policy with a sum insured of £500,000 would be as follows:

Original insurer retains	£100,000
The treaty reinsurers accept	£400,000
Total = the sum insured of	£500,000

Thus, 80 per cent of the risk is reinsured by the treaty, which receives that percentage of the premium, and bears that percentage of any claim affecting that policy. (See **32.16** below for the alternatives where the treaty and retention together do not absorb the full amount of the risk.)

While this method is widely used, it is not suitable where there is an enormous sum insured, or where the limit of indemnity is very high. With some liability insurances, for instance, the indemnity insured is unlimited in amount (thus making it impossible to calculate percentages or proportions of the exposure).

32.12 Excess of loss treaty

This is particularly suitable for liability insurances, or where very large losses may be sustained, e.g. the catastrophe risk in fire insurance. Here the reinsurance is not based on the sum insured but on the cost of individual claims. The retention (or *deductible*) is usually fairly high, e.g. £1,000,000, and the reinsurers are involved only to the extent that a single claim exceeds that retention. That is, any *excess* over and above the retention is recoverable from the reinsurers. For this protection the insurer pays the reinsurers an agreed (usually small) percentage of the annual premium income for that class of business.

NOTE: i. Such a treaty will contain an upper limit, e.g. the reinsurers will pay the excess of £1,000,000 up to £5,000,000. An additional *second (and third, etc.) layer* treaty may be arranged to cover the catastrophe risk.

ii. The insurer may be required to retain part of the cost in excess of the deductible. To keep the insurers directly involved in the cost, for instance, the treaty may provide that the reinsurers pay only 95 per cent of the excess of £1,000,000.

32.13 Excess of loss ratio (or stop loss) treaty

This is a form of excess of loss reinsurance, based upon claim costs rather than exposures (sums insured). However, instead of applying to individual claims, this system is based on the complete cost of all claims in the class of business concerned, compared with premiums for the year or other period under consideration (i.e. the claims ratio).

EXAMPLE: The reinsurers pay 90 per cent of any gross loss ratio in excess of 75 per cent. (The treaty normally does not pay all the excess above the deductible.) On this basis, a specimen year might be:

Annual premium income	£5,000,000
Claims for the year	£4,000,000

The gross claims ratio is 80 per cent, and so the reinsurance is involved. The amount under consideration is the excess of 75 per cent (£3,750,000), i.e. £250,000. Of this, the reinsurer pays 90 per cent. Thus, the insurer will recover £225,000 from the insurer.

This system protects the insurer from sustaining a crippling loss in a given year, although it does not prevent loss altogether. It may help understanding to say that the reinsurance "stops a loss becoming a disaster", hence "stop-loss" treaty. The important thing to note, however, is that it will not turn a loss year into profit. There must be a loss before the stop-loss treaty operates. (In the above example, a 75 per cent loss ratio, when added to the expense ratio, is bound to produce an overall loss).

For the protection afforded, an agreed percentage of the annual premium income is paid to the reinsurer. The stop-loss treaty (like quota share: see **32.10**) can be said to be a *portfolio reinsurance*, in that it insures whole classes of business, rather than individual risks.

32.14 Reinsurance pools

These are used for exceptionally heavy risks, such as atomic energy risks. Often the whole premium is ceded to the pool by all insurers involved with that class of business, losses or profits being shared in the same proportions as the respective contributions to the pool. Thus, there is the widest possible spread of risks, and these very hazardous classes of business are shared equitably among all participating insurers.

32.15 An alternative classification of reinsurance

The categories shown in **32.7** may be seen as one classification. Another in common international use has two categories:

(a) *Proportional* (or *pro rata*) *reinsurance*, where claims met by the reinsurer are in exactly the same proportion as premium received. Quota share, and surplus (and pools), are in this category.

(b) *Non-proportional* (or *excess of loss*) *reinsurance*, where there is no correlation between the proportion of premiums received by the reinsurer and the proportion of claims payable by him. Excess of loss and stop-loss reinsurance are in this category. Should the premium received and claims paid be in exactly the same proportion it would be by total chance. This would scarcely ever arise.

C. SOME DIFFICULTIES EXAMINED

32.16 Surplus treaty reinsurance

It must not be thought that a five-line treaty, for instance, is shared necessarily by five reinsurers, nor that the proportions accepted by the different reinsurers are necessarily equal. The term merely indicates the capacity of the treaty (in the above example, five times the insurer's retention). The income and liabilities of the treaty may be shared by any number of agreed reinsurers in any agreed proportions.

32.17 Inadequate surplus treaty reinsurance

Where the exposure (sum insured) is so large that the arranged treaty and insurer's retention do not absorb it, three possibilities exist:

(a) The treaty is fully used and facultative reinsurance is sought for any balance of risk.
(b) The insurer seeks special permission from the reinsurers to increase the basic retention, so that the number of lines of the treaty can then absorb the whole balance of risk.
(c) The insurer may retain the unaccommodated balance of the risk, after using the full extent of the treaty. This must be the position if no other action is taken. This assumes that all the risk is accepted by the insurer. He could accept only such proportion as his existing reinsurance can absorb, leaving the balance uninsured or a matter for co-insurance (see **32.21**).

32.18 Excess of loss and excess of loss ratio reinsurance

These are often confused. The former is concerned with the cost of individual claims, the reinsurer paying the balance over and above the deductible figure. The latter is operative when the combined cost of all claims exceeds a certain percentage of the year's premium income for that class of business (agreed claims-ratio).

32.19 Excess of loss and surplus treaty reinsurances

With the former, every policy in the class of business is reinsured, but reinsurance recoveries are only made for a proportion of the larger claims. With the latter, only the larger policies are reinsured, but reinsurance recoveries are made in the applicable proportions on all claims affecting such policies.

D. REINSURANCE AND CO-INSURANCE (See Fig. 19)

32.20 Reinsurance

The insured is not party to this (see **32.3**(c)). The reinsurance contract is solely between the reinsurer and insurer. Payments made by the reinsurer are only made to the insurer.

32.21 Co-insurance

This occurs where more than one insurer is in direct contractual relationship with the insured for parts of the same risk. This is often found in fire insurance where, for example, five insurers may each arrange to bear 20 per cent of the risk. In law, separate contracts exist between the insured and the five insurers, although in practice it may be that a *leading insurer* may conduct all correspondence on behalf of all the insurers, and perhaps only one policy is issued. (In such a case, there would be a *schedule* of insurers, indicating their proportion of the risk, which would be termed *scheduled*.) Thus, should one of the co-insurers fail, the insured would be directly prejudiced.

NOTE: Compare *co-insurance* as found in U.S. household policies, where the term relates to under-insurance situations rather than reinsurance (see **31.13**).

32.22 The essential difference

With reinsurance there is only one contract between the insured and insurer. With co-insurance there are a number of contracts with different insurers.

32.23 Marine insurance

Co-insurance is very widespread in marine insurance. Of course individual insurers also practice reinsurance. This is either facultative or by treaty.

32.24 Life assurance

Facultative or treaty methods are used.

32.25 Fire insurance

Surplus treaty is the most widely used, but excess of loss reinsurance is used for the catastrophe risk. Facultative reinsurance is also found.

32.26 Accident insurance

In view of the diverse nature of this class, all forms of reinsurance are practised widely. Excess of loss is particularly used with the liability classes.

E. PRESENT DAY REINSURANCE

32.27 Reduced capacity

This was touched upon earlier (see **15.13**). The great growth in specialist or *professional* reinsurers in the 1970s and early 1980s (usually as subsidiaries of direct insurers) was reversed, with considerable numbers of mergers and withdrawals. Direct insurers continue to transact "inward" and "outward"

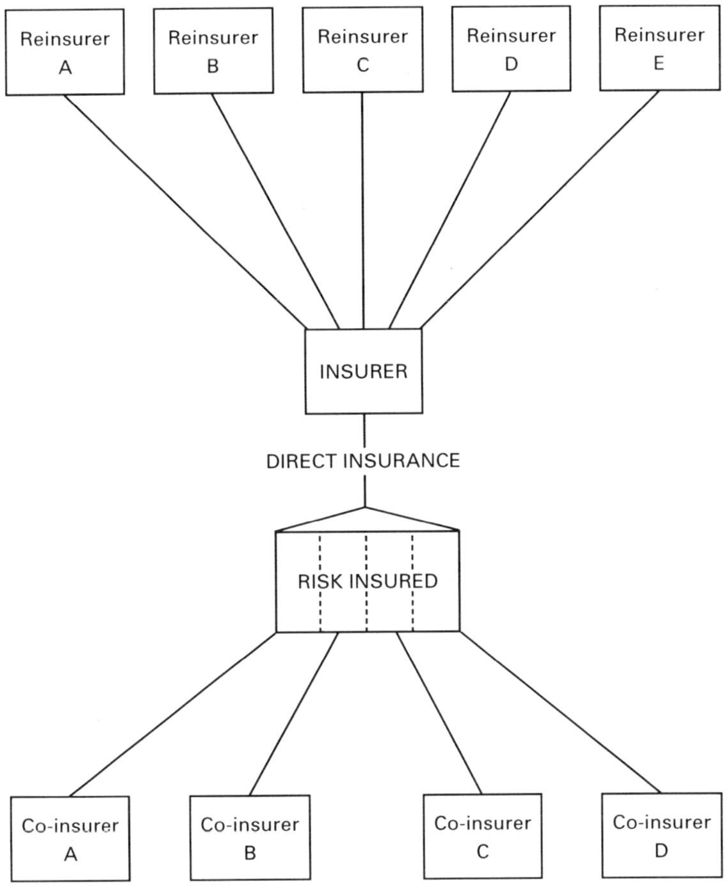

REINSURANCE
(Not necessarily in equal shares,
nor necessarily more than one reinsurer)

CO-INSURANCE
(Not necessarily in equal shares,
but must be at least two insurers)

Fig. 19 Comparison between reinsurance and co-insurance

reinsurances (the former reinsuring other insurers, the latter reinsuring their own risks), but the number of specialist insurers has decreased worldwide.

The reduction in capacity was especially felt in very high levels of cover, sometimes in the jargon of the day called "mega-risks". A noticeable development from this has been the establishment of reinsurers specialising in this type of cover, mainly based in Bermuda.

32.28 Increasing influence

It used to be said that the direct insurers had the upper hand in reinsurance arrangements and that they had the greater influence over rates and terms. To some extent this was cyclical, but in recent years it is true that reinsurers have become rather more assertive (see again **15.13**) and selective.

This is not at all bad for the industry as a whole. The days of very "soft market" reinsurance conditions sadly often led to a drop in underwriting standards by direct insurers. It has been said that the future of insurance lies in the hands of the reinsurers. While this may be an exaggeration, it is true that realistic and professional standards demanded by reinsurers will encourage a greater sense of responsibility at primary underwriting level.

32.29 Conclusion

Reinsurance has its individual features requiring much deeper study than this introductory book can provide. Readers are therefore encouraged to include other more specific publications to further their studies. This of course also applies to all specialist areas we have looked at.

F. PROGRESS TEST 32

PART 1—SHORT ANSWERS (Answer in one or two sentences)

1. If a reinsurer fails, is the insured automatically prejudiced? **(32.2)**
2. Why is reinsurance arranged? **(32.3)**
3. Why is facultative reinsurance less common than treaty reinsurance? **(32.8)**
4. Explain what is meant by a surplus reinsurance treaty. **(32.11)**
5. What is the difference between reinsurance and co-insurance? **(32.20–32.21)**

PART 2—MULTIPLE CHOICE (Choose the most correct option)

1. The practice of reinsurance:
   (a) has no implications for the insured whatsoever;
   (b) can only be carried out by specialist companies;

(c) indirectly benefits the insured as well as insurer;
(d) is exactly the same as co-insurance. **(32.2)**

2. Reinsurance commission is:
   (a) paid by the insurer to the reinsurer;
   (b) paid by the reinsurer to the insurer;
   (c) only payable if the business is profitable;
   (d) paid with every type of reinsurance. **(32.6)**
3. A quota share (or fixed share) reinsurance:
   (a) applies to the whole portfolio of business concerned;
   (b) applies only to a selection or quota of risks;
   (c) is applied to individual risks according to the exposure presented;
   (d) is no longer practised. **(32.10)**
4. "Stop-loss" reinsurance:
   (a) is a form of "sharing" individual risks;
   (b) applies to large individual claims;
   (c) guarantees that the insurer will make a profit;
   (d) is related to the claims ratio of the insurer. **(32.13)**
5. The reinsurer's influence upon the direct insurance market:
   (a) can be significant, especially with higher liability risks;
   (b) will never affect underwriting decisions;
   (c) is only important if the direct market is a "hard" one;
   (d) is and always has been negligible. **(32.28)**

(For multiple choice answers, see page 355.)

PART FIVE: OBJECTIVE TESTS (see Answers, page 356) and ASSIGNMENTS

5.1 State whether the following statements are *true* or *false*:

(a) Physical hazard is usually much easier to assess than moral hazard.

(b) Although not legally required, proposal forms are invariably used with most classes of insurance.

(c) The old "SG" (ships-goods) form of policy was in the narrative style.

(d) A condition precedent to liability goes to the root of the contract.

(e) Life and personal accident policies are normally based on the level premium system.

(f) Conventional days of grace are illegal with motor policies.

(g) *Ex gratia* payments are sometimes made by insurers in order to avoid distress and hardship that strict interpretation of their rights might cause.

(h) Average in fire and marine insurance relates to a penalty for inadequate sums insured.

(i) A retrocession is a reinsurance effected by a reinsurer.

(j) A surplus reinsurance treaty is most suitable when dealing with liability risks.

5.2 Select the *most correct* answer for the following questions:

(a) Trying to deal with adverse moral hazard is difficult because (i) proposers often do not tell the whole truth; (ii) it chiefly refers to latent factors that take time to appear; (iii) each person is different.

(b) The declaration used on fire and accident proposal forms (i) is used to extend the common law duty of utmost good faith; (ii) makes the whole proposal and contract subject to utmost good faith; (iii) has to be evidenced by an independent witness.

(c) The schedule in a scheduled policy form (i) outlines the extent of the cover provided; (ii) contains all information peculiar to that policy; (iii) is the insurer's written undertaking towards the policyholder.

(d) Cover notes in insurance (i) are required by law; (ii) will provide the police with confirmation that compulsory insurance exists; (iii) confirm that insurers are on cover for certain risks.

(e) Short period premiums (i) are proportionately more expensive than annual premiums; (ii) are charged on all policies of less than 12 months' duration; (iii) are restricted to motor policies only.

(f) Insurers send out motor renewal notices (i) because it is illegal not to do so; (ii) because policyholders would be breaking the law if they forgot to renew their policies; (iii) in order to maintain premium income.

(g) Arbitration is a method of settling disputes preferred by insurers because (i) injured third parties could otherwise gain great sympathy from the courts; (ii) very high legal expenses can thus be avoided with all claims; (iii) the hearing is confidential.

(h) The *pro rata* condition of average is so called because (i) the amount of loss paid is the same percentage as the percentage of under-insurance; (ii) the amount paid is directly proportional to the percentage of insurance arranged; (iii) not all the loss is paid.

(i) Reinsurance is practised (i) by specialist reinsurers; (ii) by virtually all insurers; (iii) because insurers could not afford to pay catastrophic claims.

(j) An excess of loss ratio reinsurance treaty (i) will only operate when the insurer has sustained a net loss; (ii) is designed to alleviate the effects of catastrophic individual claims; (iii) means that the reinsurer will pay a certain proportion of the cost of individual large claims.

5.3 Assignments

(a) Write an essay on the scheduled policy form; why it has become so popular, what the functions of the various sections are, and why insurance policy forms need to be so complicated.

(b) Discuss what you think should be an insurance company's attitude towards claims from (i) its own policyholders; (ii) third parties claiming against policyholders, particularly touching upon the merits or otherwise of *ex gratia* payments.

(c) Collect proposal forms from several insurers for the same classes of business. From them complete a report, outlining (i) the cheapest policy; (ii) which one you would recommend, and why; (iii) an improved proposal layout, using features from each.

PART SIX

INSURANCE AND THE STATE

CHAPTER 33

STATE SUPERVISION AND REGULATION

A. WHY THE STATE IS INTERESTED

33.1 Possibilities of fraud

Insurance is essentially based on trust. It also involves vast sums of money. These two factors have made insurance very attractive to the dishonest for centuries. Life assurance, particularly in the early years, was fruitful ground for fraudulent schemes, and even in recent years quite spectacular frauds have been perpetrated in this class of business.

With any business offering such incentives to the dishonest, the State is rightly concerned to maintain relatively close monitoring.

33.2 Consequences of a failure of an insurer

When any business collapses a certain amount of distress follows. When an insurer fails, the consequences for policyholders and third party claimants may be very serious indeed. The sudden collapse of a life assurer is perhaps worst of all, where policyholders and their dependants are often relying absolutely on the fund for pensions or in family tragedy.

The State therefore has a general interest and duty to try to ensure that insurance failures do not suddenly occur. Specific steps have therefore been taken to safeguard the interests of any likely to be affected.

B. HISTORICAL DEVELOPMENTS IN THE UNITED KINGDOM

33.3 Reluctance of the State to interfere

Traditionally, at least prior to the twentieth century, the State in the United Kingdom was reluctant to interfere with trade or commerce. The general attitude was that people should be free to transact business as they wished within the broad scope of what was legal and moral. The State should not intervene as long as the general public good was not threatened. At times action had to be taken, but usually the situation had to be of a grave nature to warrant any interference.

33.4 Insurable interest

Attempts to eliminate the element of gambling with insurance contracts by insisting upon insurable interest have already been studied (see **17.6–17.9**). While largely reinstating the common law position, State intervention by way of legislation was necessary to combat the unsatisfactory position that had arisen.

33.5 Life Assurance Companies Act 1870

The social significance of life assurance has already been mentioned (see **33.1–33.2**). This Act followed some disastrous failures in the 1860s and amongst other things introduced two elements attempting to secure stability and confidence:

(a) *Deposits were required*: £20,000 had to be deposited with the High Court before a new life assurer could transact any business.
(b) *Publicity was required*: life assurers were required to publish their accounts, actuarial valuations and (to their shareholders and policyholders) any intended merger or amalgamation.

33.6 Employers' Liability Insurance Companies Act 1907

This made very similar provisions to the above Act, in respect of what was becoming an increasingly important class of business.

33.7 Assurance Companies Act 1909

The measure of control exerted by minimum financial requirements and the submission of returns in respect of life business was seen to be both justified and sensible. The Assurance Companies Act 1909 extended the principle to fire insurance, personal accident insurance (termed "accident insurance" in the Act), and employer's liability insurance. Lloyd's was exempt from the provisions of the Act, since it was not an insurance company.

33.8 Industrial Assurances Act 1923

This Act made appropriate provisions for some control in industrial life assurance, including the appointment of the *Industrial Assurance Commissioner*, who has wide powers of inquiry into the affairs of industrial life assurers.

33.9 Assurance Companies (Winding up) Acts 1933–1935

Motor insurance had become a social necessity, recognised by the Road Traffic Act 1930 (see **7.4**). That statute resulted in an enormous growth of motor business, not all of it, unfortunately, being secured by stable organisations. This resulted in the failure of several motor insurers and widespread public concern. This in turn gave rise to the Assurance Companies (Winding up) Acts of 1933 and 1935. These Acts gave the Board of Trade powers to investigate the affairs of a company thought to be suspect, with a view to liquidation if necessary.

33.10 Assurance Companies Act 1946

This Act confirmed the principle outlined in the 1909 Act (see **33.6**) and brought marine, aviation and transit insurance within its scope. A further major provision was the abolition of deposits, substituting in their place a *margin of solvency*. This margin of solvency was coupled with another financial requirement, so that no insurance company could transact any class of business mentioned in the Act unless:

(a) it had a *minimum paid-up share capital* of £50,000;
(b) its assets *exceeded its liabilities* by £50,000 or 10 per cent of the previous year's premium income, whichever was the greater.

33.11 Insurance Companies Acts 1958–1982

These Acts were consolidating Acts, to bring together all the major features of existing legislation affecting insurance, as outlined above. In addition, insurers were required to submit detailed accounts, with a balance sheet, to the Board of Trade. They were also required to submit to an annual audit.

Such was the development of insurance and the relative decline in the value of money, the capital requirements and margin of solvency in earlier legislation were soon rendered inadequate. Moreover Britain's membership of the European Community required further statutory changes. The current legislation consists of the Insurance Companies Acts 1974–1982, supported by various Regulations. It is considered in more detail below.

C. THE INSURANCE COMPANIES ACTS 1974–1982

33.12 Acts and supporting Regulations

The somewhat complex accumulation of insurance supervisory law in the United Kingdom has now been consolidated and the most important statutes and statutory instruments may be considered as:

(a) The Insurance Companies Regulations 1981;
(b) The Insurance Companies Act 1982;
(b) The Insurance Companies (Accounts and Statements) Regulations 1983.

Important features are considered below.

33.13 Summary of major provisions

The complexities and rapid changes occurring in this area of the insurance industry make it inappropriate to attempt a very detailed exposition of precise statutory requirements in a study such as this. The following will therefore attempt to present only a summary of the major provisions and general concepts in this phase of regulatory control.

33.14 New classification of business

The completely new classification of business under this legislation has been mentioned before (see **2.15**).

33.15 Authorisation to transact insurance

Only duly recognised insurers are entitled to transact insurance within the scope of the Act, and they must obtain due authorisation either by the Act or as set out in the terms of the Act. Moreover, such insurers are to be owned and controlled by "fit and proper" persons.

As a consequence of an EC Life Directive, no new composites will be authorised, but it is possible for a general insurer to obtain permission to write a life account limited to reinsurance business only.

No company will receive authorisation if in the future it issues any partly paid shares.

Insurance companies authorised in the United Kingdom are prohibited from carrying out non-insurance business anywhere in the world. (It is of course possible for them to establish subsidiaries which may transact other kinds of business.)

33.16 Conditions to be met

Would-be insurers have to meet certain conditions, which will depend upon the country in which the head office is situated and whether they seek authorisation for reinsurance only.

Companies from other E.U. member states have to appoint a general representative in the United Kingdom, with authority to act and take service of suit. An individual must be so appointed, not merely a company.

33.17 Fitness screening

An important new feature, following some very unsatisfactory situations, was the insistence that persons representing or significantly involved with insurance companies should be deemed fit and suitable. This applies to representatives (see above), and to *controllers* (chief executives or owners of at least one-third share capital), *directors* and *managers*. Such persons must be judged fit and proper to hold these positions by the Department of Trade and Industry (DTI).

This *fitness screening* has been extended to *main agents* in the case of general insurers.

33.18 Solvency margins

As from 1 January 1982 new minimum solvency requirements are in force, varying according to the corporate status of the insurer and the classes of business transacted.

(a) *General business*: the solvency margin is related to the premium income of the insurer, subject to minima varying with the class of business transacted. *Additionally*, there is a second measure of solvency related to *claims costs*, which will normally apply to insurers with a reducing account or one showing very adverse results.

The anxiety to preserve adequate safety margins is thus clearly seen.

(b) *Long-term business* (mostly life assurance): the requirements are expressed as percentages of the mathematical reserves determined by the actuary of the company for the different classes of contract. Generally, the requirement is 4 per cent of the reserves, less a deduction for reassurance. Special rules apply to unit linked business.

(c) *Corporate status*: another variant for solvency margins is the corporate status of the company (e.g. UK companies, reinsurance companies, E.U. non-U.K. companies, external companies, life offices, and composite offices).

NOTE: Solvency margins are measured in ECUs (*European Currency Units*).

33.19 Conduct of business

The DTI is authorised to lay down certain conditions and the Act makes specific provisions relating to the conduct of business, including such matters as:

(a) restriction on investments of specified classes;
(b) adequate assets to be retained within the United Kingdom;
(c) assets to be held by approved person(s);
(d) limitation of premium income;
(e) specific information to be supplied to government;

(f) misleading advertisements or other statements;
(g) connected intermediaries;
(h) "cooling off" period (i.e. ten days wherein a policyholder in long-term business may cancel the contract without penalty).

33.20 Reinsurance

Reinsurance was traditionally less regulated than direct business, but adequate reinsurance facilities exist and the tendency is to require more information about such protection, in view of the serious consequences of it being uncollectable.

33.21 Actuarial valuation

In addition to the requirements earlier in the Act about the submission of returns to the DTI in respect of the specified classes of business, companies carrying on long-term business (including permanent sickness contracts) will be required to have their liabilities valued by an actuary each year.

33.22 Insolvency and winding up

A company is to be considered insolvent if it cannot attain the margin of solvency shown in **33.18**. It can then be wound up by order of the court. The Act also allows the Department of Trade to petition the court for a winding up order should the company fail to maintain the requirements of the Act in any particular.

NOTE: For the purposes of calculating the margin of solvency (see Chapter 17 above) liabilities in respect of share capital are excluded and premiums are to be considered net of approved reinsurance for other than long-term business.

33.23 Other important aspects of the Act

Other significant points are:

(a) The DTI can call upon companies to produce books and papers, or send one of its officials to investigate the company's affairs (if necessary armed with a search warrant).
(b) Severe penalties are prescribed for persons obstructing any official acting under the authority of a search warrant, and for withholding or destroying vital information. Similar penalties exist for supplying false information.
(c) The whole conduct of the business must be satisfactory and consistent with the public good.
(d) There are provisions for the criminal liability of directors.

D. THE POLICYHOLDERS PROTECTION ACT 1975

33.24 Introduction and background

Following the failure of the Nation Life in 1974, steps were taken to make the insurance industry collectively responsible for any future insurer insolvencies. No public funds were to be made available for this purpose. This was in line with government action in relation to failed travel agencies, where a levy was imposed upon that industry to compensate any future victims.

33.25 Application and limitations

The Act was intended to apply to personal policyholders only (i.e. private individuals) as far as general insurance was concerned, and the following are not within the scope of this legislation:

(a) corporate policyholders (other than in long-term business);
(b) marine, aviation and transport (other than motor vehicle) policies, and reinsurances;
(c) policies issued by Lloyd's or Friendly Societies;
(d) insurers not authorised to transact insurance in the United Kingdom;
(e) non-U.K. policies (however, the House of Lords in *Scher & Ackman* v. *Policyholders' Protection Board* (1993) held that a "U.K. policy" was one issued by an authorised U.K. insurer operating out of the United Kingdom, but the risk did not have to be located in the United Kingdom).

33.26 The Policyholders' Protection Board

This was created with responsibility for indemnifying or financially assisting personal policyholders (i.e. not corporations, except in long-term insurances), who might be prejudiced by the failure of an insurer authorised to do business in the United Kingdom.

33.27 Compensation to be paid

The basic intentions of the Act are that compensation should be payable as follows:

(a) with *compulsory insurances*: 100 per cent secured (although the Motor Insurers' Bureau (see **7.15–15.18**) continues to operate for that class of business);
(b) *all other* insurances: 90 per cent secured (if possible, arranging for long-term business to be transferred to another authorised insurer, guaranteeing at least 90 per cent protection).

33.28 Introduction of a levy

In order to fund any compensation necessary, levies upon the insurance industry can be made, up to 1 per cent of premium income, with separate levies for general and long-term business. Levies are not to be made in advance, but only in the event of policyholders being prejudiced by company failures.

NOTE: Levies can be made upon "accountable intermediaries" as well as insurers, with long-term business. This will usually refer to brokers or other intermediaries not tied to a single insurer.

33.29 Review and reaction

The Act proved extremely controversial initially within the insurance industry, many feeling that reputable and efficient insurers would be made responsible for the incompetent and perhaps dishonourable. A review of its operation was promised, and was duly carried out in 1981. It was concluded that the Act was working well and no changes were proposed. So the Policyholders' Protection Board has become an established feature, and has been brought into use on a number of occasions.

E. OTHER GOVERNMENT "INTERVENTION"

33.30 Insurance and investment intermediaries and advisers

Two Acts of importance in this area have already been considered:

(a) The Insurance Brokers (Registration) Act 1977 (see **13.15**); and
(b) The Financial Services Act 1986 (see **13.16**).

33.31 National Insurance

Although not forming part of this study, the introduction of National Insurance in the late 1940s should be mentioned. This took from the private sector the previously important Workmen's Compensation insurance. Unemployment, widows' and sickness benefits have also become the responsibility of the State (although recent developments with regard to private medical insurance should be noted: see **15.16**).

33.32 The Unfair Terms in Consumer Contracts Regulations 1994

This legislation was enacted in accordance with E.C. Directive 93/13 and became effective from 1 July 1995. While not exclusively concerned with insurance it adds statutory weight to consumer protection. As far as insurances are concerned, the regulations:

(a) apply to contracts with "natural persons" only (i.e. not companies);
(b) require policies to be in "plain intelligible language";
(c) state that "unfair terms" are not binding upon the consumer;
(d) do not affect agreed "core provisions" (except (b) above applies);
(e) appoint the Director-General of Fair Trading as enforcing officer.

It is too early to say whether these Regulations will have any significant application. The hesitancy of the U.K. Government to impose legislation on the insurance industry has already been noted (see **33.3**). Thus, for example, *The Unfair Contract Terms Act 1977* specifically excluded insurance from its provisions (see **18.29**). Also, the self-regulation by the industry, for example with the voluntary ABI Code of Practice (see **13.17**), had previously been considered adequate. Time will tell to what extent the E.C. Directive was necessary in the U.K. situation.

33.33 Insurance Premium Tax

This was a fiscal, rather than a regulatory, measure. It was also to some extent the reintroduction of an old idea for U.K. insurance (see **5.4**(c)). Raising government income from a tax on insurance has been common in many other countries for a long time. With effect from 1 October 1994 premium tax on most U.K. general insurance premiums was introduced.

This tax does not apply to life assurance, or to reinsurances. The tax is payable by the policyholder, but the insurer must account for it to the authorities. At present the tax rate is 2.5 per cent of the written premium. The insurance industry was relieved to learn that the later 1995 Budget did not increase this tax, as was widely predicted.

F. WHY NOT NATIONALISE?

33.34 The proposition

It may be argued that since a high degree of control and intervention on the part of the State is not only justified but desirable for insurance, the whole conduct of the business should be brought within the complete control of the State by nationalisation or the creation of a State monopoly. Indeed, particularly in respect of those classes of business which are made compulsory (e.g. motor), there have been several who saw nationalisation as a logical next step.

33.35 The arguments for and against

Not unnaturally, whenever the subject of possible nationalisation of insurance has arisen, the great majority of the leaders of the insurance profession have vigorously maintained that this is highly undesirable. The arguments for and against the proposition include the following:

Arguments for:

(a) much expense in compiling and submitting returns to the government would be avoided;
(b) the absence of a profit motive would ensure that premiums were as low as possible;
(c) any profits made would be to the immediate advantage of the nation;
(d) large-scale operations would eliminate wasteful competition and result in bulk economies;
(e) uniformity of practice and interpretation of documents;
(f) taxation might possibly be reduced if the vast funds available to insurers were owned by the State;
(g) all the expenses of reinsurance would not be necessary.

Arguments against:

(a) experience suggests that paperwork is not diminished by State ownership;
(b) the absence of a profit motive tends to result in inefficiency;
(c) profits are already indirectly given to the nation through thousands of shareholders (often with small holdings of shares);
(d) competition promotes efficiency and experience of nationalised industries has not always shown the anticipated savings in administration;
(e) close contact with one's public would be lost and generosity in interpretation would inevitably be reduced;
(f) insurers already pay immense amounts to the Treasury by way of taxes, which would thus be lost;
(g) it is quite possible that overseas customers would not trade with a government concern, resulting in the loss of valuable "invisible exports".

33.36 The modern scene

To a very large extent, particularly in the United Kingdom, the arguments surrounding nationalisation of insurance are at present very academic. Neither of the two largest political parties in the United Kingdom seems likely to introduce the idea in the foreseeable future, although talk on the subject was prevalent in past years.

With the dramatic changes in the communist world in recent times, even countries which monopolised insurance have totally or in lesser measure moved to a more open-market philosophy. So the idea of the State taking over the insurance industry seems very much to have receded.

G. COMPULSORY INSURANCE IN THE UNITED KINGDOM

33.37 Motor insurance

Effectively, at least some form of motor insurance has been made compulsory since the Road Traffic Act 1930 (see **7.13**).

33.38 Employers' liability insurance

The Employers' Liability (Compulsory Insurance) Act 1969 marked a complete change of society's attitude in respect of injuries at work and liability insurance generally. For details and statutory requirements see **6.13–6.16**.

33.39 Riding Establishments Act 1970

This Act further emphasises the radical change in thinking about liability insurance, requiring the proprietors of horse riding establishments to effect insurance to cover legal liability towards the hirers of their horses and towards the public. The Act further requires insurance for the liability of hirers while using or during the hire of the horses.

33.40 The Merchant Shipping (Oil Pollution) Act 1971 (see 10.7).

Certain vessels carrying oil will need to show a certificate proving the required insurance before entering or leaving ports.

33.41 The Solicitors Act 1974

From 1976 and with the approval of the Law Society, each solicitor was required to carry professional indemnity insurance to the extent of at least £50,000 (at least £30,000 per partner in any partnership).

33.42 Insurance brokers

Under the Insurance Brokers (Registration) Act 1977 (see **13.15**) insurance brokers are obliged to effect professional indemnity insurance (sometimes called *Errors and Omissions (E & O) policies*).

33.43 Nuclear Installations Act 1965

This Act imposes strict liability on the "licensee" (meaning the operator) of a nuclear reactor for injury or property damage to third parties resulting from the use of nuclear energy. This liability must be covered, up to an aggregate sum of £5,000,000, by insurance or other approved means.

33.43 State Supervision and Regulation

Such insurance risks are, by agreement, not written by individual insurers but by a "pool" of insurers. The "pool" consists of most British insurers, including Lloyd's underwriters.

33.44 Contractual "compulsory" insurance

In addition to statutory compulsory insurance, many contracts may require insurance to be effected. Loans or other assistance from banks will normally require insurance. For example, life assurance and/or fire insurance may be required in connection with a mortgage loan and marine cargo insurance will certainly be required if credit is extended with regard to shipments (see **3.17**).

H. PROGRESS TEST 33

PART 1—SHORT ANSWERS (Answer in one or two sentences)

1. Why is the failure of an insurer a more serious matter than the failure of most other commercial enterprises? **(33.2)**
2. Outline the development of State intervention in the insurance profession up to, but not including, the Insurance Companies Acts 1958–1982. **(33.3–33.10)**
3. What is meant by an insurer's "solvency margin"? **(33.18)**
4. Give two examples where the government, through the minister or under specific provisions of the law, may intervene in the conduct of an insurer's business? **(33.19)**
5. How might an insurance be "compulsory" by contract? **(33.44)**

PART 2—MULTIPLE CHOICE (Choose the most correct option)

1. The failure of an insurance company is:
   (a) a commercial matter of no consequence to government;
   (b) only important when it writes compulsory insurances;
   (c) is important and subject to several government regulatory measures;
   (d) not allowed by law. **(33.2)**
2. The U.K. Government:
   (a) was traditionally reluctant to intervene with insurance;
   (b) has always exercised very tight control over insurance;
   (c) has totally left the insurance industry to regulate itself;
   (d) has nationalised all insurance. **(33.3–33.36)**
3. The solvency margin required by the Insurance Companies Act 1982:
   (a) is the same for all kinds of insurer;
   (b) applies to Lloyd's as well as company insurers;
   (c) for life assurance relates to premium income or claims costs;

(d) relates to premium income or claims for general insurance. **(33.18)**

4. The Policyholders Protection Act 1975:
   (a) protects only personal policyholders in general insurance;
   (b) protects both personal and corporate policyholders;
   (c) provides compensation from the government if insurers fail;
   (d) requires an annual levy on all insurers. **(33.24–33.27)**
5. The insurance premium tax in the United Kingdom:
   (a) applies to all insurance premiums;
   (b) is intended to pay for insolvent insurers' liabilities;
   (c) does not apply to reinsurances or fire insurances;
   (d) does not apply to reinsurances or life assurances. **(33.33)**

(*For multiple choice answers, see page 355.*)

CHAPTER 34

U.K. SUPERVISORY BODIES AND INSOLVENCY

A. THE U.K. PHILOSOPHY OF INSURANCE SUPERVISION

34.1 Introduction

The general philosophy in the regulation of insurance in the United Kingdom has been summed up in the phrase "freedom with publicity". To a large extent this remains true, even though considerable development has taken place in the regulatory sphere in recent years. Unlike many jurisdictions, there is no control exercised over premium rates and policy wordings. The market is free to compete and while the general interests of society are not threatened the U.K. Government remains content for market forces and industry self-regulation to prevail.

34.2 Some central control is necessary

Every civilised society has recognised that some central control is necessary, in insurance as in other commercial activities. Membership of the European Union has increased the demand for government regulation. Overall, however, the general aims and objectives of insurance supervision in the United Kingdom may be considered under the headings below.

34.3 Integrity of the market

Insurance is a vital element in the U.K. economy and like most financial activities the key words are trust and confidence. Should that confidence be undermined by perceived incompetence or dishonesty, the consequences would be very serious. Important as the protection of individual consumers and investors is, there is an equally, if not more, important duty nationally and internationally to preserve confidence in the market as a whole.

34.4 Present and future claims

With general insurance particularly, there is a duty to ensure that practising insurers can meet their known and foreseeable present and future claims. Thus, the margin of solvency, premium and claim reserves and reinsurance arrangements are among vital issues to be considered.

34.5 Reasonable expectations of policyholders

With life and similar investment products, there is the element of claims but there is also a further dimension. This has been described as the need to check that insurers can "fulfil the reasonable expectations of policyholders". The benefits policyholders look for in this type of business may include bonuses and interest earnings, which may be to a greater or lesser extent discretional with the insurer. The regulations and options available in times of financial difficulty very much bear this in mind.

B. GOVERNMENT AND OTHER SUPERVISORY BODIES

34.6 Department of Trade and Industry (DTI)

This department is charged with overall responsibility for regulating the insurance industry in the United Kingdom. Many of its duties and activities have been delegated, but the Minister of State at the DTI retains ultimate responsibility.

34.7 Government Actuary

He is largely responsible for all actuarial aspects of life and pensions business in the United Kingdom.

34.8 Office of Fair Trading (OFT)

The Director-General of OFT and staff are or were closely involved with various aspects of insurance regulation, including:

(a) the various Statements of Insurance Practice (see **18.29**);
(b) the formation of the Insurance Ombudsman Bureau (IOB) and the Personal Insurance Arbitration Service (PIAS) (see **30.27–30.28**);
(c) "unfair terms" in insurance consumer contracts (see **33.32**).

34.9 The Registrar of Friendly Societies and the Office of the Industrial Assurance Commissioner

Obviously concerned with industrial life assurance matters, these offices were created by statute (see **4.13**).

34.10 The Securities and Investment Board (SIB)

While not exclusively concerned with insurance, the SIB is closely concerned with life assurance products having an investment element. A primary function of the SIB in this connection is the approval and subsequent monitoring of *Self-Regulatory Organisations* (*SROs*).

34.11 The Personal Investment Authority (PIA)

Set up to control and supervise investment by private customers (including insurance products), the PIA is intended to replace the two former SROs:

(a) The Life Assurance & Unit Trust Regulatory Organisation (LAUTRO);
(b) The Financial Intermediaries, Managers and Brokers Regulatory Association (FIMBRA).

PIA at the time of writing is formulating its own rules, which will regulate both product producers and independent financial advisers. It was planned to replace FIMBRA and LAUTRO from late 1995, but the final handover is proving to be rather protracted.

34.12 The Insurance Brokers' Registration Council (IBRC)

This was created following the Insurance Brokers (Registration) Act, 1977 and has been considered before (see **13.6**).

34.13 Investment Management Regulatory Organisation (IMRO)

This is a recognised SRO under the Financial Services Act 1986.

34.14 Various ombudsmen

The term "ombudsman" was borrowed from Scandinavia, where it relates to a government-appointed, but totally independent, official whose function is to hear and adjudicate on complaints against the government of the country concerned. The essential function is retained, without the government dimension, in relation to certain insurance matters, including:

(a) Insurance Ombudsman (IO);
(b) Pensions Ombudsman (PO);
(c) Personal Investment Authority Ombudsman (PIAO).

The first has already been considered (see **30.27**). The others perform similar functions within the area obviously implied.

34.15 Dispute resolution bodies

These are the Insurance Ombudsman and the Personal Insurance Arbitration Service (see **30.26**).

C. INSOLVENCY

34.16 Introduction

No amount of supervision or centralised control can totally remove the risk of financial collapse. Failure in business is an unavoidable possibility with trading of any kind, and insurance is no exception. In a free market situation, the incompetent and unlucky may well have to "go to the wall". This has always been so and it is an integral part of a capitalist system.

What good and efficient supervision of insurance can do is to minimise the adverse effects of business failure, by seeking to ensure that unsuitable people do not exercise undue control or influence and by having sufficient publicity and forward knowledge to give early warning of dangerous financial situations. This is extremely important when one considers the undesirable consequences of an insurer's failure (see **33.2**).

34.17 The meaning of "insolvency"

In reality, the fact that a person or a business is *insolvent* does not automatically mean financial collapse. "Solvency" is the point at which one has just sufficient assets to pay one's debts. "Insolvency" therefore means that one is not able to meet one's financial liabilities. But being "in debt" is not at all uncommon, for individuals or companies. However, as long as creditors forbear there is nothing in common law to stop an insolvent person or company continuing to do business.

34.18 If creditors will not forbear

If those to whom money is owed are not prepared to let the situation continue (and sometimes voluntarily by the person or organisation in debt), steps may be taken which could lead to:

(a) *bankruptcy* of an individual; or
(b) *liquidation* of a company.

In either case the effective procedure is to turn assets into "liquid" form (i.e. cash) and to pay debts as far as the money will go. There are likely to be some "secured creditors" and in most involuntary bankruptcies or liquidations it is unlikely that all debts will be fully paid. Instead a percentage of debts (or *dividend*) is paid, according to the money available. In the case of an individual, he or she becomes a declared *bankrupt*. In the case of a company, it is *liquidated* ("wound up" or terminated).

34.19 The position in insurance

This is not intended to be a comprehensive survey of bankruptcy law, but a basic understanding of the topic is desirable, particularly because of its increasing importance in recent years, with many insurers and reinsurers being liquidated or in *run-off* situations. (A "run-off" is virtually self-explanatory, in that no new business is transacted and debts and liabilities are gradually dealt with, as resources allow, until trading and company existence ceases.)

In insurance, "insolvency" is not permitted for an insurer. Insurance companies must not only be able to pay their debts; they must also comply with a statutory *margin of solvency* at all times (see **33.18**). Lloyd's underwriters have to meet similar stringent criteria as to their financial soundness. Should these criteria fail to be met, they cannot continue trading. Insolvency and the probable consequence of bankruptcy or liquidation in insurance require further consideration. Although technically incorrect, we will equate "insolvency" with "financial failure".

D. THE "FAILURE" OF AN INSURER

34.20 Lloyd's underwriters

As individuals, Lloyd's underwriters can be made bankrupt. Indeed, many have filed for bankruptcy in the recent troubles (see **12.26**). The security of "Lloyd's" (as a Corporation), however, remains strong. Individual financial failure has not so far affected policyholders and it seems very unlikely that it ever will, in view of the considerable assets in the Central Fund (see **12.6**(f)).

34.21 Insurance companies

In the event of liquidation, the position of claimants and policyholders could well be protected, at least in significant measure, by:

(a) The Motor Insurers' Bureau (MIB) (see **7.17**), with motor cases, or
(b) The Policyholders' Protection Board (see **33.24**).

34.22 Life insurers

The extra special position and importance of life and other long-term business is recognised, in that *voluntary liquidation* of a life insurer is not permitted (section 52(2) of the Insurance Companies Act 1982). Liquidation may only take place on the order or with the consent of the court (although 10 or more policyholders, holding policies with an aggregate value of not less than £10,000 may petition the court to have the company wound up).

A further requirement in long-term insurance is that the liquidator must (unless the court decrees otherwise) carry on business, with a view to transferring it as a going concern to another authorised insurer. Also, a Special Manager may be appointed to assist with this highly technical field of business.

34.23 The "Equitable"

This ancient life assurer (see **4.6**), in its Deed of Settlement when it began as far back as 1762, had the foresight to provide for a rateable reduction in all sums assured by its policies in the event of insolvency (it was not needed!) This possibility was copied by other insurers subsequently, and indeed survives to this day. Section 58 of the Insurance Companies Act 1982 allows this possibility in place of a winding-up order by the court and it is not restricted to life assurance.

34.24 Failure of a reinsurer

This has no direct effect upon the original insured. Its direct effect is a matter for the ceding insurer only. Effectively, this may well mean that all or part of the reinsurance money becomes uncollectable, but the original insurer's liability towards its policyholder is unchanged. (Of course, with a small insurer and high reinsurance this could affect the financial ability of the insurer to meet its obligations. Hence, the importance of checking the "security" offered by a reinsurance: see **32.6**(i).)

Conversely, if an insurer fails, the liability of a reinsurer towards the claims made on the insurer is not affected. Recent court cases have tried to reduce the liability of the reinsurer in similar proportion to the amount actually paid or payable by the insolvent insurer to its claimants, but these submissions were rejected. The reinsurer must pay in full under its contract of insurance with the insurer.

E. THE "FAILURE" OF AN INSURANCE INTERMEDIARY

34.25 Insolvency of an insurance agent

Since the agent represents one or more insurance companies and is therefore the agent of the insurer, his financial failure should not have any direct bearing upon the policyholder. Any moneys owed to the insurer must rank with other claims in any bankruptcy or liquidation proceedings.

34.26 Insolvency of an insurance broker

Potentially this is more serious for the policyholder, since the broker is normally his agent. However, the rules of the Insurance Brokers' Registration Council require all clients' moneys to be kept in a separate fund by the broker and this money is held in trust for those to whom it belongs. Should insolvency occur by reason of professional negligence, there might additionally be a right of claim against the broker's E. & O. insurance (see **33.42**).

F. THE "FAILURE" OF AN INSURED

34.27 Position of the insurer

The bankruptcy or liquidation of the insured does not affect the insurer's liability under any insurances with the insured. It could be that the policy will be cancelled or surrendered, but the contractual obligations of the insurer remain, towards the legal personal representative (either the trustee in bankruptcy, or the liquidator).

34.28 Position of third parties

Third parties have no common law right to claim on the insurance held by the policyholder. Such rights have, however, been granted with compulsory insurances (motor and employer's liability) and special provisions have been made with other liability insurances where the insured becomes bankrupt or goes into liquidation.

Under the *Third Parties (Rights Against Insurers) Act, 1930* a third party having rights against a liability insurance policyholder who goes bankrupt or into liquidation is given a direct right against the liability insurer, as though he were the insured. He has no greater rights than the insured, so any breach of utmost good faith by the insured or other policy requirement counts against him just as it would against the original policyholder. Nevertheless, his right is direct and moneys received are not required to be shared with other creditors of the insolvent estate.

34.29 Position of the insured

Normally the proceeds of any insurance policy are counted as part of the estate of the policyholder and would therefore rank as assets in the general claims of creditors. However, third parties may be protected by the terms of the Third Parties (Rights Against Insurers) Act 1930 (see above).

Additionally, if life assurances have been effected under the provisions of the *Married Women's Property Act 1882* moneys payable under such policies are not part of the life assured's estate, but are held in trust for the wife or other beneficiary. Such money is therefore beyond the reach of creditors, indeed of the assured himself.

G. PROGRESS TEST 34

PART 1—SHORT ANSWERS (Answer in one or two sentences)

1. Sum up the general philosophy of insurance regulation in the United Kingdom. **(34.1)**
2. What additional aim exists in supervising life assurance? **(34.5)**
3. What various ombudsmen operate in insurance complaints. **(34.14)**
4. What is the difference between bankruptcy and liquidation? **(34.18)**
5. What effect has the failure of a reinsurer on the original insured? **(34.24)**

PART 2—MULTIPLE CHOICE (Choose the most correct option)

1. The general philosophy of insurance supervision in the United Kingdom is:
   (a) to allow insurers as little freedom as possible;
   (b) that government does not interfere at all;
   (c) to allow freedom with publicity;
   (d) exactly the same as in all other countries. **(34.1–34.5)**
2. The Office of Fair Trading in the United Kingdom:
   (a) is the final authority in the control of all insurance matters;
   (b) is not concerned with insurance at all;
   (c) was only involved with Statement of Insurance Practice;
   (d) has had various responsibilities with insurance regulation. **(34.8)**
3. The Personal Investment Authority (PIA):
   (a) is intended to replace FIMBRA and LAUTRO;
   (b) is merely another SRO like FIMBRA and LAUTRO;
   (c) will exercise control over all types of insurance;
   (d) is a division of the DTI. **(34.11)**
4. An insurer is allowed to continue in business:
   (a) as long as it has enough money to meet its liabilities;
   (b) as long as its creditors are prepared to extend credit;
   (c) only if it satisfies the stipulated "margin of solvency";
   (d) only if a High Court judge agrees. **(34.19)**
5. A third party having a claim against a bankrupt insured in the United Kingdom:
   (a) can claim direct upon the Policyholders' Protection Board;
   (b) can claim direct against the liability insurer;
   (c) is just like any other creditor of the bankrupt person;
   (d) is a preferred creditor against the bankrupt estate. **(34.28)**

(For multiple choice answers, see page 355.)

PART SIX: OBJECTIVE TESTS (see Answers, page 356) and ASSIGNMENTS

6.1 State whether the following statements are *true* or *false*:

(a) Specific legislation regarding insurance is totally a twentieth century phenomenon.

(b) It is illegal to act as an insurer in the United Kingdom unless the requirements of the Insurance Companies Acts have been complied with.

(c) All public liability insurance in the United Kingdom is completely optional.

(d) The general philosophy of insurance supervision in the United Kingdom has traditionally been "freedom with publicity".

(e) If an insured under a public liability goes bankrupt, a third party having a claim against him cannot claim direct against the insurer.

6.2 Select the *most correct* answer for the following questions:

(a) Government is specially interested in the continued existence of insurance companies because (i) much tax revenue would otherwise be lost; (ii) substantial invisible earnings would be lost; (iii) society would suffer wide distress if an insurer failed.

(b) A margin of solvency for insurance companies is better than deposits because (i) standard deposits are inadequate for large insurers; (ii) the money which would have been deposited is available for claims; (iii) inflation and other factors soon render deposits inadequate.

(c) The state introduced the requirement for "adequate reinsurance" (i) in order to encourage reinsurers; (ii) as a safeguard against the collapse of insurers; (iii) following a number of catastrophic situations.

(d) nationalisation of motor insurance (i) would mean that comprehensive motor policies would no longer be issued; (ii) would mean that the art of individual underwriting for motorists would cease; (iii) should mean that wasteful competitive advertising would cease.

(e) The Policyholders Protection Act enables the imposition of a 1 per cent levy (i) to supplement the funds of the Motor Insurers' Bureau; (ii) to compensate policyholders likely to be financially affected by insurance company liquidations; (iii) to meet claims an insurer has declined and where genuine hardship results.

6.3 Assignments

(a) Write an essay on the increasing State intervention in insurance practice since the turn of the century, with reasons why you think these developments occurred.

(b) Discuss the likely repercussions to the insurance industry if a form of "no fault" liability insurance is introduced.
(c) Research into the number of insurer insolvencies in the United Kingdom since the passing of the Policyholders Protection Act, and to what extent levies have been made against the insurance industry.

ANSWERS TO THE PROGRESS AND OBJECTIVE TESTS

(NOTE: The tests are meant to be revision exercises rather than achievement goals. More important than the correct answers, therefore, are the reasons behind the choice. Indeed, some answers shown below may be controversial. If so, this is good—but know why you disagree.)

Progress Test	*Page*	*1*	*2*	*3*	*4*	*5*
1	10	(b)	(c)	(d)	(a)	(a)
2	20	(b)	(a)	(c)	(a)	(d)
3	33	(a)	(b)	(c)	(c)	(d)
4	49	(b)	(c)	(d)	(a)	(b)
5	58	(d)	(a)	(c)	(c)	(a)
6	72	(d)	(c)	(a)	(a)	(b)
7	83	(d)	(a)	(a)	(d)	(a)
8	87	(b)	(d)	(a)	(a)	(c)
9	91	(c)	(a)	(b)	(a)	(c)
10	97	(b)	(a)	(d)	(c)	(d)
11	110	(b)	(a)	(b)	(c)	(a)
12	120	(b)	(b)	(a)	(b)	(d)
13	131	(c)	(d)	(a)	(d)	(a)
14	No Test					
15	148	(b)	(c)	(a)	(a)	(a)
16	159	(d)	(c)	(a)	(a)	(c)
17	172	(c)	(b)	(a)	(b)	(a)
18	187	(a)	(b)	(b)	(a)	(c)
19	200	(d)	(a)	(c)	(a)	(a)
20	209	(a)	(b)	(c)	(a)	(b)
21	218	(a)	(a)	(d)	(c)	(a)
22	226	(c)	(c)	(a)	(b)	(a)
23	No Multiple Choice Questions					
24	246	(c)	(b)	(a)	(d)	(a)
25	254	(c)	(a)	(d)	(c)	(a)
26	260	(d)	(b)	(a)	(a)	(c)
27	272	(c)	(d)	(a)	(b)	(d)
28	287	(a)	(c)	(b)	(d)	(c)
29	294	(b)	(b)	(a)	(d)	(a)
30	305	(d)	(c)	(a)	(b)	(d)
31	312	(a)	(d)	(d)	(a)	(a)
32	324	(c)	(b)	(a)	(d)	(a)

33	342	(c)	(a)	(d)	(a)	(d)
34	352	(c)	(d)	(a)	(c)	(b)

Objective Test	*Page*	(a)	(b)	(c)	(d)	(e)	(f)	(g)	(h)	(i)	(j)
1.1	22	F	F	F	F	T					
1.2	22	(ii)	(iii)	(ii)	(ii)	(ii)					
2.1	99	T	F	T	F	F	T	F	F	F	F
2.2	99	(iii)	(iii)	(iii)	(i)	(iii)	(ii)	(ii)	(i)	(iii)	(i)
3.1	149	F	T	F	F	T	F	F	F	T	F
3.2	149	(ii)	(ii)	(iii)	(i)	(iii)	(iii)	(i)	(i)	(iii)	(i)
4.1	234	F	F	T	T	F	F	F	T	F	F
4.2	234	(ii)	(i)	(ii)	(iii)	(ii)	(i)	(iii)	(i)	(ii)	(iii)
5.1	326	T	F	T	F	F	T	T	F	T	F
5.2	326	(ii)	(i)	(ii)	(iii)	(i)	(iii)	(iii)	(ii)	(ii)	(i)
6.1	353	F	F	F	T	F					
6.2	353	(iii)	(iii)	(ii)	(iii)	(ii)					

INDEX

Abandonment, 192–193
  moneys recovered after, 193
Acceptance of offer, 155
Accident insurance, 18, 61–72
  average, 311–312
  building in course of erection, 57
  claims, 299
  employers' liability insurance, 66–68
  fidelity guarantee insurance, 62–65
  first-loss policies, 311–312
  history, 61–62
  indemnity, 196
  premium rating, 279
  proposal forms, 257
  public liability insurance, 68–69
  reinsurance and co-insurance, 322
  theft insurance, 69–70. *See also* Aviation insurance; Engineering insurance; Personal accident insurance
Accident Offices' Association (AOA), 72, 76
Accident waste, 72
Actuarial valuation
  requirement of the State, 336, 346
Address of proposer, 258
Agency
  law of, 126–129
  termination, 128. *See also* Agents
Agents, 123–125
  authority, 128
  commission, 128–129
  comparison with brokers, 125–126
  death, 128
  duty of disclosure, 179
  insolvency, 350
  law of agency, 126–129
  Murfitt v. *Royal Insurance Co. Ltd* case, 128
  Newsholme Brothers v. *Road Transport & General Insurance Company* case, 127
  insured or insurer, of the, 127
  insurer, of the, 127–128
  responsibilities, 128–129
  types, 124. *See also* Agency; Intermediaries
Agreed value policies, 197–198
  cargo policies, 199
  hull policies, 199
  marine insurance, 200
Air transport insurance, 89–91. *See also* Aviation insurance
"All risks" policies, 56, 70
Alteration of existing contract
  duty of disclosure, 179
Amicable Society, 37–38
Animals
  livestock insurance, 70–71, 292
Annuities, 44
  early forms, 37
Applications. *See* Proposal forms
Apportionments, 213
Arbitration
  advantages over litigation, 301–302
  disputes over claims, 300–302, 348
  procedure, 300–301
Arbitration Act 1950, 300
Arbitration condition, 301
Arbitration services
  The Insurance Ombudsman Bureau (IOB), 302, 347, 348
  The Personal Insurance Arbitration Service (PIAS), 303, 348
Assignment
  insurable interest, 170
  nominations, 171–172
  personal contract, 170, 172
Association of Average Adjusters, 137
Association of British Insurers (ABI)
  Code of Practice, 130, 339
  membership and objectives, 134
Association of Burglary Insurance Surveyors, 138
Association of Fire Insurance Surveyors, 138
Association of Insurance and Risk Managers in Industry and Commerce (AIRMIC), 137
Association of Scottish Life Offices (ASLO), 136
Assurance, 6, 35
Assurance Companies Act 1909, 332
Assurance Companies Act 1946, 333
Assurance Companies (Winding up) Acts 1933–1935, 333
Assured
  marine insurance, 31

Index

Attestation clause, 266
Average, 307–312
  major classes of insurance, 307–312
  meaning in insurance, 307–312
Average adjusters, 298
Aviation and General Insurance Co. Ltd, 90
Aviation insurance, 18, 89–91
  claims, 299
  development, 89–90
  government interest and control, 90
  proposal forms, 257
  scope, 90–91
  war risks, 97
Aviation Insurance Offices' Association, 91, 136

Bancassurance, 145
Banking plan, 97
Bankruptcy, 348–349
  insured, of, 351–352
  Lloyd's underwriters, 349
Bankruptcy bonds, 64
Banks
  marine insurance requirement, 32
Benefit policies, 189
Bloodstock
  livestock insurance, 70–71, 292
Boiler Explosions Act 1882, 86
Bonds
  court, 63, 64
  definition, 63
  government, 63, 64
Bonuses
  motor insurance, 259
  "with profits" policies, 46–47
Bottomry, 25
British Aviation Insurance Co. Ltd, 89
British Insurance and Investment Brokers Association (BIIBA), 136–137
British Insurance Association (BIA), 134
  Statement of Insurance Practice, 182, 184–185
British Insurers' International Committee (BIIC), 135
Brokerage, 125
Brokers, 123, 125
  commission, 125, 128–129
  comparison with agents, 125–126
  insolvency, 351
  law of agency, 126–129
  professional indemnity insurance, 341
  responsibilities, 129. *See also* Intermediaries
Building risk policy, 31
Building society guarantees, 63, 64
Burglary insurance, 69–70
Burst water pipes
  special peril, 55
Business interruption
  fire, 55, 57
Business premises insurance, 70

Calling system, 117–118
Capacity to contract, 156
Capacity to insure
  reduction in, 143–144, 322, 324
  reinsurance, 315
  underwriting, 242
Captain's Room, 118
Captive insurance companies, 94, 108–109
Car and General, 75
Cargo insurance, 30
  assignment of policies, 171
  indemnity, 199
  premium rating, 278
Carriage of Goods by Sea Act 1924, 168
Carriers Act 1830, 168
Cash agents, 124
Cash bonuses, 46–47
Cash flow underwriting, 96, 277
Cash value
  life policies, 47
Cassel Committee on Compulsory Insurance, 81
Casualty Book, 118
Catastrophic risk
  excess of loss treaty, 319
  reinsurance, 316, 319
Cattle
  livestock insurance, 70–71, 292
Caveat emptor, 175
Cedant (Cedent), 316
Ceding commission, 317
Ceding office, 316
Certificate of insurance, 271, 293
Cession, 316
The Chamber of Assurances, 27–28
Chance, 1
Chancery guarantees, 64
Chartered Institute of Arbitrators, 303
Chartered Institute of Loss Adjusters, 138
Chartered Insurance Institute (CII)
  membership and aims, 133
Child's deferred assurance policy, 43
Church insurances
  average, 310
Civil Aviation Act 1949, 90
Claims, 295–305
  arbitration, 300–302
  disputes, 299–300
  ex gratia payments, 297–298
  fraudulent, 303–304
  investigations, 297
  Lloyd's of London, 116
  major classes of business, 298–299
  mediation, 302
  methods of settling, 193–195, 297
  notification, 296
  procedure, 296–297

Claims—*cont.*
professional associations, 137–138
proof of loss, 296
settlement, 296
timely settlement, 297
Claims ratio, 286, 304
Classifications of insurance, 16–20
by the function it performs, 16–17
by the main classes of business, 17–18
meaning, 16
Statute, under, 18, 333–336
Climatic influences, 142
CLMI (Commercial Lines Market Initiative), 146
Clubs
Protection and Indemnity, 32, 105
Co-insurance
reinsurance, 321–322, 323
under-insurance, 309, 310–311. *See also* Pro rata average
Collapse of insurer, 331, 349–351
Collecting friendly societies, 106
College of Insurance, 133
Collision damage
marine insurance, 32
Combined ratio, 286, 305
Commercial guarantees, 63
Commercial Lines Market Initiative (CLMI), 146
Commission
agents, 128–129
insurance brokers, 125, 128–129
rebating, 129
reinsurance, 316–317
Company officers
professional indemnity insurance, 69, 141
Compensation
contingency insurance, 64–65
Policyholders Protection Act 1975, 337. *See also* Indemnity
Complete frauds, 304
Composite insurers, 106
Compulsory insurance
compensation under the Policyholders Protection Act 1975, 337
contractual, 342
employer's liability insurance, 341
insurance brokers, 341
minimum limit replacing unlimited liability, 144
motor, 75, 79–80, 341
oil-carrying vessels, 341
operators of nuclear reactors, 341
riding establishments, 341
solicitors, 341
statutory, 341–342
United Kingdom, 341–342
Conditions in a policy, 267
breach, 270
Conditions in a policy—*cont.*
classifications, 267–270
express, 268
Conditions precedent to liability, 269
breach, 270
Conditions precedent to policy, 269
breach, 270, 281
Conditions subsequent, 269
breach, 270
Consequential loss, 221–222
fire, 55, 57
Consideration, 155–156
specialty contracts, 156–157
Constructive total loss, 193
Consultancy services
insurance, 130
Contents insurance. *See* Householder's insurance
Contingency fund, 285
Contingency risks, 63, 64–65
Contra preferentum rule, 35, 263
Contract works policy, 57
Contractors all risks policy, 57
Contracts
meaning, 153
subrogation rights, 205
types, 63. *See also* Insurance contract
Contribution, 211–217
inter-insurer agreements, 215
legal position, 212
meaning, 211, 217
North British & Mercantile v. *Liverpool & London & Globe* case, 212, 216
not applicable where different interests exist, 215–216
operation of, 212–214
policy exclusion, 214–215
policy modification of common law, 214
Convertible term assurance, 42
Corporate Names, 115
Corporate surety, 63
Corporation of Insurance and Financial Advisers, 137
Corporation of Lloyd's, 113. *See also* Lloyd's of London
Counter-guarantee, 245
Court bonds, 63, 64
Court of Arbitration, 28
Court of protection bonds, 64
Cover notes, 271, 293
form of, 271
Credit agents, 124
Credit insurance, 71
Crime prevention education, 72
Customs and Excise bonds, 64

Date on proposal form, 259
Days of grace, 291–293
Declaration on proposal form, 260

Index

Declinature, 244
Deductibles, 14, 191, 244, 317
Deeds, 153–154
  definition, 63
Deferred annuities, 44
Definitions
  assignment, 170
  average, 307–312
  bonds, 63
  contingency, 64
  contract, 153
  contribution, 211, 217
  deeds, 63
  ex gratia payments, 297
  express, 270
  indemnity, 189
  insolvency, 348
  insurable interest, 161
  insurance, 3
  insurance policies, 63
  material fact, 177
  policy, 153
  premiums, 275
  proximate cause, 219
  reinsurance, 315
  reinsurance terms, 316–317
  renewals, 289
  risk, 4
  subrogation, 203
  utmost good faith, 175–176
  warranty, 180
Department of Trade and Industry (DTI), 346
Direct insurance, 123, 131
  information technology, 146
  verbal offer, 155
Direct Line, 141
Directors
  professional indemnity insurance, 69, 141
Disclosure in insurance contracts
  duty, 179
  known facts which need not be disclosed, 178
  qualification on the duty of disclosure, 177–178
Disputes over claims, 299–300
Dividends
  participating policies, 47
Double insurance, 211–212
Drilling rigs, 30
Driving offence
  St Christopher Scheme, 96
Duty of disclosure, 179
  agent, by, 179
  duration of, 179
  Law Reform Committee recommendations, 185
  revival of, 179
E.C. Directives, 338–339
  Life Directive, 334
  motor insurance, 81
Earthquake, 142
  special peril, 55
Economy
  and the insurance profession, 147
Education endowment policy, 43
Electronic Placing Support (EPS), 146
Electronic trading, 146–147
Employers' Liability Act 1880, 67
Employers' Liability Assurance Corporation, 68
Employers' Liability (Compulsory Insurance) Act 1969, 68, 341
Employers' liability insurance, 66–68
  compulsory insurance, 341
  subrogation, 208
Employers' Liability Insurance Companies Act 1907, 332
Employment
  insurance profession, 147
Endorsements, 241, 272
Endowment assurances, 41
  house purchase, 42
  Traded Endowment Policy Sales (TEPS), 142
Engineering insurance, 10, 18, 85–87
  claims, 299
  forms of insurance available, 87
  proposal forms, 257
  scope, 86
  types of cover, 87
Engineering Offices' Association, 87
Entrepreneurial risks, 4
Environment impairment insurance, 95, 140
Environmental Impairment Insurance (EII) policy, 95
EPS (Electronic Placing Support), 146
The Equitable Life Assurance Society, 38, 350
Equitas, 120
Errors and omissions (E & O) policies, 341, 351
Estimated maximum loss (EML), 242
Ex gratia payments, 215
  claims, 297–298
  John Edwards & Co. v. *Motor Union Insurance Co. Ltd* case, 209
  meaning, 297
  subrogation, 209
Excepted perils, 219
Exceptions in a policy, 266
Excess, 14, 56, 94, 191, 244
  kidnap and ransom insurance, 94
  pollution insurance, 95
Excess of loss ratio reinsurance, 319–320, 321
Excess of loss reinsurance, 319, 320, 321

Exclusions, 245
  contribution, 214–215
  Coxe v. *Employers' Liability Assurance Corporation* case, 226
  proximate cause, 226
Expense ratio, 286, 304
Explosion damage, 55
Export Credits Guarantee Department (ECGD), 71, 95
Express authority, 128
Express conditions, 268
Express warranties, 181
Extraordinary risks, 19–20

Factories Acts 1937–61, 86
Facultative reinsurance, 317–318
Failure of insurer, 331, 349–351
Family income policy, 43
Fidelity guarantee insurance, 62–65, 154
  building society guarantees, 63, 64
  commercial guarantees, 63
  contingency risks, 63, 64–65
  court bonds, 63, 64
  government bonds, 63, 64
Financial insurance, 97
Financial Intermediaries, Managers and Brokers Regulatory Association (FIMBRA), 347
Financial Services Act 1986, 129, 338
Financial supermarkets, 145
Fire insurance, 17–18, 51–58
  abroad, 55
  average, 308–311
  building in course of erection, 57
  claims, 299
  consequential loss, 55, 57
  development, 51–55
  "new for old" basis of settlement, 197
  premium rating, 278–279
  proposal forms, 256
  reinstatement insurances, 58
  reinstatement of the sum insured after a partial loss payment, 196
  reinstatement policies, 197
  reinsurance and co-insurance, 322
  rent policy, 57
  risks other than fire, 54–55
  scope, 55–58
  sprinkler leakage policies, 56
  standard fire policy, 55–56, 225–226
  stock declaration policies, 57–58
  United Kingdom, 51–55
Fire marks, 53
Fire Office, 51
Fire Offices Committee, 53
Fire policy. *See* Standard fire policy
Fire waste, 51
First-loss policies, 311–312
Fitness screening
  State regulation, 335
Fixed share reinsurance, 318
Floating policy, 31
Flood
  special peril, 56
Franchise, 191, 244
Fraudulent claims, 252, 303–304
Freight
  indemnity, 199
  marine insurance, 30
Friendly Societies Act 1955, 172
Fully paid-up policies, 48
Functions of insurance, 7–10
  means of saving, 9
  primary function 7–8
Fundamental risks, 4–5

Gambling, 229–232
Gaming Act 1845, 164, 229
General Accident, 75
General average, 25–26, 307–308
General Insurance Council, 134
Glass claims, 194
Glass insurance, 71
Glossary of terms used in connection with premiums, 285–286
Good faith, 175
Government Actuary, 346
Government bonds, 63, 64
Government involvement in operation of insurance, 144
  aviation insurance, 90. *See also* State supervision
Grace period for renewals, 291–293
  policies for which days of grace not applicable, 292
Great Fire of London, 51–52
Green Card system, 83
Group life assurances, 44
Guarantee
  reinsurance, 317
Guarantee Society, 63

Hail, 71
  special peril, 56
Health and Safety at Work etc. Act 1974, 68
Health insurance, 66
Hijack insurance, 94
Holiday insurance. *See* Travel insurance
Horse riding establishments
  compulsory insurance, 341
Horses
  livestock insurance, 70–71, 292
Hotel Proprietors Act 1956, 168
House purchase
  decreasing term assurance, 42
  endowment assurance, 42
Householder's insurance, 70

Hull insurance, 30
assignment of policies, 171
indemnity, 199
premium rating, 278
Hurricanes, 142
Husband and wife
insurable interest, 165

Illegal contract
right to a refund, 281–282
Impact damage
special peril, 56
Implied authority, 128
Implied conditions, 268–269
Implied warranties, 181
Income tax relief
life policies, 48
Indemnity, 189–200
assessment, 192–193
Castellain v. *Preston* case, 190
choice of method of provision, 195
contingency insurance, 64–65
inadequate sum insured, 191
insurable interest, 189
legal position, 190
Leppard v. *Excess Insurance Co. Ltd* case, 191–192
marine insurance, 199–200
meaning, 189
methods of providing, 193–195, 297
policies not normally subject to, 190
policies which modify, 197–199
policy excess, 191
policy franchise, 191
policy position, 191
reinstatement of the sum insured after a partial loss payment, 195–197
sum insured, 191
Independent Financial Advisers Association, 137
Industrial Assurance and Friendly Societies Act 1948, 39, 167
Industrial Assurance Commissioner, 39, 332, 346
Industrial Assurances Act 1923, 39, 332
Industrial Branch (IB), 40
Industrial injuries
employers' liability insurance, 66–68
Industrial insurance agents, 124–125
Industrial life assurance, 39–40
assignment, 171
collecting friendly societies, 106
comparison with ordinary life assurance, 40
insurable interest, 165, 167
premium payment, 276
Industrial Life Offices Association (ILOA), 40
Information technology (IT), 146–147
Insolvency
meaning, 348
Insolvency of the insurance intermediary, 350–351
Insolvency of the insurer, 349–350
rateable reduction in sums assured in the event of, 350
State regulation, 336
Inspection services, 10, 72
engineering insurers, 87
Inspector of agents, 124
Institute clauses, 30, 135
Institute of Automobile Assessors, 138
Institute of Insurance Brokers, 137
Institute of Insurance Consultants, 130, 137
Institute of London Underwriters (ILU), 30, 135
Institute of Pension Consultants, 136
Institute of Risk Management (IRM), 137
Insurability of risk, 13
Insurable interest, 13, 161–172
assignment, 170
equitable interest, 169
expectation not an insurable interest, 168
indemnity, 189
law, and, 162–164
liability, 167
limited to financial involvement, 168–169
meaning, 161
need not be shown in the policy, 169
other people, 165
the person, 164
PPI policies, 166
prerequisite for insurance, 161
property, 165–166
rights or interest, 167
statute,
affected by, 167
modified by, 168
transfer, 170
what constitutes, 161–162
when insurable interest must exist, 169
Insurance agents. *See* Agency; Agents; Intermediaries
Insurance bonds
definition, 63
Insurance brokers. *See* Brokers; Intermediaries
Insurance Brokers' (Registration) Act 1977, 125, 129, 338, 341
Insurance Brokers' Registration Council (IBRC), 125, 347, 351
Insurance capacity
reduced, 143–144, 322, 324
reinsurance cover, 144, 315, 322, 324
underwriting, 242
Insurance companies, 105
direct business, 123
liquidation, 349
State regulation on solvency margins, 335. *See also* Insurers

Insurance Companies (Accounts and Statements) Regulations 1983, 334
Insurance Companies Act 1958, 333
  aviation insurance, 90
Insurance Companies Act 1974, 333–336
Insurance Companies Act 1982, 333–336
Insurance Companies Regulations 1981, 334
Insurance consultants, 130
Insurance contract
  capacity of parties to contract, 156
  defective, 157
  legality, 156
  simple, 153, 154–156
  speciality, 153–154, 156–157
  stamp duty, 157
  subject matter of the insurance and of the contract, 158
  types, 153–157
  unenforceable, 157
  utmost good faith, 175–187
  written, 154, 156
Insurance cycle, 143
Insurance failures, 331, 349–351
Insurance history
  question on proposal form, 258–259
Insurance in reverse
  bottomry, 25
Insurance Ombudsman Bureau (IOB), 302, 347, 348
Insurance policies
  definition, 63. *See also* Conditions in a policy; Excess; Exclusions; Policy forms
Insurance Premium Tax, 339
Insurance profession
  and the economy 147
Insurance ratios, 286, 304–305
Insurance warranties, 180, 244–245
Insured perils, 219
Insurers, 3, 103–110
  collecting friendly societies, 106
  composite, 106
  Lloyd's underwriters, 104, 113–120, 123
  mutual companies, 104–105, 144–145
  mutual indemnity associations, 105
  proprietory companies, 105
  reinsurers, 106–107, 316
  self-insurers, 106, 107–108
  specialist, 106, 324
  State supervision and regulation, 331–342
  tariff and non-tariff, 106, 109–110
  types, 103–106
Inter-company agreements, 215, 303
Intermediaries, 123–130
  Association of British Insurers Code of Practice, 130
  Financial Services Act 1986, 129, 338
  insolvency, 350–351
Inventory and valuation policies, 198
  comparison with valued policies, 198–199
Investment Management Regulatory Organization (IMRO), 347
Invisible exports
  insurance services, 9
Inwards reinsurance, 322

Joint Hull Agreement, 278
Joint-life assurances, 44

"K and R" insurance, 93–94
Kidnap insurance, 93–94
Knock-for-knock agreements, 208

Lapsed policies, 290, 292
  life assurance, 293
  policies which are revived, 293
Law Accident, 75
Law Reform Committee
  recommendations on utmost good faith, 185
Leading underwriter, 116
Legal expenses insurance, 94
Level premiums, 37, 47
Levies
  Policyholders Protection Act 1975, 338
Liability
  assessment of indemnity, 192
  excess of loss treaty, 319
  indemnity, 196
Liability insurance
  marine, 31–32
Liability insurance policy, 69
Libel insurance, 94
Life assurance, 17, 35–48
  average, 312
  claims, 299
  comparison with industrial life assurance, 40
  development, 35–39
  industrial, 39–40
  late twentieth century developments, 141–142
  liquidation of insurers, 349–350
  premium rating, 277–278
  professional associations, 136
  proposal forms, 256
  regulation, 332
  reinsurance and co-insurance, 322
  renewals, 290
  scope, 41–45
  State regulation on solvency margins, 335
  suicide, 15
  Traded Endowment Policy Sales (TEPS), 142
  underwriting, 245–246
  United Kingdom, 35–39

Life assurance—*cont.*
when insurable interest must exist, 169. *See also* Life policies
Life Assurance & Unit Trust Regulatory Organisation (LAUTRO), 347
Life Assurance Act 1774, 38, 229
insurable interest, 163
Life Assurance Companies Act 1870, 39, 332
Life assurance premium relief (LAPR), 48
Life fund, 283–284
Life Insurance Association (LIA), 136
Life Insurance Council, 134
The Life Insurance Marketing and Research Association Ltd. (LIMRA), 136
Life Offices' Association (LOA), 39
Statement of Insurance Practice, 182, 184–185
Life policies
assignment, 171
fully paid-up, 48
income tax relief, 48
loans on, 48
long-term contracts, 46
nominations, 171–172
non-forfeiture clause, 48
"second-hand", 141–142, 171
stamp duty, 157
surrender values, 47
tax exemption, 48
types, 41–45
"with profits", 46
Lightning damage, 54, 55
Limitation Acts 1939–1975, 296
Limitations of insurance, 13–15
LIMNET (London Insurance Market Network), 135, 146
Line, 317
Liquidation, 348–349
insurance companies, 349
insured, of, 351–352
life insurers, 349–350
Liquidation of insurer,
right to a partial refund, 283
Liquor licence insurance, 71
Litigation
disputes over claims, 300
Liverpool Fire Salvage Association, 53–54
Livestock insurance, 70–71
renewal premiums, 292
Lloyd, Edward, 29, 113
Lloyd's agents, 119
Lloyd's Aviation Underwriters' Association, 91, 134
Lloyd's brokers, 104, 115, 123
Lloyd's Law Reports, 119
Lloyd's List, 119
Lloyd's of London, 113–120
agents, 119
calling system, 117–118
Lloyd's of London—*cont.*
Captain's Room, 118
Casualty Book, 118
claims, 116
constitution and government, 113–114
corporate "names", 115
Equitas, 120
formation, 28–29, 113
Intelligence Department, 119
Lutine Bell, 118
membership, 114–115
Names, 115
Nelson Room, 118
policy forms, 117
policy signing office, 116
professional associations, 134
publications, 119
shipping intelligence, 118–119
"slip", the, 115–116
syndicates, 114
traditions, 117
troubles of mid-1990s, 119–120
underwriting room ("the Room"), 115
"waiters", 117
Lloyd's Shipping Index, 119
Lloyd's underwriters, 104, 115, 123
bankruptcy, 349
Loans on life policies, 48
Local authorities clause, 197
London Assurance, 28
London Drilling Rig Committee, 30
London Insurance and Reinsurance Market Association (LIRMA), 135
London Insurance Market Network (LIMNET), 135, 146
London Processing Centre (LPC), 135
London Underwriting Centre Information Database (LUCID), 146
Long-term agreements (LTAs)
life policies, 46
renewals, 291
underwriting, 245–246
Long-term undertakings (LTUs), 291
Loss adjusters, 10, 295
Loss of profits insurance, 57
Loss Prevention Council
fire testing and research, 55
Losses history
question on proposal form, 259
LUCID (London Underwriting Centre Information Database), 146
Lutine Bell, 118

Machinery
engineering insurance, 85–87
Manchester Steam Users' Association, 85
MAR policy form, 30
Margin of solvency. *See* Solvency margins of insurers

Marine insurance, 17, 25–32
agreed value policies, 200
assignment of policies, 171
average, 307–308
claims, 298
De Vaux v. *Salvador* case, 31
development, 25–29
importance in trade, 32
indemnity, 199–200
insurance of liability, 31–32
insurance of property, 30
meaning of average, 307–308
partial loss payments, 195–196
perils covered, 29–30
policy document, 30, 117
PPI policies, 166
premium rating, 278
proposal forms, 256
reinsurance and co-insurance, 322
renewal premiums, 292
scope, 29–32
United Kingdom, 26–29
unvalued policies, 200
when insurable interest must exist, 169
Marine Insurance Act 1745,
insurable interest, 163
Marine Insurance Act 1788,
insurable interest, 163
Marine Insurance Act 1906, 29, 154, 164
definition of material fact, 185–187
utmost good faith, 176
Marine Insurance (Gambling Policies) Act 1909, 164, 166, 229
Married Women's Property Act 1882, 167, 172, 351
Material facts, 177–178
breaches of utmost good faith due to non-disclosure or concealment, 182–183
Container Transport International Ltd v. *Oceanus Mutual Underwriting Assn.* case, 186
definition, 177
examples, 177
known facts which need not be disclosed, 178
Lambert v. *Co-operative Insurance Society Ltd* case, 185–186, 187
Law Reform Committee recommendations, 185
Marine Insurance Act 1906 definition, 185–187
Pan Atlantic Insurance Co. Ltd v. *Pine Top Insurance Co. Ltd* case, 186
qualification on the duty of disclosure, 177–178
St Paul Fire & Marine Company (U.K.) Ltd v. *McConnell Dowell Constructors Ltd* case, 186
Mediation, 302
Merchant Shipping (Oil Pollution) Act 1971, 95, 341
Minor losses, 14
Mixed policy, 31
Modern language-style policy forms, 264
Money
theft insurance, 70
Moral hazard, 251–254
"More than one life" assurances, 44
Mortality tables, 37
Mortgage guarantees, 64, 142
Mortgage protection policy, 42
Motor insurance, 18, 75–83
"act" only, 78
claims, 299
classification of risks, 77
comprehensive, 78–79
compulsory, 75, 79–80, 341
cover notes, 271, 293
development, 75–76
E.C. Directives, 81
Green Card system, 83
indemnity, 197
motor traders' policies, 79
premium rating, 279
proposal forms, 257
renewal premiums, 292, 293
scope, 77–79
third party, fire and theft, 78
third party only, 78
types of policy, 78–79
Motor Insurers' Bureau (MIB), 81–83, 349
agreements, 82
establishment, 81–82
Green Card system, 83
third party property damage liability, 82
Motor tariff, 76–77
Motor traders' policies, 79
Motor Union, 75
Municipal Mutual, 144
Mutual assurance associations, 37–38
Mutual companies, 104–105
de-mutualisation, 144–145
Mutual Indemnity Associations, 105
Mutual Insurance Companies Association, 136

Name of proposer, 257–258
Names (Lloyd's of London), 115
Narrative style policy forms, 264
Nation Life, 337
National Boiler Insurance Co. Ltd, 86
National Employers Mutual, 144
National Health Service, 145
National Insurance (Industrial Injuries) Act 1946, 68
National insurance scheme, 68, 145, 338
Nationalisation
insurance industry, 339–340

Negotiation
disputes over claims, 300
New business inspector, 124
"New for old" basis of settlement, 58, 197
No claims discount, 259
Nominations
life policies, 171–172
Non-forfeiture clause, 48
Non-tariff insurers, 106
Normal acceptance, 244
Norwich Union Life, 38
Notification of claim, 296
Novation, 172
Nuclear Installations Act 1965, 94, 341
Nuclear insurances, 94, 341–342

Occupation of proposer, 258
Offer of insurance, 155
verbal, 155
Office of Fair Trading (OFT), 346
Ombudsmen, 302, 347, 348
Open cover
marine insurance, 31
Operative clause, 265
Ordinary Branch (OB), 40
Ordinary life assurance, 40
Outwards reinsurance, 322
"Own case" agents, 124

P & I Clubs, 32, 105
Parol contracts, 153, 154–156
Partial loss payment
fire insurance, 196
marine insurance, 195–196
reinstatement of the sum insured, 195–197
Partial losses
valued policies, 198
Participating policies, 46
Particular average, 307
Particular risks, 5
Partners
insurable interest, 165
Pecuniary insurance, 16
assessment of indemnity, 192
fidelity guarantee insurance, 62–65
indemnity, 196
Pensions Ombudsman (PO), 347
Perils
of the sea, 29
types, 219
Personal accident insurance, 65–66
indemnity, 196
types of policy, 65–66
Personal contract
assignment of policy, 170, 172
Personal Insurance Arbitration Service (PIAS), 303, 348
Personal Investment Authority (PIA), 347
authorisation of intermediaries, 129
Personal Investment Authority Ombudsman (PIAO), 347
Phenix, 51
Physical hazard, 249–251
Pluvius insurance, 71
Polaris United Kingdom, 146
Police vehicles, 80
Policies of Assurance Act 1867, 171
Policy
meaning, 153
Policy conditions. *See* Conditions in a policy
Policy document. *See* Policy forms
Policy excess. *See* Excess
Policy exclusions. *See* Exclusions
Policy forms, 263–272
basic styles, 263–264
certificates, 271
cover notes, 271
endorsements, 272
evidence of the contract, 153, 263
marine insurance, 30, 117
prepared by the insurers, 263
rectification, 270
temporary, 271. *See also* Scheduled policies
Policy franchise, 191, 244
Policy Proof of Interest policies. *See* PPI policies
Policy Signing and Accounting Centre (PSAC), 135
Policy variations
marine insurance, 31
Policyholders Protection Act 1975, 337
Policyholders' Protection Board, 337, 338, 349
Political risk insurance, 95
Pollution insurance, 95, 140, 341
Pool Reinsurance Company Limited, 143
Pools of aviation insurers, 89–90, 91
Pools, reinsurance, 320
Portfolio reinsurance, 320
PPI policies, 166, 209
Marine Insurance (Gambling Policies) Act 1909, 164, 166
Premium loading, 244
Premiums, 3, 155–156, 275–286
coverage, 276–277
full payment by the insured, representing, 275
industrial life assurance, 276
level, 37, 47
manner of payment, 275–276
rating, 9–10, 72, 241, 277–279
return of, 280–283
short-period scales, 279–280
speciality contracts, 156–157
terminology, 285–286
underwriting, 241
ratio, 286
when payable, 275

Pro rata average, 213
accident insurance, 311–312
condition, 309
fire insurance, 309
United States, 310
Pro rata reinsurance, 320
Probable maximum loss (PML), 242
Products liability insurance, 69
Professional associations, 133–138
Professional indemnity insurance
directors and officers, 69, 141
insurance brokers, 341
solicitors, 341
Professional reinsurers, 107, 316, 322
Profit commission, 317
Property
assessment of indemnity, 192
indemnity, 196
insurable interest, 165–166
Proportional reinsurance, 320
Proposal forms, 155, 255–260
contractual duty of utmost good faith, 182
structure, 257–260
use in major classes of business, 256–257
Protection and Indemnity Clubs, 32, 105
Proximate cause, 219–226
exclusions worded in wide terms, 226
Gaskarth v. *Law Union* case, 221
Johnston v. *West of Scotland Insurance Co* case, 221
legal considerations, 220–222
Leyland Shipping Co. Ltd v. *Norwich Union Fire Insurance Co. Ltd* case, 220
Marsden v. *City & County Assurance Co.* case, 221, 225
meaning, 219
modification by policy condition, 225–226
rules of application, 222–225
standard fire policy, 225–226, 225–226
Re Etherington and the Lancashire & Yorkshire Accident Insurance Co. case, 222–224
Tootal Broadhurst Lee Co. v. *London & Lancashire Fire Insurance Co.* case, 224
Yorkshire Dale S.S. Co. v. *Minister of War Transport* case, 221
Public liability insurance, 68–69
Pure endowment policies, 43–44
Pure risks, 4

Queen's Bench guarantees, 64
Quota share reinsurance, 318

Racehorses
livestock insurance, 70–71, 292
Railway Fires Acts (1905, 1923), subrogation rights, 206
Railway Passenger Assurance Company, 65
Rainfall insurance, 71
Ransom insurance, 93–94
Rating premiums, 9–10, 72, 241, 277–279
short-period scales, 279–280
Ratios, 286, 304–305
Reaction to risks, 5–6
Rebating commission, 129
Reciprocity, 317
Recital clause, 265
Recognised Professional Body (RPB)
authorisation of intermediaries, 129
Rectification, 270
Registrar of Friendly Societies, 39, 346
Regulation
insurance industry, 331–342, 345–352
Rehabilitation of Offenders Act 1974, 184
Reinstatement
method of providing indemnity, 194–195
of sum insured, 195–197
Reinstatement clause, 293
Reinstatement insurances, 58
Reinstatement policies, 197
Reinsurance, 315–324
co-insurance, and, 321–322, 323
definitions, 316–317
effect of, 315
facultative, 317–318
meaning, 315
pro rata, 320
proportional, 320
reasons for, 315–316
reduced capacity, 144, 322, 324
State regulation, 336
treaty, 318–320
types, 317–320
Reinsurance and Insurance Network (RINET), 146
Reinsurance Offices Association (ROA), 135
Reinsurance pools, 320
"Reinsurer of last resort", 143
Reinsurers, 106–107, 316
failure, 350
professional, 107, 316, 322
Reminders
renewals, 292
Remuneration. *See* Commission
Renewals, 289–293
amendments, 290–291
days of grace, 291–293
duty of disclosure, 179, 289
expiry date, 291–292
legal position, 289
life assurance, 290
long-term agreements, 291
long-term undertakings, 291
meaning, 289
motor insurance, 292, 293
not obligatory, 289
policies revived, 293

Renewals—*cont.*
premium, 291–293
premium not paid within days of grace, 292–293
procedure, 291–293
reminders, 292
underwriting considerations, 289–291
Rent insurances, 57
Repair
method of providing indemnity, 194
Repair of Benefice Buildings Measure 1972, 167
Replacement
method of providing indemnity, 194
Representations, 179–180
comparison with warranties, 181
De Hahn v. *Hartley* case, 181
Research
fire and fire-fighting, 55
Reserves, 283–285
Respondentia bonds, 25
Retention, 317
Retroactive insurances, 95–96
Retrocession, 317
Return of premiums, 280–283
legal position, 280–281
partial returns, 283
total return, 281–282
Reversionary bonuses, 47
Revival clause, 293
Revived policies, 293
life assurance, 293
Riding Establishments Act 1970, 341
Rights of recovery
against third parties, 193
RINET (Reinsurance and Insurance Network), 146
Riot
special peril, 56
Riot (Damages) Act 1886
subrogation rights, 206
Risk, 3–6
accident insurance, 71
extraordinary, 19–20
fundamental, 4–5
moral hazard, 251–254
particular, 5
physical hazard, 249–251
pure, 4
reaction to, 5–6
speculative, 4
Risk averse, 240
Risk management, 6–7, 139–140
financial insurance, 97
professional associations, 137
Risk manager, 6
Risk prone, 240
Risk reduction, 7
Risk retention, 7, 140
Road Traffic Acts 1930–91, 76, 341
motor insurance not technically compulsory, 79
Royal Charter, 105
Royal Exchange Assurance, 28
Royal Charter, 105

Safety
employers' liability insurance, 66–68
St Christopher Scheme, 96
Sale of Goods Act 1893, 175
Salvage, 192
subrogation rights, 207
Salvage experts, 10
Salvage moneys, 193
Satellite launch, 96–97
Savings
insurance policy, 9
Scheduled policies, 264
conditions in a policy, 267–270
structure, 264–267
Scottish Union & National, 105
Seal
speciality contracts, 153–154, 156–157
Securities and Investment Board (SIB), 347
authorisation of intermediaries, 129
Security
commercial guarantees, 63
reinsurance, 317
Self-insurers, 106, 140
advantages, 107
captive insurance companies, 108–109
disadvantages, 107–108
Self-Regulatory Organisations (SROs), 347
Settled Land Act 1925, 167
Seventy-five percent condition of average, 309
"SG" (Ships-Goods) policy form, 30, 117
Short-period insurances
premium rating, 279–280
renewals, 292
Signature clause, 266–267
Signature on proposal form, 259
Simple contracts, 153, 154–156
"Slip", the, 115–116
Small losses, 14
Solicitors
professional indemnity insurance, 341
Solicitors Act 1974, 341
Solvency guarantee
in lieu of compulsory motor insurance, 79–80
Solvency margins of insurers, 349
State regulation, 335
Sonic boom insurance, 96
Space satellite insurance, 96–97
Special condition of average, 309, 311
Special perils, 55–56
Specialist insurers, 106, 324
Speciality contracts, 153–154, 156–157

Speculative risks, 4
Spontaneous combustion
special peril, 56
Sprinkler leakage policies, 56
Stamp duty
insurance contracts, 157
Standard fire policy, 55
combined policies, 56
proximate cause, 225–226
special perils, 55–56
Standard premiums, 175
State supervision
Acts of Parliament on insurance, 90, 332–338
Department of Trade and Industry, 346
insurance industry, 331–342, 345–352. *See also* Government involvement in operation of insurance
Statement of Insurance Practice, 182, 184–185
Statute of Frauds 1677, 154
Steam Boiler Assurance Co., 86
Stock declaration policies, 57–58, 70
adjustable premiums, 275
Stop loss reinsurance, 319–320
Storm
special peril, 56
Sub-standard risks, 244
Subrogation, 203–209
arising under contract, 205
Burnand v. *Rodocanachi* case, 204
Castellain v. *Preston* case, 204
employer's liability insurance, 208
ex gratia payments, 209
example, 203
how rights arise, 204–207
legal position, 204
limited to 100 pence in the £, 208–209
meaning, 203
modification of common law position, 207
salvage, 207
statute, from, 205–206
tort, 205
when rights are waived, 207–208
Subsidence, 142
special peril, 56
Subterranean fire
special peril, 56
Suicide, 15
Sum insured
reduced, 245
reinstatement, 195–197
Supervision of the insurance industry, 331–342, 345–352
Surety insurance, 63
Surplus treaty reinsurance, 318–319, 320–321
Surrender values
life policies, 47
Surveys, 10, 72
professional associations, 137–138

Tariff insurers, 106, 109–110
Tax exemption
life policies, 48
Taxation
Insurance Premium Tax, 339
Temporary policies, 271
Term assurances, 41
Terminology of premiums, 285–286
Terms in contract
underwriting, 241–242
Terrorism, 143
Theft insurance, 69–70
stock declaration policies, 70
Third parties
failure of an insured, 351
rights of recovery against, 193
Third Parties (Rights Against Insurers) Act 1930, 351
Third party claim sharing agreements, 208
Threshold retention, 317
Thunderbolt
special peril, 56
Time franchise, 191
Time policy, 31
Tontine, 44
Tooley Street Fire, 54
Tort
subrogation rights, 205
Traded Endowment Policy Sales (TEPS), 142
Transit
theft insurance for cash and goods in, 70
Travel insurance, 66, 70, 169
Treaty reinsurance, 318–320
excess of loss, 319, 320, 321
excess of loss ratio, 319–320, 321
quota share (fixed share), 318
stop loss treaty, 319–320
surplus, 318–319, 320–321
"Twins" insurance, 65
Two conditions of average, 309

Uberrimae fidei, 175
Ultra vires policy
right to a refund, 282
Underlying retention, 317
Underwriter, 239
marine insurance, 26–27
Underwriting, 239–246
declinature, 244
estimated maximum loss (EML), 242
features to be considered, 243
guides and rating manuals, 239
long-term insurance, 245–246
marine insurance, 27
moral hazard, 251–254
normal acceptance, 244

Underwriting—*cont.*
options, 244–245
physical hazard, 249–251
premiums, 241
probable maximum loss (PML), 242
ratio, 286
renewals, 289–291
risk prone or risk averse, 240
sub-standard risks, 244
terms in contract, 241–242
Unearned premium reserves, 284, 285
Unenforceable contracts, 157
Unexpired risk reserve, 285
Unfair Contract Terms Act 1977, 182, 184–185, 339
Unfair Terms in Consumer Contracts Regulations 1994, 338–339
Union of Canton Insurance Company, 89
Unit trust, 44
United States
co-insurance, 310
Environmental Impairment Insurance (EII) policy, 95
Utmost good faith, 175–187
breaches of, 182–184
Carter v. *Boehm* case, 176
contractual duty, 182
duty applies to insured and insurer, 176
duty of disclosure, 179
effect of a breach of, 183–184
inherent duty, 175–179, 182
Lambert v. *Co-operative Insurance Society Ltd* case, 185–186
law, and, 176–177
Law Reform Committee recommendations, 185
London General Omnibus Co. Ltd v. *Holloway* case, 176–177
material facts, 177–178
meaning, 175–176
representations, 179–180
Rozanes v. *Bowen* case, 177
waiver of breach of, 184

Valuation
policies based on an inventory, 198
valued policies, 197–198
Valued policies, 197–198
comparison with inventory and valuation policies, 198–199
justification of, 199
partial losses, 198
Void contracts, 157
breach of utmost good faith, 176, 183
policy conditions, 270
Voidable contracts, 157
policy conditions, 270
Voyage policy, 31

Wagering
compared with insurance, 161, 164, 229–232
War risks, 97
Warranty, 244–245
breach of, 180, 185
comparison with representations, 181
De Hahn v. *Hartley* case, 181
definition, 180
insurance, 180
types, 181
Weather patterns, 142
Welfare state, 145
Westminster Society, 38
White Cross Insurance Company, 89
Whole life assurances, 41
WIN (World Insurance Network), 146
Winding up of the insurer
State regulation, 336
"With profits" policies
life assurance, 46
Wordings
standard policy, 241
Workmen's Compensation Act 1897, 68
Workmen's compensation insurance, 68, 338
World Insurance Network (WIN), 146
Worshipful Company of Insurers, 138